# THE MINI-DOCUMENTARY–
## Serializing TV News

No. 797
$12.95

# THE MINI-DOCUMENTARY–
## Serializing TV News

### By Stanley Field

TAB BOOKS
Blue Ridge Summit, Pa. 17214

791.4353
F 4 56 m
1975

FIRST EDITION

FIRST PRINTING—OCTOBER 1975

Copyright © 1975 by TAB BOOKS

Printed in the United States
of America

Hardbound Edition: International Standard Book No. 0-8306-5797-5

Library of Congress Card Number: 75-9685

# Preface

Where there is a body of literature on a given subject, a writer may engage in extensive library research and sprinkle his own manuscript with liberal quotations. This approach is particularly appropriate if the manuscript is being written in the academic tradition. But there has been little or nothing written on the mini-documentary per se. Roy Paul Madsen, in his monumental volume, *The Impact of Film* (Macmillan) devotes one or two sentences to the mini-documentary. Yet this television form has been in existence for more than a decade and it has had a profound influence on the betterment of the community. Many television news directors believe it will replace the local full-length half-hour or hour documentary as a news special. The networks may even see fit to continue the fine art form of the documentary indefinitely. The mini-documentary is almost entirely the province of the local television station, although there are scattered instances of network productions, e.g., Jay McMullen's series on pharmaceutical practices broadcast by CBS News.

Most of the mini-documentaries produced by local TV stations can be classified as investigative as opposed to purely informative. I have taken a leaf from their book and employed an investigative approach myself in the preparation of this volume. Since there is no literature on the subject, I went to the source: news directors, reporters, producers, writers, and film editors. I believed the best way to illustrate the hows, whys, and wherefores of the mini-documentary was to have the professionals who are actually engaged in the production of this unique television medium explain their methods of operation and illustrate them by the actual scripts. If there is some repetition in the various chapters, its purpose is to show the similarities of production techniques by different stations.

The logistics of my endeavors were necessarily restricted by budgetary limitations. I could not travel about the countryside for a year or two interviewing newspeople. However, I was fortunate to be located in an area where four television stations were producing, according to leading critics, some of the most vital mini-documentary series. One of them was awarded a national Emmy and others received local Emmys. I enlarged my horizons by conducting a survey of television stations in every state; the results of that survey furnish a chapter for this book.

I believe this volume is truly pragmatic, and I hope it will help to establish the mini-documentary as a production format unique to television with significant and enduring impact. The mini-documentary has played an outstanding public service role because it has been widely used by local television stations to bring community events, problems, and items of local concern to the attention of the community as a whole.

The Washington, D.C. television stations have been extremely cooperative. They have welcomed my interviews and given me transcripts of their programs and permission to reproduce them. Reporters, news directors, and film editors have taken time from their busy schedules to offer me the benefit of their experience.

I thank news directors Dave Kelly, WMAL-TV; Tom Houghton, WRC-TV; John Baker, WTOP-TV; Stan Berk, WTTG-TV; reporters Jim Clarke, WMAL-TV; Meryl Comer, WTTG-TV; Jim Michie, WTOP-TV; Clare Crawford, WRC-TV; film editors John Long, WRC-TV; Sam Brooks, WMAL-TV; Toby Weaver, WTOP-TV; and producer Madhu Damania, WTTG-TV. To Tom Paro, vice president of the National Broadcasting Company and general manager at WRC-TV; Charles A. Batson, president of Cosmos Broadcasting Corporation; Jack Harris, president of KPRC; Vann M. Kennedy, president of KZTV; and to all the TV news directors who responded to my questionnaire, a specific thanks for their assistance. To Stuart Finley, for special help. And particular gratitude to Ken W. Sessions, Jr., Editor, TAB BOOKS, who inspired this volume; and to my devoted and patient wife, Joyce.

*Stanley Field*

# Contents

# Chapter 1

# The Documentary

A great deal has been written about the television documentary. It is a creative format for factual audio-visual presentation; the hallmark of prestige for networks and individual stations and often the social conscience of television. Karel Reisz and Gavin Millar in their classic volume *The Technique of Film Editing* (Hastings House) made this distinction between drama and documentary: "A story film (drama) is concerned with the development of a *plot*; the documentary film is concerned with the exposition of a *theme*." There is a modified form of the documentary which has come to be known as the mini-documentary and which is generally the province of local station production. It is a technique that Roy Paul Madsen (*The Impact of Film*) has characterized as "unique to television."

There was a time in the early years of television when hopeful creative spirits envisioned the new medium establishing its own art forms. But this never occurred. The visual medium aped its predecessor, radio, or became a vehicle for Hollywood film productions. This trend is epitomized in the current rash of "movies made for television." Not, mind you, teleproductions per se, but again imitating another medium so that a giant like Universal Pictures utilizes the same cinema techniques for the small screen as it does for the large—except making provision for curtain scenes to permit commercial intrusions.

The mini-documentary, however, does bring a format of its own to television; and the impact, as Paul Harris writing in *Variety* has noted, is threefold: (1) It allows a station to better perform it civic responsibilities by zeroing in on a community issue to a larger audience than through the old half-hour documentaries; (2) a crack investigative news team lends prestige to a station; and (3) the series creates an important source for selling local news shows and attracting new audiences.

Since newscasts do garner a large audience, the insertion of the mini-documentary within the regularly scheduled 6, 10, or 11 o'clock programs reaches a greater viewing public than the single-shot documentary. Nevertheless, as we shall discover in this in-depth study of the mini-documentary, the local station may consolidate the series into a half-hour documentary for additional impact. Or as WMAL-TV did with its mini-series on amnesty, it may present a vigorous pro-and-con discussion with panelists and studio audience. In this instance, WMAL-TV capitalized on the interest they knew existed before the mini-series was used to present the amnesty story. This brings up another interesting point which also will be discussed more fully in following chapters: Should the mini-documentary be strictly parochial in its approach? As we observe from the above instance, the mini-documentary does deal with national issues.

On rare occasions, network newscasts will present mini-documentaries. Jay McMullen's series on the Walter Cronkite CBS newscasts revealed improper sales and distribution of amphetamines and barbiturates by pharmaceutical houses and the failure of some mail-order laboratories to make accurate diagnoses of dangerous bacilli. The investigative reports resulted in legislative action to correct the situation. Generally speaking, however, mini-documentaries are the province of the local station and are concerned with area issues.

Obviously, a crack investigative team brings added prestige to a station. Perhaps instead of investigative we might use the term *reporting* team. Some newspeople prefer *reporter* to *investigator*. The fact is, a fair proportion of the mini-documentaries are informative rather than investigative, or a combination of both. Undoubtedly the Watergate scandals raised investigative reporting to a new high. The investigative reporter was transformed into a crusading hero. Certainly the efforts of Woodward and Bernstein of the *Washington Post* brought them the proverbial fame and fortune.

The mini-documentary, because it ranges deeply and often controversially into local issues, arouses audience response and therefore assists the sales department. And, as stations are wont to do, many will schedule highly provocative mini-documentaries during rating periods. The broadcaster still plays the rating game and is guided in his choice of programing by the printout from the Nielsen calibrators or American Research Bureau reports which measure the share of audience.

The general manager soon finds out whether he has won the brass ring for that week.

The mini-documentary is comparatively new to television but many stations have been producing mini-documentaries for a decade. In point of time, of course, a decade is yesterday. Up to 1963, television stations were presenting 15-minute daily newscasts. Evidently it was the consensus at the time that a quarter-hour daily newscast represented all the news reporters could gather and producers could assemble—or perhaps simply all the audience could be expected to assimilate. But in that year the decision was made to extend the period to a half-hour. The seriousness—one might almost say solemnity—with which this judgment was made was epitomized by a 5000-word memorandum Reuven Frank, then executive producer of NBC News, sent to his staff. What Mr. Frank had to say about the news story then is applicable to the mini-documentary today: "Every news story should, without sacrifice of probity or responsibility, display the attributes of fiction and drama. It should have structure and conflict, problem and denouement, rising and falling action, a beginning, a middle, and an end. These are not only the essentials of drama; they are the essentials of narrative. We are in the business of narrative because we are in the business of communication." (*Documentary in American Television.*)

Consider the scale of current news broadcasts. WTOP-TV in Washington, D.C. presents a 90-minute daily newscast followed by a half-hour of network news. Most other local TV stations schedule an hour of news, usually during the 6 to 7 p.m. slot. The trend to enlarge newscasts, begun in 1963, has taken a giant leap. What Reuven Frank envisioned, "planned and prepared film stories," has come to pass. In addition to daily events, newscasts offer single-shot features; more importantly, the mini-documentary has sprung into being.

Whether the mini-documentary is investigative or purely informative, it is a social document. Witness such topics as drug abuse, mental health institutions, slum conditions, exaggerated land sales, auto repair overcharges. The forerunners of this type of social documentary were produced by idealists like John Grierson, who initiated social analysis in documentary films. Mini-documentaries are always, or should be, the product of careful research, and their revelations have often been the catalyst for social change.

The question has been raised: are mini-documentaries an offshoot of the station's editorial policy? On the contrary, the situation is generally the reverse. The research performed by the reporter and embodied in his mini-documentary may lead to an editorial by the station; it rarely happens the other way around. Philosophically, the reporter is seeking the truth, a word that is much maligned when we find that its essence has been squeezed into unrecognizable pulp in the highest places in the land. Edward Jay Epstein writing in *Commentary* postulates that "the problem of journalism in America proceeds from a simple but inescapable bind: journalists are rarely, if ever, in a position to establish the truth about an issue for themselves and they are therefore almost entirely dependent on self-interested *sources* for the version of reality that they report." Mr. Epstein is obviously referring to the political arena where half-truths abound and even the most perceptive mind cannot always distinguish between reality and dissimulation. Also, politics and diplomacy have developed a grammar of their own that often defies definition. Reporters will devote paragraphs to analyzing a "no comment" statement. It puts one in mind of the professor of *fine arts* who devoted pages of erudite discussion to the hidden meanings of an artist's canvas which was simply white on white.

But the mini-documentary reporter is not dependent on unrevealed sources. He speaks to the people who are directly involved: slum dwellers, land owners whose lots are flooded after every rainstorm, automobile mechanics, career school graduates unable to find the promised job. The mini-documentary can tackle social problems with exactitude and intimacy.

The early film documentaries, prior to television, often took editorial stands. They were against deteriorating social and environmental conditions. *The River*, produced by Pare Lorentz, was a study of erosion in the Mississippi River basin and its message was strong and obvious. *The City* portrayed urban blight, the result of improper planning. Some documentarists felt that television softened their stands, that they did not have the freedom of their film predecessors. Television, geared to mass audiences and subsidized by advertisers fearful of controversy, might tend to avoid investigative reporting. Unlike newspapers, station owners must consider license renewals. There is also the fairness doctrine and the requirement that when a station editorializes it must offer equal opportunity to any responsible citizen or organization wishing to rebut. It can be argued that although the newspaper does not *have* to allot editorial space to the opposition, it frequently does publish letters which espouse contrary views. When we study some of the transcripts of mini-documentaries, we will find that opposing views are presented.

Nevertheless, television has taken strong stands as exemplified by the CBS documentaries *Harvest of Shame*, *Biography of a Bookie Joint*, and *The Selling of the Pentagon*.

How strong a stand is evidenced by the attempt of Edward R. Murrow, when he headed the United States Information Agency, to prevent the British Broadcasting Corporation from showing *Harvest of Shame*, which was a penetrating indictment of the miserable conditions of migrant workers.

It brings us to the question of objectivity which we discussed in a previous volume (*Professional Broadcast Writer's Handbook*, TAB Books). Albert Wasserman, then producer for NBC News Creative Projects, stated in a panel discussion that "I do not think *objectivity* means fear of taking a stand. If the investigations of the objective documentary reports lead to definite conclusions then I think such conclusions must be reflected in the finished program." Based on my talks with television reporters, I found that most of them chose the topics of their mini-documentaries because they had a keen interest in them and believed some action should be taken about the situation. They strove to be objective in their pursuit of information. But all documentarists agree that they make subjective choices when they edit the footage they have shot.

Is it possible for a mini-documentary to be so biased that its participants are chosen arbitrarily and the film edited to make a preconceived point? After all, there are many individuals and organizations who believe so. It was the hue and cry of Spiro

USIA documentary filming of fifth anniversary of the Alliance for Progress in Panama. (Courtesy Ken Resnick)

Agnew that all media were indefensibly antiadministration—this despite the fact that the majority of newspapers were pro-Nixon during the 1972 election campaign. The Agnew adherents were led to the conclusion that the broadcasters and journalists were *making* news instead of *reporting* it.

What it comes down to is faith in the integrity of the reporter. "Newsmen," Mr. Epstein tells us, "almost invariably depict themselves not merely as reporters of the fragments of information that come their way but as active pursuers of the truth." Although Epstein is pessimistic about the foregoing concept, the reporter for a mini-documentary is a seeker after the truth. The ones I have interviewed were all imbued with a desire to present honest information to enlighten the public. Professor Bluem asserts that "the substance of responsible reporting must be in each man's independent determination of what he deems is essential for a civilization to know—and to understand." This perhaps explains the rationale of the *New York Times* in releasing its edited version of the Pentagon Papers. And, more simplistically, it explains the editing process of the mini-documentary: the choice of footage, the words, and the pictures that finally reach the screen.

Morry Roth, in an article in *Variety*, observed that the mini-documentary has largely replaced the once traditional half-hour and hour news specials on many stations and that the production of the news serials has increased tremendously. The more rigid half-hour or hour documentaries have' often faced scheduling problems, and many stations would not preempt the time. Another factor favoring the mini-documentary is that it can encompass so-called *intermediate* news: "neither timely enough for a regular newscast nor broad enough for full-length treatment." And from a budgetary standpoint the mini-documentary is more economical than the half-hour or hour special since it can be shown on the early evening news program and repeated on the late news broadcast. It is also possible to bring an element of suspense into the series and therefore help to maintain audience interest.

For the reporters, the mini-documentaries are both a challenge and an opportunity. All their investigative and "nose for news" talents are brought to bear and their reputations enhanced. The scope of their activities is broadened; they have freedom for research and time to do an in-depth story. In many instances, they are rewarded by a great sense of satisfaction in knowing their efforts have been instrumental in correcting a community problem.

It was John Grierson, the famous documentary filmmaker, who first coined the term *documentary*. He used it in February

1926 when he reviewed Robert Flaherty's *Moana*. Grierson thought of film primarily as a medium for reaching public opinion. "We were," he writes, "sociologists, a little worried about the way the world was going. We were interested in all instruments which would crystallize sentiments in a muddled world and create a will toward civic participation."

On that first historic broadcast of the CBS documentary series, *See it Now*, Edward R. Murrow's opening statement was one of momentous significance: "No journalistic age was ever given a weapon for truth with quite the scope of this fledgling television."

The philosophy of Grierson and Murrow is a credo that today's documentarists would well emulate.

# Chapter 2

# The Structure of the Mini-Documentary Series

The subjects of mini-documentaries are as varied as a day's events. Even a brief listing of topics (see final chapter) shows the wide range of community and national issues that afford the reporter/producer an unending variety of themes. Perhaps we are taking a simplistic view when we point out the obvious: newscasts—certainly on network affiliated stations—are presented twice daily. There may be a single presentation on weekends. Newspapers are published on a 7-day, year-round basis, and neither the daily newspapers nor the television stations complain about a dearth of news. The mini-documentary, as part of the television newscasts, need never fear a lack of ideas.

The structure of the mini-documentary shows a distinct similarity in production techniques by various television stations. Generally, the time element—3 minutes or so per episode—does not permit enough latitude for visual gimmickry. Time is so tight that only on occasion can the camera wander into panoramic vistas. This type of footage has to be reserved for the full-length documentary or when it is essential to the subject of the mini-documentary; for example, an aerial view of a land development which is under investigation. Since each episode, although part of an integrated whole, must be able to stand by itself, concentration on the essence of the story is necessary.

This does not mean the reporters, producers, writers, film editors, cameramen, and sound and lighting technicians are restricted in the use of their collective imaginations. Whatever they can do to enhance the appeal of the mini-documentary is more than welcome. The mini-documentary can help increase the viewing audience but it cannot do this by being dull. It is true that titillating subjects will in themselves draw an audience: prostitution in the city streets, swinging singles, the block in Baltimore that caters to the prurient, a view of homosexuality. These are all facets of our daily lives but they affect only a small segment of the population. They are spicy but highly selective subjects. More meaningful are the mini-documentaries that deal with the plight of the poor, the growing welfare rolls, the need for consumer protection, the problems of mass transit, the perils of pollution.

Although the mini-documentary is presented as a part of the daily newscast and, as such, is considered news, it does have an identity of its own. It bears a title which is used to introduce each episode. For example, WTTG's title for its series on career schools:

FADE UP ON CAMERA CARD
SUPER* TITLE:    CAREER SCHOOLS— PROMISES, PROMISES
V/O** CAMERA CARD


WRC-TV, for its *Uncle Sam is a Slumlord* series, used one of its anchormen with voice-over scenes of slum areas and the title superimposed:

| | |
|---|---|
| ANCHORMAN: ON SCREEN STUDIO SUPER SLUM APARTMENTS SUPER TITLE: UNCLE SAM IS A SLUMLORD | THE VICTORIA APARTMENTS AT 14TH AND CLIFTON STREETS NORTHWEST IS A TYPICAL EXAMPLE OF THE ROTTEN CONDITIONS UNDER WHICH THE FEDERAL GOVERNMENT FORCES MANY INNER CITY RESIDENTS TO LIVE. THE VICTORIA IS IN AN URBAN RENEWAL AREA WHERE UNCLE SAM IS THE SLUMLORD. |

Many television stations will use the title at the close of each episode also. Other stations will employ a teaser at the close which usually consists of a few seconds of footage from the next day's episode like this sequence from WTOP-TV's *The Miracle Merchants*.

| | |
|---|---|
| (CLOSING) MICHIE: VOICE OVER 3-SHOT OF REVEREND DAY, MS. AMEEN, AND MICHIE | IN OUR NEXT REPORT. WE CONTINUE WITH REVEREND MOTHER DAY—PAST THE PROMISES AND TO THE TRUTH. THIS IS JIM MICHIE. EYEWITNESS NEWS. |

---

*SUPER—superimpose
**V O—voice over

| | |
|---|---|
| (TEASER)<br>(FILM SEGMENT FROM<br>NEXT<br>EPISODE)<br>MS. AMEEN:<br>CLOSEUP<br>FADE TO BLACK | AND I GAVE YOU, REVEREND DAY, FOUR DOLLARS FOR A READING. AND YOU TOLD ME THAT I HAD VERY SEVERE MARITAL PROBLEMS. |

We have categorized mini-documentaries as either informative or investigative. There is often overlapping between the two. Some examples of informative subjects include mini-documentaries on such topics as: constitutional amendments, seabird sanctuaries, cancer signs, police training, religious missions, prevention of heart disease, solar energy, unique neighborhoods, medical centers, and the autistic child. However, based on the transcripts made available to us and the survey we have conducted, the majority of mini-documentaries are investigative in nature. Obviously, a controversial issue will engender more heat and more attention than a purely informative mini-documentary. And one of the prime reasons for the development of the mini-documentary is its potential for increasing the station's audience. Still, all due credit must be given to television stations which produce mini-documentaries. They are the most potent example of the television medium acting in the public interest. Mini-documentaries have uncovered blemishes in the community: slums, alcoholism, unscrupulous merchants, unspeakable conditions in mental health institutions, unpalatable food. At times, mini-documentaries have been scheduled in the face of possible cancellations by sponsors whose products are involved. Reporters have been diligent and unswerving in their investigations despite personal threats. All this has proved over the past decade that television stations have found the mini-documentary a most worthy and significant form of production and far reaching in its effect on the public conscience.

## OPENING STATEMENTS

The lead-in to the first episode of a mini-documentary is all important. It should be an ear catcher and possibly an eye catcher, although the visual should not be so overwhelming that it distracts from what is being said.

Let us take a pragmatic approach and examine several opening statements. Here is the introduction to the mini-documentary series on career schools produced by WTTG.

| | |
|---|---|
| REPORTER: ON<br>SCREEN<br>THEN DISSOLVE TO | AT THE OUTSET, LET US SAY THIS IS MEANT TO BE NEITHER A BROAD ALL-INCLUSIVE REPORT ON, NOR A BLANKET INDICTMENT |

**V/O MONTAGE OF VARIOUS TRADE SCHOOLS AND CLASSROOM ACTIVITIES**

OF THE MULTIBILLION DOLLAR, MULTIMILLION STUDENT VOCATIONAL OR CAREER SCHOOL INDUSTRY...WHICH, WITH IN-CLASS AND CORRESPONDENCE TRAINING, IS PLAYING A MOST VALUABLE ROLE IN A SOCIETY WHERE THE ONCE ALL-IMPORTANT COLLEGE DIPLOMA IS ALL IMPORTANT NO MORE...WHERE P - H - D's ARE A GLUT ON THE MARKET...WHERE THE VAST MAJORITY OF ALL JOBS REQUIRE SKILLED TRAINING AND NOT NECESSARILY A DEGREE. AND WHERE MOST STUDENTS WILL EITHER NEVER REACH COLLEGE OR FAIL TO GRADUATE, AMID THE GROWING REALIZATION THAT MANY WHO ARE STROLLING THE HALLS OF IVY NEVER SHOULD HAVE WALKED THAT WAY IN THE FIRST PLACE.

BUT DESPITE THESE POSITIVE ASPECTS OF THE CAREER SCHOOL INDUSTRY AS A WHOLE...WE WILL BE EMPHASIZING THE NEGATIVE...FOR WITHIN THE CONTEXT OF THIS SERIES WE ARE IN THE CONSUMER PROTECTIVE BUSINESS.

WE WILL POINT OUT THE GOOD BUT OUR PRIMARY ROLE WILL BE TO EXPOSE THE BAD AND THE UGLY...TO TELL THOSE WHO HAVE BEEN HURT HOW TO GET HELP...TO BETTER INFORM POTENTIAL STUDENTS. THEREBY INDIRECTLY GUIDING THEM TOWARD THE MAJORITY OF WELL-RUN CAREER SCHOOLS AND AWAY FROM THE BAD INSTITUTIONS AND UGLY PRACTICES THAT, IN THIS CASE, ROB SOMEONE NOT ONLY OF DOLLARS BUT OF MOTIVATION—OF THAT LAST CHANCE TO BETTER THEMSELVES AND THEIR LOT IN LIFE.

The foregoing opening statement leads off with a disclaimer because the mini-documentary series will be devoted to those career schools which have been taking advantage of students. The reporter states, "We will be emphasizing the negative." "We are in the consumer protection business."

This mini-documentary series was produced with the cooperation of young law students from George Washington University who had formed an investigative unit of their own to assist consumers in the Washington, D.C. metropolitan area. WTTG is an independent station and does not have the budgetary wherewithal of its competing network affiliates. The enlistment of knowledgeable students from a neighboring university is therefore of great assistance to WTTG and a possibility for any other independent television station similarly situated.

19

The thrust of the narration is that the station is engaged in a matter of public interest that should elicit the attention of the community. The visuals serve as a backdrop: a montage of trade schools with glimpses of varying vocational activities. The montage complements the narration so that eye and ear are attuned and one does not distract from the other.

WMAL-TV produced a mini-documentary series with the intriguing title, *Are You Eating Garbage?* Here is reporter Jim Clarke's opening statement:

CLARKE:
V/O FULL SHOT OF LIVING ROOM WITH CAMERA PANNING BOUNTEOUS THANKSGIVING DINNER.

WE AMERICANS HAVE LONG ENJOYED THE HIGHEST STANDARD OF LIVING IN THE WORLD AND ALL THE BENEFITS AFFLUENCE WILL BUY—AMONG THEM, THE GREATEST QUANTITY AND VARIETY OF FOODSTUFFS KNOWN TO MAN.

DISSOLVE TO MONTAGE OF FAST-FOOD EATING PLACES

DISSOLVE TO GRAPHICS AND GOVERNMENT CHARTS

IRONICALLY, HOWEVER, OUR DIETARY HABITS AND NUTRITIONAL HEALTH HAVE BEEN GOING TO HELL IN A HANDBASKET. A GOVERNMENT SURVEY UNDERSCORES THE POINT: BETWEEN 1955 AND 1965, THE NUMBER OF AMERICANS HAVING A GOOD DIET DECLINED BY TEN PERCENT. BY 1965, FORTY PERCENT OF THE POPULATION WAS EATING LESS THAN THE RECOMMENDED DAILY ALLOWANCES FOR THE SEVEN BASIC NUTRIENTS.

DISSOLVE TO SCENES OF CROWDS IN STREETS DURING LUNCH HOUR

DURING THE SAME DECADE, THE PERCENTAGE EATING POOR DIETS JUMPED FROM FIFTEEN TO TWENTY-ONE PERCENT OF THE POPULATION. THEY WERE EATING LESS THAN TWO-THIRDS OF THE DAILY ALLOWANCE FOR ONE TO SEVEN NUTRIENTS.

DISSOLVE TO HARVESTING SCENE

DISSOLVE TO SUPERMARKET SHELVES CROWDED WITH FOODSTUFFS

THAT'S A CURIOUS PARADOX FOR A NATION BLESSED WITH A BOUNTY OF NATURAL FOOD RESOURCES, CLUTTERED WITH SUPERMARKETS, ONE LITERALLY AWASH IN FOOD FROM THE MOST PROLIFIC AND SOPHISTICATED BREADBASKET IN THE WORLD.

The opening narration juxtaposes the nation's affluence with a statistical notation of widespread poor diets. This raises the question of why the situation exists and obviously piques our interest.

In both the preceding examples, the opening statement was straight narration using the reporter on screen or voice over film.

The visuals specifically illustrate the audio. A varied approach is employed by the following opening statement for the mini-documentary series *Home Buyer Beware*, produced by WTOP-TV.

| | |
|---|---|
| PETERSON:<br>ON SCREEN | FOR MOST PEOPLE THE PURCHASE OF A NEW HOME IS THE LARGEST SINGLE INVESTMENT OF A LIFETIME. NOW. NO ONE EVER BOUGHT A HOME. NEW OR USED. WITHOUT RUNNING INTO SOME PROBLEM. |
| MICHIE:<br>V/O SHOTS OF SLOPPY<br>HOME<br>CONSTRUCTION | BUT IN A FAST-GROWING AREA LIKE METROPOLITAN WASHINGTON. BUYING A NEW HOME FOR SOME HAS TURNED INTO A NIGHTMARE EXPERIENCE. |
| DONALD BOWERS:<br>SOUND ON FILM<br>(HOMEOWNER)<br>CLOSEUP | WE HAVE A LIST OF DEFICIENCIES THAT WE'VE RUN IN A PRIVATE ENGINEERING FIRM TO CHECK OVER THE HOUSE AND THEY CAME UP WITH EIGHT THOUSAND DOLLARS WORTH OF REPAIRS. |
| ARTHUR RAYMAN:<br>SOUND ON FILM<br>(HOMEOWNER)<br>MEDIUM CLOSEUP | WHEN THE WEATHER GOT A LITTLE COOLER. I STARTED TO TURN ON MY HEATING SYSTEM. AND I WENT TO TURN IT ON AND I FOUND OUT THERE WAS NO BLOWER INSTALLED. SO I CALLED UP THE HEATING COMPANY AND ALL THE GUYS DID WAS JUST YELL AT ME FOR CALLING THEM IN THE NIGHT. I ASKED THEM. "HOW CAN YOU INSTALL FURNACES WITHOUT A BLOWER? WHAT KIND OF WORKMANSHIP IS THAT!" |

In *Home Buyer Beware* we have a quickened pace. Peterson's opening two sentences delineate the theme of the mini-documentary series with added emphasis provided by reporter Jim Michie. This is followed immediately by the statements of two homeowners colorfully describing their problems. The visuals consist of scenes of poor home construction. Aurally and visually, the subject of *Home Buyer Beware* is presented dramatically and should capture immediate attention.

## RESEARCH

Before the reporter/writer ventures out into the field to record and film his interviews, he must prepare himself by adequate research. Many reporters are accustomed to doing their own research, which may consist of exploratory field trips and perusal of newspapers and magazines for articles on the subject of the mini-documentary, plus digging through official files.

For the mini-documentary series, *Career Schools—Promises, Promises*, we noted that WTTG had the assistance of law students, and that the station, on occasion, employs student interns to assist in research. The network affiliates can afford to hire reporters to work exclusively on mini-documentaries. In some instances, the network affiliates may engage free-lance reporters or writers for mini-documentaries. At the independent station, the reporter is often doubling in brass: producing mini-documentaries and also performing as anchor or newscaster.

In our chapter on the interview, the relationship of the reporter to the interviewee is discussed and the need for comprehensive research is stressed. In subsequent chapters, you will learn how this research is carried out by individual reporters.

## TALKING HEADS

Since the interview is a staple of the mini-documentary, the problem is to avoid a static presentation or what is known in TV parlance as *talking heads*—that is, film footage that shows nothing but the speakers themselves during a narrative. This is not to imply that interviews are not stimulating. The proliferation and popularity of talk shows prove that face-to-face encounters can be extremely lively. Panel programs such as *Face the Nation, Meet the Press*, and *Issues and Answers* are an enlargement of the interview, variety being added by having the interviewee questioned by several reporters.

The mini-documentary adds its own variations by using filmed or videotaped statements by participants either as single inserts or in a montage effect. Here is an example of the single insert from the WMAL-TV *Are You Eating Garbage?* series.

| | |
|---|---|
| CLARKE:<br>STUDIO | IN OUR FIRST REPORT WE SAID AMERICANS ENJOY THE GREATEST QUANTITY AND VARIETY OF FOODSTUFFS KNOWN TO MAN. TO THAT WE WOULD ADD: OUR FOOD IS PROBABLY MORE WHOLESOME THAN ANY OTHER. AND WE WOULD AGREE WITH THE CONCLUSION EXPRESSED BY DR. ROBERT LEE, CHIEF OF THE MARYLAND MEAT AND POULTRY INSPECTION SERVICE. |
| DR. LEE:<br>SOUND ON FILM<br>FULL SHOT<br>OFFICE | WE IN THE WASHINGTON METROPOLITAN AREA, AS WELL AS IN MARYLAND, ARE EXTREMELY FORTUNATE THAT WE HAVE AVAILABLE TO US AN EXTREMELY WHOLESOME, PLENTIFUL, AND VARIED SUPPLY OF MEAT AND POULTRY PRODUCTS. |

|  | TO SUPPLEMENT THIS INSPECTION WITHIN THE PLANT, WE ROUTINELY PICK UP SAMPLES OF MEAT AND POULTRY PRODUCTS AS WELL AS VARIOUS OTHER NONMEAT INGREDIENTS—BOTH AT THE PLANT AND OUTSIDE THE PLANT—SEND THEM TO OUR LABORATORY, WHERE THEY ARE TESTED FOR VARIOUS POSSIBLE CONTAMINANTS OR ADULTERANTS WHICH MAY BE PRESENT. |
| CLARKE:<br>STUDIO | AS DILIGENT AS DR. LEE AND HIS ASSOCIATES AND THEIR FEDERAL AND STATE COUNTERPARTS MAY BE, THEIR EFFORTS MAY NOT BE ADEQUATE. |

As an example of the montage effect, here is an excerpt from *Sunny Side Up*, another mini-documentary series produced by WMAL-TV on food contamination.

| CLARKE:<br>STUDIO | IT IS NOT FOR NOTHING THAT WE SHOULD BE CONCERNED ABOUT WHAT WE ARE EATING. BUT IT IS DIFFICULT TO FOCUS THAT CONCERN BECAUSE THE EXPERTS DISAGREE ON SO MANY THINGS: |
| CAREY:<br>SOUND ON FILM<br>CLOSEUP | COMMERCIALLY CANNED FOOD IN THIS COUNTRY, WE BELIEVE, IS AS SAFE AND AS WHOLESOME AS HUMAN INGENUITY CAN MAKE IT. OVER 17 MILLION TONS OF RAW PRODUCT IS PROCESSED ANNUALLY. |
| NELSON:<br>SOUND ON FILM<br>CLOSEUP | THE WHOLE COUNTRY IS BEING MASSIVELY MEDICATED AGAINST ITS WILL BY SOME ONE-THOUSAND FOOD ADDITIVES. THE F-D-A DOES NOT KNOW WHETHER OR NOT OR HOW MANY OF THESE ADDITIVES MAY IN FACT BE DANGEROUS. NEITHER DOES ANYBODY ELSE BECAUSE THERE HAS NOT BEEN ADEQUATE SCIENTIFIC TESTS TO DEMONSTRATE THAT. |
| BLUMENTHAL:<br>SOUND ON FILM<br>CLOSEUP | WE HAVE BEEN ACCUSED OF POISONING THE PUBLIC—MANY TIMES. I, ON THE OTHER HAND, CONSIDER MYSELF AND MY FAMILY THE PUBLIC, AND I'M NOT OUT TO POISON ANY OF THEM. AND, I WOULD SAY THAT AT THIS TIME, I PLACE NO RESTRICTIONS ON THE TYPES OF FOOD PURCHASES THAT MY WIFE MAKES FOR OUR FAMILY. |
| PETERSON:<br>SOUND ON FILM<br>CLOSEUP | I'M VERY CONCERNED AND PLEASED WITH THE CARE THAT GOES INTO IT. I JUST WATCH OUR OWN BUYERS AND OUR QUALITY CONTROL. AND WHEN I THINK OF HOW MANY MILLIONS OF PEOPLE ARE FED. I DON'T WANT ONE BAD THING TO HAPPEN. NEVERTHELESS. I THINK WE DO PRETTY WELL. |

| | |
|---|---|
| HUTT:<br>SOUND ON FILM<br>CLOSEUP | MOST OF THE FOODS WE EAT ARE NOT NECESSARY—OR. IN SOME INSTANCES. EVEN PARTICULARLY BENEFICIAL—EVEN THOUGH THEY ARE VERY DELIGHTFUL. I WOULD HATE TO TRY TO PROVE THAT CAVIAR HAD ANY USEFUL PURPOSE IN MODERN LIFE. SNACK PRODUCTS THAT WE EAT—AND THAT FRANKLY WE ALL ENJOY VERY MUCH. WHETHER IT'S CANDY BARS. POTATO CHIPS. OR SODA POP—OBVIOUSLY ARE NOT AN ESSENTIAL BIT OF OUR AMERICAN DIET FROM THE NUTRITIONAL STANDPOINT. |
| WEISBURGER:<br>SOUND ON FILM<br>CLOSEUP | IT SHOULD BE KEPT IN MIND THAT THE BODY OR THE ORGANISM IS EQUIPPED TO TAKE CARE OF THE SMALL AMOUNTS OF TOXIC MATERIALS AND CAN ELIMINATE THEM USUALLY WITHOUT ANY HARMFUL EFFECT TO THE PERSON. IT'S ONLY WHEN THERE IS AN OVERWHELMING AMOUNT THAT PERHAPS CANCER OR SOME OTHER HARMFUL EFFECT DEVELOPS. |
| CLARKE:<br>STUDIO | THE EXPERTS AREN'T LIKELY TO AGREE UPON EVERYTHING SOON. SO WE SHOULD CONTINUE TO RELY UPON THE FOOD AND DRUG ADMINISTRATION TO INSURE THE WHOLESOMENESS OF OUR FOOD. |

You will observe that a carefully balanced presentation has been maintained in the foregoing montage: three positive comments, two negative, and one statement (Weisburger) that incorporates pros and cons.

## CONTENT

A mini-documentary is an *actuality*; that is, it deals with on-going events and with the people directly concerned. Structurally, as we have noted, each episode should be an entity in itself and yet an integral part of the series. This poses something of a problem as compared with the full-length documentary, which is a single-shot presentation. Also, the full-length documentary adheres to a rigid time schedule: 30, 60, or 90 minutes. However, each segment of the mini-documentary may vary from as little as 3 minutes to as long as 10 minutes. The number of episodes may be as few as 3 or as many as 12. In several instances, television stations have edited the episodes of a mini-documentary series into a half-hour or hour full-length documentary with varying degrees of success.

There is a pattern observable in most investigative mini-documentaries. The participants generally fall into three categories: the victims of deception or misguidance, the perpetrators, and the officials who have jurisdiction in the problem area.

In the mini-documentary series, *Career Schools—Promises, Promises*, the participants were unhappy students, vocational school administrators, and Federal Trade Commission officials. Through research accomplished with the assistance of the George Washington University HELP center, the reporter was able to reach students whose promises for a rewarding career were never fulfilled. A woman who was a librarian related that she spent $2000 for a computer course, applied for dozens of jobs, and is still a librarian. A young man told of taking a $1200 course that was supposed to qualify him automatically for a government civil service rating as a computer operator, but the rating never materialized. The other side of the coin was shown: a successful disc jockey gave due credit to the training he received via a correspondence course. The foregoing incidents were presented in filmed statements, usually closeups or medium closeups of the students.

The choice of participants is extremely important to the credibility of the mini-documentary. If an entirely negative view is presented, the station could be accused of bias and selectively choosing participants to prove a point. On the other hand, if the mini-documentary involves a case of misrepresentation, witnesses must be provided who have been deceived. Where the issue is controversial, the station may send scripts, prior to broadcast, to the companies which are named as culprits and offer time for rebuttal. (For an in-depth look at how this situation is handled, see *The Auto Repair Go-Round* and *You And Auto Repair* in Chapter 4.)

The career-school series again resorts to a disclaimer in its second episode to aver that an entire industry is not being called to task—only its miscreants.

| REPORTER:<br>V/O MONTAGE OF<br>TRADE SCHOOL<br>ACTIVITIES | BOB JONES IS NOT TYPICAL OF THE MAJORITY OF CAREER SCHOOL STUDENTS. MILLIONS OF WHOM BENEFIT ANNUALLY FROM THE EXPERIENCE: BUT FOR A SIZABLE MINORITY OF THE DISILLUSIONED AND FRUSTRATED. HIS STORY IS ALL TOO TYPICAL...FOLLOWS AN ALL TOO FAMILIAR PATTERN. THE BOB JONESES ARE MOTIVATED BY THE UNDERSTANDABLE YEARNING FOR ADVANCEMENT. A BETTER JOB—IN HIS CASE. WITH COMPUTERS...FOR OTHERS—IN BROADCASTING. MOTELS. TRUCK DRIVING. AIRLINES. MEDICAL. DENTAL WORK—YOU NAME IT—IF IT GLITTERS. THERE IS POTENTIAL GOLD FOR THE STUDENT BUT FIRST FOR THE SCHOOL. |
|---|---|

| | |
|---|---|
| **CLIPPINGS OF**<br>**TRADE SCHOOL**<br>**ADVERTISEMENTS** | THE BOB JONESES ARE LURED BY PROMISES, OUTRIGHT OR IMPLIED—SOMETIMES IN ADVERTISING, MORE OFTEN TUMBLING FROM THE LIPS OF SO-CALLED GUIDANCE COUNSELORS, ENROLLMENT PERSONNEL, OR SCHOOL REPRESENTATIVES. |

Episode 2 of *Career Schools—Promises, Promises* explores the inadequate training Bob Jones received and then makes the point that brings the issue home to all viewers, whether or not they are interested in career schools.

| | |
|---|---|
| **REPORTER:**<br>**V/O FILM OF COM-**<br>**PUTER SCHOOL**<br>**ACTIVITIES** | BOB JONES RECEIVED MAYBE HALF OF THE "ON HANDS" COMPUTER TRAINING REQUIRED FOR THAT GOVERNMENT RATING HE DIDN'T GET. HE RECEIVED NO PLACEMENT ASSISTANCE AND NO JOB. |
| | HIS DREAM, PURCHASED AT 49 DOLLARS AND 56 CENTS DOWN AND 30 DOLLARS A MONTH, EVAPORATED; BUT THE LOAN PAYMENT BOOK DID NOT—AND WE THE TAXPAYERS PICK UP THE TAB FOR COUNTLESS DISILLUSIONED BOB JONESES IN MILLIONS OF DOLLARS OF DEFAULTED LOANS THAT UNCLE SAM MUST PAY OFF UNDER THE FEDERALLY INSURED LOAN PROGRAM. |

"We the taxpayers pick up the tab" is the key statement that brings the problem home to every one of us. It is not only the Bob Joneses who are affected. This point is stressed at the conclusion of the episode.

| | |
|---|---|
| **REPORTER:**<br>**V/O STACKS OF**<br>**DOCUMENTS**<br>**ON DESKS**<br><br>**DISSOLVE TO SCENES**<br>**OF TRADE SCHOOLS** | THIS MOUNTAIN OF DOCUMENTS AND THE UNSEEN LEGAL PAPERWORK JUNGLE SURROUNDING IT STEM FROM AN F-T-C CASE INVOLVING A SINGLE CAREER SCHOOL. FOR WHATEVER REASONS, THE BUREAUCRATIC SYSTEM IS QUICK TO INDIRECTLY SUPPORT CAREER SCHOOLS WITH MILLIONS IN GUARANTEED LOANS AND V-A BENEFITS, BUT SLUGGISH INDEED WHEN IT COMES TO PULLING OUT THE ROTTEN APPLE THAT STINKS UP THE INDUSTRY, THAT SAPS STUDENTS OF MOTIVATION AND TAXPAYERS OF THEIR DOLLARS. WE'LL HAVE MUCH MORE TO SAY ON THIS AS OUR SERIES CONTINUES. |

In the body of the script, we have this lead-in to a statement by a federal official regarding unscrupulous career schools.

26

| REPORTER:<br>ON SCREEN<br>STUDIO | BOB JONES COULDN'T KNOW IT AT THE TIME AND IT'S PROBABLY LITTLE SOLACE TO HIM NOW. BUT THE COMPUTER SCHOOL HE AT-TENDED WOULD LATER BE CITED IN A FEDERAL TRADE COMMISSION COMPLAINT CHARGING MISREPRESENTATION. QUOTING NEWSPAPER. DIRECT-MAIL. AND BROAD-CAST ADVERTISING THAT OFFERED: |
|---|---|
| SUPER CARD BEARING<br>ADVERTISING COPY | "JOB INSURANCE...OUR GRADUATES ARE MOST EMPLOYABLE" |
| SUPER CARD<br>CLAIM COPY<br><br>SUPER<br>DOCUMENT | AND THAT CLAIMED A SCHOOL "JOB PLACEMENT RATE OF 98-POINT-4 PERCENT." TWO YEARS AND COUNTLESS STUDENTS LATER THE F-T-C FILED ITS FIRST FORMAL COMPLAINT. NOW GOING ON FOUR YEARS AND MANY MORE STUDENTS LATER. A HEARING WILL BE HELD ON WHETHER FINALLY TO ORDER THE SCHOOL TO CEASE AND DESIST. |

The above narration is followed by a brief statement, sound on film, of a Federal Trade Commission executive describing what steps the FTC is taking to correct the situation. The use of corroborating statements by officials is not only a standard device of the mini-documentary's structure, but it serves to reinforce the credibility of the program. There is enough material in this one episode to arouse viewers, complacent or not. If they did not see any other episodes, they still would know that there was something rotten in this Denmarkian area. The reporter's concluding statement for this episode tells them there is much more to come. Thus, having given the audience a rounded story, it is still underscored as part of a series.

The actual timing of episode was 6:43. There were 6 episodes in the series, and timing varied for each one—ranging from 5:30 to over 7 minutes. The 6-part series concluded not with an abstract warning but a practical word of advice and assistance which gave added meaning to that FCC requisite, "in the public interest."

| REPORTER:<br>V/O SCENE OF<br>MAN LOOKING AT<br>BROCHURE<br><br>DISSOLVE TO CARD<br>SHOWING ADDRESS<br>DISSOLVE TO SHOTS<br>OF G.W. STUDENTS<br>SUPER<br>CONSUMER HELP | THIS ADVICE GOES FOR OTHER CAREERS AS WELL...AND THERE ARE OTHER POINTERS YOU CAN GET BY INVESTING A TEN-CENT STAMP AND WRITING FOR CAREER SCHOOL INFORMATION TO DEPT. 1. FEDERAL TRADE COMMISSION. ZIP 20580. DEPARTMENT ONE—F-T-C—20580. AND FINALLY. THESE ARE THE GEORGE WASHINGTON UNIVERSITY LAW STUDENTS WHO STAFF OUR CONSUMER HELP CENTER. THERE'S A LONG LIST OF PLACES YOU CAN COMPLAIN TO. IF YOU FEEL YOU'VE BEEN MISLED. BUT WHY NOT |
|---|---|

## VARIATIONS ON A THEME

The news department at WMAL-TV decided to tackle, via the mini-documentary, a subject of prime interest to every viewer: food. The series was presented over a period of 3 weeks, with each week devoted to a different aspect of the topic. Its structure combined all the elements of the informative and the investigative mini-documentary. The first week's series was entitled *Are You Eating Garbage?*; the second week, *Who Watches What We Eat?*; and the third week, *Sunny Side Up*.

The following excerpts and commentary will illustrate the method of presentation. A preceding section of this chapter, **Opening Statements**, included the introduction to the series. Part 2 of *Are You Eating Garbage?* employs both a forthright and humorous approach to that almost sacrosanct American product, the hot dog, and arouses a storm of protest from the food manufacturers. Reporter Jim Clarke, never one to sidestep even a time-honored institution, accomplished his usual thorough research, including the ingestion of a variety of frankfurters, and did not mince words.

| | |
|---|---|
| CLARKE:<br>V/O SHOTS<br>OF INTERIOR OF FOOD<br>MANUFACTURING<br>PLANT | IF EVER YOU NEED TO DISPROVE UGLY RUMORS YOUR STOMACH RESEMBLES A CEMENT MIXER. VISIT YOUR LOCAL FRANKFURTER FACTORY. THAT'S HOW WE STARTED OUR STUDY OF THE HOT DOG. WE DID IT FULLY AWARE IT IS A TASTE-TESTED INSTITUTION RANKING ALONGSIDE GOD. COUNTRY. MOTHERHOOD. AND THE BOY |
| SHOTS OF WORKERS<br>CUTTING MEAT | SCOUTS. FEDERAL REGULATIONS SAY YOUR HOT DOG MAY CONTAIN BEEF. PORK. CHICKEN. TURKEY. AND GOAT MEAT. IT MAY ALSO INCLUDE SUCH ANIMAL BY-PRODUCTS AS SNOUTS. LIPS. SPLEENS. CHEEKS. STOMACHS. AND—WELL. THE LIST—LIKE |
| DISSOLVE TO<br>FULL SHOT<br>MACHINE WHIRRING | THE BEAT—GOES ON.<br><br>IT ALL GOES INTO A BIG MIXMASTER WITH RAZOR SHARP BLADES—TO WHICH THE MANUFACTURER CAN ADD TEN PERCENT WATER—SUPPOSEDLY TO COOL THE BLADES. IN SECONDS. THE BLADES |
| DISSOLVE TO<br>WORKER ADDING<br>SPICES | CONVERT THE HASH TO A DULL GRAY MUSH.<br><br>AN ATTENDANT ADDS BUCKETS OF SPICES AND CORN SYRUP OR DEXTROSE TO ENHANCE THE FLAVOR AND TEXTURE...AND SEVERAL CHEMICALS TO FIX OR HOLD THE |

| DISSOLVE TO<br>SHOTS OF HOT<br>DOGS EJECTED FROM<br>MACHINE | FLAVOR. ANOTHER ADDITIVE. SODIUM NITRITE. IS USED TO INHIBIT THE GROWTH OF DEADLY BACTERIA AND HELP THE FRANK KEEP ITS "HEALTHY" RED TINT. |
| --- | --- |
| | NOW THE MUSH WHICH—EXCEPT FOR SPICES. FLAVORS. AND THINGS—COULD END UP AS SAUSAGE OR LUNCHEON MEAT. HEADS FOR A BIG SQUIRT GUN—WHERE IT IS TURNED INTO HOT DOGS. THE FINISHED PRODUCT CAN CONTAIN UP TO 54 PERCENT WATER. 30 PERCENT FAT. AND 5 PERCENT B I N D E R S .   F L A V O R E R S .   A N D PRESERVATIVES. IT USUALLY CONTAINS 11 TO 12 PERCENT PROTEIN. AT 89 CENTS A POUND. THAT WORKS OUT TO 7 DOLLARS AND 12 CENTS A POUND FOR PROTEIN. THE WATER AND FAT ARE ZERO NUTRITIONAL VALUE. AND THE SODIUM NITRITE IS OF QUESTIONABLE MERIT. |
| DISSOLVE TO<br>DR. JACOBSON'S<br>OFFICE | DR. MICHAEL JACOBSON. AN M-I-T MICROBIOLOGIST. NOW CODIRECTOR OF THE CENTER FOR SCIENCE IN THE PUBLIC INTEREST. HAS STUDIED THE HOT DOG...WITH DEPRESSING RESULTS. |
| DR. JACOBSON:<br>FULL SHOT AT OFFICE.<br>BACKGROUND OF<br>SHELVES<br>LINED WITH BOXES<br>AND<br>CANS OF FOOD<br>PRODUCTS AND<br>VIALS OF DYES | THE AMOUNT OF FAT IN THE HOT DOG HAS INCREASED FROM ABOUT 18 PERCENT UP TO THE CURRENT 29 PERCENT IN THE LAST 35 YEARS. MEANWHILE THE AMOUNT OF PROTEIN HAS GONE FROM ABOUT 19 PERCENT ALL THE WAY DOWN TO ABOUT 12 PERCENT. THE HOT DOG THE PEOPLE KNEW IN 1937 DOES NOT EXIST TODAY. |

This mini-documentary, as you will have observed from the foregoing excerpts, follows the pattern of presenting an expert with impeccable credentials to corroborate the reporter's findings. This is essential for any investigative mini-documentary. There are always two sides to a controversy, however; and as we have noted, the negative statements about the frankfurter brought a host of protests from the food manufacturers. The protests were acknowledged during the third week's series on food, *Sunny Side Up*.

| INTRO<br>ANCHORMAN:<br>STUDIO | JIM CLARKE'S EARLIER REPORT ON THE HOT DOG DREW HOWLS OF PROTEST FROM THE MEAT INDUSTRY. LETTERS CAME IN FROM AS FAR AWAY AS MILWAUKEE. |
| --- | --- |
| | JOHN F. KLEMENT. PRESIDENT OF MILWAUKEE'S KLEMENT'S SAUSAGE COMPANY. WROTE: "THE HOT DOG IS A GOOD SOURCE OF PROTEIN" AND SAID PEOPLE |

ALL OVER THE WORLD CONSIDER THE MEAT BY-PRODUCTS USED IN HOT DOGS—"GOURMET FOOD."

FROM RALPH NADER'S OFFICE CAME A REMINDER OF MARK TWAIN'S LINE—"IF YOU WANT TO KEEP YOUR RESPECT FOR HOT DOGS AND POLITICIANS, DON'T LOOK TOO CLOSELY AT HOW EITHER WAS MADE."

SO, TOSSING CAUTION TO THE WIND, JIM REVISITS THE HOT DOG TONIGHT—ONCE OVER LIGHTLY—IN PART 2 OF "SUNNY SIDE UP."

Further on in this episode of *Sunny Side Up* the president of the American Meat Institute is given rebuttal time.

| ANCHORMAN: STUDIO | THE PRESIDENT OF THE AMERICAN MEAT INSTITUTE FLEW IN FROM CHICAGO LAST WEEK TO DEFEND THE HOT DOG. DR. HERRELL DEGRAFF SAID THE HOT DOG HOLDS ITS OWN NUTRITIONALLY WHEN COMPARED TO A GOOD T-BONE STEAK. AND HE NOTED, THERE IS AN OPTION FOR THOSE WHO DON'T WANT SNOUTS, LIPS, SPLEENS AND SO FORTH IN THEIR FRANKS. |
|---|---|
| DR. DEGRAFF: SOUND ON FILM CLOSEUP | I'D LIKE TO MAKE THE POINT TO SOME FOLKS WHO HAVE OBJECTED TO SOME OF THE BY-PRODUCTS IN HOT DOGS THAT FOR MANY, THESE MATERIALS ARE OFTEN CONSIDERED DELICACIES. WE WOULDN'T BE TOO FAR OUT OF LINE TALKING TO SOME FOLKS TO SAY THESE ARE FRANKFURTERS MADE WITH GOURMET ITEMS. NOW, I'M TALKING ABOUT TRIPE AND TONGUE AND THINGS OF THIS KIND WHICH CERTAINLY IN THE EUROPEAN COUNTRIES ARE HIGHLY PRIZED. BUT HERE AT HOME, THOSE WHO DON'T LIKE THE IDEA OF THE BY-PRODUCTS IN THEIR FRANKFURTERS CAN EASILY AVOID THEM BECAUSE ABOUT 70 PERCENT OF OUR TOTAL PRODUCTION OF FRANKFURTERS ARE MADE TO THE SO-CALLED "ALL MEAT" FORMULA, WHICH PERMITS ONLY SKELETAL MEAT. AND ADDITIONALLY, IF ANY BY-PRODUCTS ARE USED, THESE HAVE TO BE LISTED BY NAME IN THE INGREDIENTS STATEMENT ON THE PACKAGE. |

The inclusion of rebuttals during the course of a mini-documentary series or as a follow-up is a factor unique to the mini-documentary. The full-length documentary does not permit such flexibility. It may present both sides of a controversial issue within the given half-hour or hour; but the scripts—the point and counterpoint—would have been prepared weeks or months before airtime.

However, a federal official or an industry executive may catch an episode of a mini-documentary series and ask to be heard in rebuttal. His or her statement can be filmed in the same manner and the same speed as any news event and then inserted within the body of an upcoming episode of the series. This adds *recency* value to the mini-documentary and contributes greatly to its newsworthiness.

The full-length documentary has no such resiliency. A case in point: A television station scheduled an hour documentary on the Navajo Indians. An Indian viewer wrote a letter to the editor of the local newspaper protesting that the documentary did the Navajos a disservice because it portrayed them as a tribe still performing ancient rites and living in the past. There were no scenes in the documentary showing the Navajos coming to grips with contemporary society, adjusting to new environments, and advancing themselves in the new technology. If this documentary had been presented as a mini-documentary series, it would have been possible to film the letter writer and his comments and insert them as part of the series or as a follow-up. Although this was a purely informative documentary, it still lent itself to dispute.

The reporter/producer of an investigative mini-documentary series may actively seek rebuttal, but the individual or organization involved may—and often does—refuse to participate. This situation occurred when WTOP-TV presented its mini-documentary series, *Home Buyer, Beware*. The reporter approached one of the builders whose home buyers were complaining of shoddy construction. The builder refused to respond. The course the reporter took was to include a statement to that effect during the episode involving that particular builder.

| REPORTER:<br>ON SCREEN | OFFICIALS OF THE COMPANY MET WITH US BUT DECLINED TO BE FILMED OR TAPED. SAYING THAT FOR THEM TO DO SO WOULD ONLY ADD FUEL TO THE FIRE. |
|---|---|

## RECAPITULATION

In this study of the structure of the mini-documentary we have underscored the maxim that each episode of a mini-documentary series should be an entity in itself and yet part of an integrated whole. This brings up the question of recapitulation. There is no standard guide. An examination of many programs shows that there are numerous variations. Some of the stations use no recapitulation on the basis that it is time-consuming and unnecessary. The audience will discover the theme of the mini-documentary from each opening statement; and since each episode is planned as a complete story, it is not essential that the viewer watch every episode even though that is what the news department is striving for.

One of the WTOP-TV mini-documentary series, *The Eye Doctor Feud and You*, deals with the problem the consumer faces in deciding whether to visit an optometrist or an ophthalmologist for an eye examination. Here is the introduction to episode 2:

| ANCHORMAN:<br>STUDIO | ILLNESS CAN MEAN A VISIT TO A PHYSICIAN. BUT IN THE CASE OF A VISION PROBLEM. IT'S NOT THAT SIMPLE FOR THE CONSUMER BECAUSE OF THE CHOICE BETWEEN TWO SEPARATE EYE CARE PRACTITIONERS—THE DOCTOR OF OPTOMETRY AND THE MEDICAL DOCTOR. HERE IS EYEWITNESS NEWS CORRESPONDENT JIM MICHIE WITH HIS SECOND REPORT ON "THE EYE DOCTOR FEUD AND YOU." |
|---|---|

The above introduction uses a brief recapitulation of the subject under investigation.

In the first episode of this mini-documentary series, the concluding statement attempts to arouse the interest of the viewer to watch succeeding episodes.

| MICHIE:<br>STUDIO<br>SUPER TITLE | BOTH SIDES—OPTOMETRY AND OPHTHALMOLOGY—DO AGREE THAT THE CONSUMER WHO REQUIRES EYE CARE IN THE WASHINGTON AREA PROBABLY FACES MORE PROBLEMS THAN THE CONSUMER IN MOST OTHER LARGE CITIES.<br><br>IN OUR NEXT REPORT. WE'LL BEGIN EXAMINING SOME OF THOSE PROBLEMS. |
|---|---|

WMAL-TV also uses a brief recapitulation for many of its mini-documentary series—for example, this introduction to part 3 of *Who Watches What We Eat?*:

| ANCHORMAN:<br>STUDIO<br>SUPER TITLE | THE RODENT HAS FIGURED PROMINENTLY IN JIM CLARKE'S RECENT INVESTIGATION OF THE FOOD WE EAT. LARGELY BECAUSE OF ITS UNWANTED "CALLING CARD" IN SOME OF OUR FOOD.<br><br>TONIGHT. IN PART 3 OF "WHO WATCHES WHAT WE EAT?". JIM GIVES US A DIFFERENT PERSPECTIVE OF BROTHER RAT. AND HE WARNS OF A PENDING COLLISION OF SCIENCE AND THE LAW. |
|---|---|

## FOLLOW-UPS

When a mini-documentary series has uncovered a particularly vulnerable situation—mistreatment of patients in an institution for the mentally retarded or neglected slum areas, for example—the television station's news department will often present a sequence of follow-ups. These follow-ups may consist of 1-minute on-location spots to demonstrate that no action has yet been taken or to show on-going improvements. If warranted, the station may develop a second series on the same subject. This helps to maintain a serious public-interest image for the station: the mini-documentary is telecast not merely to increase the viewing audience but to point up a willingness on the part of the station to help combat some of society's ills.

## CAMERA

In the *New York Times Magazine* of January 12, 1975, Earl Ubell, Director, WNBC-TV News, took to task Robert Daley who had previously written an article for the magazine (*We Deal With Emotional Facts*, December 15, 1974) on the station's news operations. Daley had said, among other critiques, that camera operators do not regard themselves as journalists. Ubell disagreed: "Their eyes and skills capture the essence of the story on film just as the reporter grasps the facts."

Obviously without the cameraman there would be no motion pictures, the essential visuals for the mini-documentary. The cameraman may or may not have a journalistic sense, that is, be first and foremost a photo-journalist, rather than a technician. In *The Work of the Motion Picture Cameraman* (Hastings House), Freddie Young, formerly chief cameraman for MGM, states that the cameraman's "most important attributes are a fully developed pictorial sense and a sound understanding of the technical basis on which it must be built. He is an artist and a technician."

The cameraman must work closely with the reporter/producer. He should be fully informed of the script requirements and should be brought in to help in planning the shooting. Ubell comments, "We advise young reporters to bring the cameraman in on a story, to ask the cameraman's advice; he wants to be asked. The reporter has to be a field producer."

Ideally, the cameraman must be able to operate with speed, precision, and an artistic eye for composition. There are times when his ingenuity will be taxed because he has to work with a hidden camera filming some aspects of an investigative mini-documentary. Usually, the reporter/producer will tell the cameraman which shots he or she desires, but the cameraman should offer his opinion as to whether the shots look good or not.

Use of hand-held camera requires high degree of skill and concentration. Note sound man at right wearing headphones.

The cameraman must be able to operate under a wide range of conditions. The mini-documentary covers such a variety of subjects that one week the cameraman will be filming the faces of retarded children in an institution and the following week, the rutted roads of a land development.

In an interview, a facial expression or gesture may be all important. It may show that the interviewee has been jolted by an incisive query. The aware cameraman will capture the look or the movement and it will not be lost on the viewer.

There is no question of the importance of the cameraman; his skill and his artistry are of immeasurable value to the impact of the mini-documentary. However, it is not within the scope of this volume to cover the technique of the camera. There are several excellent books of interest and assistance to the cameraman and apprentice.

## SUMMATION

Subsequent chapters of this book contain complete scripts of mini-documentary series to present an overall view of individual program structure. In this chapter we have outlined the basic structure of a series. We have not enunciated rigid guidelines because we are dealing with an area of creativity—and the essence of creativity is originality, the ability to combine talent and imagination in the presentation of any theme, to capture attention, and to maintain interest.

At most television stations, the reporter/producer is given wide latitude. His or her only restriction is budget: at network affiliates, budgets are large; at independent stations, budgets are slim. Perhaps this presents more of a challenge to the independent station's reporters who have to employ ingenuity to overcome economic limitations.

As in the full-length documentary, sight and sound in the mini-documentary have to be skillfully intertwined. A shot of a child whose battered face attests to a brutal beating will arouse shock and sympathy. The viewer will also be aroused by an interview with an elderly widow who has been fleeced of her life's savings.

There is no subject that the mini-documentary cannot tackle. No theme is taboo: the principal criterion is quality. Since the majority of mini-documentaries are investigative in nature, reporters will often find themselves in the midst of highly controversial issues. It will be difficult for them to be completely objective; all of us have our loves and hates. But any time a news department is accused of bias, its credibility is called into question. And credibility must be the keystone of the mini-documentary.

Hand-held camera and sound equipment for filming of crop-duster pilot in "Risk" mini-documentary series.

Use of camera on tripod demonstrated at Redskins football game by WMAL-TV.

This inevitably raises the question of sponsor influence. What if the mini-documentary is investigating the wholesomeness of food products manufactured by a company which, coincidentally, happens to be an advertiser on the daily newscast. The consensus among news directors is that sponsors do not and cannot influence newscasts. Newsman Earl Ubell affirms categorically that "Advertisers have nothing to say about news. Newspeople control the news at NBC, not station managers."

Ed Joyce, WCBS-TV, says, "If our consumer affairs correspondent does a piece knocking, say, an antacid and we happen to have an ad on for that antacid, then we will move that ad to another part of the show or even give the advertiser the option of canceling it."

Some news directors we have interviewed complained that competing stations often sacrificed newsworthiness for raciness in their mini-documentaries. However, our examination of the numerous mini-documentaries produced by those stations showed that although racy subjects were included, the majority of the mini-documentaries covered the gamut of society's shortcomings. Of course, the mini-documentary should be entertaining in the widest meaning of that word. There is no excuse for dullness. Phil Nye, news director for WABC-TV, summed up this aspect succinctly: "A degree of entertainment is inevitable in TV news. But our function is not entertainment, it's information and, hopefully, education."

There may be some differences of opinion as to the definition of a mini-documentary. In this book we have defined the mini-documentary as a series of brief integrated episodes dealing with a subject of prime interest to the local community, or of national scope, and presented within the body of daily newscasts.

News directors may at times refer to a one-time presentation as a mini-documentary. Generally, they are speaking of feature spots as against hard news. A bank robbery: hard news. How alcoholics are being rehabilitated at a local center: feature. But alcoholics are a problem to the community and it is news if alcoholism is successfully controlled. Whether you give 2 minutes to the bank robbery and 3 minutes to alcoholism, they are both news events.

The mini-documentary goes far beyond the feature spot. A series may run from 5 to 12 weeks and even longer. A reporter may be assigned to mini-documentaries exclusively. He may spend weeks or even months in researching, planning, writing, and producing a series. Under these circumstances, the mini-documentary can be singularly defined and, as Professor Madsen noted, "unique to television."

# Chapter 3
# The Interviewer

An integral part of the mini-documentary is the interview. Anyone who has cared for an inquisitive child or observed the breed will have encountered the progenitor of the interviewer. A child's questions can be a delight, a burden, or a bore. In any event, the child is eliciting information: "Why, Daddy?" "Where do babies come from, Mommy?"

A reporter's function is to ask questions to elicit information. If he is an investigative reporter, he may have to ferret out the truth. How he goes about those interviews will determine the success of his documentary series. Mike Wallace in *Television Quarterly* noted that one of the functions of the interviewer is to "talk no more than necessary." The reporter's job is to encourage the interviewee to talk.

When the reporter is working on a purely informative mini-documentary, he is generally seeking background or descriptive material. But when he is handling a controversial subject he may, as Mike Wallace does, "push, prod, and encourage" the participants to make direct statements of their views. Obviously, the reporter for the mini-documentary cannot engage in the same type of interview that Mike Wallace or Elizabeth Drew would conduct with a half-hour or hour segment at his or her disposal. Since the mini-documentary is shown in brief episodes, perhaps 3 minutes—the time will vary depending on the interest value of the sequence—the interviews must be succinct.

Although the subject may be provocative, the interviewee may prove dull. For example, real estate closing costs arouse every home buyer; however, the buyer may be angered about the situation but inarticulate. The skillful reporter will have to be adept at choosing his participants and adroit in drawing them out.

Reuven Frank has said that the best interviews are "of people reacting—not people expounding. Joy, sorrow, shock, fear—these are the stuff of news."

The interviewer should be figuratively and often literally in the background. The viewers want to know what the participants have to say. Evidently they have been chosen because they have pertinent information to impart. Questions by the reporter should be brief unless it is necessary to recapitulate a situation.

Wherever possible, it is preferable to interview one person at a time. When WMAL-TV reporter Jim Clarke went to Toronto to produce his mini-documentary series on *Americans in Exile—A Question of Amnesty*, he interviewed one exiled man or man-and-wife for each episode. In this way he was not only able to make a more cogent presentation but it was possible to deal more fully with one person's reactions. The final episode, however, was a wrapup on the feelings of those exiled about returning home.

To get the interviewee to be responsive, the reporter must himself be equally responsive, not in the number of words but in his manner—his approach. And he must come prepared. Only comprehensive research will provide him with sufficient background to ask the proper questions.

Many times because of the social significance of the mini-documentary, reporters will have to interview public officials. Usually, statements by public officials are self-serving. When an official is being questioned about a problem under his jurisdiction, he will, most likely, attempt to justify his position. A reporter should have enough awareness of the situation to know whether he is being conned or being told the truth. The reporter is not omniscient and assuredly the official will know more about his area of control than the reporter or be privy to documents withheld from the public. An abundance of tact is required to draw out the interviewee. Antagonizing a participant may induce some colorful language more suitable for an X-rated movie than a television program.

It is best to demonstrate to the official that you are fair minded and are listening willingly to his side of the story. Perhaps a footnote to the beginning reporter might not be amiss. The young man or woman reporter may be intimidated or even overcome with awe in the presence of a well-known official who has appeared often in the headlines. Simply remember that, elected or appointed, the functionary is serving directly or indirectly at the will of the people. The elected official is there because the people, through their votes, placed him in a position of responsibility to them. He is, in essence, a public servant, not a master. Too many officials are prone to forget that relationship and often assume a posture of unquestioned authority. It is the reporter's function, in a fair but decisive manner, to pierce any cautiously worded, ambiguous statement. The public official should command respect for what he does, not what he is. Some of the incisive questions asked by reporters at presidential news conferences should demonstrate to the beginner that no public official is sacrosanct.

There are some cautions that should be observed by the reporter. The public official may say that the information he is imparting is "off the record." The reporter will honor the confidentiality unless he learns that he can obtain the same information from another source. He will then either confront the official with this knowledge or if his other source is equally authoritative, go ahead and use the material. Otherwise, if he breaks his trust, he can be sure the official will consider him *persona non grata* and a fountain of information will have dried up for him.

Another problem may arise when an interviewee requests that a portion of his interview not be used. If the reporter believes

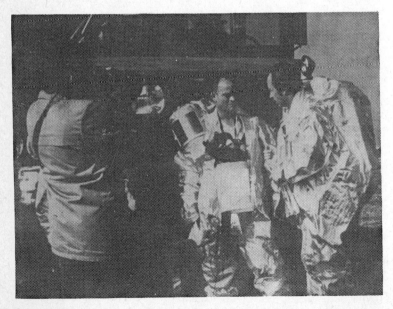

Typical distance for closeup interview shot. Interviewer takes part in fire-safety procedure.

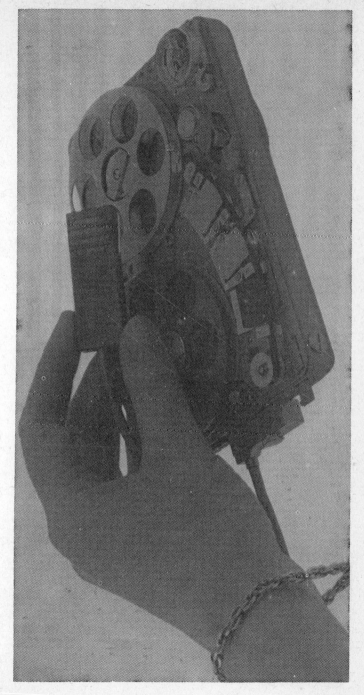

NAGRA SN miniature tape recorder for interviews.

that the requested deletion will in no way affect the impact of his mini-documentary he will probably accede. Sometimes an interviewee may make an intimate revelation about which he or she later has reservations or which may prove to be injurious to the interviewee's reputation. If this information is titillating but unessential, discretion becomes the better part of valor. However, if the reporter firmly believes that the information is absolutely necessary to the mini-documentary's significance, he should confer with his news director; it may even become an issue for the legal department. The reporter may have real estate deals and the executive may have made a statement, inadvertently or not, which verified the reporter's research. The executive might then back down and request that the statement not be used. The elimination of the statement would weaken the impact of the mini-documentary. If the reporter is convinced of the truth of the statement, he will use it. Again, he should check with the news director to get the backing of the station. The reporter must know that he cannot be shackled in bringing the truth to the community. His own integrity and credibility are at stake.

Hugh C. Sherwood has written an excellent treatise on *The Journalistic Interview* (Harper and Row). He stresses the factor that "probing is the key skill in interviewing...How can you best probe? Ask open-end questions: What do you think about? Ask reflective questions: Can you tell me a bit more about how you feel? Ask interpretive or summary questions: You're saying, then, that...? Or ask problem questions. Let's suppose that you're president of a company faced with the following situation..."

It is incumbent on the reporter to ascertain that statements made by the interviewee can be backed up by fact. The credibility of the reporter will be destroyed if he uses material which has no basis in fact. Or a self-serving public official may speak in half-truths which would eventually prove embarrassing to the reporter.

As one reporter observed, "You have to have the technique of a trial lawyer, the ability to elicit information from a hostile or uncooperative witness." It is not necessary to write down every question you have in mind, but you should be able to pose your questions in the right order. Again, like a trial lawyer, moving step by step to a final revelation.

As you ask your basic questions, responses made by the interviewee will inevitably lead to other questions you may not otherwise have formulated. The necessity for thorough research cannot be stressed too strongly. You should be so familiar with the subject that you probably know the answers to the questions you are planning to ask. This will enable you to determine whether the respondent is telling the truth. If he is not, then without hesitancy you can challenge his assertions.

Perhaps there is a reporter's instinct that guides his or her probing activities. More than likely, however, the ability to ask the proper questions and ferret out information is a matter of experience.

# Chapter 4
# The Mini-Documentary
# Approach of ABC
# Affiliate WMAL- TV

As noted in the preface, we are presenting in-depth studies of four television stations in a large metropolitan area, Washington, D.C., and a comparative analysis of their mini-documentary productions. This chapter will be devoted to WMAL-TV, a station affiliated with the American Broadcasting Company.

WMAL-TV has been producing award-winning mini-documentaries for years. Two of its series, *Shades of Gay* and *Sin City II—Baltimore's Block*, won public affairs prizes at the 1974 Atlanta International Film Festival. Who decides on the subject matter? "Suggestions come from everybody," news director Dave Kelly says. It could be a member of the staff or it could be a viewer. People complain they have been overcharged by auto repair shops or TV repairmen, and it sets the investigative wheels in motion. Or perhaps the consumer affairs reporter uncovers a bad product or a possible fraud. These are all grist for the mini-documentary mill. Many television stations have an editorial board which chooses the topics for the day's or the week's editorial. But there is no such board for deciding the themes for mini-documentaries.

Do the station's editorials influence the mini-documentary? Is the series an extension of the station's editorial policy? The answer is no. There is hardly an instance on record where a station editorial has been the catalyst for a mini-documentary. The reverse is invariably true. The facts unearthed by the reporter have often served as the basis for a station's editorial.

WMAL-TV has one or two mini-documentaries in the works at all times. Many are investigative, some purely informational, others a combination of both.

There is no arbitrary limit to the number of episodes that make up a mini-documentary series. The duration of the series depends on its scope, its importance, the amount of interesting material available. A series can run anywhere from 3 to 10 episodes, and often there are follow-ups.

There are also no arbitrary limits to the length of segments. WMAL-TV, like most stations, tends to keep episodes to 3 minutes, but there are times when a sequence may run to 10 minutes. Again, it is a question of interest value. It is possible for a 2-minute segment to be dull and seem twice its length, whereas a 5- or 10-minute episode may be filled with such engrossing material that the time seems short.

There are problems involved in investigative reports. Special techniques may be required. For example, in preparing a series on TV repair, no names of those who took advantage of their customers were used. But the names of satisfactory repair shops were given. In the series on auto repairs, however, names of exorbitant dealers were broadcast. Could this lead to lawsuits? Possibly. The news director checks any such potential hazards with the station's legal department. As Dave Kelly observed, "We don't put anything on the air we don't feel secure about." In any of the investigative series, subjects are given the opportunity to defend themselves if they so desire.

The observant reader will undoubtedly raise the question as to why the auto repair dealers' names were used and not the TV repairmen, who were equally at fault. It is a fine point. The automobile test car was especially engineered for the series, as you will note in the scripts reproduced in this chapter, and was completely under the control of the station staff. On the other hand, the station, in order to avoid any question of erroneous confrontation, took into consideration the unlikely possibility that the sensitive television set might be jarred in transportation to the repair shop. As we stated, this is a very fine point since the station employed highly skilled technicians to maintain equipment and to judge the honesty of repairs and charges. Nevertheless, that was the rationale.

It is extremely important that research be accomplished; the reports must be accurate. If there were a loss of credibility, the entire concept of mini-documentaries could be destroyed.

The mini-documentary has a definite impact on the community. One example, Dave Kelly noted, was a series surveying the number of doctors listed in the classified section of the Washington telephone directory who, it turned out, were not licensed to practice in the District of Columbia. They were medical practitioners, but each state requires a physician to be licensed under its jurisdiction. The net effect of the presentation of this series was that the telephone company changed its policy and each physician was checked prior to listing. The mini-documentaries on TV and auto repair led to a resolution by the Washington city council commending the station.

Production staffs at most of the stations are comparable in size, if not in quality. Obviously, the network affiliates are more affluent and have more film crews than independent stations. At WMAL-TV the mini-documentary crew may consist of a producer/director, a reporter/narrator/writer, cameraman, sound man, and a lighting technician for indoor locations. The news director believes that a field producer can be helpful in saving the reporter's time. The field producer can undertake the responsibility for camera angles and other technical requirements, thus freeing the reporter to concentrate on the story.

The average time for WMAL reporters in putting together a mini-documentary is 4 to 6 weeks, but the time can vary from a week to several months. Production costs are high. But the mini-documentaries do attract audiences and increase ratings. Generally, the subject of the mini-documentaries is confined to local issues; but here again there are no restrictions, as witness the series on amnesty.

A basic problem is obtaining good visuals and avoiding static scenes. However, if what the participants are saying is vital, any gimmicks or unnecessary cutaways may only prove distracting.

Dave Kelly believes the mini-documentaries will continue into the foreseeable future as an integral part of a news program. The mini-documentary affords the television audience a better opportunity to be informed. It also is scheduled at a time that is relatively convenient, since so many people do watch newscasts.

## THE REPORTER'S VIEWPOINT

What does it take to be an investigative reporter? Jim Clarke has an extensive background in journalism, including a degree in Communication Arts from Fordham University. Before joining the WMAL-TV news team, he worked as a reporter for several newspapers around the country and had general reporting assignments for several TV stations.

If you ask him for a basic distinction between broadcast news and the print media, his reply is that television is the "medium of essence" whereas the newspaper is the "medium of record." Television has to encapsulate the news because of stringent time restrictions; it extracts the essence of the news. Newspapers can go into very detailed accounts. As a reporter, there is a difference, also, in approach: an investigative reporter for television has high visibility as compared to a newspaper reporter. People will recognize the reporter they have seen on TV while a newspaper reporter may have his byline but is unknown visually. It is, therefore, a more difficult task for the TV reporter to do investigative reporting. At times, the TV reporter must have an associate accomplish research he would rather do himself. Broadcast journalists tend to be generalists. Tv news staffs are comparatively small and the TV reporter cannot cover beats in a manner similar to the newspaper reporter. The TV reporter for a local station is also limited in his sources compared to network reporters. The well-known network reporters have enormous influence. Informants bring them material or identify sources or there are official leaks to them.

Jim Clarke's procedure in preparing a mini-documentary series is both thorough and logical. He believes in full-fledged research, including poring over the files of newspapers to see what has been written on the subject—not only the local *Washington Post* and *Star News* but the *New York Times* and national magazines. He literally steeps himself in the subject. Often this all-consuming research is actually timesaving in avoiding blind alleys and additionally productive in permitting the reporter to discover whether or not there are new developments which have not been covered or questions which remain unanswered. The reporter will then be able to present a more comprehensive series and perhaps say something new about the subject. The editorial policy of the station does not influence the reporter in his choice of subject matter. Management does not intrude upon the news department. With a reporter's instinct, Jim Clarke wants to be "out on the street" where the events occur and he likes to deal with a great variety of subjects—which permits him a wider choice of theme.

His next step is to determine the visual aspects; collectively, the newspaper reporter might call them illustrative material. Clarke usually operates with a 2-man crew: cameraman and sound man. He prefers to act as his own producer/director. Deadlines are flexible since so much depends on the scope of the topic.

He then decides on the story form and begins writing. An outline or synopsis is prepared which gives an overview to the film editor. Clarke works very closely with the film editor and relies on his sensitivity and capability. However, the reporter makes the substantive decision on the content of the story and leaves the esthetics to the film editor. Clarke also decides on the number of segments the series will warrant. A consultant once hired by the station claimed that the mini-documentary should never run more than 3 episodes, on the rationale that it would be unlikely for a viewer to watch more than 3 parts, a theory Clarke discounts and believes is negated by viewer response. The fact is, as we have noted, WMAL-TV has not set arbitrary limits on the number of episodes. Nor is there an arbitrary time limit to the segments. Clarke disagrees with whoever promulgated the thesis that audience attention span to any news item is 3 minutes. The interest value is what counts. There have been times when episodes have run 7 to 10 minutes. For example, in a series on food contamination, one sequence was concerned with toxicology and time was needed to give the viewer a proper understanding of the subject.

Clarke makes the final decision as to what appears on the air. This is a delegated responsibility. He will invariably choose what is said rather than how it looks. Often a comment is made that a scene is too static. The episode should be kept moving with a great many visual images. Naturally, when you are working with a visual medium you should try to present your story in as interesting a visual fashion as possible. But no visual setting or even extraordinary photography will overcome lack of content. If a man who is evidently in desperate straits reveals he is facing financial ruin because he signed a note that turned out to be fraudulent, the audience will be intent on his tale of woe, not his surroundings.

The preparation for and production of mini-documentaries are very demanding on the reporter. Clarke finds that he does much of his work at home. He does his own transcribing. In that way he has a complete recall of the dialog, the demeanor of the participants, and the interpretation of voice inflection.


## AMERICANS IN EXILE: A REPORT FROM CANADA

Now let us examine several of the mini-documentaries as they were actually aired by WMAL-TV. One series that delivered a tremendous impact and received voluminous response dealt with the controversial issue of amnesty. Obviously, this is a national theme. There was no attempt to localize the series by interviewing exiles who may have come from the Washington metropolitan area. Reporter Jim Clarke felt that amnesty was a particularly troubling problem which would be of interest to all viewers.

This is how he approached the subject in his own words: "I went up to Canada to find out who these people are, why they are there, what they are doing, and what their thoughts are about the future. I didn't go there to argue with them. The story wasn't to defend or condone what they had done. I think I captured fairly adequately what the situation was."

We are reproducing this mini-documentary series in its entirety to give you a fully comprehensive view of what each episode contains, how the participants are handled, the types of visuals employed, and the writing quality. Note also that this series was presented on both the 6 and 11 p.m. news programs which, for budgetary purposes, conceivably halved the cost of the series.

The first episode, entitled *Preview*, was presented on a Friday evening. The rationale was that the subject matter would have enough impact to carry over the weekend and pique enough interest to lure a host of viewers the following week.

The opening visuals established the locale: Toronto. The participants were chosen for this preview with an eye and an ear for colorful background and occupation: Crazy David who built a multimillion-dollar empire in exile, Bill King who is a jazz blues pianist, Rosemary Frances, the wife of an Army deserter.

Episode 1 is exposition, a brief historical background describing what led these men into exile and comments on the question of amnesty. There is no recapitulation. Each sequence speaks for itself and is, in essence, complete in itself with a beginning, a middle, and an end. No segment depends on the previous one. We can accept each one as a totality. Also, Jim Clarke has devoted each episode to one person or one couple to give us an integrated story in the brief time allotted. Episodes 8 and 10 are exceptions. Here the reporter is attempting to obtain a consensus. Episode 8 is concerned with the possibility of a congressman coming to Toronto to take testimony. In episode 10, the final sequence, we have a wrap-up based on the exiles' reactions to going home.

With the preview there are actually 11 episodes in this mini-documentary series and each one runs approximately 3 minutes. There are variations in production technique. Both the *preview* and the first series *episode* employ straight narration by the reporter. Episode 1 is historic library footage. With episode 2 we begin to hear from the exiles. Jim Clarke met with the participants for an overall briefing and then let them express their opinions freely. What finally appeared on screen was Clarke's choice. As we have stated previously, the end product is a subjective decision on the part of the reporter. The audience must rely on his integrity and his judgment to present an issue in its proper perspective and without bias. In Clarke's case, as he has told us, he makes his own transcripts and he is therefore throughly familiar with all the dialog. He follows his own precept that television is a "medium of essence."

As anticipated, the series drew an excellent response, so much so that WMAL-TV scheduled an hour-and-a-half live discussion program on amnesty originating from Toronto and Washington.

## PREVIEW—FRIDAY

**EXTERIORS FROM ROOFTOP SHOWING NEW AND OLD CITY HALL. PHILIP NATHAN PLAZA. ICE RINK... REVERSE ZOOM FROM FLAG TO CLARKE. GROUND LEVEL VIEW CLARKE W/CITY HALL FRAMED IN BACKGROUND**

A REPORTER COMING TO TORONTO LOOKING FOR THOUSANDS OF AMERICAN DRAFT DODGERS AND DESERTERS—HAS A RUDE AWAKENING.

HE DOESN'T SLIP INTO A SCENARIO RIGHT OUT OF THE POISONED AND BITTER POLITICS OF THE SIXTIES.

HE FINDS NO COFFEE HOUSES OR RALLIES TEEMING WITH ANGRY EXILES DENOUNCING THE WAR AND DEMANDING AMNESTY.

THAT ISN'T BECAUSE THE DRAFT DODGERS AND DESERTERS AREN'T HERE. THEY ARE— TENS OF THOUSAND OF THEM. WITH THEIR WIVES AND CHILDREN. OR THEIR GIRLFRIENDS.

**PEOPLE. CHILDREN SKATING ON ICE RINK... CHILDREN FALL... CLARKE WALKS ALONGSIDE ICE RINK MONTAGE ILLUSTRATIVE OF COPY.**

THEY'RE HARD TO FIND BECAUSE THEY'VE BLENDED INTO THE EXCITING AND DISTINCTIVE CONTRASTS OF THIS QUITE REMARKABLE CITY AND CULTURE.

TORONTO IS CANADA'S FINANCIAL AND COMMERCIAL CENTER AND NORTH AMERICA'S FASTEST-GROWING URBAN INDUSTRIAL COMPLEX. IT IS FREE. OPEN. BEAUTIFUL. AND RICHLY DESERVES ITS REPUTATION AS THE CITY THAT LOVES PEOPLE.

IT WAS LIKE A MAGNET TO THE TENS OF THOUSANDS OF YOUNG AMERICANS WHO FLED AMERICA IN THE SIXTIES TO ESCAPE THE WAR IN VIETNAM.

BUT YOU DON'T FIND THESE DRAFT DODGERS AND DESERTERS CLUSTERED IN NEATLY DEFINED COLONIES OR COMMUNITIES. DRAWN TOGETHER BY LONELINESS AND DESPERATION.

ALTHOUGH MANY ARE LONELY. AND SOME LIVE FURTIVE. DESPERATE LIVES. FOR THE MOST PART. THEY ARE A REMARKABLE HUMAN MOSAIC: YOUNGSTERS AS DIFFERENT AS ANY YOU MIGHT COME ACROSS IN DOZENS OF RANDOM INTERVIEWS HERE.

50

SOUND FULL, CRAZY
DAVID
SINGING AND PLAYING
PIANO...PULL WIDE TO
SHOW WHOLE BAND,
THEN BACK
TO CRAZY...HOLD :10
THEN CLARKE FULL
V/O

HE IS CALLED CRAZY DAVID. A 27-YEAR-OLD
DRAFT DODGER FROM BIRMINGHAM. HE
FLED TO TORONTO IN 1970 WITH A 300-
DOLLAR BANKROLL. HE HAS PARLAYED
THAT INTO A MULTIMILLION-DOLLAR EM-
PIRE BASED ON THE SALE OF CRAZY DAVID
T-SHIRTS. NEXT MONTH HE WILL BECOME A
CANADIAN CITIZEN.

SILENT

V/O HAL
AND ROSEMARY
FRANCES

EXILE AS AN ARMY DESERTER HAS NOT
BEEN AS HAPPY AND SUCCESSFUL FOR HAL
FRANCES AND HIS WIFE ROSEMARY:

ROSEMARY FRANCES:

...IT'S BEEN HARD BECAUSE WE'VE BEEN
ISOLATED COMPLETELY FROM OUR
FAMILIES. LIKE ALL THE NORMAL THINGS
PEOPLE DO WITH THEIR FAMILIES. THE
BIRTHDAYS. THE NORMAL HOLIDAYS. WE
MISS EVERYTHING. AND FOR THAT OUR
LIVES ARE EMPTY.

SUPER
JACK COLHOUN:
(DESERTER, SCHOLAR,
WRITER)

...THEY WANT TO BE ABLE TO ATTEND
THEIR PARENTS FUNERALS OR THEIR IL-
LNESSES. AND WITHOUT AMNESTY YOU
CAN'T DO THAT. EVEN AS A CANADIAN
CITIZEN. YOU CAN'T GO BACK TO THE
STATES. OTHER PEOPLE HAVE BEEN ABLE
TO ACCEPT IN THEMSELVES THE FACT THAT
THEY WOULD LIKE TO GO BACK TO AMERICA
IF AMERICA ISN'T THAT WHICH IS
REPRESENTED BY RICHARD NIXON.

SOUND FULL, BILL
KING
PLAYING PIANO,
SINGING
"GOODBY
SUPERDAD"...
SOUND UNDER V/O

AS A YOUNGSTER....JAZZ BLUES PIANIST BILL
KING TOOK HIS PIANO LESSONS FROM W.C.
HANDY AND PIANIST AVA SMITH. LATER HE
WOULD STUDY AT THE UNIVERSITY OF
LOUISVILLE ACADEMY OF MUSIC. THEN
WITH OSCAR PETERSON. AND FINALLY GO
ON TOUR WITH THE JANIS JOPLIN BAND.

NOW 28 YEARS OLD. HE IS AN ARMY DESERTER LIVING IN EXILE IN TORONTO. HIS FIRST SONG IN CANADA MADE THE TOP 20 SINGLES. "GOODBY SUPERDAD"—IT WAS A SONG ABOUT G. GORDON LIDDY.

SOME OF THE PEOPLE YOU'LL BE MEETING NEXT WEEK ON OUR SERIES. "AMERICANS IN EXILE: A REPORT FROM CANADA." THIS IS JIM CLARKE ON THE SCENE IN TORONTO.

## EPISODE 1—MONDAY

PAN DOWN FROM FULL FRAME
ANGEL OF MERCY TO THREE
DOUGHBOYS AT FOOT OF MEMORIAL.

IT IS AN EXPLOSIVE ISSUE. AMNESTY. SPAWNED BY WHAT MANY CONSIDER AMERICA'S MOST COSTLY WAR. IN A DECADE OF BITTER FIGHTING IN VIETNAM. MORE THAN 45,000 AMERICANS LOST THEIR LIVES. 300-THOUSAND WERE WOUNDED. 600 IMPRISONED IN PRISONER-OF-WAR CAMPS.

AS THE WAR RAGED. AMERICA WAS GOING THROUGH WHAT ONE CRITIC WOULD CALL A CESSPOOL OF A DECADE.

MAYDAY DEMOS

HUNDREDS OF THOUSANDS ENGAGED IN ANTIWAR DEMONSTRATIONS. THEY WOULD CULMINATE HERE IN THE MAYDAY PROTEST OF 1971.

THE ATMOSPHERE WAS ELECTRIC. A RAG-TAG ARMY OF THE MORE RADICAL AND DISRUPTIVE ELEMENTS OF THE ANTIWAR MOVEMENT DESCENDED ON THE CAPITAL. THREATENING TO SHUT DOWN THE PENTAGON AND THE GOVERNMENT. THEY FAILED. BUT THE CLASSIC SHOWDOWN WAS COSTLY. THERE WAS SPORADIC VIOLENCE AS POLICE AND MILITARY UNITS SECURED THE CITY AND ARRESTED DEMONSTRATORS.

ARRESTS—PENS
JAMMED WITH
DETAINEES

IT WOULD END IN THE LARGEST MASS ARREST IN AMERICAN HISTORY. POLICE ARRESTED AND PLACED IN MAKESHIFT COMPOUNDS DEMONSTRATORS WHOSE NUMBERS WOULD SWELL TO 7000 BEFORE THE DAY ENDED.

STILLS—WOUNDED,
ETC.
ON ANIMATION
FOOTAGE

IT WAS THE TWILIGHT OF THE WAR AND ANTIWAR MOVEMENT—REFLECTING EVENTS THAT WOULD LEAVE SCARS AND BITTERNESS FOR YEARS TO COME.

| | |
|---|---|
| **INSERT SOME OF ANIMATION CUTS "AMEX" MAGAZINE WITH HEADS RAISING QUESTIONS ABOUT AMNESTY... CARTOON UNCLE SAM... AMERICA WILL MISS YOU.** | THE QUESTION OF AMNESTY CALLS IT ALL BACK TO A NATION RAPIDLY TRYING TO FORGET IT ALL. THE FIGHTING. THE DYING. THE SUFFERING AND THE LOSS. |
| **COVERS OF "AMEX"... HEADS FROM MAGAZINE** | TENS OF THOUSANDS WENT INTO HIDING OR FLED TO OTHER COUNTRIES.<br><br>MOST OF THE EXILES WENT TO CANADA.<br><br>NOW. THEY ARE SEEKING AMNESTY TO ERASE CRIMINAL RECORDS. AVOID PRISON. AND RESTORE CIVIL RIGHTS. |
| **SILENT FOOTAGE SENATOR ROBERT TAFT CONGRESSMAN ROBERT DRINAN... EXTERIOR WAR COLLEGE FOOTAGE PRESIDENT NIXON** | CONGRESS HAS BEGUN A DEBATE ON WHETHER AND UNDER WHAT CONDITIONS AMNESTY MIGHT BE EXTENDED. PRESIDENT NIXON SAYS THERE WILL BE NO AMNESTY GRANTED BY HIM—THAT THOSE WHO DESERTED IN TIME OF NEED MUST PAY THE FULL PENALTY. |
| **"AMEX" HEADLINE ON NATIONAL SERVICE...OR ANIMATION FOOTAGE OF SENATOR TAFT'S BILL.** | AUTHORS OF LEGISLATION TO EXTEND AMNESTY WOULD—FOR THE MOST PART— LIMIT IT TO DRAFT DODGERS. AND THEN THEY WOULD REQUIRE THAT SOME KIND OF NATIONAL SERVICE BE PERFORMED TO ACHIEVE IMMUNITY FROM PROSECUTION. DESERTERS WOULD BE LEFT TO THE COURT MARTIAL PROCEDURES AND MILITARY JUSTICE.<br><br>FOR MANY. JUSTICE WOULD BE GAINED IN PRISON. AS THE DEBATE PROCEEDS. ONE THING IS MISSING. THE VOICES AND PLEAS OF THE INTENDED BENEFICIARIES OF AMNESTY. THE EXILES.<br><br>WE WENT TO CANADA TO FIND WHO THEY ARE. WHY THEY THINK THEY DESERVE AMNESTY. AND UNDER WHAT CONDITIONS IT WOULD BE ACCEPTABLE. IN MANY CASES WE FOUND THE UNEXPECTED. |
| **SOUND ON FILM** | THE AMERICAN EXILES HERE IN TORONTO ARE ALWAYS REMINDING YOU THAT AMNESTY IS A LEGAL ACTION THAT SIMPLY ERASES A PRIOR CRIMINAL RECORD. IT DOES NOT FORGIVE AND IT DOES NOT CON- |

DONE. THEY ALSO REMIND YOU THAT AMNESTY HAS BEEN GRANTED BY TEN AMERICAN PRESIDENTS. RANGING FROM GEORGE WASHINGTON AND ABRAHAM LINCOLN TO HARRY TRUMAN.

THIS IS JIM CLARKE ON THE SCENE IN TORONTO.

## EPISODE 2—TUESDAY

STREET SCENES.
PEOPLE WALKING.
SKYSCRAPERS.
STREETCARS—
TORONTO
SOME SHOTS OF SOUND-ON-FILM
SUBJECTS

MOST OF THE YOUNG EXILES CAME HERE TO TORONTO. SOME 30-THOUSAND DRAFT DODGERS AND DESERTERS.

A MODERN. BEAUTIFUL CITY. TORONTO IS THE CENTER OF CANADIAN COMMERCE. IT OFFERED JOBS. A SOCIETY AND CULTURE MUCH LIKE OUR OWN. AND FEW OF THE ENORMOUS SOCIAL AND POLITICAL PROBLEMS DIVIDING AMERICA.

CANADIANS GENERALLY WELCOMED THEM. BUT IN THE EARLY YEARS. THEY WERE HAUNTED BY THE FEAR OF DEPORTATION AND THE INABILITY TO GET WORK PERMITS AND JOBS. SOME SUFFERED TERRIBLY.

GERALD GERSHOWITZ:
MAGNETIC SOUND ON
FILM

WE SAW PEOPLE WHO WERE SUFFERING. WE SAW 40 OR 50 OF THEM IN A HOSTEL. THESE PEOPLE DIDN'T HAVE ANYTHING TO EAT. AND WE TOOK FOOD TO THEM. AND WE WEREN'T DOING THAT WELL OURSELVES AT THE TIME.

THESE WERE PEOPLE WHO HADN'T SCORED HIGH ENOUGH ON THE POINT SCALE WHERE THEY COULD AUTOMATICALLY BECOME CANADIAN LANDED IMMIGRANTS. AND THESE PEOPLE HAD NO WAY OF GETTING PERMISSION TO WORK.

KERRY GERSHOWITZ:
MAGNETIC SOUND ON
FILM

WE HAVE SUFFERED. WE'VE ACCEPTED A SELF-IMPOSED PENALTY BY COMING HERE AND LIVING IN EXILE. ANYONE WHO THINKS THAT EXILE ISN'T A PENALTY OR PUNISHMENT ISN'T THINKING VERY HARD.

CLARKE:
V/O SILENT
GERSHOWITZES

GERALD AND KERRY GERSHOWITZ ARE FROM A SMALL TOWN IN EAST TEXAS. HE BECAME A DRAFT DODGER IN 1968.

THAT WAS A CRITICAL YEAR FOR HIM AND THE NATION. IN THE STREETS AND ON CAMPUS ACROSS THE COUNTRY STUDENTS REBELLED AGAINST THE WAR AND THE DRAFT.

54

| | |
|---|---|
| **MAGNETIC SOUND ON FILM OF DR. BENJAMIN SPOCK FILM: VIETNAM GI'S IN COMBAT** | PROMINENT AMERICANS JOINED THEIR PROTEST: |
| | THE VIETNAM WAR HAD BECOME A KIND OF MONSTER BITTERLY DIVIDING THE NATION. IN 1968 AMERICAN CASUALITIES EXCEEDED THOSE OF THE KOREAN WAR. BY MARCH. THE WAR AND THE PROTESTS WOULD FORCE THE RETIREMENT OF PRESIDENT LYNDON JOHNSON. |
| | THE SUMMER AND FALL WERE MARKED BY RACE RIOTS IN 125 CITIES AND THE MURDERS OF DR. MARTIN LUTHER KING AND SENATOR ROBERT KENNEDY. |
| | GENERAL WILLIAM WESTMORELAND WAS RELIEVED OF COMMAND IN VIETNAM AFTER ASKING FOR 200-THOUSAND MORE TROOPS. |
| | IN AUGUST. ANTIWAR PROTESTORS AND NATIONAL GUARDSMEN BATTLED IN THE STREETS OF CHICAGO. BLIGHTING THE DEMOCRATIC NATIONAL CONVENTION. |
| | IT WAS A YEAR OF AGONY. ENDING IN THE ELECTION OF RICHARD NIXON AS THE NATION'S 37TH PRESIDENT. PROTEST WAS UNPOPULAR—AND THE THEME WAS LAW AND ORDER. |
| **GERALD GERSHOWITZ: MAGNETIC SOUND ON FILM** | IN THE SPRING OF 1968. I WAS TAKING MY FINAL EXAMS. AT THAT POINT. I GOT MY NOTICE TO REPORT FOR A PHYSICAL. |
| | I FELT IT WAS AN UNDECLARED UNJUST WAR REALLY. THAT'S HOW I LOOKED AT IT. I ALSO FELT THERE WAS NO WAY I COULD KILL ANYONE. AND THE ONLY REAL ALTERNATIVE I HAD WAS TO COME TO CANADA. |
| **HOLD SILENT ON GERSHOWITZ CLARKE: V/O** | HOLDING A DEGREE IN ENGLISH. GERALD GERSHOWITZ HELD SEVERAL MENIAL JOBS IN TORONTO BEFORE LANDING A POSITION AS A COMPUTER PROGRAMMER. HE AND HIS WIFE KERRY NOW LIVE A COMFORTABLE. MIDDLE-CLASS LIFE. BUT THEY HAVE FEW FRIENDS AND STILL FEEL LIKE ALIENS. |
| | THEY'RE LONELY FOR AMERICA. AND WANT TO COME HOME. |
| **CLARKE: SOUND ON FILM CLOSE** | FOR MANY OF THESE EXILES. UNTIL THE QUESTION OF AMNESTY IS FINALLY SETTLED. THEY WILL BE UNABLE TO LEAD |

MEANINGFUL AND PURPOSEFUL LIVES. RIGHT NOW IT IS AS THOUGH THEY WERE RUNNING IN PLACE: IN TROUBLE IF THEY STOP. AND IN TROUBLE IF THEY KEEP ON RUNNING. THIS IS JIM CLARKE ON THE SCENE IN TORONTO.

## EPISODE 3—WEDNESDAY

JOE JONES:
MAGNETIC SOUND ON
FILM

WELL, AT THE BEGINNING OF MY LAST YEAR OF UNIVERSITY, I REALIZED THERE WAS NO WAY IN GOOD CONSCIENCE THAT I COULD SERVE THE AMERICAN MILITARY. AND I BEGAN TO CONSIDER ALL OF THE ALTERNATIVES. I LOOKED AT EVERYTHING FROM GOING TO PRISON TO CONSCIENTIOUS OBJECTION TO—WHAT I FINALLY DID GOING TO CANADA. AMONG THE THINGS I ATTEMPTED WAS TO JOIN THE PEACE CORPS.

CLIP SOUND, BUT CONTINUE
FILM OF JONES WITH
CLARKE V/O

JOE JONES. A 26-YEAR OLD DRAFT DODGER NOW IN HIS FOURTH YEAR AS AN AMERICAN EXILE IN CANADA. HE GREW UP IN THE HILL COUNTRY OF WILKESBORO. NORTH CAROLINA. FROM A RELIGIOUS FAMILY. JOE HAD AN 8-YEAR PERFECT ATTENDANCE RECORD AT SUNDAY SCHOOL. A BOY SCOUT WHO BELIEVED IN THE PLEDGE OF ALLEGIANCE. HE WAS AS AMERICAN AS APPLE PIE.

BUT. ALONG WITH MILLIONS OF OTHERS HE BEGAN QUESTIONING THE WAR IN VIETNAM WHILE IN COLLEGE. AT DAVIDSON COLLEGE HE GRADUATED IN THE TOP 5% OF HIS CLASS—WAS OFFERED THREE SCHOLARSHIPS AND A GRADUATE* FELLOWSHIP.

HIS FIRST THREE YEARS IN CANADA WERE MARKED BY THE FEAR AND PARANOIA THAT HAUNTED MOST. FEAR OF DEPORTATION AND GOING TO PRISON. HE BECAME A LONER—HAD NOTHING TO DO WITH ANY AMERICANS.

NOW A GRADUATE STUDENT ON GOVERNMENT FELLOWSHIP AT THE UNIVERSITY OF TORONTO. JOE JONES HAS FALLEN IN LOVE WITH A CANADIAN GIRL. NEXT MONTH THEY WILL MARRY AND JOE WILL TRY TO FIND WORK AS A SCHOOL TEACHER. MEANWHILE. HE IS A LEADER IN THE EXILE MOVEMENT FOR AMNESTY.

JOE JONES:
MAGNETIC SOUND ON
FILM

AS FAR AS THE RIGHTNESS OR WRONGNESS OF WHAT I DID—LEGALLY. PERHAPS. I WAS WRONG: MORALLY I WAS NOT. AT THIS

| | |
|---|---|
| | POINT, I CAN'T SEE THAT I SHOULD PAY ANY PENALTY. I FEEL THAT WATERGATE AND THE EVENTS SURROUNDING IT HAVE DEMONSTRATED THE CORRUPTION OF THE AMERICAN GOVERNMENT. |
| CLARKE: V/O | YOU ARE AWARE SOME PEOPLE BACK HOME ARE SAYING "WE'RE NOT GOING TO FORGIVE THESE DRAFT DODGERS AND DESERTERS." HOW DO YOU RESPOND TO THAT? |
| JONES | "I WOULD SAY NOT SO MUCH FORGIVE AS FORGET. THE ROOT MEANING OF AMNESTY IS RELATED TO AMNESIA, AND WOULD IMPLY A FORGETTING ON BOTH PARTS. I COULD SEE THAT IT WOULD BE DIFFICULT FOR SOME TO FORGET, BUT IT IS ALSO GOING TO BE VERY DIFFICULT FOR ME TO FORGET WHAT AMERICA DID TO VIETNAM. |
| JEANETTE: (JOE'S FIANCE) | THE ONLY TIME I'VE SEEN JOE'S PARENTS WAS VERY BRIEFLY WHEN THEY CAME TO VISIT HIM. I'VE REALLY DONE VERY LITTLE TRAVELING IN THE STATES AND NONE AT ALL IN THE SOUTH. I WOULD CERTAINLY LIKE TO BE ABLE TO VISIT THEM THERE. |
| CLARKE: V/O | JOE JONES. HILLBILLY. INTELLECTUAL, CONSCIENTIOUS OBJECTOR. DRAFT DODGER. AMERICAN EXILE. A CASUALTY OF THE WAR IN VIETNAM. |
| CLARKE: SOUND ON FILM CLOSE | MANY DRAFT DODGERS AND DESERTERS WILL—LIKE JOE JONES—MARRY CANADIAN GIRLS. START TO RAISE A FAMILY, AND BEGIN A WHOLE NEW FUTURE. FOR THEM THE WHOLE QUESTION OF AMNESTY WILL SOON BE A LESS COMPELLING ISSUE. |
| | THIS IS JIM CLARKE ON THE SCENE IN TORONTO. |

## EPISODE 4—THURSDAY

| | |
|---|---|
| SOUND FULL, CRAZY DAVID AT ORGAN LEADING BAND IN PERFORMANCE AT SUBURBAN TORONTO SHOPPING CENTER | |
| HOLD TO FADE UNDER CLARKE: V/O | THEY CALL HIM CRAZY DAVID. HE IS A 27-YEAR-OLD DRAFT DODGER FROM BIRMINGHAM, AND HIS REAL NAME IS DAVID |

KELLER. CRAZY DAVID IS ALSO A MILLIONAIRE. BETWEEN PROMOTIONAL GIGS LIKE THIS, HE DOES BUSINESS ABOARD A LEAR JET AS IT SAILS FROM TORONTO TO PARIS, ROME, AND TOKYO.

IT ALL BEGAN FOUR YEARS AGO, WHEN HE SKIPPED TO CANADA TO EVADE THE DRAFT. DAVID BROUGHT WITH HIM A SMALL BANKROLL AND A GENIUS FOR ODD-BALL HUMOR.

HE BEGAN MAKING "CRAZY" T-SHIRTS. HE AND THE SHIRTS ARE FAST BECOMING A WORLDWIDE SENSATION.

IN PEAK SEASON, CRAZY DAVID'S PRESSES TURN OUT 24-THOUSAND NUTTY T-SHIRTS A DAY—BARELY ENOUGH TO KEEP AHEAD OF DEMAND. HE SAYS THE SHIRTS ARE AN "EGO TRIP"—AND EVERYBODY WANTS THEM AND WANTS TO BE SEEN IN THEM.

THIS YEAR THE CRAZY DAVID T-SHIRTS WILL GROSS 4-MILLION DOLLARS IN SALES IN CANADA, EUROPE, AND ASIA. HE RECENTLY BOUGHT HIS OWN RECORD COMPANY AND FORMED THIS BAND. TO KEEP IT ALL ROLLING IN, CRAZY DAVID HAS A STAFF OF 100 IN CANADA, 500 IN EUROPE, AND 60 IN JAPAN.

DAVID KELLER REPRESENTS A VERY NAR-ROW DIMENSION OF THE EXILE COLONY IN CANADA—THE VERY FEW WHO HAVE REALLY MADE IT BIG. SOME CALL THEM OP-PORTUNISTS.

HERE IN EXILE THEY HAVE PURSUED, SUC-CESSFULLY, CAREERS THEY MIGHT HAVE FOLLOWED IN THE STATES HAD IT NOT BEEN FOR THE WAR:

CLARKE: DAVID, YOU WERE A GO-GETTER BEFORE YOU SKIPPED TO CANADA. WHAT WERE YOU DOING?

DAVID: I WAS IN THE ROCK-AND-ROLL BUSINESS. WE HAD 9 ROCK HALLS AND 24 ROCK BANDS, AND PART INTEREST IN A RECORDING STUDIO. WE WERE SCOOPING IT EVERY WAY WE COULD.

CLARKE: WHEN YOU CAME HERE, HOW MUCH MONEY DID YOU HAVE?

DAVID: ABOUT $300.

CLARKE: YOU MEAN YOU GOT ALL THIS GOING WITH JUST $300?

| | |
|---|---|
| **DAVID** | YES. BUT IT WAS A MATTER OF COMPOUNDING THE MONEY ONCE OR TWICE. |
| **CLARKE:** | DAVID. IT'S GOT TO BE A LONG WAY FROM BIRMINGHAM TO DOING BUSINESS IN YOUR LEAR JET. JETTING FROM TORONTO TO LONDON OR PARIS OR TOKYO. HAS IT BEEN A BIG ADJUSTMENT FOR YOU? |
| **DAVID:** | NOT REALLY. I CAN'T EVEN SAY THAT I MISS THE SOUTHEASTERN UNITED STATES TOO MUCH. |
| **CLARKE:** | IT HASN'T BEEN HARD LIVING WITH ALL OF THIS SUCCESS AND MONEY? |
| **DAVID:** | WELL. NO. BUT IT HASN'T BEEN CONSTANT. IT WAS JUST RECENTLY THAT WE HAD ENOUGH MONEY TO PAY THE PHONE BILL. |
| **CLARKE:** | ARE YOU BOTHERED BY THE FACT THAT YOU HAVE A CRIMINAL RECORD BACK IN THE STATES AND SOME PEOPLE MAY CONSIDER YOU A COWARD OR TRAITOR? |
| **DAVID:** | WELL. NO. I REALLY DON'T CARE WHAT THOSE PEOPLE THINK. |
| **CLARKE:** | DO YOU HAVE ANY URGE TO GO BACK TO THE STATES? |
| **DAVID:** | NOT UNTIL THEY CLEAN UP THE WATER AND THE AIR. |
| **CLARKE:** | WHAT DO YOU THINK ABOUT THE QUESTION OF AMNESTY? SHOULD THERE BE AMNESTY AND WHY? |
| **DAVID:** | OH. DEFINITELY I THINK THERE SHOULD FOR ALL THE GUYS WHO AREN'T DOING THAT GOOD OUTSIDE THE COUNTRY. SO THEY CAN GO BACK AND SEE THEIR FAMILIES AND THAT SORT OF THING. I ALSO THINK RICHARD MIGHT GET HIMSELF OUT OF A HELLUVA JAM IF HE GRANTS AMNESTY. ARE YOU GOING TO BE HERE ON MAY 8TH? |
| **CLARKE:** | NO. NOT REALLY. WHY? |
| **DAVID:** | THAT'S WHEN I BECOME A CANADIAN CITIZEN. |
| **CLARKE:** | CONGRATULATIONS. HOW LONG HAVE YOU BEEN HERE? |
| **DAVID:** | WELL. I'VE BEEN HERE FOUR YEARS IN MAY. |
| **CLARKE:** | CRAZY DAVID. AN AMERICAN DRAFT DODGER WHO PARLAYED A $300 BANKROLL INTO A MULTIMILLION-DOLLAR BONANZA— AS AN AMERICAN EXILE. NEXT YEAR HE'LL |

| | |
|---|---|
| MAGNETIC SOUND ON FILM CLOSE | BECOME CHAIRMAN OF THE BOARD AND DO WHAT HE LIKES BEST—NEXT TO MAKING MONEY—PLAY THE ORGAN. THIS IS JIM CLARKE ON THE SCENE AT A SUBURBAN TORONTO SHOPPING CENTER. |

## EPISODE 5—FRIDAY

| | |
|---|---|
| HAL AND ROSEMARY WALKING IN THE PARK CLARKE: V/O | HAL FRANCES GREW UP IN HOLYOKE. MASSACHUSETTS. IN 1968 HE GRADUATED FROM COLLEGE. WAS CERTIFIED AS A TEACHER. MARRIED HIS GIRLFRIEND. ROSEMARY. AND WAS DRAFTED INTO THE ARMY. HE OPPOSED THE WAR. BUT DIDN'T WANT TO DODGE THE DRAFT. HE GAMBLED ON NOT BEING CALLED TO FIGHT IN VIETNAM. BUT HE LOST. SO. IN SUMMER OF 1969. UNDER ORDERS FOR VIETNAM. HE DESERTED TO CANADA. HE AND ROSEMARY BECAME CANADIAN LANDED IMMIGRANTS. THAT GAVE THEM A LEGAL STATUS. WORK PERMITS AND—IN FIVE YEARS— ELIGIBILITY FOR CITIZENSHIP. HE NOW EARNS 95 HUNDRED DOLLARS A YEAR HERE IN TORONTO AS A COMPUTER PROGRAMER. ROSEMARY WORKS AS A SECRETARY. EXILE HAS BEEN LONELY AND PAINFUL FOR THEM. THEY LEARNED QUICKLY THAT IT WOULD BE BEST TO HIDE THE PAST. |
| HAL FRANCES: MAGNETIC SOUND ON FILM | MANY OF THE JOBS ASKED FOR CANADIAN EXPERIENCE AND I DID RUN INTO SOME PREJUDICE WITH AMERICAN COMPANIES THAT WEREN'T WILLING TO HIRE ME BECAUSE OF MY STATUS. AND EVEN SOME PREJUDICE WITH CANADIAN COMPANIES. WHERE THERE WERE PEOPLE WHO JUST WERE SIMPLY CONFUSED ABOUT MY STATUS—AFRAID THAT THE F-B-I WOULD COME UP AND ARREST ME. |
| ROSEMARY: MAGNETIC SOUND ON FILM | IT'S BEEN HARD BECAUSE WE'VE BEEN ISOLATED COMPLETELY FROM OUR FAMILIES. LIKE ALL THE NORMAL THINGS PEOPLE DO WITH THEIR FAMILIES. THE BIRTHDAYS. THE NORMAL HOLIDAYS—WE MISS EVERYTHING. FOR THAT OUR LIVES ARE EMPTY. |
| HAL: MAGNETIC SOUND ON FILM | WE DIDN'T DESERT AMERICA. WE DESERTED THE ARMY AND ITS ROLE IN VIETNAM. WE DON'T OPPOSE AMERICA AND THE AMERICAN IDEALS. AND THE AMERICAN SYSTEM. AND THAT'S THE SYSTEM WE'LL WANT TO BE LIVING WITH. |

60

| | |
|---|---|
| CLARKE:<br>V/O FILM | NOT POLITICALLY MOTIVATED. HAL AND ROSEMARY HAD NO DESIRE TO RAISE THE WAR AS AN ISSUE WHILE IN CANADA. THEY AVOIDED MAKING FRIENDS BECAUSE THAT LED FINALLY TO DISCUSSING THE PAST. AND THE FACT THAT HE IS A DESERTER. BUT RECENTLY. THEY CAME OUT OF HIDING. |
| HAL:<br>MAGNETIC SOUND ON FILM | WE THOUGHT IT WAS VERY IMPORTANT TO PRESENT OURSELVES AS AN ALTERNATIVE TO WHAT THE MEDIA HAVE SHOWN SO FREQUENTLY—THAT WE'RE JUST ORDINARY. STRAIGHT-LIVING PEOPLE. AND THAT WE'RE NOT POLITICALLY ACTIVE OR RABBLE-ROUSERS OR ANYTHING LIKE THAT. |
| ROSEMARY:<br>MAGNETIC SOUND ON FILM | WE HAVE BEEN MISREPRESENTED ON TV. AND WHENEVER ANYTHING HAS BEEN WRITTEN ABOUT US. IT'S ALWAYS BEEN CAST OFF AS A FEW HUNDRED UNDESIRABLE PEOPLE—PEOPLE WHO WOULDN'T MAKE GOOD CITIZENS IN CANADA. AND WE THOUGHT MAYBE BECAUSE WE SEEM LIKE AVERAGE PEOPLE THAT MAYBE IF THEY SAW OTHER PEOPLE. PEOPLE LIKE THEMSELVES THAT MAYBE THEY WOULD TAKE A SECOND LOOK. MAYBE A FIRST LOOK...TAKE A LOOK AT US AS PEOPLE...AND GIVE US A SECOND CONSIDERATION. |
| CLARKE:<br>SOUND ON FILM<br>CLOSE | HAL AND ROSEMARY FRANCES ARE AMONG THE CASUALTIES OF THE WAR IN VIETNAM. SO LONG AS THEY SUFFER SEPARATION FROM COUNTRY AND FAMILY. IT WILL BE DIFFICULT TO CLOSE THE BOOKS ON THE WAR. AND ONE WONDERS. AFTER TALKING WITH THEM. ABOUT THE JUSTICE OF TREATING ALL DRAFT DODGERS AND DESERTERS WITH EQUAL INDIFFERENCE OR THREATS.<br><br>THIS IS JIM CLARKE ON THE SCENE IN TORONTO. |

## EPISODE 6—MONDAY

| | |
|---|---|
| BILL KING:<br>MAGNETIC SOUND ON FILM<br>SOUND FULL.<br>FADE UNDER CLARKE. | AS A YOUNGSTER IN INDIANA AND KEN-TUCKY. JAZZ PIANIST BILL KING TOOK HIS PIANO LESSONS FROM W.C. HANDY AND PIANIST AVA SMITH. LATER HE STUDIED AT THE UNIVERSITY OF LOUISVILLE ACADEMY OF MUSIC. THEN WITH OSCAR PETERSON AND. FINALLY. HE WENT ON TOUR WITH THE |

JANIS JOPLIN BAND. NOW 28 YEARS OLD. HE IS AN ARMY DESERTER LIVING IN EXILE HERE IN TORONTO. HIS FIRST SONG IN CANADA MADE THE TOP 20 SINGLES. CALLED "GOODBY SUPERDAD" IT WAS A SONG ABOUT G. GORDON LIDDY.

**SOUND UP FULL**

**SILENT BOOTH AT RECORDING STUDIO...**
**DISSOLVE FROM SPINNING TAPE TO Q&A.**

I MET BILL KING LATE ONE NIGHT AT THIS TORONTO RECORDING STUDIO WHERE HE WAS CUTTING HIS SECOND ALBUM FOR CAPITOL RECORDS. HE TALKED ABOUT HIS WORK WITH THE ARMY BAND. JUST BEFORE DESERTING TO CANADA.

**BILL KING:**
**MAGNETIC SOUND ON FILM**

LIKE I'M A REALLY RELIGIOUS PERSON. I DON'T DRINK. I DON'T TAKE DRUGS. I DON'T TAKE COFFEE. I DON'T DO ANY OF THESE THINGS. SO I GO IN THE ARMY. I ENJOYED THE ARMY. I ENJOYED THE FIRST TWO MONTHS. I COULD LOOK PAST ALL THE JARGON AND ALL THAT'S GOING DOWN. THAT DIDN'T BOTHER ME. THEN TURNING AROUND AND SEEING ALL THESE ALCOHOLICS AROUND YOU. CHEATING ON THEIR M.O.S. AND YOU'D HAVE THE GUY. THE COMPANY COMMANDER. SIT THERE AND STRAIGHTEN OUT HIS POINT SO THE GUY COULD STAY IN THE BAND AND PLAY FRENCH HORN INSTEAD OF BE IN THE IN-FANTRY. AND HERE I AM. I AM A SERIOUS MUSICIAN AND ALL I'M DOING IS BEING SENT TO PLAY FOR COLONELS' AND GENERALS' PARTIES AND LUAUS. AND TOLD THAT MY WIFE CAN'T COME ALONG BECAUSE I'M NOT A. I'M NOT A NONCOM-MISSIONED OFFICER. YOU KNOW. KEEP HER AWAY. THINGS LIKE THAT. IT TURNED MY STOMACH. MAN. IT REALLY DID.

**CLARKE:**

WHAT DO YOU SAY TO THE PEOPLE BACK HOME WHO REGARD YOU AS A COWARD AND TRAITOR BECAUSE YOU LEFT AND CAME TO CANADA?

**KING:**

NOW I'VE PUNISHED MYSELF FOR FIVE YEARS. AND I'VE TAKEN ABUSE. AND HAD TO START FROM SCRATCH AGAIN WITH MY WIFE AND MY KID AND EVERYTHING. AND WE'VE SUFFERED ENOUGH FROM IT. OUR FAMILIES SUFFERED TOO. I THINK WE'RE THE REAL HEROES BECAUSE WE THOUGHT THIS WHOLE WAR OUT. AND IT HAS BEEN A FARCE. AND. SO FAR. NIXON HAS PROVEN HIMSELF TRUE. LOOK AT ALL HIS PEOPLE. YOU KNOW. IT'S LIKE GOD HAS SORTA

| | SPOKE. HE'S SORTA CLEANSING AMERICA RIGHT NOW. |
|---|---|
| CLARKE: | WELL. YOU WERE SO DISCONTENTED WITH THE COUNTRY. THE WAR. WHEN YOU LEFT. WHAT WOULD MAKE YOU WANT TO COME BACK NOW? |
| KING: | YOU DON'T DISLIKE THE COUNTRY. AND YOU DON'T DISLIKE THE PEOPLE. YOU JUST DISLIKE THE DISHONESTY. YOU KNOW. AND ONCE YOU BECOME A CERTAIN AGE. WHERE YOU'RE ABLE. YOU SORT OF FOCUS IN AND SEE WHAT'S GOING ON AROUND YOU. YOU REALLY SEE WHAT HAPPENS AND IT JUST KILLS YOU. IT REALLY BREAKS YOUR HEART OUT. BUT. I LOOK AT THE U.S. AS BEING THE MOST BEAUTIFUL COUNTRY IN THE WORLD. FROM COAST TO COAST... |
| CLARKE: V/O | LIKE MANY I TALKED WITH. BILL KING WANTS TO BE ABLE TO RETURN HOME. BUT NOT AT THE COST OF GOING TO PRISON. |
| DISSOLVE TO KING AT PIANO, WITH SOUND UNDER... | I'LL STAY HERE. I'LL STAY ANYWHERE IN THE WORLD...I'LL TELL YOU. MAN. IT'S LIKE I DID ENOUGH SUFFERING. YOU KNOW. I WORK FOR PEOPLE NOW. I'M NOT MAKING MONEY. YOU KNOW I'M JUST MAKING ENOUGH TO GET BY ON—$3400 A YEAR I MADE LAST YEAR WITH MY TAXES. I LIKE WORKING WITH PEOPLE AND MAKING MUSIC WITH THEM. |
| CLARKE: MAGNETIC SOUND ON FILM<br><br>CLOSE | BUT MOST OF THESE EXILES ARE NEARING THEIR THIRTIES. MANY HAVE BEEN HERE LONGER THAN FIVE YEARS. SOON THEY MUST DECIDE WHETHER TO BECOME CANADIAN CITIZENS OR FACE THE PROSPECTS OF COMING HOME TO AN AMERICA MORE FOREIGN THAN THEIR ADOPTED COUNTRY. THIS IS JIM CLARKE ON THE SCENE IN TORONTO. |

## EPISODE 7—TUESDAY

| CLARKE: EXTERIOR SOUND ON FILM WITH ANGEL OF MERCY STATUE FRAMED IN REAR | MOST OF THE AMERICAN EXILES HERE IN TORONTO ARE BITTER ABOUT WHAT THEY CALL THE POLITICS OF AMNESTY. AND THEY CLING TO THE HOPE THAT PRESIDENT NIXON WILL BE FORCED BY THE WATERGATE SCANDAL AND THE IMPEACHMENT INVESTIGATION TO EXTEND AMNESTY TO THEM AS THEY SAY HE HAS SOUGHT IT FOR HIS CLOSE FORMER ASSOCIATES NOW UNDER INDICTMENT. |
|---|---|

| | |
|---|---|
| **LARRY KEARLEY:**<br>**MAGNETIC SOUND ON**<br>**FILM**<br>**(DESERTER,**<br>**LAWYER-IN-EXILE)** | I DON'T HAPPEN TO THINK IN MY PARTICULAR SITUATION THAT I CAN AT ALL ACCEPT PUNISHMENT FOR SOMETHING THAT WAS A HUMANITARIAN ACT AS LONG AS LT. CALLEY IS OUT ON A $1000 BAIL DOING WORKS FOR THE GOOD OF THE COMMUNITY AFTER KILLING UPWARDS OF 108 PEOPLE. SO LONG AS PEOPLE LIKE RICHARD NIXON AND SPIRO AGNEW ARE GETTING SUSPENDED SENTENCES. NOLO CONTENDRE. AND JUST RUNNING AROUND LOOSE. I DON'T SEE THAT THOSE ACTS ARE ANY LESS DESERVING OF PUNISHMENT THAN WHAT I HAVE DONE. |
| **CLARKE:** | IF YOU FELT THE WAR WAS UNJUST AND ILLEGAL AND YOU HAD TO OPPOSE IT. WHY NOT ACCEPT THE PRICE AND GO TO JAIL. SAY LIKE MARTIN LUTHER KING? |
| **KERRY GERSHOWITZ:**<br>**MAGNETIC SOUND ON**<br>**FILM** | WELL. NOT EVERYBODY IS A MARTIN LUTHER KING. NOT ONLY THAT. IF IT WAS AN IMMORAL AND UNJUST WAR. IT WOULD BE EQUALLY WRONG TO PROSECUTE US FOR RESISTING THAT WAR. JUST LIKE IN NAZI GERMANY. PEOPLE WHO RESISTED THAT REGIME WERE CRIMINALS. TECHNICALLY AND YET IS IT RIGHT TO PROSECUTE THE PEOPLE THAT RESISTED THE NAZIS? |
| **GERALD GERSHOWITZ:**<br>**MAGNETIC SOUND ON**<br>**FILM** | I THINK IT WOULD HAVE BEEN A DEHUMANIZING THING FOR ME TO HAVE GONE TO JAIL. FOR INSTANCE. IT WOULD HAVE DESTROYED ME. |
| **CLARKE:** | THERE ARE A LOT OF PEOPLE BACK HOME WHO REGARD YOU GUYS AS COWARDS AND TRAITORS. |
| **JACK COLHOUN:**<br>**MAGNETIC SOUND ON**<br>**FILM**<br>**(EDITOR, "AMEX"**<br>**CANADA)** | THAT MAY VERY WELL BE: HOWEVER. I THINK IN A DEMOCRATIC SOCIETY YOU HAVE THE DUTY AND THE RIGHT WHEN YOU SEE SOMETHING THAT IS VERY WRONG. WHEN YOU KNOW THE STATEMENTS THAT COME OUT OF THE ADMINISTRATIONS IN WASHINGTON ARE LIES. AND THAT THESE LIES HAVE BEEN COVERED UP—IT'S YOUR DUTY AS A CITIZEN IN A DEMOCRATIC SOCIETY TO DO YOUR BEST TO MAKE THESE LIES KNOWN AND TO WORK TO REDRESS THESE GRIEVANCES AND CHANGE THESE POLICIES. |
| **HAL FRANCES:**<br>**MAGNETIC SOUND ON**<br>**FILM**<br>**(DESERTER)** | A CONTINUOUS EXILE AND PUNISHMENT IS NEVER GOING TO BRING BACK THE SONS THAT HAVE BEEN KILLED. AND IT'S NEVER GOING TO REPAIR THE SONS THAT HAVE BEEN MAIMED. IT'S JUST PURE REVENGE. |

| | |
|---|---|
| **ROSEMARY FRANCES:**<br>**(WIFE OF DESERTER)** | I HATE TO BRING THIS UP. BUT WITH WATERGATE AND ALL THE THINGS THAT HAVE HAPPENED TO NIXON. IT HARDLY SEEMS HE'S IN A POSITION TO EXPECT US TO PAY PENALTIES WHEN HE'S NOT EXPEC- TING HIMSELF OR ANY OF HIS AIDES OR PEOPLE...IT SEEMS VERY IRONIC TO ME THAT HE CAN DO ONE THING AND THEN TURN AROUND AND EXPECT US TO PAY THE FULL PRICE FOR WHATEVER HE THINKS WE'VE DONE. |
| **CLARKE:**<br>**SOUND ON FILM**<br>**CLOSE** | MOST OF THE EXILES SEEM TO THINK THE REAL ISSUE IS NOT NATIONAL SERVICE. BUT WHETHER OR NOT AMERICANS ARE FINALLY WILLING TO REPUDIATE THE WAR IN VIETNAM AND THE MEN WHO WAGED IT. BUT THE FACT OF THE MATTER IS. FOR THE EXILES SOME KIND OF NATIONAL SERVICE MAY BE THEIR ONLY HOPE OF RETURNING HOME AS FREE CITIZENS. THIS IS JIM CLARKE ON THE SCENE IN TORONTO. |

## EPISODE 8—WEDNESDAY

| | |
|---|---|
| **CLARKE:**<br>**MAGNETIC SOUND ON**<br>**FILM**<br>**(FROM SYNC TRACK)** | DEMOCRATIC CONGRESSMAN ROBERT DRINAN HAS SUGGESTED THAT THE HOUSE SUBCOMMITTEE HOLDING HEARINGS ON AMNESTY COME HERE TO TORONTO TO TAKE TESTIMONY. MOST OF THE VIETNAM DESERTERS AND DRAFT DODGERS WHO FLED AMERICA RATHER THAN FIGHT IN VIETNAM CAME HERE TO TORONTO. AND MOST OF THOSE WE SPOKE WITH AGREED WITH CONGRESSMAN DRINAN THAT THE INTENDED BENEFICIARIES OF AMNESTY SHOULD BE HEARD BY THE SUBCOMMITTEE. |
| **JACK COLHOUN:**<br>**MAGNETIC SOUND ON**<br>**FILM**<br>**(DESERTER)** | I CERTAINLY WOULD BECAUSE AS REPRESENTATIVE DRINAN STATED. THERE WERE VERY. VERY FEW OF THE REAL BENEFICIARIES OF AMNESTY WHO WERE ALLOWED TO TESTIFY IN WASHINGTON. EVEN THOSE WHO RESIDED IN THE U.S. SOMEHOW WEREN'T ALLOWED TO TESTIFY. |
| **KERRY GERSHOWITZ:**<br>**(WIFE OF DRAFT**<br>**DODGER)** | I THINK THERE SHOULD BE AMNESTY SIMPLY TO RIGHT A MORAL WRONG. THE WAR IN VIETNAM WAS UNJUST AND IM- MORAL. IT WAS AN UNDECLARED WAR. I THINK ONE OF THE THINGS THAT BLOCKS AMNESTY IN THE U.S. IS THAT OTHER PEOPLE HAVE LOST LOVED ONES AND THEY CAN'T ACCEPT THE FACT THAT THESE PEOPLE THEY LOVED DIED FOR SOMETHING THAT WAS TOTALLY MEANINGLESS. |

**LARRY KEARLEY:**
MAGNETIC SOUND ON FILM
(DESERTER)

I DON'T KNOW HOW ANY COMMITTEE OR SUBCOMMITTEE CAN CONSIDER WHAT MAY BE THE FATE OF A LOT OF US WITHOUT TALKING TO ANY OF US. AND THEY'RE NOT GOING TO BE ABLE TO TALK TO US DOWN IN THE STATES. I THINK IT WOULD BE A COPOUT IF THEY DIDN'T AT LEAST TRY TO MAKE ANY EFFORT TO SPEAK TO US.

**NORMAN HARTLEY:**
(REPORTER, "TORON-TO GLOBE & MAIL")

I THINK IT WOULD BE RECEIVED VERY CAUTIOUSLY BY THE EXILES. I DOUBT IF MANY WOULD BE WILLING TO TESTIFY. THEY (THE CONGRESSMEN) COULD WELL RUN INTO EITHER WHAT YOU MIGHT CALL PROFESSIONAL SPOKESMEN OR JUST SIMPLY THOSE WHO'VE ALREADY TAKEN A STRONG POLITICAL STAND IN PUBLIC. AND WHO HAVE NOTHING ELSE TO FEAR FROM APPEARING IN PUBLIC AND MAKING THOSE KINDS OF STATEMENTS.

**RICHARD WEISS:**
SOUND ON FILM
(DRAFT DODGER)

I THINK TESTIMONY FROM PEOPLE UP HERE MIGHT BE VERY REVEALING TO PEOPLE DOWN THERE. WE READ JOURNALS AND THINGS AND WE SEE THAT THERE IS SOME MISUNDERSTANDING. AT LEAST ABOUT OUR ATTITUDES.

**HAL FRANCES:**
MAGNETIC SOUND ON FILM
(DESERTER)

I WOULDN'T BE AFRAID TO COME OUT MYSELF. BECAUSE I'M INCLINED TO THINK THAT IT MIGHT BE MY ONLY CHANCE...TO REALLY BE HEARD BY THE VERY PEOPLE WHO MIGHT DECIDE WHERE I HAVE TO LIVE FOR THE REST OF MY LIFE.

**ROSEMARY FRANCES:**
MAGNETIC SOUND ON FILM

THERE'S A LOT AT STAKE AND. LIKE HAL SAID. IT MAY BE THE ONLY CHANCE...REAL CHANCE. IT'S ONE THING TO DISCUSS IT HERE AMONG OURSELVES. BUT IT DOESN'T MEAN A THING UNLESS THE PEOPLE THAT CAN DO SOMETHING ABOUT IT HEAR WHAT WE HAVE TO SAY. IF WE HAVE A CHANCE TO MEET THEM FACE TO FACE. IT MAY MAKE A DIFFERENCE...I DON'T KNOW. IT'S WORTH A CHANCE.

**CLARKE:**
MAGNETIC SOUND ON FILM
CLOSE

AS LANDED IMMIGRANTS HERE IN CANADA. COMPETING WITH CANADIANS FOR SOME OF THE BETTER JOBS. AMERICAN EXILES ARE UNDER PRESSURE TO APPLY FOR CANADIAN CITIZENSHIP. IF THEY DO AND AMNESTY IS GRANTED. THEY WILL HAVE RENOUNCED THEIR U.S. CITIZENSHIP. IF THEY DON'T. MANY FEAR IT WILL BLIGHT THEIR FLEDGLING CAREERS IN A COUNTRY THAT HAS EXTENDED THEM FRIENDSHIP. HOPE. AND MANY OPPORTUNITIES.

THIS IS JIM CLARKE ON THE SCENE IN TORONTO.

# EPISODE 9—THURSDAY

| | |
|---|---|
| CLARKE V/O SILENT COLHOUN WALKS FROM CAR INTO "AMEX" OFFICE | JACK COLHOUN IS A 28-YEAR OLD ARMY DESERTER FROM MADISON, WISCONSIN. FOR SEVEN YEARS. HE AVOIDED FIGHTING IN VIETNAM THROUGH R-O-T-C AND STUDENT DEFERMENTS. HIS CALL FINALLY CAME AFTER THE U.S. INVASION OF CAMBODIA AND THE SHOOTINGS AT KENT AND JACKSON STATES. |
| INSIDE "AMEX" OFFICE... COLHOUN TYPES AT A PORTABLE TYPEWRITER. JOE JONES WORKS ON LAYOUT. CAMERA PANS WALL SHOWING "AMEX" ISSUES DATING BACK SIX YEARS. INTERCUT WITH ANIMATION FOOTAGE | COLHOUN SAID NO PURPOSE WOULD BE SERVED BY GOING TO JAIL—SO HE DESERTED TO TORONTO. NOW A SENIOR TEACHING ASSISTANT AT YORK UNIVERSITY. HE IS STUDYING AMERICAN HISTORY. HE IS ALSO EDITOR OF "AMEX" MAGAZINE. THE LARGEST EXILE PUBLICATION. TWO YEARS AGO. HE WROTE OF THE EXILES: "WE ARE BEGINNING TO DIVIDE INTO TWO CAMPS. ONE SIDE WANTS TO FORGET THEY ARE AMERICANS. THE OTHER SIDE HAS NOT FORGOTTEN." HE SAID THE DIVISION SURFACED BECAUSE OF THE DEBATE OVER AMNESTY. |
| CLARKE: MAGNETIC SOUND ON FILM (REVERSAL) | THERE IS PERHAPS AN ASSUMPTION BACK HOME THAT IF AMNESTY WERE GRANTED. TENS OF THOUSANDS OF AMERICANS WOULD COME STREAMING ACROSS THE BORDER. IS THAT A MISAPPREHENSION? |
| COLHOUN: | WELL. I DON'T THINK IT'S POSSIBLE TO TELL AT THIS POINT AS LONG AS IT'S ABSTRACT AND IN THE DISTANT FUTURE. NONE OR VERY FEW ARE GOING TO MAKE RIGID DECISIONS. |
| CLARKE: | PRESIDENT NIXON TOLD ONE OF HIS NEWS CONFERENCES THAT THOSE WHO DESERTED THEIR COUNTRY IN TIME OF PEACE WOULD HAVE TO PAY A PRICE AND NOT A JUNKET IN THE PEACE CORPS...BUT A PENALTY FOR HAVING DISOBEYED THE LAWS OF THE LAND. |
| COLHOUN: | I THINK FIRST OF ALL THAT'S A RATHER SEVERE SLAP IN THE FACE OF THE PEACE CORPS—CALLING IT A JUNKET. AND I THINK THAT KIND OF ATTITUDE TOWARD A SERVICE TO HUMANITY PERHAPS EXPRESSES SOME OF THE REAL PROBLEMS AMERICA SUFFERED DURING THE NIXON YEARS. |
| CLARKE: | JACK. ARE YOU GOING BACK TO AMERICA WITH OR WITHOUT AMNESTY? |

| | |
|---|---|
| COLHOUN: | WELL, I KNOW I'M GOING BACK SOMETIME. I'M NOT QUITE CERTAIN WHEN. I THINK A LOT DEPENDS ON MY WORK IN CANADA. HOW LONG IT'S FRUITFUL. SAY IF NEXT YEAR AT THIS TIME MY WORK AT "AMEX" FOR AMNESTY ISN'T FRUITFUL, WHEN PERHAPS IF THERE'S A CONDITIONAL AMNESTY, I'LL GO BACK FOR A CONDITIONAL AMNESTY ON ONE GROUND ONLY. AND THAT'S TO WORK FOR AN UNCONDITIONAL AMNESTY THAT WOULD INCLUDE AMNESTY FOR DESERTERS, DRAFT RESISTERS, AND VETS WITH LESS THAN HONORABLE DISCHARGE. |
| CLARKE: | THIS IS JIM CLARKE ON THE SCENE IN TORONTO. |

## EPISODE 10—FRIDAY

| | |
|---|---|
| CLARKE:<br>MAGNETIC SOUND ON FILM<br>OPEN<br>STANDING IN DOORWAY<br>SUPREME COURT OF ONTARIO | AMNESTY WILL NOT BE ACCEPTED BY SOME. THEIR LIVES AND THEIR ATTITUDES TOWARD THE U.S. HAVE BEEN INTERRUPTED AND ALTERED BY EXILE. MANY SAY THEY HAVE ALREADY SUFFERED MORE THAN ENOUGH. AND THAT COMPULSORY NATIONAL SERVICE WOULD SUGGEST ATONEMENT... AND DENIAL OF THE RIGHTNESS OF THEIR CAUSE—OPPOSITION TO THE WAR IN VIETNAM. |
| LARRY KEARLEY:<br>MAGNETIC SOUND ON FILM<br>(DESERTER) | WELL, I MYSELF WOULDN'T BE GOING BACK. AND I ONLY KNOW OF ONE PERSON FOR SURE WHO WOULD BE GOING BACK. AND HE'S IN AMERICAN HISTORY. AND THAT SEEMS TO BE THE ONLY PLACE TO DO IT. IN THE UNITED STATES. FOR MYSELF. I'M PERFECTLY HAPPY HERE. I MIGHT GO BACK TO VISIT. BECAUSE WE HAVE FRIENDS THERE. I'M NOT INTERESTED IN LIVING THERE AGAIN. |
| KERRY GERSHOWITZ:<br>MAGNETIC SOUND ON FILM<br>(WIFE OF DRAFT DODGER) | A QUALIFIED YES. WE DON'T WANT TO GO CRAWLING BACK ON OUR KNEES ASKING FOR FORGIVENESS FOR SOME SIN...THAT WE DON'T FEEL IS A SIN. IN FACT, WE FEEL OUR ACTION WAS THE ONLY MORAL THING TO DO. |
| DRAFT DODGER: | THERE'S NOT GOING TO BE ANY LOSS OF CONFIDENCE. ANY DEGRADING OF MORAL VALUES. A PRECEDENT SET WHEN YOU HAVE A LAW CHANGED. OR ANYTHING OF THAT NATURE. INSTEAD, WHAT YOU HAVE IS AN EXPRESSION OF THE PEOPLE'S WILL. AND THIS IS THE SORT OF THING WE FEEL IT SHOULD BE. |
| JOE JONES:<br>MAGNETIC SOUND ON | HAVING BEEN HERE FOR FOUR YEARS, I'VE DEVELOPED SOMETHING OF A WAY OF LIFE. |

| | |
|---|---|
| **FILM**<br>**(DRAFT DODGER)** | I'M NOT GOING TO IMMEDIATELY DISRUPT THAT WAY OF LIFE IF AMNESTY IS DECLARED. I WOULD CERTAINLY USE THE OPPORTUNITY TO GO BACK HOME AND VISIT MY SISTER WHOM I HAVEN'T SEEN FOR 4 YEARS. AND HER CHILDREN. WHOM I'VE NEVER SEEN. |
| **JACK COLHOUN:**<br>**SOUND ON FILM** | I THINK CANADIANS SHOULD UNDERSTAND THAT IF THERE ARE AMERICAN WAR RESISTERS IN CANADA WHO WANT TO GO BACK. THE BEST WAY TO GET THEM BACK IS WITH AN UNCONDITIONAL. UNIVERSAL AMNESTY. |
| **HAL FRANCES:**<br>**SOUND ON FILM**<br>**(DESERTER)** | NO. I WOULDN'T GO BACK UNDER ANY CIRCUMSTANCES. JAIL WOULDN'T SERVE ANY PURPOSE. IT WOULDN'T BRING BACK ALL THE MEN THAT WERE WOUNDED. IT WOULD JUST FURTHER RUIN MY LIFE. AND FURTHER HURT MY FAMILY AND ROSEMARY'S FAMILY. AND IT WOULD JUST BE WRONG. |
| **CLARKE:** | IF AMNESTY WERE DECLARED DO YOU HAVE THE IMPRESSION MOST OF THE DRAFT DODGERS AND DESERTERS WOULD GO BACK TO AMERICA? |
| **NORMAN HARTLEY:**<br>**SOUND ON FILM** | YES. I WOULD THINK SO. I WOULD SAY THERE WOULD BE A SMALL NUMBER. A VERY SMALL PERCENTAGE WHO WOULD HAVE DEFINITELY MADE A COMMITMENT TO CANADA AND WHO WOULD STAY. REGARDLESS. MOST. I THINK. WOULD GO BACK. CERTAINLY FOR A WHILE. SOME MIGHT COME BACK TO CANADA EVEN-TUALLY. BUT ON THE WHOLE I WOULD SAY MOST WOULD GO BACK. |
| **CLARKE:** | THE EXILES ARE FIRM IN THEIR BELIEF THAT THE WAR WAS WRONG AND THAT THEY WERE RIGHT IN REFUSING TO GO FIGHT IN IT. MANY OF THEM ARE UNWILLING TO RETURN HOME IF THE PRICE OF THEIR RETURN IS SOME FORM OF NATIONAL SERVICE. THEY WOULD REGARD THAT AS PENANCE FOR SINS THEY HAVE NOT COM-MITTED. IT IS A NO-COMPROMISE POSITION. AND IT IS ALMOST AS THOUGH THE EXILES HAVE FORGOTTEN IT IS THEY WHO SEEK AMNESTY FROM THE NATION. BECAUSE THE FACT IS THAT THE NATION HAS NOT YET SEEN FIT TO ASK THE EXILES FOR AMNESTY. IT IS A STALEMATE LOGIC THAT SEEMS UNLIKELY TO BREAK. BUT IT IS ONE THAT MIGHT SUCCUMB TO JUSTICE WITH COMPASSION. THIS IS JIM CLARKE ON THE SCENE IN WASHINGTON. |

# THE CAMERA PERSPECTIVE

The background of newsfilm cameramen varies widely. Some have college degrees and have majored in communication. Others have attended technical schools, and still others have learned their craft solely as apprentices.

Paul Fine, head cameraman for WMAL-TV, gained his basic knowledge from his father, who himself was a photographer. He also worked in motion picture laboratories for several years. As he explained, he wanted to "learn what happens to your film after you've shot it." His familiarity with the camera and with film processing enabled him to qualify for an opening in the WMAL-TV news department where he was immersed in newsfilm operation for two years. For the next 4 years he was part of the station's documentary unit.

There is a good deal of difference between shooting straight news and filming the mini-documentary, Fine tells us. The mini-documentary series requires much more in the way of production values. There are also differences in filming the full-length documentary as compared to the mini-documentary. You do not have as much control over the camera sequences for a mini-documentary as you do for the documentary. There is much more planning time for a documentary. The cameraman should go out on location a day or two previous to the actual filming and plan his shots with a great deal of precision. That type of preplanning is rare in filming the mini-documentary. Usually, you are on location the very day of your shooting schedule. Timeliness is, therefore, more of a factor for the mini-documentary series. In Paul Fine's experience with mini-documentary series, he found that he could not be with the reporter for more than 2 or 3 weeks. On the other hand, he has often worked for 4 or 5 months on the production of a full-length documentary.

There is also an important difference between the mini-documentary and the documentary which affects the film editor. There is no workprint stage for the mini-documentary series. Cutting is done from the original footage. For the full-length documentary, a workprint is put together and the master remains intact. This, obviously, permits more creative editing to be accomplished. We must always bear in mind that the mini-documentary series is part of the daily newscast while the documentary is a program unto itself. As part of the newscast, timeliness is an essence of the mini-documentary series and, as such, it is often as ephemeral as any news event.

Fine uses the Eclair ACL 16 mm motion picture camera and an Arriflex. The Eclair ACL is a portable and sturdy silent camera that can take almost any lens in any mount. It weighs 7½

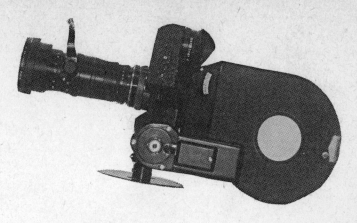

Paul Fine also uses the smaller 16 mm Eclair for undercover filming.

pounds and measures less than a foot from front to back. Its coaxial magazine can rest on the shoulder with the viewfinder right at eye level. The magazine can be changed in 5 seconds. It is a very convenient camera to use for aerial shooting. A lightweight pocket-sized battery affords readily available power. The camera, with crystal control, can shoot synchronized sound. An identical crystal on the tape recorder puts a sync signal on the tape. No connection is needed between the camera and the tape recorder.

The Arriflex Fine uses is the 16BL—a 16 mm lightweight camera designed especially for on-location sync-sound shooting. It is suited for either hand-held or tripod mounted filming. The 16 S/B model, according to Arriflex, is the "world's smallest fully professional 16 mm mirror-shutter reflex camera." Despite its size, it can use 200- and 400-foot magazines and interchangeable lenses.

Paul Fine never lets himself forget that television is an entertainment medium. "I feel that the person at home has to be entertained. I don't shoot talking heads. I feel that if I were sitting at home, I would want to be entertained. Sure you can get a talking head in an interview that's interesting to listen to; but 90% of the time, you'll be bored."

The technique he employs is to have the interview recorded on sound tape. Then he will shoot scenes relevant to the content. Again, the axiom is underscored that sound and film must complement each other. Fine insists that, in almost every instance, the cameraman can shoot scenes to illustrate the interview. "You get your ideas across more effectively that way and at least the person at home will be entertained. I know the

71

The Arriflex S/B model is the "world's smallest fully professional 16 mm mir-ror-shuttered reflex camera."

The 16 mm Arriflex 16M/B used by Paul Fine at WMAL-TV can be fitted with 200, 400, or 1200 ft magazines.

networks have used talking heads. But I believe the interview can still be factual and entertaining. The problem is that the average interviewee is not scintillating and then the viewer's attention begins to wander.''

Recently, WMAL-TV planned a mini-documentary series on airline safety. The catalyst was the crash of an airliner en route to Washington, D.C. The station's crew went to Denver, Colorado to a pilot-simulator school. The shooting was not confined to the pilot trainee. The reporter joined the pilot in the simulator and the filming covered all aspects of takeoff and flying. During these sequences, the reporter and the pilot discussed the versatility and the verisimilitude of the simulator. The theme of the series was to show what the airlines are doing to achieve total safety, rather than concentrating on air crashes. The scenes with the pilot were not talking heads. The pilot was always in conversation with the reporter and the visuals portrayed the instrumentation of the simulator.

In a prior chapter, we noted that the news director for WNBC emphasized that the cameraman should be involved in planning sessions. This is the situation at WMAL-TV. Paul Fine attends planning sessions where the ideas for mini-documentaries are discussed. These conferences include the news director, the executive producer, and the reporter.

Close shot of ground control tower personnel in action for mini-documentary series on air safety.

Shoulder strap steadies camera for hand-held shots.

There are television stations, Fine points out, where the cameraman is, in essence, a mechanical robot. He shoots what he is told by the reporter or the director. But Fine considers himself a photo-journalist and firmly believes that the cameraman's expertise and creativity are so essential to the success of a mini-documentary series that he must definitely be involved in the production from the very inception of the project.

In *The Work of the Motion Picture Cameraman* (Hastings House) by Freddie Young and Paul Petzold, the writers state that the camera's influence on what happens in a film "is so strong that, carelessly used, it can, by implication at least, infuse quite another feeling or meaning into a scene...It is important that the cameraman be as well informed and involved as possible at all stages."

Fine is an integral part of the production team at WMAL-TV. But he is the first to admit that the reporter's personality has a great deal to do with the success or failure of a mini-documentary series.

"When I started with the documentary unit," he says, "I insisted on being part of any planning for a project. Perhaps some cameramen are happy just going out and shooting what they're told to shoot. But I think the cameraman should be creative. He's the one who looks through the lens. He's the one who sees the shot."

Nevertheless, the cameraman's final product is dependent on the film editor. The cameraman may do a superb job of filming but his accomplishments may be ruined or heightened by a poor or a good film editor. Again, teamwork is the keynote. Fine would agree with Joseph V. Mascelli's dictum in *The Five C's of Cinematography (Cine/Grafic Publications)*:

> A competent cameraman should thoroughly understand film editing from a visual rather than a technical standpoint. He need not know how to assemble A&B rolls or even make a splice, but he should be able to break down an event into a series of shots that can be cut into a presentable sequence.

The cameraman may, at times, serve as the producer/director besides being a photographer. This depends on the camerman's ambitions or inclinations.

Many investigative mini-documentaries require undercover shooting. One mini-documentary series produced by WMAL-TV was based on the activities of the police homicide squad. The cameraman rode with policemen in a squad car. Most of the shooting was done using the hand-held Eclair camera.

Fine prefers shooting in natural light whenever possible even if he has to *push* the film. (Pushing refers to a technique of allowing extra developing time for underexposed film.) For example, in obtaining footage of a murder that had been committed, the film was pushed 3 stops. It was grainy in development but the feeling of being on the scene was there. If a sun gun or other lighting were to be used, it would, literally, reflect the presence of a technician setting up a picture rather than the natural look—the appearance of spontaneity.

In the mini-documentary series on prostitution, the cameraman was hidden in a van in a parking lot across the street from the action site. In this way, prostitutes and their solicitors were unaware of being filmed, and scenes could be taken of policewomen, who posed as prostitutes, arresting men.

The cameraman, as much as the reporter, must be aware of the structure of the mini-documentary series: the fact that each episode should be self-contained. There is rarely any recapitulation within the episode itself. As Paul Fine expressed it, "I think you can watch just one episode of our series and know what it is we're trying to say."

He is less sanguine about turning a mini-documentary series into a full-length documentary:

> I would think it is definitely better to plan a full-length documentary by itself rather than develop it from a mini-documentary series. In working on a mini-documentary series, the film editor has to cut original film—there is no workprint. Once you've cut the original film, you've limited yourself. With a workprint, you can do all the cutting you need.

The advent of videotape is of paramount concern. However, Fine's comment is that it does not matter to the cameraman whether he is shooting film or videotape; he is still "making pictures." The problem, at the moment, is that videotape equipment is not as compact as film. Also—and film editors have corroborated this finding—film is more flexible for editing than videotape. That factor is important to the cameraman, since the cameraman and the film editor work in tandem.

Fine has another interesting observation about the relationship of film to videotape. Videotape doesn't have the feel of film. "It's too real. Film creates an illusion. Videotape gives you that live feeling, the same image your eyes see. It doesn't have the fantasy-world image of film."

Some television stations, Fine said, expect their cameramen to be engineers, too. That is, they believe the cameraman ought to be able to take the equipment apart and repair it. That would require a cameraman to attend electronics school. There is nothing really wrong with that concept, but the emphasis should be on the cameraman's creativity, not his ability as a maintenance man. There is little point in having a cameraman who knows the ins and outs of his equipment but who does not have the talent for properly composing a picture. As Joseph V. Mascelli (*The Five C's of Cinematography*) noted, "A carefully

Use of crane solves problems in many special photographic situations.

76

chosen camera angle can heighten dramatic visualization of the story. A carelessly picked camera angle may distract or confuse the audience by depicting the scene so that its meaning is difficult to comprehend. Therefore, selection of camera angles is a most important factor in constructing a picture of continual interest."

With emphasis on economy, some TV stations prefer using single system equipment or have a videotape cameraman carry all the equipment he needs for sight and sound. Fine believes that single system is acceptable for a brief interview or a news event but not for any production as complex as a mini-documentary series. He definitely prefers working with an audio expert.

## SOUND

One of the audio experts at WMAL-TV is Clyde Roller, who was a radio engineer for 9 years before he decided to move into television. At first he spent most of his time in the studios but he liked the idea of going out on location. The news department proved to be the best place for his talents. He began to specialize in creative services and public affairs programing.

Roller uses the Nagra for sound recording and Sony lavalier microphones for interviews. He is enthusiastic about the WMAL-TV team concept. The crew he is part of has worked together for six years and each member coordinates with each other to the best advantage.

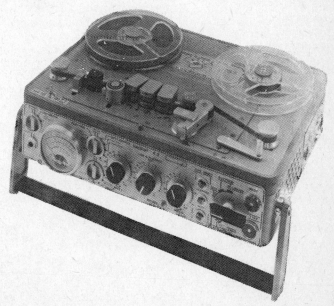

Nagra 4.2L tape recorder used by WMAL-TV sound technician.

Reporter flanked by camera and sound men to capture crop-dusting sequence.

The audio technician must know how to keep his microphones from view and still obtain the best possible sound. It adds to the spontaneity and realism of the sequences for a mini-documentary series if microphones are not obvious, in the same way that the viewer does not see the camera.

Also, microphones should not block the camera angle. However, audio and visual are two-way streets and if the sound were to be ruined by shifting the microphones, then the cameraman would have to bring his ingenuity to bear in order to obtain the most effective sight and sound.

The sound technician generally is not involved in the early planning stages of the mini-documentary series. The cameraman, usually, meets with his audio counterpart immediately after the planning session and informs him of the scope of the mini-documentary. If there is an opportunity to examine the location before shooting, the audio technician accompanies the cameraman.

Clyde Roller believes that it is highly effective to begin a mini-documentary series with ear catching sound:

> For example, we did a hospital emergency series and we started off with a bang: the cry of a child screaming in pain. Then the sound of the ambulance siren as the vehicle sped through the city. Sure, you hit people right off with that kind of opening. But you have to maintain the pace. You can't kick off with a striking opening and let the rest of your show go downhill.

Sound man aims mike at helicopter sound source.

He agrees with Fine that videotape is excellent for the immediacy of news events, but he cannot see videotape, as yet, taking the place of film for the documentary.

## THE AUTO REPAIR GO-ROUND

One of the mini-documentary series produced by WMAL-TV, which inspired a resolution by the District of Columbia city council, was devoted to an investigation of the auto repair industry. It is a far cry in subject matter from amnesty. Although it deals with a problem of concern to every car owner in the United States, this investigative report was confined to one metropolitan area. Transitions also differ from *Americans in Exile*. There is a recapitulation for every episode. It was essential that the viewer know what had transpired previously in relation to repairs of the test car; otherwise, the cumulative impact would be lost. As Jim Clarke explained, "We had to let them know that what they were seeing tonight was part of a puzzle and we would have its solution at the conclusion of the series."

*The Auto Repair Go-Round* opens with an introductory segment on a Friday evening—similar to the preview for *Americans in Exile*—and then runs the following week on a daily basis. It is actually a 2-part series consisting of a total of 12 episodes. There is a hiatus of a week between parts. The second series was an outgrowth of the previous week's investigatory series. The basic question raised in the first series was whether the exorbitant charges for auto repairs were a matter of dishonesty or incompetence. The second series offered the industry an opportunity to respond—to criticize the mini-documentary freely. Industry spokesmen preferred to talk about aspects of their workload rather than criticize the television program.

Each part of this mini-documentary series does involve a different aspect. The first deals with ripoffs by auto repairmen. The second advises the consumer on car maintenance. These are examples then of both the investigative and the informative mini-documentary.

The gimmick employed in the investigative series—that of a test car—is necessary to the theme of the mini-documentary. It is certainly a more scientific approach than simply asking consumers to relate their experiences with auto repair shops. Also, from a legal standpoint, the consumer's complaint might be considered hearsay. The use of a test car and the employment of a master mechanic as a consultant assured the credibility of the mini-documentary.

Remember that we are dealing with a touchy subject, particularly in naming culprits. Obviously, the firms involved would not voluntarily give access to camera crews, so Clarke had

Investigative reporter Jim Clarke and the **Blue Goose.**

to film the exteriors of auto repair shops. Most of the shops chosen were located in or adjacent to shopping centers. The shop owner could not readily discern what the camera crew was filming. To be prepared for any contingency, the reporter had brought with him a script on urban renewal. In one or two instances, the shop manager came out to ascertain what was being said; in these cases, one of the crew would alert the reporter, who would hurriedly switch to the script on urban renewal. An obvious deception, but the reporter was convinced that the end justified the means.

Each company involved received a copy of the transcript and the opportunity for rebuttal 48 hours before each episode was scheduled.

The effectiveness of the series was twofold: viewers commended the station for its ingenuity in exposing consumer harassment and the repair shops reformed their operations. As an example, car owners were provided with plastic bags containing the used parts which had actually been replaced.

The production of a mini-documentary calls on the imagination, the drive, and all the talent a reporter possesses. Investigative reports by a television station conscious of its public service obligations can go far in alerting the community and acting as the catalyst for essential reforms.

The interlocking series, *The Auto Repair Go-Round* and *You and Auto Repair* are reproduced below for study purposes.

## INTRODUCTION—FRIDAY

| | |
|---|---|
| CLARKE:<br>SOUND ON FILM | THIS IS A 1970 FORD MAVERICK WITH A 6-CYLINDER ENGINE AND A MANUAL TRANSMISSION. |
| VARIED SHOTS<br>OF MAVERICK | PRIOR TO ITS PURCHASE 3 MONTHS AGO BY THE SCENE TONIGHT IT HAD ONLY A SINGLE OWNER. IT HAD BEEN DRIVEN 45.500 MILES AND WAS IN GENERALLY EXCELLENT CONDITION. SINCE THEN. IT HAS BEEN TESTED AND RETESTED. OUTFITTED WITH NEW PARTS. WORKED ON BY MECHANICS IN THREE STATES AND A DOZEN GARAGES. EXCLUDING RACING CARS. CARS OWNED BY PRESIDENTS AND MECHANICS. THIS CAR MAY HAVE HAD MORE PROFESSIONAL ATTENTION IN LESS TIME THAN ANY OTHER PRIVATELY OWNED CAR IN HISTORY. |
| | IT ALL BEGAN THREE MONTHS AGO WHEN WE DECIDED TO TEST THE WIDELY HELD BELIEF THAT TAKING YOUR CAR IN FOR REPAIRS CAN BE AS HAZARDOUS AS JUMPING INTO A POOL OF BARRACUDA. |

MOTORISTS ROUTINELY BELIEVE THEY ARE VICTIMS OF AUTO REPAIR RIPOFFS. ONE REASON IS THE INCREASING SOPHISTICATION AND COMPLEXITY OF CARS. WE REALLY DON'T UNDERSTAND THEM OR HOW THEY WORK. OFTEN, REPAIRS ARE EXPENSIVE. ANOTHER REASON FOR DISCONTENT IS INDUSTRY'S PHILOSOPHY OF PLANNED OBSOLESCENCE. CARS AREN'T BUILT AS WELL AS THEY ONCE WERE NOR INTENDED TO LAST AS LONG AS THEY ONCE DID. UNTIL RECENTLY, OUR AF-FLUENCE, RESOURCES, AND ENVIRONMENT ALLOWED US TO ACCEPT ALL THAT. BUT AS THESE HAVE BEEN THREATENED, CONSUMERS HAVE BECOME LESS TOLERANT AND MORE VOCAL.

THE DISTRICT, MARYLAND, AND VIRGINIA ARE NOW CONSIDERING REGULATION OF THE AUTO REPAIR INDUSTRY. SOME CRITICS OF REGULATION SAY WHAT IS NEEDED IS COMPETENT MECHANICS, NOT LAWS THAT WOULD DRIVE MECHANICS OUT OF THE FIELD. YET THE AUTO-MAINTENANCE-AND-REPAIR INDUSTRY IS BIG BUSINESS.

**MRS. PACKARD:**
**SOUND ON FILM**

PAT, SUPPOSE SOMEBODY TAKES A CAR IN LIKE THIS—WELL THIS CAR—THAT YOU'VE PERFECTLY TESTED. SAY IT'S RUNNING A LITTLE ROUGH AND I'M GOING ON VACATION. IF I TELL THE GARAGE TO FIX IT UP FOR ME, WHAT KIND OF DAMAGE CAN THEY DO?

**PAT GOSS:**
**SOUND ON FILM**

WELL, THEY CAN DO A LOT OF DIFFERENT THINGS. FIRST OF ALL ONE OF THE PRIMARY THINGS THIS CAR IS GOING TO GO IN WITH ABSOLUTELY NOTHING WRONG WITH IT. I'M NOT GOING TO BUG IT OR ANYTHING. AND THEY'RE GOING TO SAY THEY WANT THE BRAKES AND FRONT END CHECKED. AND HERE THERE'S A GOOD PROBABILITY THAT THEY'LL BE SOLD BALL JOINTS, OR AN IDLER ARM, POSSIBLY A COMPLETE BRAKE JOB.

**MOTORIST WHO TOOK CAR IN FOR REPAIRS-ON PHONE, IN MID-CONVERSATION.**

OKAY, WHAT ARE YOU GOING TO HAVE TO DO TO IT? FOUR SHOCK ABSORBERS, FRONT WHEEL BRAKE SHOES...YOU SAY YOU'RE GOING TO TURN THE DRUMS. HOW MUCH IS ALL OF THIS GOING TO COST ME?

**CLARKE:**
**SOUND ON FILM**

WHAT WOULD YOU SAY OF OUR TV 7 EXPERIENCE? WAS IT AN UNUSUAL EXPERIENCE OR WOULD YOU SAY IT'S A TYPICAL EXPERIENCE?

**SENATOR PHILIP HART:**

UNHAPPILY, IT'S TYPICAL. OUR HEARINGS INDICATED THAT YOU AND I SPEND ABOUT

| | |
|---|---|
| (CHAIRMAN, SENATE ANTI-TRUST SUBCOMMITTEE) | BETWEEN 8 AND 10 BILLION DOLLARS A YEAR FOR JUST THE SORT OF STUFF THAT YOU'RE DESCRIBING: WORK THAT WAS UNNECESSARY OR IMPROPERLY DONE OR DONE AND DONE WELL BUT NOT NEEDED. THAT'S 8–10 BILLION DOLLARS OUT OF A 30–35 BILLION–DOLLAR TOTAL CONSUMER PAYMENT FOR AUTO REPAIRS. |
| CLARKE: SOUND ON FILM | KEEPING A CAR RUNNING IS EXPENSIVE ENOUGH IF REPAIRS ARE NECESSARY AND COMPETENTLY DONE. IF REPAIRS ARE UNNECESSARY AND THE WORK IS POORLY DONE, IT CAN BE MURDER. YOU'LL SEE WHAT WE MEAN BEGINNING MONDAY NIGHT AT 6 ON "THE SCENE TONIGHT—THE AUTO REPAIR GO-ROUND." |
| CLOSE | THIS IS JIM CLARKE REPORTING. |

# EPISODE 1—MONDAY

| | |
|---|---|
| CLARKE: STUDIO | YOU HAVE JUST SEEN THE FINAL TEST RUN OF THE BLUE GOOSE. THAT'S THE AFFECTIONATE NAME THAT I AND HALF-A-DOZEN COLLEAGUES AND MECHANICS GAVE THIS 1970 FORD MAVERICK. |
| V/O AERIAL SHOTS OF TEST RUN | THREE MONTHS AGO WHEN WE BEGAN TESTING THE AUTO REPAIR BUSINESS IN THE DC AREA. THE BLUE GOOSE BECAME THE EXCLUSIVE PROPERTY OF THE SCENE TONIGHT. PREVIOUSLY, SHE HAD ONLY A SINGLE OWNER, HAD BEEN WELL CARED FOR, DRIVEN 45,500 MILES. NOW, 1500 MILES LATER SHE HAS BEEN OUTFITTED WITH DOZENS OF NEW PARTS AND WORKED ON BY MECHANICS IN THREE STATES AND A DOZEN GARAGES. ALL IN THE INTEREST OF TESTING THE VIEW HELD BY MANY OF YOU—THAT VENTURING OUT TO HAVE YOUR CAR REPAIRED IS LIKE WALKING BLINDFOLDED THROUGH A MINE FIELD. |
| STUDIO | OUR EXPERT AND GUIDE TO THIS GO-ROUND OF THE AUTO REPAIR INDUSTRY WAS PAT GOSS—AN OVERNIGHT SENSATION—WHEN CBS NETWORK'S "60 MINUTES" PROGRAM TWO YEARS AGO PICKED HIM FROM AMONG ALL THE MECHANICS IN THE NATION TO CONDUCT ITS AUTO REPAIR TEST. |
| | PAT ESTIMATES HE SPENT TEN TIMES AS MUCH TIME ON OUR CAR—THE BLUE GOOSE—AS HE DID ON THE CBS TEST CAR. THE SON OF A MECHANIC, PAT DID HIS FIRST |

ENGINE OVERHAUL WHEN HE WAS 9 YEARS OLD. NOW, RECOGNIZED NATIONWIDE AS AN EXPERT ON AUTO REPAIRS, HE OWNS A GULF SERVICE STATION AND GARAGE IN RIVERDALE, MARYLAND. SINCE AUGUST 9TH, PAT HAS SPENT MUCH OF HIS TIME WORKING ON THE BLUE GOOSE—GETTING HER IN TOP-NOTCH CONDITION. THERE WERE SCORES OF ELECTRONIC, HANDS-ON, EYEBALL, AND ROAD TESTS OF THE CAR.

**SUPERVISORS WATCHING CHECKOUT**

FAIRFAX COUNTY SUPERVISORS CHAIRMAN JEAN PACKARD AND MRS. BARBARA GREGG, DIRECTOR OF THE MONTGOMERY COUNTY OFFICE OF CONSUMER AFFAIRS, WITNESSED PAT'S FINAL CHECKOUT OF THE CAR.

SEPTEMBER 4TH. OUTFITTED WITH A PAIR OF DELIBERATELY RUSTED BUT BRAND NEW FRONT SHOCK ABSORBERS, THE BLUE GOOSE PASSES VIRGINIA INSPECTION. SHE IS TUNED LIKE A FINE SWISS WATCH.

**EXTERIOR AUTO REPAIR SHOP**

SHE GOES INTO THE FIRESTONE STORE GARAGE AT 9400 MAIN STREET IN FAIRFAX, VIRGINIA. OUR DRIVER ASKS FOR A BRAKE AND FRONT-END CHECK—SAYS HE'S LEAVING ON VACATION.

THE NEXT DAY, FOLLOWING REPAIRS, PAT EXAMINES THE CAR:

**CLARKE: EXAMINATION OF CAR**

PAT, HERE IS OUR FIRST BILL AND YOU KNOW I BET YOU'RE NOT GOING TO BELIEVE THE DAMAGE—$65.10.

**GOSS:**

WOW.

**CLARKE:**

LET ME GIVE YOU THE DETAILS. THEY REPLACED A LEFT SIDE UPPER BALL JOINT. THEY SAY FOR A PRICE OF $27.50. THEY CHECKED THE ALIGNMENT OF THE CAR AND THEY PUT TWO NEW FRONT SHOCK ABSORBERS ON THE CAR FOR A CHARGE OF $19.76.

**GOSS:**

FIRST OF ALL, THE LEFT UPPER BALL JOINT HAS DEFINITELY BEEN REPLACED. THIS IS A NEW BALL JOINT.

**CLARKE:**

I CAN SEE IT NOW. IT'S THE ONLY SHINY THING UP THERE, ISN'T IT?

**GOSS:**

RIGHT. AND THE SHOCKS HAVE BEEN REPLACED. YOU CAN SEE HERE...

**CLARKE:**

I SEE THE NEW FITTINGS THERE. I CAN SEE THOSE ARE BLUE AND OURS WERE PRETTY FILTHY WHEN THEY WERE IN THERE.

**GOSS:**

ABSOLUTELY.

84

| CLARKE: | AND I'VE GOT ANOTHER LITTLE SURPRISE FOR YOU. THE SERVICE MANAGER AT THIS REPAIR SHOP YESTERDAY TRIED TO SELL US A BRAKE JOB. HE SAID THE BRAKE LINERS WERE 85% WORN. DOES THAT SURPRISE YOU? |
|---|---|
| GOSS: | NOT REALLY. |
| CLARKE: | WHEN WE TESTED THEM OUT. THEY WERE ABOUT—WHAT—60% OF NEW. WHAT DO YOU THINK? I'M SURE YOU ARE NOT AS SURPRISED ABOUT THIS AS I AM. AND I FRANKLY AM SURPRISED. |
| GOSS: | WELL. I SEE THIS TYPE OF THING DAY IN AND DAY OUT. SO IT DOESN'T REALLY COME AS THAT MUCH OF A SURPRISE TO ME. AS A MATTER OF FACT. THIS SEEMS PRETTY MILD COMPARED TO SOME OF THE THINGS I SEE. |
| CLARKE: | TOMORROW NIGHT FOLLOW THE TRAIL OF THE BLUE GOOSE AS. STILL IN EXCELLENT CONDITION. SHE HEADS FOR MORE REPAIRS AND GOES INTO GARAGES IN THE DISTRICT OF COLUMBIA. |
| CLOSE | THIS IS JIM CLARKE ON THE SCENE. |

## EPISODE 2—TUESDAY

| STUDIO INTRODUC-TION: | LAST NIGHT AS WE BEGAN JIM CLARKE'S SERIES. "THE AUTO REPAIR GO-ROUND." WE FOLLOWED THE SCENE TONIGHT'S TEST CAR THROUGH ITS FIRST REPAIR RUN. YOU WILL RECALL THAT THE BLUE GOOSE. A 1970 MAVERICK. WAS IN PERFECT OPERATING CONDITION WHEN IT WAS TAKEN TO A FIRESTONE STORE GARAGE ON MAIN STREET IN FAIRFAX. IT CAME OUT WITH A $65 REPAIR BILL. A NEW BALL JOINT. A FRONT-END ALIGNMENT. AND TWO NEW FRONT SHOCK ABSORBERS. |
|---|---|
| | TONIGHT. IN PART 2. JIM RESUMES THE TEST—WITH FILMS SHOT 54 DAYS AGO. |
| CLARKE: EXTERIOR, AUTO REPAIR SHOP | ON SEPTEMBER 7TH OUR DRIVER DROPS OUR CAR AT CALL CARL'S GARAGE AT 30TH AND M STREETS IN GEORGETOWN. SHE ASKS FOR A SAFETY CHECK. NOTING SHE IS LEAVING ON A TRIP. SHE KNOWS OF NOTHING WRONG EXCEPT THE CAR'S A BIT BUMPY AT HIGH SPEEDS ON THE BELTWAY. AND THE BRAKES DON'T FEEL QUITE RIGHT. |
| | EARLIER. OUR EXPERT. PAT GOSS. HAD MADE A THOROUGH CHECK OF THE BRAKES. |

ONE TEST MEASURED THE AMOUNT OF WEAR LEFT IN THE BRAKE SHOES:

GOSS:
SOUND ON FILM
DEMONSTRATING

WE FIRST ADJUST IT, THEN WE MEASURE THE THICKNESS OF THE BRAKE SHOES. AND HERE THIS IS SHOWING US THAT WE HAVE BETWEEN 55 AND 60 PERCENT OF THE WEAR LEFT IN THE BRAKE SHOES, WHICH MEANS THEY'RE IN VERY GOOD CONDITION.

CLARKE:

THE BRAKE DRUMS WERE ALSO MEASURED FOR WEAR. A TEST THAT SHOWED THEM PRACTICALLY NEW. CALL CARL'S BILL SHOCKED US—$149.63. THEY CHARGED FOR THE CAR'S SECOND ALIGNMENT IN TWO DAYS. FOR ROTATING AND BALANCING ITS TIRES—BUT FAILED TO DETECT AND ROTATE OUR WORN RIGHT REAR TIRE. WE GOT EIGHT NEW BRAKE LINERS. TWO NEW FRONT WHEEL CYLINDERS—AND WERE CHARGED FOR OVERHAUL OF THE TWO REAR CYLINDERS. A JOB THEY DID NOT DO.

IN ADDITION, PAT GOSS FOUND SOME OF THEIR WORK SHODDY AND SOME DANGEROUS: THOUGH THEY PUT AN EXCESSIVE AMOUNT OF GREASE ON THE SPINDLE, A POTENTIAL PROBLEM LATER, THEY DID NOT LUBRICATE ANY OF THE BRAKE PARTS AS THEY SHOULD HAVE.

AND THERE WERE OTHER PROBLEMS.

PAT GOSS:
SOUND ON FILM

DEMONSTRATING

YOU'LL NOTICE HERE THE BRAKE SHOE RETURN SPRINGS. THESE ARE THE SPRINGS THAT PULL THESE BRAKE SHOES BACK TOGETHER AFTER THEY HAVE PERFORMED THEIR FUNCTION. THE SPRING ENDS ARE EXTENDED—THEY'RE SPREAD OUT—WHICH COULD BE A VERY SIMPLE THING FOR THE MECHANIC TO CORRECT. ALL HE WOULD HAVE TO DO AS HE FINISHED UP EACH WHEEL WAS TAKE A PAIR OF PLIERS, SUCH AS I'M DOING HERE, AND SQUEEZE THE ENDS OF THE SPRINGS TOGETHER LIKE THAT SO THEY FIT PROPERLY AROUND THIS PIN.

CLARKE:

ADDING INSULT TO INJURY, CALL CARL'S CHARGED US FOR "TURNING"—THAT IS GRINDING USABLE METAL OUT OF OUR BRAKE DRUMS. THEY DID GRIND THEM. HALF THE USABLE LIFE WAS GROUND FROM THE FRONT DRUMS, AND THE LEFT REAR DRUM GOT A CLASSIC "TURN."

PAT GOSS:
SOUND ON FILM

ON THIS ONE—THIS IS THE LEFT REAR— THEY REALLY DID A JOB HERE. THIS PARTICULAR ONE IS READING AP-

| | |
|---|---|
| **DEMONSTRATING** | PROXIMATELY 59 THOUSANDTHS OF AN INCH. NOW THE MAXIMUM LIFE EXPECTANCY OF THIS DRUM IS 60-THOUSANDTHS OF AN INCH. SO THIS DRUM HAS BEEN TOTALLY DESTROYED. JUST BY THE TURNING OF IT. |
| **CLARKE:** | EXAMINATION OF THE RIGHT FRONT WHEEL REVEALED MORE INCOMPETENT WORK: |
| **PAT GOSS: SOUND ON FILM** | NOW HERE WE CAN SEE THE SELF-ADJUSTOR CABLE. IT'S SUPPOSED TO COME AROUND THIS LITTLE BLOCK HERE. IT'S SUPPOSED TO BE COMPLETELY ON THE BACK SIDE OF IT. AS YOU CAN SEE. IT ONLY |
| **DEMONSTRATING** | COMES OVER THE TOP PORTION. AND THEN JUST RIDES RIGHT OVER THE EDGE OF IT. THIS COULD BE VERY DANGEROUS BECAUSE THIS COULD JUMP OUT OF HERE. THE CABLE THEN COULD GET WOUND UP IN THE BRAKE MECHANISM OR VARIOUS PARTS OF THE BRAKE MECHANISM COULD FALL OUT. WHICH COULD BE EXTREMELY DANGEROUS. |
| **CLARKE: SOUND ON FILM** | FOUR DAYS LATER. HOPING AT LEAST WE MIGHT GET A NEW BRAKE DRUM. OUR CAR WAS LEFT HERE AT CALL CARL'S DIAGNOSTIC CENTER AT HALF AND L STREETS SOUTHWEST. AGAIN. WE REPORTED THE SAME SYMPTOMS FOR THE |
| **EXTERIOR AUTO REPAIR SHOP** | BLUE GOOSE. IT WAS LATE IN THE DAY AND WE WERE TOLD THEY DIDN'T HAVE MUCH TIME TO WORK ON THE CAR. THEY CHARGED US $8 TO REMOVE EXCESSIVE GREASE CALL CARL'S HAD PUT ON IN GEORGETOWN AND $12 TO BALANCE THE TIRES THEY HAD ALREADY BALANCED. THE TOTAL BILL WAS $23.10. WE LEFT CALL CARL'S FEELING WE HAD BEEN HAD. |
| **CLOSE** | THIS IS JIM CLARKE ON THE SCENE. |

## EPISODE 3—WEDNESDAY

| | |
|---|---|
| **STUDIO INTRODUCTION:** | TONIGHT. IN PART 3 OF THE AUTO REPAIR GO-ROUND. OUR TEST CAR HEADS SOUTH INTO VIRGINIA. |
| **SHOTS OF CAR DRIVING ON HIGHWAY** | SO FAR. SHE HAS BEEN SOLD TWO FRONT-END ALIGNMENTS. TWO SHOCK ABSORBERS. A BALL JOINT. EIGHT BRAKE SHOES. AND TWO BRAKE CYLINDERS. HER TIRES HAVE BEEN BALANCED TWICE: HALF THE USABLE LIFE HAS BEEN GROUND OUT OF HER FRONT BRAKE DRUMS AND GRINDING HAS DESTROYED THE LEFT REAR DRUM. AND SHE HAS PICKED UP REPAIR BILLS TOTALING $237. |

<table>
<tr><td></td><td>JIM CLARKE REPORTS AS THE BLUE GOOSE HEADS INTO MORE TROUBLE IN VIRGINIA AND MARYLAND:</td></tr>
<tr><td>CLARKE:<br>SOUND ON FILM<br><br><br>EXTERIOR<br>AUTO REPAIR SHOP</td><td>SPORTING 4 NEW BUT DIRTY SHOCK ABSORBERS. THE CAR IS LEFT HERE AT THE MEMCO AUTOMOTIVE CENTER NEAR OLD LEE HIGHWAY IN FAIRFAX. VIRGINIA. LEAVING ON VACATION. THE DRIVER WANTS A FRONT-END CHECK FOR A BUMPY RIDE AND A SAFETY CHECK ON BRAKES. LATER MEMCO'S BILL SHOCKS US: $79.60. $18.95 FOR TIE-ROD END BUSHINGS. OUR EXPERT. PAT GOSS. SAYS THEY WERE UNNECESSARY AND COULD CAUSE EXCESSIVE STRESS AND WEAR:</td></tr>
<tr><td>CLARKE:</td><td>COULD IT CONCEIVABLY BE DANGEROUS FOR US TO HAVE THEM ON THERE?</td></tr>
<tr><td>GOSS:</td><td>YES. IT COULD. BECAUSE THIS SPRING PUTS AN EXTRA STRAIN ON THIS CONNECTION WHICH ACTUALLY IN MANY CASES CAN MAKE THE TIE-ROD END WEAR MORE RAPIDLY THAN IT WOULD NORMALLY.</td></tr>
<tr><td>CLARKE:</td><td>YOU KNOW. I'M GETTING A LITTLE AFRAID OF DRIVING THIS CAR.</td></tr>
<tr><td>GOSS:</td><td>RIGHT.</td></tr>
<tr><td>CLARKE:</td><td>FOR $8 MEMCO BALANCED OUR TIRES AND FOR $8.95 GAVE US A FRONT-END ALIGNMENT. THE THIRD BALANCE AND THIRD ALIGNMENT IN A WEEK. BUT MEMCO'S BIG SURPRISE—$41.69 FOR REPLACING OUR DIRTY BUT BRAND-NEW SHOCK ABSORBERS.</td></tr>
<tr><td>CLARKE:</td><td>I JUST CAN'T BELIEVE IT. BECAUSE WE HAD FOUR NEW SHOCKS ON THIS CAR AND THEY REPLACED THEM. WHICH MEANS THEY OBVIOUSLY DIDN'T TEST THE CAR TO SEE IF IT NEEDED SHOCKS AND IT'S A VERY SIMPLE TEST. WHY ARE THEY DOING THIS TO US?</td></tr>
<tr><td>GOSS:</td><td>WELL (LAUGHS). MONEY IS THE BIG REASON.</td></tr>
<tr><td>CLARKE:<br><br><br>EXTERIOR<br>AUTO REPAIR SHOP</td><td>THE NEXT DAY. OUTFITTED WITH OUR NEW BUT DIRTY SHOCK ABSORBERS. THE BLUE GOOSE GOES INTO THIS FIRESTONE GARAGE AT RIVERDALE PLAZA IN RIVERDALE. MARYLAND. PAT GOSS HAD MADE HER NEW PARTS DIRTY. OUR DRIVER SAYS HE IS BUYING THE CAR FOR A THOUSAND DOLLARS. LESS WHAT IT COSTS TO PUT IN GOOD OPERATING CONDITION.</td></tr>
<tr><td>CLARKE:</td><td>THE CAR IS RETURNED LATE THE NEXT DAY WITH A STAGGERING BILL OF $201.75. WE ARE</td></tr>
</table>

| | |
|---|---|
| **STUDIO** | CHARGED FOR FOUR NEW SHOCK ABSORBERS. REPLACING THE FOUR NEW ONES ALREADY ON THE CAR. THEY INSTALLED NEW TIE ROD ENDS AND TIE ROD SLEEVES. THEY GAVE THE CAR ITS FOURTH ALIGNMENT IN A WEEK. PUT IN NEW WINDSHIELD WIPER BLADES. AND SOLD US NEW FRONT BRAKE DRUMS. REPLACING WORN BUT SAFE BRAKE DRUMS. THEY DID NOT DISCOVER OUR LEFT REAR DRUM WHICH HAD BEEN DESTROYED IN AN EARLIER JOB. RUBBING SALT INTO AN OPEN WOUND. THESE MECHANICS LEFT OUR WHEEL-BEARING DUST COVERS JUST BARELY HANGING ON AND BOTH FRONT-BEARING RETAINING NUTS WERE IM-PROPERLY INSTALLED. |
| **GOSS·** | AS TIGHT AS THAT WAS. WITHIN A MATTER OF PROBABLY 100 MILES OR SO IT WOULD HAVE DESTROYED THE FRONT WHEEL BEARINGS. |
| **CLARKE:** | IS THAT RIGHT? |
| **GOSS:** | UH-HUH. IT WAS VERY BAD. |
| **CLARKE:**<br><br>**EXTERIOR**<br>**AUTO REPAIR SHOP** | THIS FIRESTONE STORE CHARGED US FOR TURNING—THAT IS. GRINDING—OUR NEW BRAKE DRUMS. BUT PAT GOSS FOUND THEY HAD NOT BEEN TURNED. THE RIVERDALE PLAZA FIRESTONE ALSO TRIED TO SELL US TWO NEW REAR TIRES. DECLINING THAT OF-FER. WE ASKED INSTEAD THAT THEY REPLACE THE WORN RIGHT REAR TIRE WITH THE SPARE TIRE WHICH WAS IN THE TRUNK. INSTEAD. THEY REPLACED A GOOD RIGHT FRONT TIRE AND LEFT OUR REAR TIRE RIGHT WHERE IT WAS. AND SO WE AND THE BLUE GOOSE LEAVE THE FIRESTONE STORE AT RIVERDALE PLAZA. CERTAIN WE'VE BEEN HAD AND WONDERING WHETHER THINGS MIGHT GET BETTER. |
| **CLOSE** | THIS IS JIM CLARKE ON THE SCENE IN RIVERDALE. |

## EPISODE 4—THURSDAY

| | |
|---|---|
| **STUDIO INTRODUCTION**<br>**SUPER**<br>**VARIED SHOTS OF CAR** | AS YOU'VE SEEN OR HEARD. THIS WEEK THE SCENE TONIGHT IS DOCUMENTING THE HAZARDS YOU FACE WHEN TAKING YOUR CAR OUT FOR REPAIRS. THUS FAR. OUR TEST CAR—THIS 1970 FORD MAVERICK—HAS BEEN TO FIVE AREA GARAGES. THE CAR. WHICH WE'VE DUBBED THE BLUE GOOSE. LEFT OUR TEST FACILITY IN EXCELLENT CON-DITION. THE ONLY THING IT NEEDED WAS |

89

REPLACEMENT OF A WORN TIRE. IN FIVE VISITS TO REPAIR SHOPS. IT HAS ROLLED UP A TOTAL BILL OF $519. IN NINE DAYS SHE HAS HAD FOUR FRONT-END ALIGNMENTS. TEN SHOCK ABSORBERS. EIGHT BRAKE SHOES. TWO BRAKE DRUMS. TWO BRAKE CYLINDERS. NEW TIE ROD ENDS AND SLEEVES. AND NEW WINDSHIELD WIPER BLADES. ALL OF IT WAS UNNECESSARY. MUCH OF THE WORK WAS POORLY DONE AND IN SOME INSTANCES THE CAR WAS LEFT IN A DANGEROUS CONDITION.

TONIGHT. IN PART 4 OF THE AUTO REPAIR GO-ROUND. JIM CLARKE REPORTS WHAT HAPPENED WHEN WE STARTED TO ''BUG'' THE CAR:

**CLARKE:**
**V/O FILM**

WHEN WE SENT THE BLUE GOOSE OUT IN EXCELLENT CONDITION. OUR REPAIR BILLS AVERAGED MORE THAN A HUNDRED DOLLARS A VISIT. NOW. ON SEPTEMBER 18TH. OUR EXPERT—PAT GOSS— DELIBERATELY BUGS THE CAR FOR THE FIRST TIME.

**GOSS:**
**SOUND ON FILM**


**DEMONSTRATING**

NOW WHAT I'M GOING TO DO IS TO DISABLE THE CHARGING SYSTEM BY A VERY SIMPLE MEANS SO WHAT WILL BE HAPPENING IS THAT THE ALTERNATOR WILL NOT BE RECHARGING THE BATTERY AND THE IDIOT LIGHT INSIDE THE CAR WILL BE GLOWING RED. THE REGULATOR ON THE CAR. WHICH IS IDENTICAL TO THIS ONE. HAS THESE CON-NECTIONS ON THE SIDE OF IT. NOW THIS HAS ONE COMMON CONNECTOR THAT PLUGS INTO IT. I'M GOING TO BEND ONE OF THESE LITTLE CONNECTORS SO THAT WHEN THIS PLUG-IN CONNECTOR IS ATTACHED TO IT. THIS ONE WILL NOT BE MAKING CONTACT. SO THIS WILL DISABLE THE SYSTEM. THE ONLY THING THAT WOULD BE NECESSARY TO REPAIR IT WOULD BE TO BEND THIS UP AND RECONNECT IT.

**CLARKE:**
**V/O FILM**


**EXTERIOR**
**AUTO REPAIR SHOP**

THE CAR GOES INTO THE MARKET TIRE COMPANY GARAGE AND DIAGNOSTIC CENTER AT 5709 LEESBURG PIKE. BAILEY'S CROSSROADS IN VIRGINIA. A FEW HOURS LATER IT COMES OUT WITH A BILL—$67.55. WE WERE SOLD A NEW VOLTAGE REGULATOR AND A REBUILT ALTERNATOR- —REPLACEMENTS FOR PARTS THAT HAD NOTHING WRONG WITH THEM. WE REJECTED MARKET TIRE'S OFFER TO SELL US A NEW BATTERY. WE KNEW IT WAS OKAY AND WE WANTED TO TRY THIS ELECTRICAL PROBLEM AGAIN WITHOUT A NEW BATTERY.

| | |
|---|---|
| **GOSS:**<br>**SOUND ON FILM** | IN MOST CASES. IF A MECHANIC IS COMPETENT. THE NORMAL TEST PROCEDURE IS FIRST TO DETERMINE IF THE SYSTEM IS OR IS NOT WORKING. THEN TO CHECK ALL CONNECTIONS ON THE REGULATOR AND THE ALTERNATOR. IF THE MECHANIC DOES THIS. HE WOULD FIND THIS VERY QUICKLY. |
| **CLARKE:**<br><br><br><br>**EXTERIOR**<br>**AUTO REPAIR SHOP** | TWO DAYS LATER. PAT CUTS THE WIRE LINKING THE ALTERNATOR AND VOLTAGE REGULATOR. HE RECONNECTS IT WITH AN OLD ELECTRICAL TAPE THEN PULLS IT APART. OUR IDIOT LIGHT IS GLOWING WHEN THE BLUE GOOSE ROLLS INTO THE COLUMBIA PIKE SHELL STATION AT 7023 COLUMBIA PIKE IN ANNANDALE. HERE WE GET OUR FIRST COMPETENT AND FAIR BILL FROM A MECHANIC WHO QUICKLY IDENTIFIED THE PROBLEM AND FIXED IT. HE CHARGED US ONLY $8.06 AND THIS AFTER WE HAD TOLD HIM AN EARLIER ESTIMATE FOR FIXING THE CAR WAS $150. |
| **CLARKE:**<br>**V/O FILM**<br>**EXTERIORS OF**<br>**AUTO REPAIR SHOPS** | THREE DAYS LATER. DISABLING THE SAME WIRE WE DROP THE CAR AT CALL CARL'S AT CONNECTICUT AND NEBRASKA AVENUES IN WASHINGTON. THEY FIX IT AND CHARGE US ONLY $5.20. OUR LUCK IS PICKING UP. LATER. PAT BENDS THE TERMINAL ON OUR NEW VOLTAGE REGULATOR AGAIN CAUSING THE IDIOT LIGHT TO BURN. A MECHANIC AT THE MOBILE STATION AT 7209 LITTLE RIVER TURNPIKE IN ANNANDALE THUMPS IT A COUPLE OF TIMES WITH HIS HAND. CAUSES THE LIGHT TO GO OUT AND PRONOUNCES IT DEFECTIVE. HE DID NOT CHECK THE CONNECTION. OUR BILL: $19.08 FOR A NEW VOLTAGE REGULATOR. |
| | EQUIPPED WITH EXCELLENT FRONT BRAKE SHOES AND DRUMS. THE BLUE GOOSE GOES INTO THIS MERCHANT'S FIRESTONE STORE AT 210 HUNGERFORD DRIVE IN ROCKVILLE. HER SHOCKS ARE NEW BUT DIRTY. LATER. WE'RE TOLD THE CAR NEEDS FOUR NEW SHOCKS. FRONT BRAKE SHOES. DRUM TURNS. AND GREASE SEALS. WHEN PICKED UP. THE $51 CHARGE FOR SHOCKS HAS BEEN SCRATCHED OFF THE BILL. WE'RE TOLD THEY HAD JUST BEEN SPRAYED WITH UNDERCOATING AND HAD PICKED UP DIRT. THE TOTAL BILL: $69.62—ALL OF IT UNNECESSARY. |
| | PAT GOSS FOUND 40–50 PERCENT OF THE USABLE LIFE HAD BEEN GROUND OUT OF OUR GOOD FRONT BRAKE DRUMS: THEY |

HAD IMPROPERLY INSTALLED THE FRONT BRAKES. AND HAD FAILED TO DETECT OUR BAD LEFT DRUM. THEY ALSO DAMAGED THE NEW GREASE SEALS WHEN PUTTING THEM IN.

SO IN TEN VISITS TO AREA GARAGES WE HAVE RUN UP REPAIR BILLS TOTALING $688.69. IN SIX OF THESE VISITS, THE CAR NEEDED NOTHING BUT REPLACEMENT OF A WORN TIRE. IN FOUR OTHERS, SHE HAD AN EASILY DISCERNIBLE AND SIMPLE ELECTRICAL PROBLEM.

**CLOSE**

THIS IS JIM CLARKE ON THE SCENE IN ROCKVILLE.

## EPISODE 5—FRIDAY

**CLARKE:**
**STUDIO**

THE FLIGHT OF THE BLUE GOOSE HAS ENDED. BUT I CAN REPORT. SHE IS ALIVE AND WELL.

**MONTAGE OF BILLS**
**ANIMATION**
**TECHNIQUE**

WHEN WE TOTE UP THE BILLS. WE FIND THE FOLLOWING: FIRST. FOR LABOR AND REPLACEMENT OF PARTS IN WORK DONE ON THE CAR IN GARAGES IN MARYLAND. VIRGINIA. AND THE DISTRICT OF COLUMBIA. THE TOTAL: $668.69. AND TO THAT WE ADD ANOTHER $232—THE WHOLESALE COST OF GOOD PARTS REMOVED FROM THE CAR AND DISCARDED DURING HER REPAIRS. AND THE COST OF PARTS DAMAGED DURING INSTALLATION AND REPAIR.

OUR FINAL COST FOR THE FLIGHT OF THE BLUE GOOSE: A THOUSAND ONE HUNDRED DOLLARS AND 92 CENTS.

WE BEGAN THIS SERIES WITH THE BLUE GOOSE BY TELLING YOU THAT WE WERE GOING TO TEST A WIDELY HELD BELIEF THAT TAKING YOUR CAR OUT FOR REPAIRS IS A HAZARDOUS EXPERIENCE. WE BELIEVE OUR EXPERIENCE CONFIRMS THAT BEYOND A SHADOW OF A DOUBT.

WE WOULD NOTE TOO THAT REPRESENTATIVES OF ALL THE COMPANIES VISITED BY OUR CAR TOLD US THAT THEIR POLICY IS NOT TO SELL THE CUSTOMER ANYTHING HE DOESN'T NEED. WE ACCEPT THOSE CLAIMS IN GOOD FAITH. HOWEVER, OUR TEST CAR WAS SOLD HUNDREDS OF DOLLARS WORTH OF PARTS AND LABOR IT DID NOT NEED. THAT TELLS THAT WE CONSUMERS HAVE A PROBLEM AND THOSE RUNNING THE AUTO REPAIR BUSINESS ALSO HAVE A PROBLEM.

| | |
|---|---|
| **FREEZE FRAMES**<br>**FORD ENGINE** | NOW, WE AT W-M-A-L WERE VERY FORTUNATE IN DOING THIS TEST ON THE AUTO REPAIR GO-ROUND, IN HAVING PAT GOSS, AN AUTOMOTIVE REPAIR EXPERT, ASSIST US IN THE TEST. FOR THOSE OF YOU WHO HAVE CALLED IN RECENT DAYS TO ASK FOR MORE INFORMATION ABOUT PAT, LET ME SIMPLY SAY THAT, AS I RECOLLECT, HE DID HIS FIRST ENGINE OVERHAUL WHEN HE WAS 9 YEARS OLD. HE WAS THE SON OF A MECHANIC AND I GUESS THAT BEGAN A LONG LOVE AFFAIR WITH CARS AND ENGINES FOR PAT. |
| **CLARKE:** | PAT ALSO IS THE OWNER OF A GULF SERVICE STATION IN RIVERDALE, MARYLAND. HE WAS RECENTLY NAMED DEALER OF THE YEAR BY THE GULF OIL COMPANY. HE IS A CONSULTANT TO THE PRINCE GEORGES COUNTY CONSUMER PROTECTION COMMISSION. HE HAS HAD A LOT OF EXPERIENCE. |
| **STUDIO INTERVIEW:** | PAT, I REMEMBER WHEN WE STARTED PREPARING THIS TEST SEVERAL MONTHS AGO, YOU STARTED BY TELLING ME WHAT YOU THOUGHT ABOUT THE INTEGRITY OF THOSE PEOPLE IN THE AUTO REPAIR INDUSTRY, ESPECIALLY MECHANICS. I'D LIKE TO HAVE YOU REPEAT THAT FOR OUR VIEWERS. AND HAS THIS TEST CHANGED YOUR IDEAS ABOUT THAT? |
| **GOSS:** | WELL, FIRST OF ALL, THIS TEST HASN'T CHANGED MY IDEAS AND MY IDEAS ARE THAT, IN MY PERSONAL EXPERIENCE, I'VE FOUND THAT THE BIGGEST PROBLEM IN THIS AUTO REPAIR BUSINESS IS NOT SO MUCH THE DISHONEST ASPECT OF IT AS IT IS INCOMPETENCY. I FIND THAT PROBABLY 80 TO 85 PERCENT OF THE CASES THAT I COME IN CONTACT WITH ARE AS A RESULT OF A MECHANIC THAT EITHER DOESN'T KNOW TOTALLY WHAT HE'S DOING, DOESN'T HAVE THE PROPER EQUIPMENT, OR SOMETHING LIKE THIS. |
| **CLARKE:** | DON'T WE HAVE A SERIOUS SHORTAGE OF MECHANICS IN THIS COUNTRY? |
| **GOSS:** | YES. AS A MATTER OF FACT WE DO—A VERY, VERY SERIOUS SHORTAGE. |
| **CLARKE:** | WELL, WHAT ARE SOME OF THE THINGS THAT WE MIGHT THINK IN TERMS OF DOING TO CORRECT THAT PROBLEM? |
| **GOSS:** | WELL, THERE HAS TO BE A COUPLE OF THINGS. FIRST OF ALL, THERE HAS TO BE SOME INCENTIVE TO GET YOUNG MEN INTO |

| | THIS FIELD. THE WAY IT IS AT THE MOMENT. THERE ISN'T ANYTHING THAT REALLY IS INTERESTING THAT WOULD MAKE THE YOUNG PERSONS WANT TO GET INTO THE FIELD. |
|---|---|
| **CLARKE:** | THE TRADES HAVE BEEN DOWNGRADED IN THIS COUNTRY FOR A LONG TIME. AND THAT'S GOT TO BE A PROBLEM. DON'T YOU THINK? |
| **GOSS:** | RIGHT. WE HAVE THIS STIGMA THAT UNLESS WE'RE WHITE COLLAR. COLLEGE GRADUATES. WHATEVER. THAT WE DON'T HAVE A GOOD STATUS. THIS SHOULD BE DONE AWAY WITH BECAUSE THERE'S GOOD MONEY TO BE MADE IN THE TRADE AND IT'S A VERY REPUTABLE BUSINESS. REALLY. |
| **CLARKE:** | DO YOU THINK THERE MIGHT BE A NEED TO CHANGE SOME OF THE METHODS BY WHICH MECHANICS ARE PAID NOW? THERE'S A FLAT-RATE SYSTEM WHERE A MANUAL SAYS IT TAKES A CERTAIN AMOUNT OF TIME TO DO A BRAKE JOB AND WHETHER THE MAN SPENDS HALF THAT TIME OR TWICE THAT TIME THE CUSTOMER IS CHARGED THE FLAT RATE. |
| **GOSS:** | WELL. ABSOLUTELY. THIS FLAT RATE IS A REAL PROBLEM. IT DOES A NUMBER OF THINGS. AS YOU MENTIONED. THE CONSUMER USUALLY PAYS FOR WHATEVER THIS FLAT-RATE BOOK SAYS. IT SAYS THAT THE CUSTOMER PAYS AN HOUR. EVEN IF THE MECHANIC CAN DO THIS JOB IN HALF AN HOUR OR EVEN FIFTEEN MINUTES. ALSO. IT DOES AWAY WITH MOST OF THE COMPETITION IN THE BUSINESS BECAUSE MOST EVERYONE WORKS FROM THIS BOOK AND REGARDLESS OF WHERE YOU GO. YOU GET PRETTY MUCH THE SAME PRICE ON THINGS. |
| **CLARKE:** | PAT. THANK YOU VERY MUCH. |
| | IT IS LONG PAST THE TIME WHEN WE SHOULD HAVE BEGUN WORKING TOGETHER TO SOLVE THE PROBLEMS OF THE AUTO REPAIR INDUSTRY. THE AUTOMOBILE AND ITS PROBLEMS ARE CENTRAL TO OUR WAY OF LIFE. VARIOUS LEGISLATIVE BODIES ARE NOW MOVING TOWARD REGULATION OF THIS INDUSTRY. WE WONDER WHETHER THERE HAS BEEN SUFFICIENT DISCUSSION OF THE ISSUES INVOLVED TO DRAFT GOOD LEGISLATION. WE'LL EXAMINE THAT AND GIVE YOU SOME TIPS ON MAINTAINING |

CLOSE                    THIS IS JIM CLARKE.

## YOU AND AUTO REPAIR

Jim Clarke's series on auto repair ripoffs was hardly inclined to win friends in the industry but it did influence influential people. It led the District of Columbia government to enact legislation regulating auto repair shops. An article by Craig R. Walters in the extensively circulated *TV Guide* extolled Clarke's investigative reporting. District Attorneys in many other cities contacted Clarke for advice on establishing their own tests. One of the auto repair corporations under fire requested copies of the series to use in a course for their service personnel. Thousands of phone calls and letters commended WMAL-TV for the series.

There was the other side of the coin: Clarke was harassed by threats, his car's tires were slashed, WANTED notices with his picture were posted in many garages. But threats, veiled or otherwise, never fazed this investigative reporter as long as he believed he was bringing the truth to the community he served. And he was being fair, since equal time was always offered to industry spokesmen for rebuttal.

The outgrowth of the series on auto repair overcharges and inefficiencies led to another series called *You and Auto Repair*. This mini-documentary employs techniques similar to those of its predecessor: opening with an introductory episode on a Friday

Pat Goss explains motor repair problems to reporter Jim Clarke for "You and Auto Repair."

evening newscast and then running for five installments the following week. However, it does not employ any recapitulation. That was necessary in the *Auto Repair Go-Round* in order to build up and bring to a climax the mounting repair costs. The episodes of *You and Auto Repair* each consist of a different aspect of the central theme. The visuals are necessarily restrictive since much time is devoted to comments by concerned officials. This is the script:

## INTRODUCTION—FRIDAY

**CLARKE:**
**STUDIO**

WE GOT LOTS OF VIEWER REACTION ABOUT THE AUTO REPAIR GO-ROUND. MOST. BUT NOT ALL OF IT. WAS COMPLIMENTARY. AN UNIDENTIFIED SERVICE STATION OPERATOR PHONED TO SAY. ``IF JIM CLARKE EVER DRIVES A CAR INTO MY PLACE. I'LL FIX HIS WAGON.``

**BLOWUP OF ENGINE OF BLUE GOOSE**

A GENTLEMAN FROM SPRINGFIELD COMMENDED US FOR WHAT HE TERMED AN ``EXCELLENT`` AND ``LONG OVERDUE`` REPORT. BUT HE WONDERED WHY WE HAD OMITTED DEALERS OR NEW CAR REPAIR SHOPS. THE REASON: OUR CAR WAS A 1970 MODEL. STUDIES SHOW THE GREAT MAJORITY OF MOTORISTS DON'T TAKE CARS LONG OUT OF WARRANTY BACK TO DEALERS FOR REPAIRS.

A MR. D.S. OF GAITHERSBURG WRITES: ``JIM CLARKE'S RESEARCH ON THE AUTOMOTIVE REPAIR INDUSTRY DOESN'T HAVE US FOOLED. THE BENDING OF THE REGULATOR TERMINAL WAS BLATANT TRICKERY!``

**ZERO IN VARIOUS PARTS OF ENGINE**

A MECHANIC FROM ROCKVILLE PHONED TO SAY: |QUOTE| PART OF THE REASON FOR SLOPPY REPAIRS AND UNNECESSARY PARTS IS THE SYSTEM USED TO COMPUTE MECHANIC'S PAY. WORKING ON A COMMISSION. THE FASTER YOU WORK THE MORE YOU MAKE. THE SAME GOES FOR PARTS SALESMEN. THE MORE YOU SELL. THE MORE YOU MAKE. END QUOTE.

T.G. RILEY. OF THE GOODYEAR TIRE AND RUBBER COMPANY. WRITES: ``CONGRATULATIONS ON YOUR AUTO SERVICE SURVEY. YOU HAVE DRAMATICALLY BROUGHT THE MECHANIC INTO THE SPOTLIGHT.`` MR. RILEY ADDS THAT GOODYEAR HAS 20 ``PHANTOM`` CARS THAT GO TO ITS STORES AROUND THE COUNTRY TO TEST THE REPAIRS AND SALES OF GOODYEAR EMPLOYEES. JUST THE WAY WE DID WITH THE BLUE GOOSE.

MR. R.H.. AN AUTO EQUIPMENT SALESMAN. PHONED TO SAY DRIVERS SHOULD BE COMPELLED TO LEARN SOMETHING ABOUT CARS BEFORE THEY ARE GIVEN A LICENSE. IF THEY DID. THEY'D TAKE BETTER CARE OF THE CAR. HAVE FEWER PROBLEMS AND LESS EXPENSIVE BILLS.

AND THERE WERE OTHER REACTIONS:

**TEDSON MEYERS:**
**(D.C. CITY COUN-**
**CILMAN)**
**SOUND ON FILM**

OBVIOUSLY. IT'S ONE OF RAGE TO DISCOVER THAT ALL OF THE THINGS YOU THOUGHT WERE TRUE—ARE. I THINK THE SERIES WAS. FIRST OF ALL. AN EXCEPTIONAL PUBLIC SERVICE. AND I THINK IT WILL BE OF IMMENSE HELP TO LEGISLATORS IN THE AREA AND THE CITIZENS IN UNDERSTAN-DING WHAT IT IS WE ARE AFTER. I THINK I'VE NOT SEEN ANYWHERE BEFORE SUCH A CAREFULLY DOCUMENTED PIECE OF WORK.

**HAL HART:**
**(DIRECTOR,**
**AUTOMOTIVE**
**INFORMATION COUN-**
**CIL)**
**SOUND ON FILM**

THE INDUSTRY AS A WHOLE. NOT JUST PARTS OF IT. WANTS THE CAR OWNER TO HAVE A CAR SERVICED PROPERLY. THERE IS SO MUCH BUSINESS TO BE DONE. WE DON'T HAVE ENOUGH SHOPS. WE DON'T HAVE ENOUGH EQUIPMENT IN THE FIELD REALLY TO DO A HUNDRED PERCENT JOB NOW THE WAY WE LIKE TO DO IT. WE NEED MORE PEOPLE. WE NEED THEM TO BE TRAINED BETTER. WE DON'T CONDONE— AND NOBODY IN THE INDUSTRY CON-DONES—REPAIRS BEING DONE THAT SHOULDN'T BE DONE OR REPAIRS THAT ARE NOT DONE PROPERLY.

**DON RANDALL:**
**(AUTOMOTIVE SERVICE**
**COUNCILS OF**
**AMERICA)**

**SOUND ON FILM**

AUTO REPAIRS ARE THE LEADING CONSUMER COMPLAINT THROUGHOUT THE NATION AND IT'S REGRETTABLE THAT WE HAVE THE KIND OF SYSTEM THAT GIVES US HANG-ON. HIT-AND-MISS REPAIRS. THERE ARE SOME ANSWERS AND POINTING THE FINGER OF BLAME AT THE MECHANIC ISN'T THE CORRECT ANSWER ALTOGETHER. IT STARTS WITH THE DRAWING BOARD IN DETROIT. WHERE THE CAR IS NOT DESIGNED TO BE DIAGNOSED OR REPAIRED.

**DONALD PARKER:**
**(FORD MOTOR CO)**
**SOUND ON FILM**

JIM. I WOULD LIKE FIRST TO COMMEND YOU ON YOUR SERIES WITH THE BLUE GOOSE. I THINK IT WAS VERY OBJECTIVE. THOROUGH. AND I THINK IT HIGHLIGHTED A LOT OF AREAS OF WHICH THE AUTOMOTIVE INDUSTRY HAS BEEN VERY MUCH AWARE— AREAS IN WHICH WE HAVE MANY PLANS TO IMPROVE.

CLARKE:
STUDIO

A LAWMAKER CONTEMPLATING LEGISLATION OF THE REPAIR INDUSTRY AND AN INDUSTRY SPOKESMAN SAY EDUCATION. NOT LEGISLATION. IS THE ANSWER—SUBJECTS WE'LL BE DEALING WITH NEXT WEEK IN "YOU AND AUTO REPAIR."

## EPISODE 1—MONDAY

CLARKE:
STUDIO

ONE OF THE FIRST THINGS WE DID AFTER FINISHING THE "AUTO REPAIR GO-ROUND" WAS TAKE PHONE CALLS FROM VIEWERS. SEVERAL CAME FROM MECHANICS. SERVICE-STATION OPERATORS. AND OTHERS IN THE AUTOMOTIVE INDUSTRY. RECALLING RECENT WOES LIKE THE FUEL SHORTAGE AND RISING PRICES. THEY SAID TO US. "PLEASE TELL THE OTHER SIDE OF THE STORY." WELL. WE WENT OUT AND TALKED TO A LOT OF PEOPLE IN THE IN- DUSTRY AND HERE ARE SOME SAMPLES OF WHAT WE GOT:

CLARKE:
INTERVIEWS
SOUND ON FILM

WHAT ABOUT THE WAY MECHANICS ARE PAID? DO YOU THINK THAT HAS SOMETHING TO DO WITH THE QUALITY OF THE WORK DONE ON CARS?

MECHANIC:
SOUND OF FILM

YES. BECAUSE THE FLAT-RATE MANUAL AL- LOWS A MAN A CERTAIN AMOUNT OF TIME TO DO IT AND IF HE DOESN'T DO IT IN THAT AMOUNT OF TIME. HE'S GOING TO LOSE MONEY. SO THE THING HE'S GOT TO DO IS BEAT THAT BOOK. GET THAT JOB DONE. AND GET ANOTHER JOB IF HE'S GOING TO MAKE ANY MONEY.

MECHANIC:
SOUND ON FILM

I THINK...THE WAY CARS ARE MADE TODAY. THERE NEEDS TO BE MORE SPECIALIZATION. LIKE IGNITIONS. TRANSMISSIONS. AND STUFF LIKE THAT. IF HE SPECIALIZES. HE KNOWS THE PART BET- TER AND CAN DO IT FASTER.

MECHANIC:
SOUND ON FILM

WHEN THE CUSTOMER BRINGS THE CAR IN TO HAVE IT REPAIRED. WE HAVE SERVICE WRITERS WRITE THE TICKETS. THE TICKET IS THEN SENT TO THE CONTROL TOWER. AND THEN TO A MECHANIC. WE HAVE A LACK OF COMMUNICATION BETWEEN THE CUSTOMER AND THE MECHANICS. SOMETIMES THE SERVICE WRITERS CAN'T INTERPRET WHAT THE CUSTOMER'S TRYING TO PUT ACROSS.

DON RANDALL:
(AUTOMOTIVE SERVICE
COUNCILS)

LET'S COMPARE THE MECHANICS EARNINGS OF ABOUT $4.75 PER HOUR WITH THE TECHNICIAN THAT COMES TO REPAIR YOUR

98

AIR CONDITIONER. I HAD ONE THE OTHER DAY. HE HANDED ME A PAD AND SAID, "SIGN HERE." I LOOKED AT IT, AND IT SAID $17.50 PER HALF-HOUR FROM PORTAL TO PORTAL TO WORK ON MY AIR-CONDITIONING UNIT. AND IT ISN'T NEARLY AS COMPLEX AS MY $3000 CAR.

**MECHANIC: SOUND ON FILM**

I THINK A LOT OF PEOPLE EXPECT US TO DO SO MUCH WORK TO THEIR CARS. AND THEY WANT IT DONE IN SUCH AN AMOUNT OF TIME THAT YOU JUST CAN'T GET TO IT. PEOPLE ALSO COMPLAIN ABOUT THE AMOUNT OF MONEY THEY'RE PAYING YOU FOR THE LABOR. THEY DON'T REALIZE THE MONEY YOU'RE SPENDING FOR THE EQUIPMENT TO DO THIS WORK ON CARS.

**MECHANIC: SOUND ON FILM**

A MECHANIC STAYS A YEAR OR SO BEHIND TO RELEARN EACH YEAR BECAUSE THERE ARE SO MANY CHANGES MADE IN ALL THE DIFFERENT MANUFACTURERS' CARS. THEY JUST KEEP CHANGING THEM, WITH THE RESULT THAT IT KEEPS NEW GUYS. WHO ARE TRYING TO GET THE ON-THE-JOB EXPERIENCE, FROM LEARNING WHAT THEY NEED TO KNOW ABOUT THE LATEST MODELS. A LOT OF GUYS GET DISCOURAGED AND GO INTO THINGS, LIKE BRICKLAYING, THAT DON'T CHANGE ALL THE TIME.

**MECHANIC: SOUND ON FILM**

LET ME SAY RIGHT NOW: JUST WAIT UNTIL ALL THE SMOG STUFF STARTS BREAKING DOWN. WAIT UNTIL THESE RESTRAINT SYSTEMS ON THE SEAT-BELT SYSTEMS START BREAKING DOWN AND THAT $143 RESTRAINT BOX HAS TO BE REPLACED. THEN YOU'RE GOING TO REALLY HEAR SOME SCREAMING.

**MECHANIC: SOUND ON FILM**

EVERYTHING IS ON A TIME BASIS. A CUSTOMER COMES IN. HE SAYS. "I WANT IT FIXED, I WANT IT FIXED RIGHT NOW, AND I'M NOT GOING TO TAKE NO FOR AN ANSWER." SO YOU HAVE A SITUATION WHERE THE MECHANIC IS RUSHED. YOU HAVE THE SERVICE WRITERS. SERVICE MANAGERS, AND MANAGEMENT IN GENERAL PUSHING HIM TO KEEP THE CUSTOMER HAPPY. AND IN THE PROCESS YOU MIGHT GET HIM HAPPY BECAUSE YOU MIGHT NOT REPAIR IT.

**HAL HART: (AUTOMOTIVE IN- FORMATION COUNCILS) SOUND ON FILM**

SOMETIMES I THINK WE OUGHT TO REALIZE THAT NOT ONLY DOES THE MECHANIC HAVE TO HAVE A LOT OF KNOWLEDGE. BUT EVERY DAY HE'S GETTING NEW TECHNICAL BULLETINS ON NEW CHANGES; ON

SOMETHING ELSE THAT'S BEEN PUT ON THE CAR: ON A REFINEMENT: ON AN IMPROVEMENT. HE HAS TO KNOW SOMETHING ABOUT ALMOST 400 DIFFERENT ENGINE MODELS. THOUSANDS OF DIFFERENT MODELS OF AUTOMOBILES. HE HAS TO KNOW SOMETHING ABOUT THE PEOPLE WHO OWN THEM. HE HAS TO KNOW SOMETHING ABOUT HOW MANY MILES THE CARS HAVE BEEN DRIVEN: WHAT'S BEEN DONE TO THEM BEFORE. OR WHAT HASN'T BEEN DONE THAT SHOULD HAVE BEEN DONE. AND HE NEVER HAS A HAPPY CUSTOMER COME IN. NOBODY IS HAPPY WHEN LOSING HIS TRANSPORTATION: WHEN IT'S GOING TO COST MONEY: WHEN IT'S TAKING THEM TIME. SO. OUR POOR MECHANIC NEVER SEES A HAPPY PERSON UNTIL HE GOES HOME AT NIGHT.

**CLARKE:**
**STUDIO**

SPEND AN HOUR WITH A DOZEN MECHANICS AND IT ISN'T HARD TO COME AWAY SYMPATHIZING WITH THEM. YOU HAVE THE FEELING THAT WHATEVER THE PROBLEMS OF THE AUTO REPAIR INDUSTRY—THE MECHANIC IS CAUGHT SOMEWHERE IN THE MIDDLE. MORE. TOMORROW. ON "YOU AND AUTO REPAIR."

**CLOSE**

THIS IS JIM CLARKE.

# EPISODE 2—TUESDAY

**CLARKE:**
**V/O FILM**

IF YOU GOT THROUGH THE SUMMER WITHOUT RUNNING OUT OF GAS IN A HIGH-CRIME DISTRICT. THEN YOU MAY THINK YOUR MOTORING WORRIES ARE OVER.

**SHOTS FROM HIGHWAY OVERPASS SHOWING CAR SPEEDING ALONG MULTILANES**

BEFORE GETTING TOO COMFORTABLE WITH THAT IDEA. ASK YOURSELF HOW MUCH YOU KNOW ABOUT YOUR CAR AND HOW WELL YOU TAKE CARE OF IT. AND. REMEMBER. WINTER IS HERE.

CHANCES ARE YOU DON'T KNOW MUCH ABOUT YOUR CAR AND YOU PUT IT THROUGH A MINIMUM OF MAINTENANCE. CHANCES ARE YOU LIKE IT THAT WAY AND DON'T INTEND TO CHANGE. WITH THAT IN MIND. WE'VE GOT SOME TIPS ON THINGS YOU SHOULD KNOW AND DO:

**GOSS:**
**SOUND ON FILM**

WELL. THE FIRST THING AND PROBABLY THE MOST IMPORTANT THING IS THE ENGINE AND ITS RELATED SYSTEMS. TO BEGIN WITH. ONE OF THE KEY THINGS—IF YOU REALLY WANT TO KEEP THE CAR GOING FOR A LONG PERIOD OF TIME—IS PREVENTIVE MAINTENANCE. NUMBER ONE.

100

CHANGING THE OIL. IT MUST BE CHANGED REGULARLY. IT SHOULD BE CHANGED EVERY 90 DAYS IN THE SUMMER OR EVERY 2000 MILES OR EVERY 60 DAYS IN THE WINTER.

**CLARKE:**
**V/O FILM**
**OUTSIDE OF GOSS'**
**SHOP**

THAT IS A MUCH MORE FREQUENT CHANGE OF OIL THAN NEW CAR MANUFACTURERS CALL FOR. PAT ALSO RECOMMENDS CHANGING THE OIL FILTER WITH EACH OIL CHANGE OR AT LEAST WITH EVERY OTHER OIL CHANGE. HE SAYS IT WILL MEAN LESS ENGINE WEAR AND FEWER ENGINE PROBLEMS.

**CLARKE:**
**SOUND ON FILM**
**CAR STRIPPED DOWN**

IF YOU'VE GOT AN ENGINE THAT IS VIBRATING WHEN IT RUNS, IT'S RUNNING VERY ROUGH. WHAT WOULD THAT LEAD YOU TO SUSPECT?

**GOSS:**

IN MOST CASES EITHER A BAD SPARK PLUG, AN IMPROPERLY ADJUSTED CARBURETOR, OR SOMETHING LIKE THAT. USUALLY IT'S RELATIVELY MINOR, ESPECIALLY IF IT COMES ON ALL OF A SUDDEN.

**CLARKE:**

WELL, WHAT IF YOU HAVE A COUGHING AND A CHOKING ENGINE?

**GOSS:**

HERE YOU WOULD NORMALLY BE CONCERNED WITH IGNITION TIMING OR THE ADJUSTMENT OF THE IGNITION POINTS.

**CLARKE:**

HOW ABOUT THE CHOKE?

**GOSS:**

THE CHOKE WILL USUALLY ONLY BE RELATED TO PROBLEMS THAT OCCUR WHEN THE CAR IS COLD—WHEN YOU FIRST START IT. IF IT COUGHS AND DIES TWO OR THREE TIMES BEFORE YOU CAN ACTUALLY GET IT TO MOVE OR SOMETHING LIKE THAT. THEN USUALLY YOU'RE CONCERNED WITH THE CHOKE. IF THESE PROBLEMS OCCUR AFTER THE CAR HAS WARMED UP, USUALLY IT IS NOT THE CHOKE.

**CLARKE:**

WHAT ARE SOME OF THE OTHER THINGS THAT SHOULD BE CHECKED REGULARLY?

**GOSS:**

WELL, THE IGNITION SYSTEM. THE PLUGS AND THE POINTS SHOULD BE CHECKED EVERY 5 TO 10 THOUSAND MILES BECAUSE THESE ARE THE THINGS THAT ARE VITAL AS FAR AS PERFORMANCE IS CONCERNED. AND THE BATTERY SHOULD BE CHECKED EVERY TIME YOU FILL THE CAR WITH GAS...AND THE BATTERY CABLES AND CONNECTION, TO MAKE SURE THEY'RE SECURE. THESE ARE THE MOST IMPORTANT THINGS.

| | |
|---|---|
| **CLARKE:**<br>**V/O FILM** | A LITTLE CHECKLIST FOR THOSE OF US WHO DON'T KNOW MUCH ABOUT OUR CARS AND PROBABLY DON'T INTEND TO LEARN MUCH. WE WONDERED, WHILE TALKING WITH PAT GOSS, WHY THE MAJOR AUTOMOTIVE |
| **GLOVE COMPARTMENT**<br>**ANIMATION OF**<br>**MANUAL** | MANUFACTURERS HAVEN'T PUT SUCH TROUBLESHOOTING IDEAS IN BOOKLETS IN GLOVE COMPARTMENTS OF NEW CARS. WE LOOKED IN THE GLOVE COMPARTMENT OF THE BLUE GOOSE, THE TEST CAR USED IN OUR SERIES TWO WEEKS AGO. THERE WE FOUND ONE. IT CONTAINED A FULL 41 PAGES ON MAINTENANCE—COMPLETE WITH DRAWINGS, DIAGRAMS, CHARTS, TABLES, AND MAINTENANCE RECORDS. WHY DON'T YOU LOOK. MAYBE YOU'VE GOT ONE, TOO. |
| **CLOSE** | THIS IS JIM CLARKE ON THE SCENE. |

## EPISODE 3—WEDNESDAY

| | |
|---|---|
| **CLARKE:**<br>**SOUND ON FILM**<br>**SUPER**<br>**A S S E M B L Y   L I N E**<br>**FOOTAGE** | THE AUTOMOTIVE INDUSTRY IS FACING A CONSUMER REVOLT. IT IS FIRED BY PROBLEMS BOTH DETROIT AND CONSUMERS HAVE CREATED. DETROIT'S SOPHISTICATED AND LUXURIOUS MACHINES HAVE COLLIDED WITH POLLUTION CONTROL DEVICES—ON THE EDGE OF A MONUMENTAL FUEL SHORTAGE. SMOG CONTROLS MAKE |
| **SUPER**<br>**TRAFFIC ON HIGHWAYS** | THE MAGNIFICENT MACHINES ROUGH RUN-NING, PRONE TO BREAKDOWNS, AND MORE EXPENSIVE TO OPERATE. THE HIGHWAYS ARE CONGESTED WITH A HUNDRED MILLION CARS. AND DRIVING ISN'T THE FUN IT USED TO BE. |
| **V/O  H O U S E W I V E S**<br>**TAKING**<br>**L E S S O N S   A T   G O S S'**<br>**SERVICE**<br>**STATION** | ALL THIS SETTLES AND EXPLODES, FINALLY, WHEN THE CAR HAS TO GO IN FOR REPAIRS. THEY ARE EXPENSIVE, AND GOING UP. AND OFTEN, THE WORK IS LOUSY. SO, CONSUMERS, FED UP WITH IT ALL, ARE GRADUALLY SEEKING OUT ALTERNATIVES. INCREASINGLY, WHITE-COLLAR WORKERS AND HOUSEWIVES ARE SHOWING UP AT SERVICE STATIONS, COMMUNITY COLLEGES, AND ANYWHERE ELSE THEY CAN GET A LAYMAN'S COURSE IN AUTO MECHANICS. |
| | AT HIS RIVERDALE GULF STATION, PAT GOSS SAYS HE HAS TAUGHT TWO THOUSAND OF THEM IN THE PAST FOUR YEARS. AND 40 PERCENT OF THEM HAVE BEEN WOMEN WHO ARE NOW CHANGING THEIR OWN OIL AND FILTERS AND DOING MINOR ENGINE TUNEUPS. FOR THEM IT MEANS A SHARP REDUCTION IN THE COST OF OPERATING THEIR CARS AND A FEELING OF EQUALITY WHEN THEY ROLL THE FAMILY CHARIOT IN-TO A GARAGE. |

| | |
|---|---|
| **CLARKE:**<br>**SOUND OF FILM**<br>**V/O DART DRUG** | AS PRICES HAVE CLIMBED. ONE OF THE FASTEST GROWING PARTS OF THE AUTOMOTIVE SERVICE INDUSTRY HAS BEEN AIMED AT THIS DO-IT-YOURSELF CAR FIXER. NOWHERE IS IT MORE EVIDENT AND IRONIC THAN IN THE LARGE AND WELL STOCKED AUTOMOTIVE SECTIONS OF DRUG STORES LIKE THIS ONE AT DART DRUG'S CHANTILLY STORE. |
| **JOSEPH GWIZDZ:**<br>**(VICE PRESIDENT**<br>**DART DRUG)**<br>**SOUND ON FILM** | WE HAVE GONE IN THE LAST 10 YEARS FROM SEVERAL ITEMS CONSISTING CHIEFLY OF WAXES, POLISHES, AND CHAMOIS TO A DEPARTMENT THAT WE FEEL IS A COMPLETE, TOTAL DEPARTMENT. THIS DEPARTMENT CARRIES ANYTHING FROM THE SIMPLE ITEMS OF MOTOR OIL, ALL THE WAY TO TESTING KITS, FILTERS, SHOCK ABSORBERS, CAR BATTERIES, BRAKE SHOES, ET CETERA. WE CAN SAVE THE CUSTOMER MONEY TWO WAYS. WE DISCOUNT THE NATIONAL BRANDS ON A DAILY BASIS. IN ADDITION TO THIS, WE OFFER OUR OWN PRIVATE BRANDS. THESE ARE ALL QUALITY PRODUCTS—SEVERAL OF THEM ARE ACTUALLY MADE BY THE NATIONAL MANUFACTURER. |
| **DON RANDALL:**<br>**(AUTO SERVICE COUN-**<br>**CILS)**<br>**SOUND ON FILM** | UNFORTUNATELY, THE SYSTEM WE HAVE IN THIS COUNTRY IS ONE DESIGNED FOR MERCHANDISING PARTS. WE SELL ABOUT 14 BILLION DOLLARS WORTH OF AUTOMOTIVE PARTS ANNUALLY. WE HAVE ABOUT 14 BILLION MORE IN SERVICE AND LABOR COSTS. WE DON'T KNOW WHAT THE PROFIT RATIO IS, BUT WE KNOW IT'S PRETTY HIGH ON THE PARTS. WE DO KNOW THE AVERAGE YEARLY EARNING OF A MECHANIC IN THE U.S. IS ABOUT $7000. |
| **MECHANIC:**<br>**SOUND ON FILM** | I BELIEVE AN INDIVIDUAL WHO OWNS A CAR SHOULD TAKE SOME TYPE OF AUTOMOTIVE COURSE WHICH, AS I SAY, FAIRFAX COUNTY OFFERS. AND IT'S A GOOD ONE. IT WOULD BE WORTH THE TIME EFFORT AND MONEY EVEN IF IT GAVE ONLY A BASIC KNOWLEDGE OF HIS CAR, SO HE CAN TALK INTELLIGENTLY TO A SERVICE WRITER OR ANYONE IN THE AUTO INDUSTRY AS FAR AS REPAIRS TO HIS CAR ARE CONCERNED. |
| **CLARKE:**<br>**STUDIO** | SO, LURED BY SAVINGS UP TO A HUNDRED PERCENT, A LOT OF AMERICANS ARE GOING BACK TO SCHOOL TO BEAT THE HIGH COST OF AUTO REPAIR AND MAINTENANCE. |
| **CLOSE** | THIS IS JIM CLARKE. |

# EPISODE 4—THURSDAY

CLARKE:
V/O FILM

CONSUMER COMPLAINTS ABOUT AUTO REPAIRS TOP THE LIST OF GRIPES FILED WITH CONSUMER PROTECTION AGENCIES AROUND THE COUNTRY. COMPLAINTS RANGE FROM ALLEGATIONS OF FRAUD TO PLAIN SLOPPY WORK. THEY ARE THE MAJOR REASON LAWMAKERS ARE PREPARING TO IMPOSE STIFF REGULATIONS ON THE INDUSTRY.

TEDSON MEYERS:
(D.C. CITY COUN-
CILMAN)
SOUND ON FILM

WE ARE STRESSING NOT JUST THE LICENSING OF SHOPS. BUT THE COMPETENCY OF A CLASS OF PEOPLE THAT WE'VE CREATED. WE CALL THEM THE SUPERVISORY MECHANIC OR THE SUPERVISORY INSPECTOR. THEY'D BE PRESENT IN ALL THE LICENSED IN-DUSTRIES OR CATEGORIES. BE THEY AUTOMOTIVE. ELECTRONIC. OR HOME AP-PLIANCES.

DONALD PARKER:
(DISTRICT MGR., FORD
MOTOR CO.)
SOUND ON FILM

WELL. GENERALLY. I DON'T FEEL THIS IS THE TOTAL ANSWER—IN LICENSING MECHANICS. THE BIGGEST PROBLEM IS TO IMPROVE THE COMPETENCE OF THE MECHANIC. WE'RE DOING SEVERAL THINGS IN ORDER TO IMPROVE THE COMPETENCE OF AUTOMOBILE MECHANICS. THIS IS ONE OF 34 SCHOOLS IN THE NATION.

LOWELL DODGE:
(CENTER FOR STUDY
OF AUTO SAFETY)
SOUND ON FILM

THE SITUATION AS WE SEE IT IS THAT ALMOST ANY PERSON CAN PUT ON A PAIR OF OVERALLS AND CALL HIMSELF A MECHANIC. THIS LEADS TO THE PROBLEM OF GROSS IN-COMPETENCE AND. IN SOME CASES. DISHONESTY IN THE PROFESSION. WE THINK ALL MECHANICS SHOULD. THEREFORE. BE LICENSED.

HERBERT FUHRMAN:
(NATIONAL INSTITUTE
AUTOMOTIVE SERVICE
EXCELLENCE)
SOUND ON FILM

LICENSING WILL NOT IN ANY WAY IMPROVE THE LEVEL OF COMPETENCE OF AUTO MECHANICS. THERE ARE GRANDFATHER CLAUSES WITH LICENSING: ANYBODY WHO SAYS HE'S A MECHANIC AT THE TIME THE LAW GOES INTO EFFECT IS AUTOMATICALLY LICENSED.

HAL HART:
(AUTO INFORMATION
COUNCILS)
SOUND ON FILM

WE THINK THE CERTIFICATION OF MECHANICS VOLUNTARILY GIVES HIM AN OPPORTUNITY TO TAKE A POSITIVE STEP FORWARD. WE HAVE TWO CERTIFICATION PROGRAMS NOW IN THE INDUSTRY WHERE YOU CAN TAKE TESTS. THEY'RE TOUGH. IF YOU PASS THEM YOU GET AN ARM PATCH TO SHOW YOU REALLY KNOW WHAT YOU'RE DOING IN THAT AREA.

| | |
|---|---|
| **TEDSON MEYERS:**<br>**SOUND ON FILM** | OUR ANSWER IS THE POSITION TITLE I CREATED CALLED THE SUPERVISORY MECHANIC. HE WOULD BE THE MAN WHO MUST BE COMPETENT TO PASS A HANDS-ON TEST IN THE FIELD. HE MUST BE EMPLOYED IN A SHOP. WITH HIM THE BUCK STOPS. HE MUST CERTIFY THAT THE WORK IS DONE RIGHT AND THAT IT IS DONE HONESTLY. |
| **DON RANDALL:**<br>**SOUND ON FILM** | WE DON'T HAVE A MASSIVE SYSTEM OF TRAINING PROGRAMS IN THIS COUNTRY FOR THE MECHANICS WE HAVE. MOST OF THE MECHANICS WE HAVE ARE SELF-TAUGHT. WE DON'T REALLY HAVE A GOOD TRAINING PROGRAM. |
| **HAL HART:**<br>**SOUND ON FILM** | THIS IS A TYPICAL PLACE. IT'S A GENERAL MOTORS TRAINING CENTER. THERE ARE 30 OF THEM ACROSS THE COUNTRY. THE CAR FACTORIES HAVE THEM. THE PARTS MANUFACTURERS HAVE THEM. THERE ARE SOME 3400 VOCATIONAL SCHOOLS ACROSS THE COUNTRY SPECIALIZING IN AUTO MECHANICS. AMONG OTHER THINGS. WE HAVE TO SEE AN ATTITUDE CHANGE IN THE PEOPLE OF THE COUNTRY—THAT THERE'S NOTHING WRONG WITH WORKING WITH YOUR HANDS. NOT EVERYONE SHOULD BE AN ENGLISH PROFESSOR. |
| **CLARKE:**<br>**V/O FILM**<br>**GENERAL MOTORS**<br>**TRAINING**<br>**FACILITY** | THE NUMBER OF VEHICLES PER MECHANIC HAS RISEN FROM 75 IN 1950 TO 150 NOW. ALL THE WHILE. CARS HAVE BECOME MORE COMPLEX. HARDER TO REPAIR. AND MORE PRONE TO BREAK DOWN. THERE IS A TREMENDOUS GAP BETWEEN THE SUPPLY OF AND THE NEED FOR MECHANICS. LAWS REQUIRING THE LICENSING OF MECHANICS CERTAINLY WON'T CHANGE THAT. SOMETHING ELSE IS NEEDED. MORE ON THAT TOMORROW NIGHT ON "YOU AND AUTO REPAIR." |
| **CLOSE** | THIS IS JIM CLARKE. |

## EPISODE 5—FRIDAY

| | |
|---|---|
| **CLARKE:**<br>**STUDIO** | CONSUMERS COMPLAIN ABOUT IN-COMPETENT AND OVERPRICED REPAIRS. INDUSTRY COMPLAINS OF A CRITICAL SHORTAGE OF TRAINED MECHANICS. BOTH COMPLAINTS ARE JUSTIFIED. THE PRESSURE IS ON TO IMPOSE LICENSING ON REPAIR SHOPS AND MECHANICS. BUT LICENSING WILL NOT PROVIDE THE TENS OF THOUSANDS OF SKILLED MECHANICS WE NEED. INDUSTRY OFFERS EXCELLENT |

PROGRAMS FOR TRAINING. TESTING. AND CERTIFYING MECHANICS. THEY ARE UNDERUTILIZED.

FEW INCENTIVES NOW EXIST FOR MECHANICS TO IMPROVE THEIR STATUS AND SKILLS. BUT TONIGHT. THE NATIONAL INSTITUTE FOR AUTOMOTIVE SERVICE EXCELLENCE IS ANNOUNCING A STEP IN THIS REPORT THAT SHOULD PROVIDE SOME INCENTIVE FOR BOTH MECHANICS AND SHOP OWNERS.

**HERBERT FUHRMAN:**
**SOUND ON FILM**

WE WILL PUBLISH IN EARLY SPRING OF 1974 A NATIONAL DIRECTORY OF REPAIR ESTABLISHMENTS THAT EMPLOY CERTIFIED MECHANICS. THESE DIREC-TORIES WILL BE UPDATED EVERY 6 MONTHS. AFTER EACH TEST SERIES. AND WILL BE AVAILABLE FOR PURCHASE BY CAR OWNERS. THIS DIRECTORY WILL BE AN INSTANT REFERENCE FOR THE CAR OWNER. SHOWING WHERE HE CAN TAKE HIS CAR FOR REPAIR BY A CERTIFIED MECHANIC.

**CLARKE:**
**STUDIO**

THIS NATIONAL DIRECTORY COULD SWING THE LION'S SHARE OF AUTO REPAIR WORK TO A SMALL PERCENTAGE OF REPAIR SHOPS. THAT COULD HAPPEN UNLESS THERE IS AN INDUSTRY-WIDE MOVE TO HAVE MECHANICS TRAINED AND CERTIFIED. BUT IT REMAINS A PROBLEM OF DEMAND FOR MECHANICS FAR OUTSTRIP-PING THE SUPPLY. PART OF THE PROBLEM IS A SOCIETY THAT DISCOURAGES ITS YOUNG FROM ENTERING THE TRADES WHERE MANY OF THEM MIGHT BE HAPPY.

**DON RANDALL:**
**SOUND ON FILM**

WE NEED A NATIONAL PROGRAM AT THE FEDERAL LEVEL WITH FEDERAL FUNDS AD-MINISTERED THROUGH STATE PROGRAMS SO WE CAN TRAIN OUR TECHNICIANS. NOT ONLY AUTO TECHNICIANS. BUT SERVICE TECHNICIANS GENERALLY. OUR PROGRAMS HAVE BEEN TOO LONG ORIENTED TOWARD WHITE-COLLAR PROGRAMS FOR TRAINING STUDENTS TO BECOME EXCUTIVES. WE NEED TECHNICIANS AND THEY NEED TO BE TRAINED: OTHERWISE. OUR MACHINES. OUR MOBILITY. AND OUR ECONOMY IS GOING TO GRIND TO A SCREECHING HALT. I'M AFRAID.

**CLARKE:**
**V/O VARIOUS SHOTS OF**
**MECHANICS ON JOB**

BEYOND BOLD MOVES TO TRAIN MORE MECHANICS. THERE ARE THINGS INDUSTRY CAN DO. DESIGNING A MORE EQUITABLE PAY SCALE FOR MECHANICS MIGHT BE A GOOD START. THEY COULD ELIMINATE THE PRESENT SYSTEM OF ALLOWING SOME

| | |
|---|---|
| | MECHANICS TO CHARGE FOR 16 HOURS OF WORK IN A SINGLE 8-HOUR DAY. A PAY SYSTEM THAT ENCOURAGES RAPID WORK. COMMISSIONS ON LABOR. AND THE SALE OF PARTS IS OBVIOUSLY CAUSING MUCH UNNECESSARY AUTOMOTIVE WORK AND EXORBITANT REPAIR BILLS. THE AUTO INDUSTRY CAN AND SHOULD CHANGE THIS. MECHANICS SHOULD BE PAID ACCORDING TO THEIR ABILITY AND FOR THE HOURS THEY ACTUALLY WORK. |
| **FILM OF SENATOR HART** | A LAW. AUTHORED BY MICHIGAN SENATOR PHILIP HART. SHOULD BE QUICKLY IMPLEMENTED. IT WOULD SET UP PILOT INDEPENDENT DIAGNOSTIC CENTERS. THESE PLACES WOULDN'T SELL PARTS OR MAKE REPAIRS—JUST FIND THE CAR'S PROBLEM. YOU WOULD THEN SHOP AROUND TO HAVE IT FIXED. |
| **MOVING SHOTS ASSEMBLY LINE** | THE AUTOMOTIVE INDUSTRY IS A HUNDRED-BILLION-DOLLAR-A-YEAR BUSINESS. IT CAN ELIMINATE A LOT OF THE REPAIR INDUSTRY'S PROBLEMS BY PROVIDING LEADERSHIP AND HELPING CUSTOMERS GET A FAIR SHAKE. IT CAN ALSO START DESIGNING CARS EASIER TO REPAIR AND LESS PRONE TO BREAK DOWN. MEANWHILE. LEGISLATION SEEMS TO BE THE ONLY ANSWER AND IT WON'T BE A COMPLETE ANSWER. |
| **CLOSE** | THIS IS JIM CLARKE. |

## TIME SPAN

In studying the mini-documentary series, *Americans in Exile*, *Auto Repair Go-Round*, and *You and Auto Repair*, you will observe that the episodes are of almost uniform length, approximately 3 minutes. But in our discussion with Jim Clarke he emphasized that length would depend on the interest value. If he felt very strongly that a sequence deserved more time, he would insist on it. In the series *Alcoholism: D.C. Area*, he firmly believed that the first episode required 10 minutes, and that was how it reached the screen. This first installment is reproduced in its entirety. The scenes are shocking, but the script maintains a matter-of-fact tone and lets the visuals speak for themselves. Only in the final dialog between Clarke and the rehabilitation-center director and in the closing statement does the reporter permit his own emotions to surface.

# ALCOHOLISM: DC AREA

CLARKE:
V/O BLACK-AND-WHITE
FILM—
AN ALCOHOLIC
STUMBLES DOWN
A BACK ALLEY. HE
SPOTS A
GARBAGE CAN AND
BEGINS
RUMMAGING THROUGH
IT.
HE FINDS A BOTTLE,
HOLDS IT
UP TO SEE IF THERE'S
ANYTHING
IN IT.
THERE ISN'T. HE SLAMS
THE BOTTLE AGAINST
THE WALL.

FREEZE/FRAME:
SUPER
THE ALCOHOLIC

ALCOHOLIC PATIENT
WITH DELIRIUM
TREMENS BEING AT-
TENDED
BY A DOCTOR AND A
NURSE

PHYSICIAN TREATING
ALCOHOLIC

REHABILITATION
CENTER

BACK IN 1966, THE U.S. APPEALS COURT HERE HEARD THE CASE OF 61-YEAR-OLD DEWITT EASTER. EASTER, A CHRONIC ALCOHOLIC, HAD BEEN ARRESTED 77 TIMES FOR PUBLIC INTOXICATION. HIS ATTORNEYS ARGUED HE HAD AN ILLNESS CALLED ALCOHOLISM—AN ADDICTION TO ALCOHOL THAT CAUSED HIM TO LOSE CONTROL OF HIS DRINKING AND SUBSEQUENT BEHAVIOR.

IN AN HISTORIC DECISION, THE COURT RULED UNANIMOUSLY IN EASTER'S FAVOR, DECLARING ALCOHOLISM AN ILLNESS AND NOT A CRIME. THE RULING PROHIBITED THE JAILING OF ALCOHOLICS FOR BEING DRUNK.

BEFORE THAT DECISION, HALF OF ALL THE CITY'S NONTRAFFIC ARRESTS WERE FOR PUBLIC INTOXICATION. MANY OTHERS WERE ALCOHOL-RELATED CRIMES OF VIOLENCE; PERHAPS HALF THE TRAFFIC ACCIDENTS INVOLVED 44 THOUSAND PERSONS A YEAR FOR PUBLIC DRUNKEN-NESS. IN ONE YEAR, 16 DRUNKS DIED WHILE IN POLICE CUSTODY.

THE EASTER DECISION WAS TO CHANGE ALL THAT IN A SINGLE STROKE. TWO YEARS LATER, CONGRESS PASSED A LAW ORDERING THE CITY TO ESTABLISH A COM-PREHENSIVE PROGRAM FOR THE TREATMENT AND REHABILITATION OF ALCOHOLICS AND THE PREVENTION OF ALCOHOLISM.

IT DIRECTED THAT CHRONIC ALCOHOLICS BE GIVEN MEDICAL, PSYCHIATRIC, INSTITUTIONAL, AND REHABILITATIVE TREATMENT SERVICES OF THE HIGHEST CALIBER. THE CITY'S RESPONSE TO THAT LAW WAS SOON TO BE HAILED AS A MODEL FOR THE NATION.

CALLED THE REHABILITATION CENTER FOR ALCOHOLICS, IT IS LOCATED IN A BUCOLIC SETTING AT OCCOQUAN, VIRGINIA—25 MILES AWAY FROM THE ALCOHOLICS IT WAS DESIGNED TO SERVE.

| | |
|---|---|
| **PRISON** | THE FACILITY IS SURROUNDED BY THE CITY'S LORTON PRISON COMPLEX. THE FIRST THING AN ALCOHOLIC SEES WHEN HE ARRIVES HERE IS A MAXIMUM-SECURITY PRISON. |
| **PRISON FENCE, GUARD TOWERS** | A HUNDRED YARDS AWAY AN 18-FOOT BARBED-WIRE FENCE SURROUNDS IT, AND IT IS FLANKED BY THE TRADITIONAL PRISON GUARD TOWERS. THE ALCOHOLIC WILL SEE IT EVERY DAY SO LONG AS HE STAYS AT R-C-A. THE CENTER ITSELF IS LOCATED IN WHAT USED TO BE THE OLD PRISON WORKHOUSE. THAT'S WHERE THEY USED TO SEND ALCOHOLICS—FOR 32 DAYS AT A TIME—BEFORE THE EASTER DECISION. |
| **PATIENTS ALONG RCA MALL** | FOR OLD-TIMERS—THE REPEATERS AT R-C-A—TALK TO THEM ABOUT THE EASTER DECISION AND THEY'LL LAUGH IN YOUR FACE. FOR THEM LITTLE HAS CHANGED. THE STIGMA OF CRIMINALITY STILL HANGS OVER THE ALCOHOLIC. THREE TIMES A DAY IT IS REINFORCED WHEN ALCOHOLIC PATIENTS ARE REQUIRED TO SERVE MEALS TO PRISON INMATES. |
| **ALCOHOLICS GOING THROUGH FOOD LINE** | ALCOHOLICS EAT IN THE SAME DARK AND CAVERNOUS DINING HALL USED BY PRISON INMATES, BUT NOT AT THE SAME TIME. THIS COMINGLING IS A CLEAR VIOLATION OF TREATMENT AND ETHICS THAT TROUBLES THE CENTER'S DIRECTOR, DR. JAMES VANDERPOOL: |
| **DR. JAMES VANDERPOOL: SOUND ON FILM** | OUR PATIENTS ARE REQUIRED TO SERVE INMATES. I CONSIDER THIS MOST SERIOUS BECAUSE THE INTENT OF THE LAW WAS THAT PATIENTS SHOULD NOT BE MIXED WITH INMATES. FREQUENTLY, OUR PATIENTS ARE THREATENED. FORTUNATELY, NOTHING HAS HAPPENED. |
| **CLARKE:** | PATIENTS ARE REQUIRED TO WORK AT R-C-A AS COOKS, SERVERS, MAINTENANCE MEN, HOUSEKEEPERS, GROUNDS KEEPERS, AND MESSAGE RUNNERS. THE CENTER IS SO SHORT OF STAFF IT COULDN'T OPERATE WITHOUT USING PATIENTS AS LABORERS. IT IS CHEAP LABOR: THE PATIENTS GET PAID ONLY 35 CENTS AN HOUR. |
| **DR. JAMES VANDERPOOL: SOUND ON FILM** | THERE IS ONE SIDE OF THIS DOMICILIARY THAT IS VERY IMPORTANT. WITHOUT THIS DOMICILIARY, WE COULD NOT OPERATE R-C-A. WE HAVE A SYSTEM HERE WHEREBY WE SAVE AT LEAST A MILLION DOLLARS A YEAR. |

| | |
|---|---|
| **CLARKE:**<br>**V/O PATIENT**<br>**DORMITORY** | HOMELESS DOMICILIARY PATIENTS HOLD 235 BEDS AT R-C-A: BEDS THAT CANNOT BE USED FOR ALCOHOLICS REQUIRING INTENSIVE CARE AND TREATMENT. BUT THE CENTER IS SO SHORT OF STAFF AND FACILITIES THAT 235 NEW PATIENTS WOULD PUT IT ON THE BRINK OF COLLAPSE. IN THE WINTER MONTHS. THEY OPERATE ON THE EDGE OF CRISIS—LITERALLY PRAYING FOR ABOVE-NORMAL TEMPERATURES. IN COLD WEATHER. ALCOHOLICS FLOCK THERE IN DROVES. |
| | PRAYING COMES EASY TO DR. VANDERPOOL. WHO IS AN ORDAINED CATHOLIC PRIEST ON WORK LEAVE FROM HIS DIOCESE IN ROCKFORD. ILLINOIS. THE LAW THAT CREATED R-C-A ANTICIPATED 800 PATIENT BEDS. LAST WEEK IT HAD ONLY 620 FOR MALE PATIENTS ANOTHER 50 FOR FEMALES. DR. VANDERPOOL RECALLED THAT ONCE BEFORE. DURING A COLD WAVE. SOME PATIENTS WHO HAD BEEN THERE FOR A WHILE WERE DISCHARGED EARLY TO MAKE WAY FOR OTHERS IN MORE CRITICAL NEED. |
| **DR. VANDERPOOL:**<br>**SOUND ON FILM** | TRAGICALLY ENOUGH. WE DIS-CHARGED 31 MEN IN JANUARY OF 1970. 30 WERE BACK WITHIN TWO WEEKS AND ONE DIED FROZEN TO DEATH ON THE STREETS. WE DON'T WANT THIS TO HAPPEN AGAIN. |
| **CLARKE:**<br>**INTERIOR OF**<br>**DETOXIFICATION**<br>**CENTER** | THE CENTER'S DETOXIFICATION UNIT IS SO OVERCROWDED THAT PATIENTS HAVE ONLY 60 SQUARE FEET FOR THEIR BED AND LOCKERS. THEY SHOULD HAVE 80 SQUARE FEET. BUT THERE SHOULD NOT EVEN BE A DETOXIFICATION UNIT AT THE CENTER. PATIENTS ARE SUPPOSED TO BE SOBERED UP BEFORE THEY ARRIVE AT OCCOQUAN. THEY CAN'T BE BECAUSE THE UPTOWN DETOX CENTER HAS ONLY 75 BEDS WHERE THERE SHOULD BE 250. |
| | COMPOUNDING ITS DILEMMA. R-C-A IS CRITICALLY UNDERSTAFFED. ANY GOOD MEDICAL FACILITY SHOULD HAVE A STAFF-TO-PATIENT RATIO OF 1 TO 1. R-C-A HAS A RATIO OF 1 TO 3.2. IT MEANS MOST PATIENTS RECEIVE ONLY CUSTODIAL CARE. THE CENTER HAS NO SECURITY PERSONNEL OR FACILITIES. AND R-C-A CANNOT FORCE ANY PATIENT TO STAY THERE. YET 10 PERCENT OF THE PATIENT POPULATION IS COMMIT-TED BY THE COURTS: SOME OF THEM ARE VERY DANGEROUS. SOME ARE ACCUSED OF MURDER. |

| | |
|---|---|
| **DR. VANDERPOOL:**<br>**SOUND ON FILM** | PATIENTS HAVE BEEN HURT AND SO HAVE SEVERAL OF OUR STAFF MEMBERS. I FEEL THEY OUGHT TO GET SPECIAL SECURITY PAY FOR DANGEROUS AND HAZARDOUS DUTY. SEVERAL OF OUR COUNSELORS' AND SOME OF OUR NURSES HAVE BEEN HURT VERY BADLY. |
| **CLARKE:**<br>**V/O CELL BLOCK,**<br>**INDIVIDUAL CELLS—**<br>**PATIENTS IN TWO**<br>**CELLS** | THOUGH THE CENTER IS NOT SUPPOSED TO HAVE A SECURITY FACILITY, PHOTOGRAPHER BERNIE GMITER AND I FOUND ONE—AND IT WAS IN USE. |
| | THIS CELL BLOCK CONTAINED TWO PATIENTS NOT YET DETOXIFIED OR CONSIDERED HARMFUL TO THEMSELVES OR OTHERS. WHEN I LOOKED AT THEM AND THE CELLS, I REMEMBERED THAT THE EASTER DECISION HAD DECLARED ALCOHOLICS WOULD NOT BE JAILED FOR DRUNKENNESS. CONFRONTED WITH OUR DISCOVERY, VANDERPOOL ADMITTED THE CELLS ARE USED REGULARLY FOR PATIENTS WHO PRESENT PROBLEMS FOR THE STAFF AND OTHER PATIENTS. |
| **INTERIOR OF**<br>**RENOVATED**<br>**BUILDING** | PRESSED FOR FACILITIES TO HOUSE PATIENTS SHOULD A COLD WAVE HIT, VANDERPOOL HAS OPENED AN OLD PRISON OFFICE BUILDING. BEDS HAVE BEEN JAMMED INTO SMALL ROOMS IN THIS BUILDING THAT WILL HOUSE 50 MEN—WITH ONLY THREE TOILETS. AND THERE ARE NO SHOWERS. AT THE REAR OF THE BUILDING, I SAW THE CLOTHING SUPPLY STORE. HERE, CLOTHES FOR PATIENTS—CLOTHES SCROUNGED FROM UNDERTAKERS AND CHURCHES—ARE REPAIRED AND ISSUED TO THE PATIENTS. HERE, AS EVERYWHERE ELSE, THE HEAT FROM THE ANTIQUATED STEAM-HEAT SYSTEM WAS OPPRESSIVE. |
| **MONTAGE OF**<br>**PATIENTS, DOCTOR**<br>**EXAMINING PATIENT,**<br>**EXTERIOR AND**<br>**INTERIOR**<br>**SCENES, RCA** | MANY OF THE PATIENTS AT THE CENTER ARE OLD. SEVERAL HAVE SERIOUS PHYSICAL AILMENTS. BUT THERE IS NO MEDICAL DOCTOR AT THE CENTER AT NIGHT. ONE PATIENT COMPLAINED TO ME THAT IT WOULDN'T MAKE MUCH DIFFERENCE "BECAUSE THE ONES THEY HAVE DON'T UNDERSTAND ENGLISH—THEY'RE CUBAN." BUT THERE ARE NOT DOCTORS ON DUTY AT NIGHT AT A HOSPITAL FACILITY WITH NEARLY 700 ALCOHOLIC PATIENTS. |
| | ON PAPER, R-C-A'S 90-DAY PROGRAM OF INTENSIVE CARE AND TREATMENT IS A MODEL. IN REALITY, IT IS SOMETHING ELSE INDEED. PATIENTS ARE DISCHARGED FROM |

THE CENTER FOR ADMINISTRATIVE. RATHER THAN MEDICAL REASONS. IN OTHER WORDS. BECAUSE OF OVERCROWDING. THE AFTER-CARE FACILITIES TO EASE ALCOHOLICS INTO THE COMMUNITY ARE VIRTUALLY NONEXISTENT. PATIENT RECORDS DON'T LIST ANY REASON FOR THEIR DISCHARGE: A SERIOUS ADMINISTRATIVE OVERSIGHT. IF NOT A COVER-UP FOR WHAT HAS ACTUALLY BEEN HAPPENING HERE.

**CLARKE:**
**SOUND ON FILM**

DR. VANDERPOOL. YOUR PATIENTS ARE COMINGLING WITH PRISON INMATES: SOME ACTUALLY SERVING PRISON INMATES IN THE SAME CAFETERIA WHERE ALCOHOLIC PATIENTS EAT THEIR MEALS. YOU'RE USING PATIENTS AS CHEAP LABOR. YOU HAVE THEM JAMMED TOGETHER IN TIGHT QUARTERS. YOU'RE UNDERSTAFFED. THAT SOUNDS LIKE THE 19TH CENTURY TO ME.

**DR. VANDERPOOL:**
**SOUND ON FILM**

THE FACTS SPEAK FOR THEMSELVES. JIM. I'M NOT GOING TO COMMENT ON THAT. I WOULD LIKE TO SAY THAT WE HAVE A DEDICATED STAFF AT THIS INSTALLATION. OUR DEPARTMENT. HUMAN RESOURCES. IS DOING ALL IT CAN WITHIN THE LIMITED BUDGET THAT CAN BE PROVIDED. FINALLY. I FEEL LIKE ONE PATIENT SAID TO ME THIS MORNING: THIS ISN'T MUCH. BECAUSE HE'S HAVING TO LIVE IN A DORMITORY WHERE THERE ISN'T EVEN A SHOWER: BUT IT'S BETTER THAN BEING OUT IN THE STREET.

**CLARKE:**
**STUDIO**
**CLOSE**

MAYBE SO. BUT THE REHABILITATION CENTER FOR ALCOHOLICS FALLS LAMENTABLY SHORT OF BEING THE MODEL FACILITY IT IS SUPPOSED TO BE. IN THE HEART OF OUR METROPOLITAN AREA WITH ITS 200.000 ALCOHOLICS. IT IS ALSO OPERATING IN FLAGRANT VIOLATION OF THE LAW THAT CREATED IT. THE LAW THAT CALLED FOR TREATMENT OF THE HIGHEST CALIBER FOR ALCOHOLICS. CONGRESS CREATED R-C-A AND CONGRESS HAS STARVED IT BY FAILING TO FUND ITS GROWTH AND DEVELOPMENT. IT MAY TAKE ANOTHER EASTER DECISION TO SET THINGS RIGHT.

## EDITING THE MINI-DOCUMENTARY

One very basic difference in editing the mini-documentary, explains Sam Brooks, film editor at WMAL-TV, is that you shoot so much more footage per sequence than you do for straight news film. The policy at the station is to shoot minimal news film so that it can be edited as quickly as possible. It is just the opposite with a mini-documentary. The reporter has all the time he needs to get the material he wants. The deadlines are much more flexible. And the film editor is not pressured.

Another difference is that the mini-documentary has a theme, a point to be made; with news film it is simply a matter of recording a current event. The mini-documentary series also has to provide complete episodes, yet each episode must relate to the other—which can present a problem. The burden lies with the reporter/writer rather than the film editor.

In the WMAL-TV mini-documentary series on *digestive diseases*, an individual patient suffering from stomach cancer was chosen as the focal point. The film report involved on-the-scene sequences in the operating room, and the final episode showed the patient in the recovery room. Each segment was complete in itself, and yet each was dependent on the other to demonstrate the progress of the operation. The theme of the mini-documentary was that digestive disorders can be treated early. It explored the questions of why people don't go for treatment and why they wait until massive surgery is required.

The reporter, as we have noted, makes the final decision in regard to the content of the mini-documentary, but the film editor has a great deal to say about the visuals. For a straight news story, though, the reporter is much more of a decision-maker. He was on the scene and he usually knows precisely what he wants in the way of sound and picture. During the production of a mini-documentary, there are times when the reporter will not accompany the crew; this occurs if only background or location shooting is required.

Often, because of the subject, visuals are static and the mini-documentary could prove boring. The reporter can heighten interest by writing a good script. The film editor can help move the story by skillful pacing. If drama is not present, often it must be injected into the story to maintain interest.

On occasion there is an embarrassment of riches as, for example, in the series on amnesty. There was an abundance of good footage, but only a fraction could be used. The most expressive moments were excerpted. However, expressive should not be equated with sensational. As Brooks described it, "We chose a very quiet scene, for instance, where someone had something very profound to say."

The film editor constantly tries to enhance the visual. It is not always possible. Sometimes a participant is both photogenic and articulate, but often he or she may be dull. Then it may be advisable to cut away from the participant, show scenes of his or her occupation and use the reporter's commentary off screen.

Sam Brooks is a graduate of the University of North Carolina with majors in TV/*film* and *psychology*. He worked as a TV engineer and then came to WMAL-TV as a trainee, eventually specializing in film editing. To him, news film editing is a very exciting and rewarding experience, but it is very strenuous. It entails working at an extremely rapid pace. He recommends that the embryo film editor learn all the facets of television production before he specializes. He believes there will always be a need for film despite the advances of videotape. "There are a lot of things you can do with film which you can't do with videotape," he says. "As far as I'm concerned, I can edit more quickly and effectively with film. Also, I can do more with effects through the different exposures of film which I cannot get from videotape. Also, the lab manages smoother dissolves with film. Videotape may replace news film, but I don't think it will replace documentary film."

The mini-documentary is an interest-builder. It encourages the viewer's desire to watch the following night. Most of the news staff at WMAL-TV believe that the mini-documentary is more effective for a local station than the full-length documentary.

# Chapter 5
# The Mini-Documentary Approach of NBC Owned WRC-TV

During the research stage of this book, Tom Houghton was news director for WRC-TV in Washington. Houghton is a high-minded young man idealistic about the presentation of mini-documentaries as a public service rather than as a rating builder. It is no secret that broadcast stations put their best programs forward during rating periods. Since all of them do, it can hardly be labeled unfair competition. All of us tend to wear our Sunday best when we're out to make an impression.

Houghton states that he was working on mini-documentaries in Minneapolis a decade ago. The local station had been producing news specials at great expense but reaching a small audience. The mini-documentary series presented the topics in a more compelling manner, i.e., they intrigued the viewer to watch future episodes. When Houghton came to Washington, he started a probe unit which he believes was the first investigative crew of its kind. The probe unit does not operate on any formula or regular basis. It concentrates on substantive, investigative themes. For example, it was the probe unit that broke the story on cyclamates. That was followed by an expose of conditions at an institution for the mentally retarded; and *Uncle Sam is a Slumlord* dealt with federally owned property which was unfit for human habitation. Transcripts of both these series are reproduced in this chapter. The slum series was rebroadcast on NBC network news and won a national Emmy. Obviously, WRC-TV does not limit its mini-documentary themes to local issues. Houghton would like to see important mini-documentaries turned into prime-time specials.

The ultimate decision regarding themes for the mini-documentaries rests with the news director. The staff suggests ideas and then the news director decides whether any of them are worth a series or a single shot. It is not a question of whether a proposal will generate a high rating but whether it is a strong issue of paramount interest to the community.

At WRC-TV, an editorial supervisor is involved in all investigative reports. One or two researchers are assigned to the production. There is the usual film crew consisting of cameraman, sound and lighting technician, and, naturally, the film editor. On occasion a field producer accompanies the film crew. But some reporters who have the ability prefer to act as their own field producers. WRC-TV has four film crews, with one of those crews out almost continually on assignment to a mini-documentary series. In regard to time required to produce a series, Houghton's guidance has been, "Do it as well as possible, as soon as possible, with the least possible expense." And he adds as a footnote, "Then I close the door and pray!"

Like his colleagues at the other network affiliates, Houghton sets no arbitrary time limits for the production of a mini-documentary series. The time can range from a week to 6 months but the longer series have cost $50−60 thousand.

Most of the mini-documentaries produced by WRC-TV are confined to the metropolitan area; the series on mental retardation, which is a national topic, centered about the operations of a local institution. The series on cyclamates was an exception; it was not a local story, nor could it very feasibly be forced into that category.

A good reporter, according to Houghton, has to have the ability and the facility to cut through the double-talk, the ambiguous verbiage of officialdom, the passing of the buck. One pungent President of the United States had the forthrightness to say, "The buck stops here." But many lesser officials are too prone to pass the onus on to some other official. That was what Clare Crawford, a free-lance reporter for WRC-TV, discovered when she was researching the series on the institution for the mentally retarded. The institution's admistrator blamed lack of funds and staff for the inadequacies of the institution. The state legislature claimed it had received no request for additional funds. The governor said the legislature had not sent him an appropriation bill to sign.

The production crew shot film which showed the abject despair of the inmates. It was not the intention of the station to ask why the situation is permitted to exist, but rather: What is the institution going to do about it? Officials were offered equal time to make their case. Somehow they had expected that the mini-documentary would show them in a good light, doing a satisfactory job. That would have negated the credibility of the probe unit. The institution's officials insisted on previewing the program. The news director did not want to acquiesce but he did permit them to view portions of the film.

A difficult problem arose when the officials promised releases for the visuals of the inmates but then 24 hours before air time refused to grant them. Since many of the inmates were mentally retarded juveniles, Houghton believed the station would be faced with a legal problem. The station's lawyers tried to convince the officials to grant the releases but to no avail. Finally, the attorneys told the news director to go ahead with the program as scheduled. The news director's philosophy is that if you are performing a public service and convinced of its rightness then you should be willing to chance a lawsuit.

As it turned out, there was no suit. The governor launched an investigation. The administrator of the institution resigned. The ancient, inadequate buildings were torn down and the children were transferred to new buildings. The Department of Justice began a suit on the basis that the children's civil rights were being violated...a prime example of how a mini-documentary series can influence the community.

With *Uncle Sam is a Slumlord*, WRC-TV tackled another basic problem: inadequate shelter for humans. Inadequate must surely be the understatement of the century. The slum apartment chosen as the subject for the mini-documentary was on Washington's 14th Street. It was under control of a governmental agency. The neighborhood eventually was to become the city's urban renewal master plan. It had once been an all-white neighborhood; now it was all black. The building was filthy and overrun with rats and roaches. And, as happens so many times in dealing with bureaucracies, each agency involved claimed the other had jurisdiction. It took a great deal of persuasion on the reporter's part to get public officials to appear on the series. But they did, and the upshot was that the apartment building was abandoned and the residents relocated.

In this instance and several others, WRC-TV returned from time to time to the slum area for a progress report. It was not permitting sleeping dogs to lie. It is this sort of substantive reporting that Houghton believes should be the function of the mini-documentary.

There is no arbitrary limit to the length of a series or the time of each segment. Interest value, as always, is the criterion. Episodes have run from 3 to 10 minutes. The news director points out that since WRC-TV presents its newscasts in half-hour intervals, 3 minutes is 10% of the program; and when you subtract the time for commercials, the percentage is even greater. On the assumption that not everybody watches every night, episodes of the mini-documentary generally open with a brief recapitulation. The series is also repeated on later newscasts.

The station has never faced a problem with a sponsor due to debatable material. Its policy has been not to schedule a commercial within 10 minutes of a controversial statement which might involve that sponsor. Also, it is against NBC policy—and WRC-TV is an owned and operated station of the network—for anyone from management or sales to influence the news department.

There is no question in Houghton's mind about the value of the mini-documentary. It is here to stay. He has a word of advice for anyone who wants to become an investigative reporter. It is not as glamorous a profession as it sounds. It often requires working round the clock, plodding research—with many arid, dull days. Nevertheless, all the investigative reporters I have spoken to are very enthusiastic about their work.

What the news director avoids is advocacy reporting. The credibility of the reporter is maintained if he is not an advocate of a cause but a purveyor of information. That information may lead authorities or the general public to take steps to attack the problem. And that, in essence, is what a mini-documentary series can do.

## UNCLE SAM IS A SLUMLORD

Clare Crawford, free-lance investigative reporter for WRC-TV, almost seems to come by her vocation naturally. Her father was a White House correspondent. She teaches investigative reporting at the George Washington University in the nation's capital. To get at the truth of a situation, she has sometimes placed herself in jeopardy as she did when she infiltrated the White Citizens Council or posed as an unwed mother. But perhaps her most trying experience occurred when she worked on the mini-documentary series *Uncle Sam is a Slumlord*. She spent a night in the slum apartment, a sleepless night, fighting off voracious rats that considered her a gourmet repast and fidgety roaches that attempted to burrow into her ears. It was a living nightmare, and when the news director asked her to return for another night, she literally went down on her knees in protest.

The transcripts reproduced below are the second part of the series; they include the episode describing Ms. Crawford's stay in the slum apartment. The reports were broadcast both on the 6 p.m. and 11 p.m. newscasts. They ran on a 3-day basis—Monday through Wednesday—for two weeks. You will note that each episode has a brief introduction by the newscaster.

# EPISODE 1—MONDAY

**GLENN RINKER:**
**STUDIO**
**SUPER**
**SHOTS OF SLUM AREAS**

EARLIER THIS YEAR. THE NEWS 4 WASHINGTON PROBE UNIT PRESENTED A SERIES ENTITLED "UNCLE SAM IS A SLUMLORD." DURING THE NEXT TWO WEEKS. WE WILL CONTINUE THAT SERIES WITH AN INTERESTING LOOK AT AN APPALLING SITUATION IN ONE BUILDING. THE VICTORIA APARTMENTS AT 14TH AND CLIFTON IN THE DISTRICT.

THIS WEEK REPORTER CLARE CRAWFORD EXAMINES THE SITUATION AT THE VICTORIA AND THE PEOPLE WHO LIVE THERE. HERE IS HER FIRST PROBE REPORT.

**CLARE CRAWFORD:**
**V/O PAN OF SLUM DWELLINGS**

IN 1968. THE CITY AND COUNTRY WERE SHOCKED BY RIOTING. JUST BLOCKS FROM THE WHITE HOUSE. FOURTEENTH STREET CAME TO SYMBOLIZE THESE CONDITIONS AND GOVERNMENT OFFICIALS MADE IT A MODEL TO SOLVE INNER CITY PROBLEMS. YET FIVE YEARS AND TWENTY-EIGHT MILLION DOLLARS LATER. THE AREA LOOKS MORE RAVISHED. NOT ONLY HAS THE COSTLY PROJECT FAILED. URBAN RENEWAL ITSELF HAS MADE THE AREA WORSE THAN

**CHILDREN AND ADULTS LIVING IN SHACKS**

EVER. WITH A MANDATE TO HELP 14TH STREET. THE REDEVELOPMENT LAND AGENCY HAS TORN DOWN. BOARDED UP. AND EMPTIED HUNDREDS MORE BUILDINGS THAN WERE EVEN SLIGHTLY DAMAGED IN THE RIOT. FAMILIES HAVE BEEN FORCED FROM POOR HOUSING INTO EVEN MORE CROWDED. UNSAFE. AND BROKEN DOWN APARTMENTS.

**SHOTS OF SLUM DWELLINGS SHOWING IMPOVERISHED CONDITIONS**

THERE IS AN IRONY HERE. JUST BY PLANNERS DESIGNATING AN URBAN-RENEWAL AREA AND SAYING IT'S GOING TO BE A WONDERFUL PLACE SOMEDAY. EVERYDAY MAINTENANCE STOPS AND THINGS GET WORSE. BUILDING. HEALTH. AND FIRE

**SHOTS OF ABANDONED CARS**

CODES AREN'T ENFORCED. ABANDONED CARS ARE NOT MOVED. TRASH PILES UP AND THE AREA IS OVERRUN WITH RATS AND BUGS. AND CHILDREN ARE AFFLICTED WITH LEAD POISONING.

**CHILDREN PLAYING**

THIS SMALL BARE PATCH IS THE ONLY PLACE TO PLAY FOR THE 60 OR SO KIDS WHO LIVE IN THE VICTORIA APARTMENTS AT 2526 14TH STREET. THE LANDLORD HERE IS THE

**CRAWFORD ON SCREEN AT VICTORIA APTS.**

REDEVELOPMENT LAND AGENCY. R-L-A; AND THE LAW REQUIRES THAT R-L-A MAKE CERTAIN THE PEOPLE WHO LIVE IN ITS BUILDINGS AND THE PEOPLE WHO HAVE

MOVED OUT OF BUILDINGS IT TEARS DOWN ARE DECENTLY HOUSED. BUT OBVIOUSLY R-L-A DOESN'T MAINTAIN A DECENT HOUSE. AND SO HUNDREDS OF FAMILIES IN THIS NEIGHBORHOOD ARE FORCED TO EXIST IN UNSAFE FILTHY DUMPS OWNED AND OPERATED BY THE UNITED STATES GOVERNMENT.

**DISSOLVE TO ROBINSON APT. MEDIUM CLOSEUP MRS. ROBINSON**

A TYPICAL FAMILY IS THIS ONE IN THE VICTORIA. HEADED BY BERTHA ROBINSON. MRS. ROBINSON IS A PRACTICAL NURSE AND DIVORCED. SHE LIVES HERE WITH SIX CHILDREN. A GRANDDAUGHTER. AND RATS AND ROACHES AND TRASH. TWO OF HER CHILDREN HAVE LEAD POISONING. THE SECOND YOUNGEST. EDNA. WAS BORN A WEEK AFTER THE RIOTS AND THIS IS THE ONLY LIFE SHE KNOWS. HER BROTHERS AND SISTERS HAVE LIVED THIS WAY FOR FIVE YEARS. TOO.

**FULL SHOT: DEBORAH AND BABY**

MRS. ROBINSON IS PROUD OF HER UNMARRIED DAUGHTER. DEBORAH. AND HER BABY. IT WOULD HAVE BEEN MUCH EASIER. MRS. ROBINSON SAYS. FOR HER 17-YEAR-OLD TO HAVE BECOME A PROSTITUTE. A DRUG ADDICT. OR AN ALCOHOLIC IN THIS NEIGHBORHOOD.

**PAN OF KITCHEN**

AT NIGHT. EVEN WHEN THE FAMILY GOES TO BED HUNGRY. MRS. ROBINSON LEAVES FOOD IN THE KITCHEN FOR THE RATS SO THEY WON'T MOVE INTO THE BEDROOM AND BITE HER SLEEPING CHILDREN.

CLARE CRAWFORD. NEWS 4 WASHINGTON.

**JIM VANCE: STUDIO**

TONIGHT AT 11:00 THE PROBE UNIT EXAMINES THE QUALITY OF LIFE AND THE LACK OF SERVICES AT THE VICTORIA. NEXT WEEK REPORTER CRAWFORD AND A NEWS 4 CAMERA CREW WILL MOVE INTO THE VICTORIA IN AN ATTEMPT TO LIVE THERE FOR AS LONG AS THEY CAN STAND IT.

## EPISODE 2—MONDAY

**GLENN RINKER: STUDIO**

A NEWS 4 PROBE REPORT OUTLINING HOW UNCLE SAM IS A SLUMLORD WHEN NEWS 4 CONTINUES.

**JIM VANCE: STUDIO SUPER SLUM AREAS**

THE VICTORIA APARTMENTS AT 14TH AND CLIFTON STREETS. NORTHWEST IS A TYPICAL EXAMPLE OF THE ROTTEN CONDITIONS UNDER WHICH THE FEDERAL GOVERNMENT FORCES MANY INNER-CITY RESIDENTS TO LIVE. THE VICTORIA IS IN AN URBAN-RENEWAL AREA WHERE UNCLE SAM IS THE SLUMLORD.

REPORTER CLARE CRAWFORD AND THE NEWS 4 PROBE UNIT HAVE EXPOSED AND WILL CONTINUE TO COVER THIS GOVERNMENTAL NEGLECT. HERE'S THE STORY.

**CLARE CRAWFORD:**
**V/O VICTORIA**
**EXTERIORS**

THE REDEVELOPMENT LAND AGENCY HAS SPENT MORE THAN 28 MILLION DOLLARS IN THIS SMALL 14TH-STREET NEIGHBORHOOD IN THE PAST FIVE YEARS. BUT LIFE FOR MOST OF THE PEOPLE HERE IS WORSE THAN IT WAS FIVE YEARS AGO, WHEN R-L-A STARTED BUYING LAND AND TEARING DOWN BUILDINGS.

**SHOTS OF SLUM ALLEY**

R-L-A IS A GOVERNMENT AGENCY. AND FOR PEOPLE LIKE JUANITA JOHNSON, WHO HAVEN'T BEEN ABLE TO FIND ANOTHER PLACE TO LIVE, R-L-A IS AS BAD AS THE WORST SLUMLORD.

**PAN OF APARTMENTS**

SOMEDAY, MAYBE IN 5, MAYBE IN 15 YEARS, URBAN RENEWAL WILL MEAN A BETTER LIFE FOR THE PEOPLE WHO LIVE HERE. BUT IN THE MEANTIME, UNCLE SAM'S TENANTS ARE GROWING UP AND GROWING OLD AMONG PILES OF TRASH, RATS, AND HOUSES THAT ARE FALLING DOWN.

**SCENE OF CHILDREN**
**CARRYING FOOD BAGS**

SO JUANITA JOHNSON TRIES TO EKE OUT SOME SEMBLANCE OF A LIVING FOR HER 7 CHILDREN AND GRANDCHILD IN A TWO-BEDROOM APARTMENT. SHE LIVES ON THE SIXTH FLOOR. AND THE ELEVATOR HAS BEEN BROKEN FOR A COUPLE OF YEARS. CARRYING FOOD IN AND OUT IS A MAJOR JOB. AND SHE LIVES IN FEAR THAT ONE OF HER SMALL CHILDREN WILL FALL SIX FLOORS FROM AN UNSCREENED WINDOW. WHEN SHE WAS A YOUNG GIRL, MRS. JOHNSON WANTED TO BE AN INTERIOR DECORATOR. SHE DOESN'T LIKE THE APARTMENT THE GOVERNMENT RENTS HER.

**JUANITA JOHNSON:**
**MCU***
**THEN PAN APARTMENT**
**SHOWING PEELING**
**PLASTER**
**AND HOLES IN WALLS**

THEY'RE SUPPOSED TO BE STRIPPING THE WALLS FOR LEAD BECAUSE LEAD POISON WAS FOUND IN THE WALLS. SO THEY CAME OUT AND IT TOOK 'EM ABOUT A WEEK TO DO ALL THIS, YOU KNOW, SCRAPING. I THOUGHT THEY WOULD PUT SOMETHING OVER IT, YOU KNOW, SO IT WOULDN'T LOOK SO BAD. BUT THEY JUST LEFT IT LIKE THAT. AND THEN THEY TRIED TO START FIXING THESE HOLES HERE. BUT THEY PUT PLASTER WHICH FALLS OUT THE MINUTE YOU BUMP AGAINST IT. THE LEAST LITTLE BUMP MAKES IT FALL RIGHT BACK OUT. SO I DON'T

*MCU—medium closeup

121

KNOW WHAT GOOD THAT DID. AND NOW THE PLASTER AND STUFF UP THERE PEELS. AND AFTER IT PEELS SO MUCH IT FALLS OUT ON THE FLOOR ALL OVER EVERYTHING.

**SHOT OF SCREENLESS WINDOW**

WELL, YOU SEE, THIS WINDOW HAS NO SCREEN. THAT'S WHAT WE HAVE TO BE CONCERNED WITH. IN THE DAYTIME IF YOU WANT TO LIE DOWN AND TAKE A NAP, IT'S IMPOSSIBLE BECAUSE THE FLIES ARE ALL OVER YOU. THEY'RE IN YOUR FACE; THEY'RE ON YOUR LEGS; THEY'RE EVERYWHERE. SO YOU JUST GET UP AND KEEP MOVING AROUND BECAUSE YOU CAN'T REST.

**FULL SHOT BABY IN CRIB**

AND THIS IS WHERE MY GRANDSON SLEEPS. ALL THIS IS COMING DOWN. IT LEAKS. IT POURS THERE WHEN IT RAINS. IT POURS TERRIBLY WHEN IT RAINS. IT RUNS ALL DOWN THE WALL, ALL DOWN HERE. THE WALL IS SOAKED AND IT RAINS UNDER

**SHOTS OF CHILDREN IN BEDS AND CRACKS IN WALLS BEHIND BEDS**

THERE. AND IT RAINS IN THE KIDS' ROOM. IN THEIR CLOSET, ON THEIR CLOTHES. AS LONG AS I STAY, I DON'T FEEL LIKE I HAVE A FUTURE REALLY. IT'S JUST LIVING FROM DAY TO DAY.

**CRAWFORD: ON SCREEN**

WHAT ABOUT YOUR CHILDREN?

**JOHNSON: CLOSEUP**

I FEEL THE SAME FOR THEM. LIKE, YOU KNOW, IF WE COULD GET AWAY OR EVEN GET A BETTER PLACE, I FEEL LIKE THEY WOULD PROBABLY DO BETTER IN A LOT OF THINGS: IN THEIR SCHOOL WORK, THEIR BEHAVIOR, EVERYTHING. IT WILL BE ENTIRELY DIFFERENT.

**VANCE: STUDIO**

TOMORROW NIGHT AT 11 THE PROBE UNIT REPORTS ON HOW THE DISTRICT BUILDING AND FIRE CODES ARE NOT ENFORCED AT THE VICTORIA. AND NEXT WEEK REPORTER CRAWFORD AND A NEWS 4 CAMERA CREW WILL MOVE INTO THE VICTORIA IN AN ATTEMPT TO LIVE THERE.

## EPISODE 3—TUESDAY

**RINKER: STUDIO SUPER SLUM AREAS**

LIVING IN A GOVERNMENT-OWNED HOUSE ON 14TH STREET IN NORTHWEST WASHINGTON IS NOT ONLY FILTHY, INCONVENIENT, AND UNHEALTHY: IT'S OFFICIALLY UNSAFE. REPORTER CLARE CRAWFORD AND A NEWS 4 PROBE TEAM HAVE MORE ON THE STORY ABOUT A TYPICAL BUILDING WHERE UNCLE SAM IS THE SLUMLORD.

| | |
|---|---|
| **CRAWFORD:**<br>**V/O EXTERIOR OF VIC-**<br>**TORIA APTS** | THE VICTORIA APARTMENTS MAY HAVE BEEN ALMOST ELEGANT WHEN THEY OPENED IN 1908. BUT NOWADAYS EVERYONE USES THE TRADESMEN'S ENTRANCE HERE AT THE SIDE OF THE BUILDING. THE FRONT DOOR HAS BEEN CLOSED IN VIOLATION OF FIRE REGULATIONS. R-L-A PAYS A JANITOR $427 A MONTH TO KEEP THE PLACE CLEAN. HE SAYS HE TRIES. BUT IT'S IMPOSSIBLE. |
| **JANITOR:**<br>**MCU IN FRONT OF**<br>**BUILDING AT TRASH**<br>**CAN** | WELL. FIRST. PEOPLE NEED TO BE INDOC-TRINATED IN THE DO'S AND DON'TS. A LOT OF PEOPLE HERE HAVE NEVER HAD ANYTHING. FOR MANY. THE POSSESSIONS THEY NOW HAVE ARE MORE THAN THEY'VE EVER HAD BEFORE. THE TROUBLE IS THAT THEY HAVEN'T LEARNED THAT THERE IS SOMETHING BETTER OR THAT THEY HAVE TO TAKE CARE OF THE THINGS THEY HAVE. |
| **CRAWFORD:**<br>**OFF SCREEN** | IS IT THE R-L-A'S FAULT OR THE PEOPLE'S FAULT? |
| **JANITOR:**<br>**CLOSEUP** | IT'S BOTH. I SAY BOTH BECAUSE IF R-L-A WOULD BE MORE ALERT IN DEALING WITH THE PROBLEMS AND THE PEOPLE WOULD TAKE MORE PRIDE IN WHAT R-L-A FINALLY GETS AROUND TO DOING. IT'D BE A MUCH EASIER THING FOR ALL. AND CONDITIONS WOULD BE MUCH BETTER. |
| **CRAWFORD:**<br>**V/O SHOTS OF INSPEC-**<br>**TORS**<br>**GOING THROUGH**<br>**BUILDING** | R-L-A OFFICIALS SAY WHEN THEY BOUGHT THE VICTORIA IN 1970. THERE WERE 500 BUILDING CODE VIOLATIONS. AND THEY SAY THEY CORRECTED THEM. BUT BUILDING INSPECTORS. AT NEWS 4'S REQUEST. RECENTLY VISITED A THIRD OF THE APARTMENTS AND FOUND OVER 300 VIOLATIONS IN JUST THOSE. |
| **PAN OF INTERIOR**<br>**OF BUILDINGS** | THE HEAD OF R-L-A. MELVIN MISTER. SAYS HE DOESN'T THINK R-L-A SHOULD SPEND MONEY ON A BUILDING THAT'S GOING TO BE TORN DOWN. BUT THERE'S NO DATE SET TO TEAR DOWN THE VICTORIA. |
| | TENANTS SAY SINCE R-L-A TOOK OVER. THE BUILDING IS DIRTIER AND UNLOCKED. THERE ARE NO HALL LIGHTS. THE ELEVATOR DOES NOT WORK. AND THERE IS NO HOT WATER MOST OF THE TIME. ON THE THREE OR FOUR DAYS A WEEK THE WATER'S HOT. SO ARE THE RADIATORS. EVEN DURING THE SUMMER. AND DURING THE WINTER THERE IS NEITHER HEAT NOR HOT WATER HALF THE TIME. BUT MORE IM-PORTANT THAN THE INCONVENIENCE. DISCOMFORT. AND FILTH. THE BUIDLING IS ACTUALLY NOT SAFE TO LIVE IN. AND R-L-A |

| | DOESN'T SEEM TO BE DOING ANYTHING ABOUT IT. |
|---|---|
| | THESE FIRE INSPECTORS VISITED HERE AT NEWS 4'S REQUEST OVER A MONTH AGO. |
| **FIRE INSPECTOR:** <br> **MCU** | THERE WERE 85 FIRE CODE VIOLATIONS. HOWEVER, THERE WERE APPARENT HOUSING OR ELECTRICAL CODE VIOLATIONS THAT WOULD REQUIRE A REFERRAL BY OUR OFFICE. |
| **CRAWFORD:** <br> **OFF SCREEN** | HOW UNSAFE IS IT FOR THE 80 PEOPLE WHO LIVE HERE AT THE VICTORIA? |
| **INSPECTOR:** <br> **MCU** | I WOULD SAY IT'S VERY UNSAFE BECAUSE OF THE BLOCKING OF THE EXITS OUT OF THE BUILDING. THE FIRE ESCAPES BEING BLOCKED. IF SOMETHING SHOULD HAPPEN. ON SOME OF THE FLOORS IT'S ALMOST IMPOSSIBLE TO GET OUT IF THERE WAS A SERIOUS FIRE OF ANY TYPE. SO IT IS IN A PRETTY BAD CONDITION. |
| **VANCE:** <br> **STUDIO** | TOMORROW AT 11 THE PROBE UNIT SURVEYS THE RATS AND THE ROACHES WHO ALSO LIVE AT THE VICTORIA. AS WELL AS THE UNLAWFUL SANITATION PROBLEMS. AND NEXT WEEK REPORTER CRAWFORD AND A NEWS 4 CAMERA CREW WILL MOVE INTO THE VICTORIA IN AN ATTEMPT TO LIVE THERE. |

## EPISODE 4—WEDNESDAY

| | |
|---|---|
| **VANCE:** <br> **STUDIO** <br> **SUPER SLUM AREAS** | THERE'S A LOT MORE TO LIVING IN THE VICTORIA APARTMENTS ON 14TH STREET NORTHWEST THAN JUST BROKEN ELEVATORS AND CLOSED-OFF FIRE EXITS. THE BUILDING IS NOT ONLY UNSAFE. IT IS ALSO OVERRUN WITH RATS AND ROACHES AND FILTH. REPORTER CLARE CRAWFORD AND THE NEWS 4 PROBE TEAM CONTINUE THEIR STORY ON THE LIVES OF UNCLE SAM'S TENANTS IN WASHINGTON. |
| **CRAWFORD:** <br> **V/O INTERIOR OF APARTMENT** <br> **SHOT OF RAT COMING THROUGH WALL** | THIS IS A WOMAN WHO FEEDS THE RATS THAT BITE THE CHILDREN WHO LIVE IN THE HOUSE THE GOVERNMENT OWNS. <br><br> AND THIS IS THE RAT. HE IS ONLY ONE OF MANY. HE COMES OUT AT NIGHT IN BERTHA ROBINSON'S KITCHEN. SHE LEAVES FOOD FOR HIM SO HE WON'T GO INTO THE TWO |
| **PAN OF CHILDREN IN APARTMENT** | BEDROOMS AND BITE THE 7 CHILDREN. THESE PICTURES WERE TAKEN IN THE DARK WITH A SPECIAL LENS. |
| **CHILDREN STUFFING SHEETS** | UPSTAIRS JUANITA JOHNSON'S CHILDREN SHOWED NEWS 4 HOW THEY STUFF THEIR EARS WITH SHEETS BEFORE THEY GO TO |

|  | SLEEP SO COCKROACHES WON'T CRAWL INTO THEIR EARS. |
|---|---|
| **JOHNSON: TWO SHOT** | IF YOU WAKE UP AND IT COMES OUT. YOU STICK IT BACK IN. |
| **CHILD:** | OKAY. |
| **CRAWFORD:**<br>**V/O CLOSE SHOT OF**<br>**BATHROOM SHOWING**<br>**POOR CONDITION** | MANY OF THE RESIDENTS ALSO HAVE SANITATION PROBLEMS WITH BROKEN BATHROOM AND KITCHEN EQUIPMENT. AND SOME OF THE MOTHERS WITH MANY YOUNG CHILDREN CROWDED INTO TINY APARTMENTS FRANKLY HAVE GIVEN UP TRYING TO KEEP THEIR HOMES CLEAN. |
| **DISSOLVE TO**<br>**BASEMENT AREA,**<br>**TRASH STREWN ABOUT** | THERE ARE ALSO PILES OF TRASH IN THE BASEMENT. BUT RATS AND OVERCROWDING ARE NOT THE ONLY HEALTH PROBLEMS. THERE ARE ANIMAL WASTE AND FLEAS IN THE BASEMENT ALSO AND TWO OF THE ROBINSON CHILDREN HAVE LEAD POISONING. TENANTS SAY CONDITIONS WERE NOT LIKE THIS BEFORE THE GOVERNMENT BECAME THE LANDLORD. |
|  | LAST MONTH NEWS 4 ASKED THE DISTRICT HEALTH INSPECTOR TO CHECK. HE FOUND SWOLLEN CANS IN THE YARD WHICH HE SAID PROBABLY CONTAINED DEADLY BOTULISM POISONING. |
|  | WHAT VIOLATIONS HAVE YOU FOUND HERE AT THE VICTORIA APARTMENTS? |
| **ROBERT WHITE:**<br>**CLOSEUP** | NUMEROUS VIOLATIONS RANGING FROM INFESTATION OF RATS. ABANDONED VEHICLES. TRASH. DEBRIS. POSSIBLY UN-BARRICADED ENTRANCES TO THE BUILDING. |
| **CRAWFORD:**<br>**ON SCREEN**<br>**VICTORIA APTS** | THE HEALTH INSPECTOR SAID THE GOVERNMENT'S REDEVELOPMENT LAND AGENCY OWNS MANY BUILDINGS LIKE THIS IN THE NEIGHBORHOOD. R-L-A IS IN CHARGE OF URBAN RENEWAL. FIRE OF-FICIALS SAY THE VICTORIA'S A FIRE TRAP. BUT NOBODY SEEMS TO BE DOING ANYTHING ABOUT IT. |
|  | ONE DISTRICT OFFICIAL. JAMES ALEXANDER. SAYS THIS IS TYPICAL OF URBAN-RENEWAL PROGRAMS ACROSS THE COUNTRY. HE SAID TOO MUCH EMPHASIS IS PLACED ON THE FUTURE WHILE THE PEOPLE WHO ARE LIVING IN THE RENEWAL AREA RIGHT NOW ARE IGNORED. HE SPOKE ABOUT UPPER 14TH STREET. |
| **JAMES ALEXANDER:** | TWO WAYS OF ANSWERING IT. ONE IS. FROM A GOVERNMENT POINT OF VIEW. |

| CLOSEUP<br>OFFICE | BUREAUCRATICALLY. MAYBE: IT'S BETTER THAN IT WAS "X" MONTHS AGO. BUT THE FACT IS, CLARE, THAT IF YOU GO OUT AND WALK IT, YOU KNOW IT'S IN ROTTEN CONDITION. AND I SOMETIMES FEEL THAT IF WHAT WE SEE OUT THERE HAD BEEN CAUSED BY AN EARTHQUAKE OR OTHER DISASTER THAT WE PROBABLY WOULD HAVE HAD THE MILITARY AND EVERY RESOURCE WE HAVE IN THERE CLEANING IT UP, WHICH IS ABOUT WHAT'S NEEDED. |
|---|---|
| LEE McCARTHY:<br>STUDIO<br>SUPER VICTORIA APTS | NEXT WEEK REPORTER CRAWFORD AND A NEWS 4 CAMERA CREW WILL MOVE INTO THE VICTORIA AND TRY TO LIVE THERE. |

On the Sunday prior to the second week of the series, WRC-TV used a promotion teaser.

| LEE McCARTHY:<br>STUDIO<br>SUPER VICTORIA APTS | LAST WEEK THE NEWS 4 PROBE UNIT DETAILED THE FILTHY AND DANGEROUS CONDITIONS AT THE VICTORIA APARTMENTS, OPERATED BY THE REDEVELOPMENT LAND AGENCY, AT 14TH AND CLIFTON STREETS, NORTHWEST. TONIGHT REPORTER CLARE CRAWFORD AND A NEWS 4 CAMERA TEAM MOVED INTO THE VICTORIA TO LIVE THERE FOR AS LONG AS THEY CAN, AND THEY MOVED IN OVER THE OBJECTIONS OF THE R-L-A. TOMORROW EVENING ON NEWS 4 WASHINGTON AT 6, REPORTER CRAWFORD WILL REPORT ON A NIGHT IN THE VICTORIA. |
|---|---|

## EPISODE 5—MONDAY

| VANCE:<br>STUDIO<br>SUPER SLUM AREAS | THE NEWS 4 PROBE TEAM REPORTING ON THE UNHEALTHY AND ILLEGAL CONDITIONS AT THE VICTORIA APARTMENTS AT 14TH AND CLIFTON STREETS, NORTHWEST, MOVED INTO THOSE APARTMENTS LAST NIGHT IN AN ATTEMPT TO LIVE THERE. THE REDEVELOPMENT LAND AGENCY, THE AGENCY OR THE LANDLORD THERE AND AT SIMILAR BUILDINGS THROUGHOUT THE CITY DID NOT WANT REPORTER CLARE CRAWFORD AND CAMERA CREW TO MOVE IN. HOWEVER, THE RESIDENTS OF THE BUILDING HAVE BEEN CHALLENGING THE TEAM TO SPEND A NIGHT THERE. HERE IS WHAT HAPPENED. |
|---|---|
| CRAWFORD:<br>ON SCREEN<br>IN FRONT OF VICTORIA<br>ENTRANCE | IN ADDITION TO THE RATS AND ROACHES, I WAS NEVER VERY ENTHUSIASTIC ABOUT THE IDEA: IT SEEMED RATHER MELODRAMATIC. BUT I LEARNED A LOT |

126

SCENES OF CONSTRUC-
TION
WORKERS INSIDE APTS

LAST NIGHT. THE MOST OUTSTANDING. IF NOT IMPORTANT. IMPRESSION I HAVE IS OF HOUSE FLIES. THERE SEEMED TO BE HUNDREDS AND HUNDREDS AND HUNDREDS OF FLIES. I DIDN'T SLEEP WELL. AND ABOUT 6 A.M. THE RAT IN MRS. ROBINSON'S KITCHEN WENT FLIPPING THROUGH THE POTS AND PANS LIKE A ROCK-AND-ROLL BAND.

THE LANDLORD. THE REDEVELOPMENT LAND AGENCY. HAS FIRED THE OLD JANITOR AND HIRED A NEW ONE. THEY HAD MEN BOARDING UP VACANT APARTMENTS TODAY. AND THEY'VE HAULED SOME TRASH AWAY. THERE'S BEEN HOT WATER FOR THE LAST THREE OR FOUR DAYS. ONE R-L-A EMPLOYEE SAID THIS MORNING THEY INTEND TO BOARD UP ALL THE WINDOWS ON THE FIRE ESCAPE. WHICH MEANS IT WILL BE AN EVEN WORSE FIRETRAP.

THE PROBE TEAM STAYED IN MRS. ROBINSON'S APARTMENT LAST NIGHT. R-L-A REFUSED US ENTRY TO THE REST OF THE BUILDING. THE MOST OVERWHELMING FEELING I HAVE IS THAT THE WOMEN I'VE GOTTEN TO KNOW HERE ARE THE SAME AGE I AM AND THEY HAVE KIDS THE SAME AGE AS MY KIDS. WE WERE ALL RAISED HERE IN WASHINGTON SIX OR SEVEN MILES APART. IT'S VERY. VERY FRIGHTENING. I WON'T BE COMING BACK HERE TONIGHT.

CLARE CRAWFORD FOR NEWS 4 WASHINGTON AT THE VICTORIA APARTMENTS.

RINKER:
STUDIO

ALTHOUGH THE PROBE TEAM WON'T BE LIVING THERE. IT WILL RETURN EVERY DAY TO THE VICTORIA APARTMENTS TO CONTINUE REPORTS ON THE BUILDING AND ITS HUNDREDS OF VIOLATIONS OF DISTRICT HEALTH. FIRE. AND BUILDING LAWS. AND THE FLIGHT OF ITS RESIDENTS.

# EPISODE 6—TUESDAY

RINKER:
STUDIO
SUPER VICTORIA APTS

TODAY TWO PROMINENT MEMBERS OF CONGRESS SAID CONDITIONS AT THE VICTORIA APARTMENTS ARE INTOLERABLE. NEWS 4 CONTINUES ITS PROBE REPORT ON THE VICTORIA AT 14TH AND CLIFTON STREETS. NORTHWEST. THE REDEVELOPMENT LAND AGENCY IS THE LANDLORD. AND THERE ARE HUNDREDS OF HEALTH. SAFETY. AND BUILDING VIOLATIONS AT THE VICTORIA.

TODAY THE SENATOR AND CONGRESSMAN WHO VOTE MONEY FOR THE DISTRICT GOVERNMENT AND URBAN RENEWAL MADE TOURS OF THE VICTORIA WITH THE NEWS 4 PROBE TEAM. HERE IS REPORTER CLARE CRAWFORD WITH THE STORY.

**CRAWFORD:**
**ON SCREEN AT FRONT OF VICTORIA APTS**

THE CHAIRMAN OF THE SENATE'S DISTRICT APPROPRIATIONS SUBCOMMITTEE. SENATOR BIRCH BAYH, CAME TO THE VICTORIA APARTMENTS TO PERSONALLY INSPECT CONDITIONS THERE. HE TALKED TO THE REDEVELOPMENT LAND AGENCY PROPERTY MANAGER. GEORGE JOHNSON. JOHNSON TOLD HIM THE AGENCY WAS DOING ITS BEST. BUT THE RESIDENTS SAID THE BUILDING WAS UNLIVABLE: AND THEY SHOWED SENATOR BAYH SOME OF THEIR PROBLEMS.

**SENATOR BIRCH BAYH:**
**TWO SHOT**

CAN YOU OPEN IT?

**WOMAN:**

JUST BARELY.

**WOMAN:**

WATER THERE IS DRIPPING DOWN FROM THE REFRIGERATOR. SEE? ALL THE STUFF IS GONE AND THE AIR GETS IN THERE AND IT'S READY TO DEFROST ALL THE TIME AND IT RUNS OUT ON THE FLOOR.

**SENATOR BAYH**

AUTOMATIC DEFROSTING.

**WOMAN:**

YEAH. YEAH.

**CRAWFORD:**
**ON SCREEN AT VICTORIA APTS**

REPRESENTATIVE WILLIAM SCHERLE. A MEMBER OF THE CONGRESSIONAL COMMITTEE DEALING WITH URBAN RENEWAL. MADE AN INSPECTION TOUR. TOO. HE SAID THE BUILDING WAS IN DREADFUL SHAPE AND THAT THE POOR WERE BEING USED TO GET URBAN-RENEWAL MONEY. SENATOR BAYH WASN'T HAPPY ABOUT THE VICTORIA EITHER.

**SENATOR BAYH:**
**CLOSEUP**

WELL. I'M ASHAMED. I REALLY AM. I CAN'T SEE WHY THIS KIND OF CONDITION CAN EXIST IN THE NATION'S CAPITAL.

**REPRESENTATIVE SCHERLE:**

PEOPLE LIKE THE ONES WE SAW ARE LIVING LIKE ANIMALS. OR THEY'RE NOT ANIMALS. BUT THEY'RE LIVING IN CONDITIONS—WELL. YOU KNOW. I COME FROM A FARM IN WESTERN INDIANA. AND I WOULD NOT KEEP THE STABLES WHERE I KEPT MY CATTLE IN SUCH CONDITIONS. ONLY THE HOUSES I KEPT MY HOGS IN RESEMBLED WHAT WE SAW. THE STORAGE PLACES YOU

POINTED OUT IN THE BASEMENT OF THIS PLACE CONTAIN FLEAS. DOG EXCREMENT. AND EVERYTHING ELSE. IT'S JUST TOO BAD THAT EVERY AMERICAN FAMILY JUST WOULDN'T WALK THROUGH THIS OR HAVE TO SPEND THE NIGHT HERE LIKE YOU HAVE. THEN WE'D HAVE ENOUGH PUBLIC RESPONSE THAT THIS KIND OF THING COULD BE CHANGED. 'CAUSE I THINK THE AVERAGE AMERICAN WOULD FEEL ALMOST LIKE THROWING UP. LIKE I DO. HAVING SEEN A PLACE LIKE THAT.

VANCE:
STUDIO

TOMORROW PRESIDENT NIXON'S REPORT ON HOUSING WILL BE RELEASED AND THE NEWS 4 PROBE SERIES WILL REPORT ON WHETHER IT WILL AFFECT THE VICTORIA AND SIMILAR SITUATIONS HERE IN THE DISTRICT.

## EPISODE 7—WEDNESDAY

RINKER:
STUDIO
SUPER SCENES OF SLUM AREAS

REPRESENTATIVE WILLIAM SCHERLE. A CONSERVATIVE REPUBLICAN FROM IOWA. HAS CALLED ON CONGRESS TO DO SOMETHING IMMEDIATELY ABOUT THE VICTORIA APARTMENTS AT 14TH AND CLIFTON STREETS. NORTHWEST. REPRESENTATIVE SCHERLE TOURED THE RUNDOWN APARTMENTS WHERE THE GOVERNMENT IS THE LANDLORD WITH A NEWS 4 PROBE TEAM YESTERDAY.

IN A SPEECH ON THE HOUSE FLOOR AFTER THE TOUR. SCHERLE SAID THE APARTMENTS WERE A NATIONAL DISGRACE AND THAT THE GOVERNMENT SHOULD BE FORCED TO TREAT TENANTS BETTER. HE HAS ASKED THE GENERAL ACCOUNTING OFFICE TO AUDIT THE REDEVELOPMENT LAND AGENCY WHICH OWNS THE VICTORIA AND RUNS URBAN RENEWAL IN WASHINGTON.

TODAY PRESIDENT NIXON SAID THE GOVERNMENT IS THE BIGGEST SLUMLORD IN HISTORY IN A MESSAGE ON HOUSING THAT HE SENT TO CONGRESS.

HERE IS REPORTER CLARE CRAWFORD WITH THE STORY.

CRAWFORD:
ON SCREEN IN STREET

IN HIS HOUSING MESSAGE. THE PRESIDENT ASKED CONGRESS TO PUT MORE MONEY INTO THE TIGHT HOME MORTGAGE MARKET. AND HE PROPOSED A NEW SYSTEM OF CASH PAYMENTS FOR THE POOR SO THEY COULD BUY OR RENT BETTER HOUSING. THIS WOULD TAKE SEVERAL YEARS TO GET UNDERWAY AND. IF IT WERE PASSED. IT

PROBABLY WOULDN'T HELP PEOPLE LIKE THOSE WHO LIVE IN THE VICTORIA APARTMENTS FOR LONGER THAN THAT.

FOR VICTORIA-TYPE POOR. THE PRESIDENT PROPOSED CAUTION AND MORE STUDY. THIS WASN'T A SOLUTION. AS SENATOR BIRCH BAYH HAD WHEN HE VISITED THE VICTORIA YESTERDAY. HE SAID PRESIDENTIAL LEADERSHIP WAS NEEDED TO CLEAR UP SLUMS LIKE THE VICTORIA. HE SAID AMERICANS SHOULD BE MORE CONCERNED WITH REBUILDING THEIR OWN INNER CITIES THAN REBUILDING NORTH VIETNAM.

**SENATOR BAYH:**
**MCU**

I'M CONVINCED THAT THIS KIND OF THING IS DEPLORABLE FROM A HUMAN COMPASSION STANDPOINT. I DON'T LIKE TO SEE LITTLE HUMAN BEINGS LIVING LIKE LITTLE ANIMALS. OR WORSE THAN LITTLE ANIMALS. BUT FROM A DOLLAR-AND-CENTS' STANDPOINT. FOR SOMEBODY THAT DOESN'T HAVE A BIT OF HUMAN COMPASSION. THIS KIND OF BUSINESS IS GOING TO BLEED US DRY IN THIS COUNTRY. IT PERPETUATES ONE GENERATION OF WELFARE. ONE GENERATION OF SICK HUMAN BEINGS THAT AREN'T ABLE TO PARTICIPATE AND MAKE A CONTRIBUTION TO OUR ECONOMICS OR TO OUR SOCIETY.

At the conclusion of the series, it was given national release by John Chancellor on his NBC nightly newscast.

## NBC NIGHTLY NEWS—WEDNESDAY

**CHANCELLOR:**
**OPEN ON SCREEN**
**SUPER SCENES OF SLUM**
**AREAS AND VICTORIA APTS**

PRESIDENT NIXON SENT A MESSAGE ON HOUSING TO CONGRESS TODAY. THE PRESIDENT ANNOUNCED ACTION TO MAKE FIVE-AND-A-HALF-BILLION DOLLARS MORE IN MORTGAGE MONEY AVAILABLE ALMOST IMMEDIATELY. HE IS DOING THIS BY GIVING SAVINGS AND LOAN ASSOCIATIONS MORE LENDING AUTHORITY AND BY ORDERING GOVERNMENT SUBSIDIES FOR LENDERS. HE ALSO ASKED CONGRESS TO GIVE LENDERS TAX CREDITS.

THE PRESIDENT ALSO DECLARED THAT FEDERAL HOUSING PROGRAMS. IN HIS WORDS. HAVE MADE UNCLE SAM THE BIGGEST SLUMLORD IN HISTORY. AND HE PROPOSED AN EXPERIMENTAL PROGRAM OF CASH PAYMENTS TO THE POOR FOR HOUSING INSTEAD OF BUILDING MORE PUBLIC HOUSING. THAT PLAN WILL BE STUDIED FURTHER BEFORE IT GOES TO CONGRESS.

SOME FEDERAL HOUSING PROGRAMS HAVE BEEN SUCCESSFUL, BUT MANY HAVE FAILED. CLARE CRAWFORD HAS BEEN LOOKING INTO THE SITUATION. SHE REPORTS ON ONE FEDERAL PROJECT IN WASHINGTON THAT'S TURNED INTO A SLUM.

**CRAWFORD:**
**ON SCREEN AT VIC-**
**TORIA APTS**

THE VICTORIA APARTMENTS WERE BOUGHT IN 1970 BY THE REDEVELOPMENT LAND AGENCY, A GOVERNMENT AGENCY FUNDED BY THE DEPARTMENT OF HOUSING AND URBAN DEVELOPMENT. THE URBAN-RENEWAL PROGRAM THAT WAS SUPPOSED TO FIX AND CLEAN UP THE NEIGHBORHOOD HERE HAS REALLY NEVER STARTED.

**DISSOLVE TO INTERIOR**
**OF APARTMENTS**
**SHOWING**
**DETERIORATION**

PEOPLE LIVING HERE PAY RENT TO THE GOVERNMENT. THE BUILDING IS ONE OF THOUSANDS THE GOVERNMENT LEASES. SOME ARE BETTER; SOME ARE WORSE. PLASTER IS FALLING OUT OF THE WALLS; PLASTIC PAINT PEELING EVERYWHERE; FAULTY ELECTRICAL WIRING; AND NUMEROUS OTHER HEALTH-AND-SAFETY VIOLATIONS. A FIRE MARSHAL RECENTLY SAW THE BUILDING AND SAID THE PLACE WAS A DEATH TRAP.

**CLOSEUP OF RAT**

RATS LIVE HERE, TOO. ONE RESIDENT PUTS OUT FOOD FOR THE RATS IN HER APARTMENT SO THEY WON'T COME INTO THE BEDROOM AND BITE HER CHILDREN.

THIS PICTURE OF THE RAT WAS TAKEN AT NIGHT WITH A SPECIAL LENS.

BESIDES RATS THERE ARE COCKROACHES. ONE MOTHER HAS HER CHILDREN STICK SHEETS IN THEIR EARS SO THE ROACHES WON'T CRAWL IN THEIR EARS WHEN THEY ARE SLEEPING.

THE GOVERNMENT IS AWARE OF THE PROBLEMS IN THE BUILDING BUT DOESN'T WANT TO SPEND THE MONEY ON FIXING A BUILDING THAT'S GOING TO BE TORN DOWN. THE GOVERNMENT HAS OWNED THIS BUILDING FOR THREE YEARS AND SO FAR NO DATE HAS BEEN SET TO TEAR IT DOWN.

THE PEOPLE LIVING HERE SAY THAT CLEANING UP IS USELESS IN AN OVERCROWDED, FALLING-DOWN BUILDING. URBAN-RENEWAL PROGRAMS HAVE A HISTORY OF BEING SLOW AND INEFFEC-TIVE. IN THIS CASE, AS WELL AS OTHERS IN THE COUNTRY, IT FORCES THE GOVERNMENT'S TENANTS TO LIVE AMONG PILES OF TRASH, RATS, AND FALLING-DOWN HOUSING.

CLARE CRAWFORD. NBC NEWS.
WASHINGTON.

At approximately 3-week intervals, WRC-TV continued interest in the mini-documentary series by brief follow-ups, two samples of which are reproduced below.

## FOLLOW-UP 1—NEWS 4 WASHINGTON

**RINKER:**
**STUDIO**
**SUPER EXTERIOR OF**
**VICTORIA APTS**

LIFE AT THE VICTORIA APARTMENTS. WHERE THE GOVERNMENT IS THE LANDLORD. IS FILLED WITH UNEXPECTED DANGER EVERY DAY. ONE OF THE YOUNG TENANTS TOLD THE NEWS 4 PROBE TEAM HOW EARLIER THIS WEEK HE RESCUED A LITTLE GIRL WHO HAD FALLEN THROUGH A HOLE IN THE ROOF OF ONE OF THE BOARDED-UP SHOPS THAT FACE 14TH STREET.

**TENANT:**
**MCU**

THE LITTLE GIRL WAS STANDING HERE. SHE WAS HANGING ONTO THIS PART RIGHT HERE. WHEN I CAME OUT THE DOOR. I PICKED HER OUT. AND WHEN I PICKED HER OUT HER LITTLE BROTHER SAID. "WAS THERE ANY HARM DONE?" I TOLD HIM NO. THERE WAS NO HARM DONE—BUT THE LITTLE SISTER COULD HAVE BEEN KILLED.

**CRAWFORD:**
**ON SCREEN AT VIC-**
**TORIA APTS**

OTHER THINGS HAPPENED AT THE VICTORIA THIS WEEK TOO. THE REDEVELOPMENT LAND AGENCY. WHICH RUNS THE BROKEN-DOWN BUILDING. HAS SENT MOST OF THE TENANTS BACK-RENT BILLS FOR ABOUT $2000 EACH. THE TENANTS HAVE BEEN ON A RENT STRIKE IN AN EFFORT TO GET SERVICES AND REPAIRS.

R-L-A ALSO SENT FORMAL NOTIFICATION THEY MUST BE OUT OF THE BUILDING BY THE END OF THIS MONTH. THE TENANTS SAY R-L-A REPRESENTATIVES TOLD THEM THE BUILDING WILL BE TORN DOWN BECAUSE CONGRESS ORDERED IT DEMOLISHED AFTER NEWS 4 REPORTS OF UNHEALTHY AND ILLEGAL CONDITIONS. R-L-A HAS PROMISED TO HELP THE FAMILIES FIND NEW QUARTERS. BUT SO FAR NONE HAS BEEN FOUND. R-L-A HAS ALSO TOLD THE RESIDENTS TO PACK THEIR BELONGINGS TO PREPARE FOR THE MOVE.

AND SO THE VICTORIA RESIDENTS CONTINUE TO WAIT. MOST DON'T EXPECT TO MOVE BY THE END OF THE MONTH. FEW OF THEM HAVE THE MONEY TO PAY RENT SOMEPLACE ELSE AND NONE OF THEM

|   |   |
|---|---|
| | HAVE THE MONEY TO PAY THE AP-PROXIMATE $2000 EACH OWES IN BACK RENT. THEY ARE CURIOUS ABOUT THE NEW OFFICIAL INTEREST IN THEIR PLIGHT. BUT THEY STILL HAVE LITTLE HOPE FOR THE FUTURE. |
| **CLOSE** | CLARE CRAWFORD. NEWS 4 WASHINGTON. AT THE VICTORIA APARTMENTS. |

## FOLLOW-UP 2—NEWS 4 WASHINGTON

|   |   |
|---|---|
| **RINKER:**<br>**STUDIO**<br>**SUPER EXTERIOR VIC-TORIA APTS** | FOR MORE THAN A MONTH. NEWS 4 PROBE TEAM HAS BEEN INVESTIGATING LIVING CONDITIONS AT THE VICTORIA APARTMENTS AT 14TH AND CLIFTON STREETS. NORTHWEST. THE VICTORIA IS OWNED AND OPERATED BY A GOVERNMENT AGENCY. THE REDEVELOPMENT LAND AGENCY. R-L-A HAS FINALLY TAKEN SOME STEPS TO HELP THE RESIDENTS HERE. |
| | REPORTER CLARE CRAWFORD HAS THAT STORY. |
| **CRAWFORD:**<br>**V/O INTERIOR OF APT** | R-L-A HAS FOUND BETTER HOUSING FOR THE 18 FAMILIES WHO LIVE HERE. SENATOR BIRCH BAYH PRESSURED R-L-A TO CLOSE DOWN THE VICTORIA AFTER THE PROBE REPORT. THE RESIDENTS HAVE MIXED FEELING ABOUT THE MOVE. |
| **WOMAN:**<br>**MCU** | WE'RE PLEASED. BUT WE'RE NOT SO HAPPY. THAT TEMPORARILY—THIS IS WHAT THE PROBLEM IS AND YOU KNOW WHAT "TEM-PORARILY" CAN MEAN. WE COULD BE THERE A COUPLE OF DAYS AND HAVE TO MOVE AGAIN. SO WE'RE PLEASED BUT NOT HAPPY BY ANY MEANS. |
| **CRAWFORD:**<br>**ON SCREEN AT VIC-TORIA APTS** | SO BERTHA ROBINSON. WHO FEEDS THE RAT IN HER KITCHEN SO IT WON'T BITE HER CHILDREN. WILL MOVE INTO THIS HOUSE NEXT MONTH—AFTER R-L-A FINISHES REPAIRING IT. OTHER RESIDENTS WILL MOVE INTO HOUSES LIKE THIS ONE. AND THIS ONE. THE HOUSES ARE BETTER THAN THE UNSAFE VICTORIA. BUT THE BASIC TRASH AND CRIME PROBLEMS REMAIN. |
| | LIFE SEEMS TO BE GETTING BETTER FOR THE RESIDENTS OF THE VICTORIA APARTMENTS. BUT THE VICTORIA APARTMENTS WERE JUST A SYMBOL OF THE THOUSANDS OF PEOPLE WHO LIVE IN BROKEN-DOWN. RAT-INFESTED HOUSES OWNED BY UNCLE SAM. R-L-A HAS NOT SAID WHAT IT WILL DO. IF ANYTHING. FOR THESE OTHER PEOPLE. |

133

## THE MENTALLY RETARDED

A problem faced by every urban community is the care of the mentally retarded children and adults. In many cities, the approach is ostrich-like: hide the unfortunates away and bury our collective head in the sand of forgetfulness.

The News 4 probe team exposed the utterly distressing conditions at Rosewood, an institution for the mentally retarded in nearby Maryland. The mini-documentary series was very effective laying bare one of society's hidden failures; then the probe team turned to the District of Columbia and its institution at Forest Haven. The transcripts reproduced here illustrate the thoroughness of the investigation and its aural and visual impact.

Almost all episodes in this 2-week series, *The Mentally Retarded*, are prefaced by a brief introduction, usually backed by an equally brief film sequence from the preceding episode. Clare Crawford, the reporter, begins the series with a general outline of the situation and a few pertinent statistics. The technique, in continuing episodes, is to talk to a parent or parents about their handicapped children. This is a sound approach. Any story is better told through the eyes of an individual than through a mass gathering.

The reporter has covered a wide range: several parents, superintendent of the institution, director of mental health services, director of the Bureau of Human Resources. Even in the brief 3 minutes or so allotted to each episode, there is sufficient material to make a strong impression on the viewer. Visually, particularly in episode 1, the camera is unsparing in revealing the pitiful circumstances of the mentally retarded.

Another factor is the flexibility of the mini-documentary. Observe that episode 7 is devoted to an interview with the District of Columbia Bureau of Human Resources director. The director had been watching the series and was anxious to comment. The probe team reacted quickly, obtaining a filmed statement and adding commentary by the reporter. This episode brought an additional newsworthiness to the series and was a tribute to its impact.

## EPISODE 1—MONDAY

| | |
|---|---|
| NEIL BOGGS: | GOOD EVENING. A FEW WEEKS AGO OUR PROBE TEAM EXAMINED THE TREATMENT |
| STUDIO | OF MENTALLY RETARDED IN MARYLAND. THIS EVENING, CLARE CRAWFORD HAS THE |
| STILLS OF MENTALLY RETARDED NEWBORN CHILD | FIRST IN A NEW SERIES OF PROBE REPORTS ON CONDITIONS IN THE DISTRICT: THEY'RE NOT ANY BETTER. |

| | |
|---|---|
| **CRAWFORD:** | THE KIND OF CARE THE MENTALLY |
| **V/O FILM SEQUENCE** | RETARDED RECEIVE IN MARYLAND |
| **BOYS** | BECAME AN URGENT QUESTION IN |
| **DORMITORY** | NOVEMBER WHEN PARENTS REFUSED TO |
| | PERMIT DOCTORS TO PERFORM SIMPLE |
| **SEMICLAD CHILDREN** | STOMACH SURGERY ON A MONGOLOID BABY |
| | AND THE BABY WAS ALLOWED TO STARVE |
| | TO DEATH. |

WHAT WERE THE PARENTS' ALTERNATIVES? THEY COULD HAVE PLACED THE CHILD IN AN INSTITUTION. MARYLAND'S WORST AND OLDEST INSTITUTION IS ROSEWOOD. OUTSIDE OF BALTIMORE. THERE ARE VIRTUALLY NO PROGRAMS AT 19TH CENTURY KING COTTAGE AND IT IS ALSO TREMENDOUSLY OVERCROWDED.

*(labels:* **INADEQUATE BATHROOM FACILITIES**)*

ROSEWOOD ITSELF IS A LARGE INSTITUTION. BUT IT DOES HAVE AN ELEMENTARY SCHOOL AND SOME PROGRAMS FOR OTHER INMATES. ELSEWHERE. THE STATE HAS DAY-CARE CENTERS. AND THERE IS A REGIONAL HOSPITAL SCHOOL AT GREAT OAKS IN MONTGOMERY COUNTY. IT OFFERS NUMEROUS SERVICES AND PROGRAMS FOR BOTH RETARDED CHILDREN AND THEIR FAMILIES.

*(label:* **EXTERIOR SHOTS OF BUILDINGS**)*

MARYLAND ALSO IS IN THE PROCESS OF SETTING UP HOME VISITS. CONSULTATIONS. AND OTHER SERVICES FOR HANDICAPPED CHILDREN. THERE ARE SPECIAL CLASSES FOR THE LESS RETARDED CHILDREN IN THE COUNTY SCHOOL SYSTEM.

*(label:* **ZOOM IN ON KING COTTAGE**)*

IN THE NATION'S CAPITAL. THE STORY OF THE MENTALLY RETARDED OR. SPECIFICALLY. THOSE PEOPLE WHO NEED SPECIAL HELP TO LIVE WITH OTHER PEOPLE. IS NOT A SIMPLE STORY. IT'S NOT THE ANCIENT. FILTHY KING COTTAGE AT ROSEWOOD. AND IT'S NOT THE ALMOST MIRACULOUS HELP AT GREAT OAKS IN MONTGOMERY COUNTY. IT IS THE STORY OF WHAT ISN'T BEING DONE. IT IS THE STORY OF YOUNG PEOPLE WITH MENTAL. EMOTIONAL. OR PHYSICAL PROBLEMS. THEY NEED EXPERT CARE AND SPECIAL EDUCATION TO SOLVE THESE PROBLEMS.

*(label:* **MONTAGE OF CROWDS OF PEOPLE IN DOWNTOWN WASHINGTON**)*

THERE ARE MORE THAN 700 THOUSAND PEOPLE LIVING HERE. ONE-HUNDRED-FORTY-FIVE THOUSAND GO TO PUBLIC SCHOOLS. THE DISTRICT'S STORY OF EDUCATION FOR PEOPLE WHO NEED

|  | SPECIAL HELP IS REALLY A STORY OF WAITING LISTS. THERE IS A WAITING LIST FOR SPECIAL EDUCATION CLASSES IN THE PUBLIC SCHOOLS. THERE IS A WAITING LIST FOR TUITION GRANTS TO PRIVATE SCHOOLS. THERE IS A WAITING LIST FOR TRANSPORTATION. |
|---|---|
| **EXTERIORS OF FOREST HAVEN** | THERE IS A RESIDENTIAL HOME FOR THE MENTALLY RETARDED CALLED FOREST HAVEN. AND THERE IS A WAITING LIST FOR THAT. TOO. BECAUSE THE LISTS ARE SO LONG. MANY PEOPLE DON'T EVEN BOTHER TO APPLY. THERE IS YET A VAGUE STATISTIC OF LESS THAN 100: THAT'S SUPPOSED TO BE THE NUMBER OF CHILDREN WHO DON'T GO TO SCHOOL AT ALL. SOMETHING IS WRONG WITH THAT TOTAL BECAUSE IT DOESN'T EVEN INCLUDE ALL THE WAITING LISTS. IN FACT. IT IS SUCH AN UNRELIABLE ESTIMATE THE DISTRICT GOVERNMENT IS MAKING A NEW LIST. |
| **INTERIOR SHOTS OF CHILDREN PLAYING GAMES** | SO. WITH ALL THE WAITING LISTS AND THE CHILDREN WHO AREN'T EVEN ON THE WAITING LISTS. THERE ARE THOUSANDS NOT BEING HELPED. PEOPLE CONDEMNED TO EMPTY LIVES. ACCORDING TO ONE DISTRICT FIGURE THERE WERE 17.620 HANDICAPPED CHILDREN HERE LAST YEAR. BUT EVERYONE HAS THEIR OWN ESTIMATES. IT WOULD SEEM IMPOSSIBLE TO HELP THESE PEOPLE WHEN DISTRICT OFFICIALS AND EXPERTS CAN'T EVEN AGREE HOW MANY THERE ARE. |
| **MAN: SOUND ON FILM** | I WOULD ASSUME THAT THERE ARE 24 THOUSAND PEOPLE WHO WOULD FALL IN THAT CATEGORY. |
| **WOMAN: SOUND ON FILM** | ACCORDING TO OUR LAST STATISTICAL REPORT. THERE ARE APPROXIMATELY 1501 STUDENTS WHO ARE ON THE WAITING LIST FOR SPECIAL EDUCATION. THERE ARE MANY MORE IF WE WERE TO TAKE OFFICE OF EDUCATION INTO THOSE FIGURES AND TO DETERMINE THAT THERE ARE PROBABLY ABOUT 15- TO 18-THOUSAND CHILDREN WHO PERHAPS NEED SPECIAL EDUCATION. ACCORDING TO THE SIZE OF THE POPULATION. |
| **SECOND WOMAN: INTERVIEW SOUND ON FILM** | BASED ON NATIONAL SURVEYS THAT HAVE BEEN CONDUCTED. IT WOULD APPEAR THAT THERE WOULD BE AROUND 16 THOUSAND CHILDREN AND YOUNG ADULTS THAT WOULD FALL INTO THE CATEGORY OF DEVELOPMENTALLY DISABLED. MANY OF |

THEM ARE AT HOME. MANY OF THEM IN THE
SCHOOLS AND HAVE NOT BEEN IDENTIFIED.
AND, WELL, I JUST COULDN'T TELL YOU
EXACTLY WHERE THEY ARE. WE NEED TO
EDUCATE THE PUBLIC AND TELL THE COM-
MUNITY ABOUT THE PROBLEM, SO THAT
PERHAPS MANY OF THESE CHILDREN ARE
HIDDEN CHILDREN.

**CRAWFORD:** WHAT HAPPENS WHEN THE RETARDED
CHILD IS LEFT AT HOME, AND IS HOME WITH
A FAMILY? WHAT DOES IT DO TO THE CHILD
AND THE FAMILY?

**SECOND WOMAN:** WELL, IT'S A VERY TRAUMATIC
EXPERIENCE FOR THE FAMILY BECAUSE
WE HAVE NO DAY CARE FOR THE HANDICAP-
PED. WE DON'T HAVE HOMEMAKER
SERVICE. MANY OF THESE PARENTS WHO
ARE HOME 24 HOURS A DAY CANNOT EVEN
GET OUT TO THE STORE. PARTICULARLY
WHEN YOU'RE DEALING WITH A CHILD WHO
MIGHT BE VERY PROFOUNDLY HANDICAP-
PED.

**CRAWFORD:** WHAT HAPPENS TO THE RETARDED CHILD
WHO IS IN A CLASSROOM WITH SO-CALLED
NORMAL CHILDREN?

**SECOND WOMAN:** UNFORTUNATELY, MANY OF THEM ARE
FALLING THROUGH THE CRACKS. I THINK
THAT THESE CHILDREN ARE IN MANY
INSTANCES BEING PROMOTED, AND FIND
THEMSELVES IN HIGH SCHOOL—PERHAPS
WITHOUT KNOWING HOW TO READ OR
WRITE. MANY OF THEM BEGIN TO ACT UP IN
THE CLASSROOM AND END UP IN JUVENILE
COURT AND PERHAPS ARE SENT TO LAUREL
WHEN THERE MIGHT WELL BE SOME
EMOTIONAL DISTURBANCE THAT COULD BE
HANDLED WITH AN EFFECTIVE PROGRAM.

**CRAWFORD:**
**ON SCREEN—**
**STANDUP IN FRONT**
**OF FOREST HAVEN**
EFFECTIVE PROGRAMS ARE POSSIBLE. TEN
DAYS AGO SECRETARY OF HEALTH,
EDUCATION, AND WELFARE, ELLIOT
RICHARDSON, REPORTED TO PRESIDENT
NIXON THAT MENTAL RETARDATION CAN, IN
A GREAT MEASURE, BE PREVENTED OR
MODIFIED. HE SAID IF OUR CURRENT AC-
CELERATING KNOWLEDGE OF HUMAN
DEVELOPMENT WERE UTILIZED, THE
BURDEN OF MENTAL RETARDATION WOULD
DECLINE SIGNIFICANTLY AND THE QUALITY
OF LIFE FOR ALL SOCIETY WOULD BE
UPLIFTED. THERE'S NO MEANINGFUL STAN-
DARD TO MEASURE THE CARE FOR THE
RETARDED IN AMERICA. BUT ONE OFFICIAL
SAYS THE CITY OF WASHINGTON IS ONE OF
THE WORST.

## EPISODE 2—TUESDAY

| | |
|---|---|
| **CRAWFORD:**<br>V/O STILLS OF MEN-<br>TALLY RETARDED<br>NEWBORN CHILD | PERHAPS THE RETARDED PEOPLE IN THE DISTRICT WHO NEED HELP THE MOST ARE THE ONES FOR WHOM THERE IS VIRTUALLY NO PUBLIC HELP—THE PROFOUNDLY RETARDED. SOME ARE BEDRIDDEN AND CAN'T TAKE CARE OF EVEN THEIR MOST BASIC NEEDS. SOME CAN'T TALK. THEY ARE A CRUSHING BURDEN ON THEIR FAMILY AND THE COMMUNITY. |
| **SHOTS OF GIRL**<br>WATCHING<br>TV, BUT MOVING<br>UNCONTROLLABLY | THIS GIRL IS 17 YEARS OLD. SHE'S NEVER BEEN TO SCHOOL...8 OR 9 YEARS AGO, VIOLA—THAT'S HER NAME—WENT TO THE DISTRICT'S RESIDENTIAL HOME, FOREST HAVEN. BUT HER MOTHER WASN'T SATISFIED WITH HOW SHE WAS BEING TREATED. SHE SAYS ON HER FIRST VISIT HOME VIOLA WAS ONLY SKIN AND BONES, AND SHE COULDN'T BEAR TO EVEN GO BACK TO GET HER DAUGHTER'S CLOTHES. |
| **CRAWFORD:**<br>INTERVIEW<br>SOUND ON FILM | SHE CARES FOR VIOLA AROUND THE CLOCK; A VIRTUAL PRISONER IN HER OWN HOME. SHE HAS TRAINED VIOLA TO DRESS AND FEED HERSELF. SHE ATTENDED A RECREATION DEPARTMENT PLAY PROGRAM FOR A FEW YEARS, BUT SHE WAS EXPELLED WHEN SHE SCRATCHED ANOTHER GIRL. BUT HER MOTHER IS AWARE SHE'S GETTING OLDER AND WEAKER, AND VIOLA IS GETTING STRONGER. SHE WANTS A BETTER, MORE REWARDING LIFE FOR HER DAUGHTER. |
| **MOTHER:** | I'VE BEEN TRYING TO GET HER INTO SCHOOL, BUT THEY WON'T ACCEPT HER—THEY JUST WON'T ACCEPT HER IN SCHOOL. |
| **CRAWFORD:** | WELL, WHO TAKES CARE OF HER? |
| **MOTHER:** | I TAKE CARE OF HER. |
| **CRAWFORD:** | WHAT DO YOU THINK THE FUTURE IS FOR VIOLA? |
| **MOTHER:** | I DON'T KNOW. I HAVE BEEN TRYING TO GET SOME HELP FOR HER SO SHE CAN BE ABLE TO DO SOMETHING FOR HERSELF. |
| **CRAWFORD:** | WHAT DO YOU THINK SHE CAN LEARN? |
| **MOTHER:** | OH, PROBABLY SHE CAN LEARN HOW TO...SHE WAS CRAWLING. I DON'T KNOW WHETHER SHE CAN LEARN. SHE WAS |

|  |  |
|---|---|
|  | CRAWLING. SHE WAS PLAYING BALL AND SHE WAS...I DON'T KNOW WHAT ELSE SHE CAN DO. |
| **CRAWFORD:** | WHAT DOES SHE DO MOST OF THE DAY? |
| **MOTHER:** | SHE LIKES TO SUCK HER CLOTHES. TEAR UP HER CLOTHES. HER SOCKS. TAKE OFF HER SHOES. AND PULL OUT HER HAIR. SHE GETS SO NERVOUS SOMETIMES SHE TAKES BOTH HER FISTS AND GOES UP THE SIDE OF HER FACE AND THEN BANGS HER FACE WITH HER FISTS. |
| **CRAWFORD:** | HOW DO YOU CONTROL HER WHEN SHE WON'T MIND YOU? |
| **MOTHER:** | WELL. WHEN SHE WON'T MIND ME. I CONTROL HER LIKE THIS. I SAY. VIOLA COME HERE AND BE A NICE GIRL NOW. |
| **CRAWFORD:** | AS SHE'S GOTTEN OLDER. IS SHE MORE DIFFICULT TO MANAGE? |
| **MOTHER:** | OH. YES. SHE'S AWFULLY STRONG NOW. I CAN HARDLY DO ANYTHING WITH HER. I CAN'T EVEN WHIP HER NOW BECAUSE SHE TAKES THE BELT AWAY FROM ME. SHE'S STRONG. WHEN I HIT HER SHE TAKES THE BELT. SHE HOLDS THE BELT AND SHE WON'T GIVE IT BACK TO ME. |
| **CRAWFORD:** **V/O SEQUENCES OF** **CHILD** **IN CRIB** **VEGETATING** | DANIELLE WAS A VERY ADVANCED BABY. HER MOTHER SAYS SHE BEGAN TO TODDLE EARLY AND WAS STARTING TO SAY RECOGNIZABLE WORDS WHEN SHE WAS STRICKEN WITH MENINGITIS AT 12 MONTHS. SHE'S 7 YEARS OLD NOW BUT SHE FUNCTIONS AT ABOUT A 6-MONTH LEVEL. |
|  | SINCE HER ILLNESS. HER MOTHER HAS TAKEN HER TO A PUBLIC DIAGNOSTIC CLINIC. SHE HAS GOTTEN MEDICATION BUT NO HELP IN TRAINING DANIELLE. SHE SAYS DANIELLE BRIEFLY ATTENDED THE U-G-F SUPPORTED SOCIETY FOR CRIPPLED CHILDREN'S FREE SCHOOL. BUT SHE HAD TO DROP OUT BECAUSE THERE WAS NO TRANSPORTATION. FINALLY. HER MOTHER QUIT HER CLERK'S JOB AND WENT ON WELFARE TO CARE FOR DANIELLE. |
|  | SHE HAS TWO OTHER CHILDREN: ONE 10 AND ONE 3. DANIELLE'S MOTHER IS RARELY ABLE TO LEAVE THE APARTMENT. SHE DOESN'T COMPLAIN. IN FACT. SHE'S VERY GRATEFUL THAT THE DISTRICT GOVERNMENT HAS GIVEN HER A HOSPITAL BED. BUT SHE DOESN'T UNDERSTAND WHY SHE CAN'T GET MORE HELP FOR DANIELLE. |

THERE ARE SCHOOLS AND THINGS FOR EVERYTHING ELSE. I THINK WE SHOULD HAVE A SCHOOL FOR SPECIAL EDUCATION. I DON'T SEE WHY WE DON'T HAVE ONE. I GUESS I SOUND ANGRY ABOUT IT. AND I GUESS I AM. I MEAN. HERE'S A CHILD THAT JUST LIES IN BED. UNLESS I MOVE HER OR UNLESS SOMEONE ELSE MOVES HER. SHE CAN'T DO ANYTHING. BUT SOME DOCTORS TELL YOU SHE CAN BE HELPED. BUT THERE ARE NO SCHOOLS TO HELP HER. I MEAN. THERE ARE REHABILITATION CENTERS FOR EVERYTHING ELSE. THEY HAVE ALL THESE PLACES AND STUFF FOR THESE DRUG ADDICTS AND THINGS LIKE THAT. WHY NOT OPEN A SCHOOL FOR A CHILD LIKE HER?

**CRAWFORD:**

HOW MANY MORE YEARS DO YOU THINK YOU'LL BE ABLE TO CARE FOR DANIELLE?

**MOTHER.**

AS MANY YEARS AS I HAVE TO. SHE'S MY CHILD. AND I HAVE TO FIND OUT WHETHER THERE IS SOMETHING THAT CAN BE DONE FOR HER. I GET IMPATIENT. I GET ANGRY. YOU KNOW. WITH MYSELF. I GET ANGRY WITH HER EVEN, YOU KNOW. SHE HASN'T DONE ANYTHING. BUT I GET ANGRY. I GET IMPATIENT. AND I GET TIRED. BUT I STILL KNOW. YOU KNOW. THAT SHE'S MINE. AND THEN. TOO, THE DOCTORS TELL ME HER LIFESPAN IS ONLY UNTIL SHE GETS 11 YEARS OLD. AND THAT'S NOT LONG. REALLY. AND SHE'S 7 NOW. SO THAT'S NOT TOO LONG. AND SO I THINK I CAN WAIT UNTIL THEN.

**CRAWFORD:**
**CLOSEUP**

DISTRICT OFFICIALS SAY THERE ARE LESS THAN A HUNDRED CHILDREN LIKE VIOLA AND DANIELLE WHO HAVE NEVER ATTENDED SCHOOL AT ALL. BUT THIS FIGURE IS SO UNRELIABLE THEY ARE MAKING A NEW SURVEY. THEY ARE DOING IT NOT BECAUSE THEY WANT TO. BUT BECAUSE THE COURT HAS ORDERED THEM TO.

THERE IS A CASE PENDING WHICH ARGUES THAT EVERY CHILD. REGARDLESS OF HANDICAPS. HAS A RIGHT TO BE EDUCATED TO THE FULLEST POTENTIAL. THAT CERTAINLY IS NOT TRUE HERE. THE ONLY PUBLIC TRAINING PROGRAM FOR THE PROFOUNDLY RETARDED IS A SINGLE EXPERIMENTAL CLASS FOR 8 PUPILS. OTHERWISE THERE IS NO DAY CARE. NO COUNSELING. AND NO TRAINING PROGRAMS FOR THESE CHILDREN.

THE DISTRICT HOME FOR THE RETARDED. FOREST HAVEN. IS OVERCROWDED WITH 11

|  |  |
|---|---|
|  | HUNDRED RESIDENTS. ADMISSIONS WERE CLOSED MONTHS AGO. AND THERE IS A WAITING LIST OF 123. |
| VANCE: STUDIO | TOMORROW NIGHT THE PROBE SERIES CONCENTRATES ON FOREST HAVEN AND DOCUMENTS THE CASE OF AN INJURED RESIDENT. IT IS THE STORY OF A GIRL WHO HER PARENTS BELIEVE HAS DETERIORATED BECAUSE SHE HAS RECEIVED NO HELP. |

## EPISODE 3—WEDNESDAY

|  |  |
|---|---|
| RINKER: STUDIO | CLARE CRAWFORD AND THE NEWS 4 PROBE TEAM TONIGHT CONTINUE THEIR REPORTS ON CARE AVAILABLE FOR THE MENTALLY RETARDED IN THE DISTRICT. THE MAJOR FACILITY FOR THOSE WHO NEED HELP IS A CONTROVERSIAL INSTITUTION IN SUBURBAN LAUREL. MARYLAND. |
| CRAWFORD: V/O EXTERIORS OF BUILDINGS AND GROUNDS | THE DISTRICT'S RESIDENTIAL HOME FOR THE RETARDED IS CALLED FOREST HAVEN. IT HAS BEEN THE CENTER OF MUCH CONTROVERSY. AND LAST FALL A SPECIAL TASK FORCE WAS APPOINTED TO REORGANIZE IT. SOME CHANGES HAVE BEEN MADE AND MORE ARE PLANNED. BUT STILL THE MOST COMPLIMENTARY WAY TO DESCRIBE IT IS THAT IT ISN'T AS BAD AS IT USED TO BE. THERE HAVE ALWAYS BEEN PROBLEMS. |
| INTERIOR OF RECEIVING AND CORRIDORS | FOREST HAVEN WAS OPENED IN 1925 FOR THE CARE AND TRAINING OF FEEBLE-MINDED DISTRICT RESIDENTS. IT WAS DELIBERATELY LOCATED 20 MILES OUT IN THE MARYLAND COUNTRYSIDE TO SEGREGATE THE RESIDENTS FROM THE COMMUNITY AND GIVE THEM LAND TO FARM. |
| SHOTS OF RETARDED TEENAGE GIRL AT DESK WRAPPING PACKAGES | THE STORY OF FOREST HAVEN IN RECENT YEARS IS ALSO THE STORY OF JOY EVANS. JOY IS 13. SHE CAME HERE 5 YEARS AGO AND LIVED AT OLD. DIRTY. AND UNDERSTAFFED DOGWOOD COTTAGE. JOY WAS REPEATEDLY INJURED AND HER PARENTS SUCCESSFULLY FOUGHT TO HAVE THE COTTAGE CLOSED. SHE IS NOW LIVING IN A NEW BUILDING WITH A LARGER STAFF. BUT STILL HER PARENTS AREN'T HAPPY AND THEY DON'T THINK JOY IS. |
| SHOT OF JOY WALKING WITH CRUTCHES DOWN RAMP | THE EVANSES BELIEVE THE STAFF IS DEDICATED. BUT THEY FEEL JOY. WHO USED TO SAY A FEW WORDS AND CARRY OUT SIMPLE COMMANDS. HAS DETERIORATED. |

THEY BELIEVE IF THEY HAD GOTTEN HELP FROM THE DISTRICT GOVERNMENT WHEN SHE WAS YOUNGER, SHE WOULD HAVE HAD A MORE NORMAL LIFE. THEY DEVOTE MUCH OF THEIR TIME TO TRYING TO IMPROVE FOREST HAVEN. THOUGH THEY FEEL THAT JOY'S CHANCE IS GONE. THEY ARE STILL ANGRY ABOUT HOW SHE WAS TREATED HER FIRST YEARS THERE.

**MRS EVANS:**
**INTERVIEW**
**SOUND ON FILM**

ONE PARTICULAR TIME WE WENT OUT THERE TO VISIT JOY AND I TOOK HER TO THE BATHROOM. AND I NOTICED THAT SHE SEEMED TO BE IN PAIN. AND WHEN I TOOK HER CLOTHES DOWN, HER ENTIRE BACK WAS OPEN—IT WAS A MASS OF OPEN SKIN. AND WE ASKED THEM WHAT HAD HAPPENED AND THEY ASKED US IF SHE HAD A SKIN DISEASE, A BLOOD DISEASE. SO, WE BROUGHT HER IN TOWN TO OUR OWN PRIVATE PHYSICIAN AND HE TOOK ONE LOOK AND HE SAID THESE ARE URINE BURNS. HE SAID THAT SHE WAS TIED, EVIDENTLY, ON A RUBBER SHEET FOR A LENGTH OF TIME AND THIS IS WHAT HAPPENED. SO WE TOOK HER BACK OUT TO FOREST HAVEN AND THEY ASSURED US THAT THIS WOULD NOT HAPPEN AGAIN. THE DAY WE TOOK HER OUT WAS HER DISCHARGE FROM D.C. GENERAL HOSPITAL AND THIS WAS DUE TO A SEVERELY BLACKED EYE, HEMATOMA ON THE BACK OF HER HEAD. AND WE KNEW...

**CRAWFORD:**

WHAT IS THAT?

**MRS. EVANS:**

A HEMATOMA IS A BLOOD TUMOR. AND THEY SENT HER TO D.C. GENERAL HOSPITAL FOR TREATMENT.

**CRAWFORD:**

MR. EVANS, WHEN DID YOU DECIDE...AND WHY...TO TAKE JOY OUT OF FOREST HAVEN?

**MR. EVANS:**

NOT KNOWING IN WHAT CONDITION WE WOULD RECEIVE OUR DAUGHTER EACH SUNDAY. IT GOT TO BE SUCH AN EMOTIONAL THING THAT WE DECIDED IT WOULD BE BETTER IF WE BROUGHT JOY HOME. WE TRIED TO WORK WITH HER AT HOME, BUT UNFORTUNATELY, IN D.C. WE COULD NOT GET ANY TYPE OF COUNSELING ON HOW TO WORK WITH THE RETARDED. WE DIDN'T RECEIVE ANY HELP FROM THE DISTRICT GOVERNMENT. FOR EXAMPLE, AFTER TWO OR THREE WEEKS OF HAVING JOY AT HOME UNDER 24-HOUR CONSTANT CARE, WE FOUND THAT THERE WAS NO TYPE OF FACILITY WHERE WE COULD TAKE JOY JUST FOR A DAY TO GIVE SOME RELIEF FOR THE

| | |
|---|---|
| | FAMILY—IT BECAME A PROBLEM OF EITHER SPLITTING THE FAMILY OR PUTTING JOY BACK INTO FOREST HAVEN. WE HAD TO MAKE THE THREAT THAT EITHER THEY TAKE CARE OF MY DAUGHTER PROPERLY OR BE SUED. |
| **CRAWFORD:** | WELL. HOW IS JOY LIVING TODAY. MR. EVANS? |
| **MRS. EVANS:** | THE CONDITIONS HAVE IMPROVED TREMENDOUSLY. WE DO HAVE A NEW PHYSICAL PLANT. BUT WE ARE BACK TO THE SAME OLD PROBLEMS THAT WE HAD AT DOGWOOD COTTAGE. WE DON'T HAVE ANY TYPE OF RECREATIONAL PROGRAMS TO STIMULATE THE MIND. DON'T HAVE AN ORAL HYGIENIST TO TAKE CARE OF THE TEETH. IN OTHER WORDS. THERE IS NO TYPE OF PROGRAM AT ALL—WHICH RESULTS IN THE RESIDENTS JUST SITTING THERE VEGETATING. |
| **CRAWFORD:** | THE PRESENT AND THE FUTURE AT FOREST HAVEN SEEM TIED TO MONEY: MONEY FOR AN ADEQUATE STAFF. MONEY FOR RETURNING RESIDENTS TO THE COMMUNITY. AND MONEY FOR TRAINING AND RECREATION PROGRAMS. MEANWHILE. TODAY JOY AND HER FELLOW RESIDENTS SIMPLY EXIST. |
| **RINKER:** **STUDIO** | TOMORROW NIGHT THE PROBE TEAM WILL SHOW HOW FOREST HAVEN IS TODAY. THEY WILL EXPLAIN WHY MOST RESIDENTS THERE SIMPLY EXIST HOPELESSLY WITH LITTLE CHANCE TO RETURN TO THE COMMUNITY OR TO ENJOY LIFE AT ALL. |

## EPISODE 4—THURSDAY

| | |
|---|---|
| **BOGGS:** **STUDIO** | NOW CLARE CRAWFORD AND THE PROBE TEAM CONTINUE THEIR SERIES ON THE LACK OF CARE AVAILABLE TO THE RETARDED IN THE DISTRICT. TONIGHT SHE REPORTS ON THE PROBLEMS AT FOREST HAVEN. THE DISTRICT'S ONLY INSTITUTION FOR PEOPLE WITH THESE PROBLEMS. PORTIONS OF THE FILM YOU ARE ABOUT TO SEE MAY BE OBJECTIONABLE. AND SOME MAY NOT WANT TO SEE IT. |
| **CRAWFORD:** | OFFICIALS AT FOREST HAVEN HAVE REFUSED TO ALLOW PICTURES TO BE TAKEN OF RESIDENTS WITHOUT THE CONSENT OF THEIR PARENTS OR GUARDIAN. THEY DID NOT GIVE US THE NAMES OF THE RESIDENTS OR THEIR PARENTS. |

143

| | |
|---|---|
| **V/O SHOTS OF FOREST HAVEN EMPLOYEES GETTING ON BUS, GOING TO WORK** | FOREST HAVEN WORKERS ARE POORLY PAID AND HAVE TO TRAVEL A LONG WAY TO WORK. OFFICIALS SAY THAT'S WHY IT'S HARD TO FILL 103 STAFF VACANCIES. THERE IS AN ABSENTEE PROBLEM, TOO. BUT EVEN IF ALL THE VACANCIES WERE FILLED AND PEOPLE SHOWED UP TO DO THEIR HARD AND FREQUENTLY UNPLEASANT WORK, THAT STILL WOULD NOT SOLVE THE UNDERSTAFFING PROBLEM. OFFICIALS SAY THEY NEED NEARLY TWICE THE NUMBER OF PEOPLE BUDGETED TO EVEN START TO HELP THE RESIDENTS TO GET BETTER. |

THE SIX-THIRTY MORNING SHIFT IS ARRIVING AT FOREST HAVEN. ONE OF THE NURSE'S AIDES LIVES IN NORTHWEST WASHINGTON, AND GOT UP AT 4 A.M. TO CATCH A BUS TO D.C. GENERAL HOSPITAL. THERE SHE BOARDED A PANEL TRUCK FOR THE 20-MILE TRIP TO LAUREL; AND SHE WON'T GET HOME AGAIN UNTIL FOUR-THIRTY IN THE AFTERNOON. SHE CLEARS ABOUT $75 A WEEK.

PINE COTTAGE IS ONE OF THE OVER-CROWDED, UNDERSTAFFED BUILDINGS HERE. THIS NIGHT TWO STAFFERS WERE IN CHARGE OF 82 SEVERELY AND PROFOUNDLY RETARDED BOYS AND YOUNG MEN. SOME NIGHTS, AND EVEN DAYS, WHEN THE RESIDENTS ARE AWAKE THERE IS ONLY ONE STAFF PERSON RESPONSIBLE FOR ALL 82—PINE IS OVERCROWDED BY 22 BOYS, ACCORDING TO FOREST HAVEN STANDARDS. BUT IT SEEMS MORE OVERCROWDED THAN THAT BY ANY REASONABLE CRITERIA.

| | |
|---|---|
| **SHOT OF RETARDED CHILD TIED TO CRIB CLOSEUP CALLUSED HAND** | THIS LITTLE BOY IS TIED IN HIS BED. OTHERS ARE KEPT IN STRAITJACKETS TO STOP THEM FROM HURTING THEMSELVES. THE HEAD NURSE SAYS THAT WITH MORE STAFF TO SUPERVISE THE CHILDREN, THIS WOULDN'T BE NECESSARY. |
| **EXTERIOR OF BUILDING, BARS AT WINDOWS** | THE HELEN CURLEY BUILDING LOOKS A LOT LIKE A PRISON. THESE CEMENT WALLS ENCLOSE A SMALL OUTDOOR RECREATION AREA. IT COST MORE THAN 3 MILLION DOLLARS AND OPENED LAST JULY. SOME EXPERTS SAY THE MONEY WOULD BE BETTER SPENT ON SMALL GROUP HOMES AND DAY CARE CENTERS IN THE CITY OF WASHINGTON. |

THIS SECTION OF THE CURLEY BUILDING IS FOR SEVERELY AND PROFOUNDLY RETARDED ACTIVE GIRLS AND WOMEN. IT'S MUCH CLEANER AND MORE MODERN THAN A FACILITY FOR MEN WITH SIMILAR PROBLEMS AT ROSEWOOD IN MARYLAND. HOWEVER, THERE IS THE SAME LACK OF PROGRAM FOR THE RESIDENTS. AND THE RESIDENTS HERE SEEM MORE BATTERED THAN THOSE AT ROSEWOOD. FOREST HAVEN OFFICIALS HAVE NO EXPLANATION FOR THIS. THEY HAVE A FEW MORE TOYS HERE AT FOREST HAVEN, THOUGH MOST IGNORE THEM. AND THE TOYS BROUGHT OUT THE DAY THE TELEVISION CAMERAS WERE THERE, WERE NEW.

THIS IS HOW THE RESIDENTS SPEND MOST OF THEIR TIME. MANY ARE NOT TOILET-TRAINED AND A NUMBER REFUSE TO KEEP THEIR CLOTHES ON. A RECREATION AIDE VISITS A FEW HOURS A WEEK. BUT THE STAFF SPENDS MOST OF ITS TIME TRYING TO KEEP THE PLACE AND THE PEOPLE CLEAN.

SMALL ROOMS IN THIS NEW BUILDING REQUIRE MORE STAFF. THERE IS NO SINGLE LARGER ROOM WHERE ALL THE RESIDENTS CAN BE HERDED AND SUPERVISED BY A SINGLE PERSON. THIS IS THE ONLY ONE OF THE 16 BUILDINGS AT FOREST HAVEN WITHOUT AN OFFICIAL STAFF SHORTAGE. BUT IT'S OBVIOUS WITH THE LACK OF A PROGRAM THAT MORE PEOPLE ARE NEEDED IF THESE VERY RETARDED PEOPLE ARE TO BE HELPED.

THE AIDES TRY TO HELP THE INMATES LEARN TO FEED THEMSELVES. BUT STILL, FEEDING TIME, AS IT'S CALLED HERE, IS A STOMACH-WRENCHING EXPERIENCE.

THE INFIRMARY DOWN THE STREET OPERATES WITH HALF THE OFFICIAL STAFF. BUT THESE PEOPLE ARE BEDRID-DEN AND NOT HARD TO CONTROL. SOME MAY NOT EVEN BE SEVERELY RETARDED. AGAIN, THERE IS NO PROGRAM, NO STIMULATION. EXPERTS SAY THESE PEOPLE, AND THE VERY ACTIVE PEOPLE IN CURLEY BUILDING, WILL ALWAYS HAVE TO BE IN INSTITUTIONS. HOWEVER, THERE IS EVIDENCE THAT WITH TRAINING PROGRAMS THEY CAN BE HELPED. BUT THERE IS NO ONE TO WORK WITH THE RESIDENTS HERE.

| SCENES OF<br>VEGETATING<br>CHILDREN<br>IN CRIBS | THE SADDEST PLACE AT FOREST HAVEN IS THE NURSERY. HERE ARE REAL LITTLE CHILDREN. FROM 6 TO 16 YEARS OLD. AGAIN, THERE IS NO PROGRAM TO HELP OR TEACH THE YOUNG CHILDREN HERE. THERE IS NO PHYSICAL THERAPY: AND CHILDREN WITH MUSCULAR PROBLEMS DETERIORATE. SOME WHO CAN NOW WALK WILL EVEN-TUALLY MOVE INTO WHEELCHAIRS UNLESS THEY CAN GET HELP. OTHERS WILL ALWAYS BE IN DIAPERS. UNLESS THEIR PARENTS TAKE THEM AWAY. OR SOME SORT OF TRAINING IS BEGUN. THEY ARE CONDEMNED TO SPEND THEIR LIVES VEGETATING AT FOREST HAVEN. AND THERE IS NO HELP FOR THEM NOW. AND THERE IS NO PLAN TO GET HELP FOR THEM. |
|---|---|
| CLOSE | CLARE CRAWFORD FOR NEWS 4<br>WASHINGTON. |

## EPISODE 5—FRIDAY

| BOGGS:<br>STUDIO | CLARE CRAWFORD AND THE NEWS 4 PROBE TEAM CONTINUE THEIR REPORT ON THE CARE AVAILABLE FOR THE MENTALLY RETARDED IN THE DISTRICT OF COLUMBIA. TONIGHT. THEY RETURN TO FOREST HAVEN. WHERE SOME RESIDENTS ARE GETTING AN ADEQUATE EDUCATION. BUT IS FOREST HAVEN. AN INSTITUTION FOR THE MEN-TALLY RETARDED. THE PLACE FOR THEM? |
|---|---|
| CRAWFORD:<br>V/O INTERIOR FOREST HAVEN<br>NURSES DISPENSING TRANQUILIZERS | OFFICIALS AT FOREST HAVEN REFUSE TO ALLOW PICTURES TO BE TAKEN OF RESIDENTS' FACES WITHOUT THE CONSENT OF THEIR PARENTS OR GUARDIANS. THEY DID NOT GIVE US THE NAMES OF THE RESIDENTS OR THEIR PARENTS. |
| | THE MOST ALARMING FACT ABOUT FOREST HAVEN IS THAT OFFICIALS SAY THAT AS MANY AS 400 RESIDENTS AND MAYBE MORE ARE TOO COMPETENT TO BE IN THIS INSTITUTION FOR THE RETARDED. IN FACT. THE 225 STUDENTS WHO ATTEND THIS SCHOOL ARE LUCKY TO BE HERE. |
| | ALL RIGHT. LET'S SPEAK UP SO WE CAN HEAR YOU. HOW MANY BOYS? |
| TEACHER:<br>SOUND ON FILM<br>CRAWFORD:<br>V/O FILM | THEY ARE LUCKIER THAN THOUSANDS OF DISTRICT PUBLIC SCHOOL STUDENTS WHO ARE RECEIVING NO EDUCATION AT ALL. FOREST HAVEN'S ACTING SUPER-INTENDENT. RIMSKY ATKINSON. SAYS THAT IF THERE WERE A SCHOOL LIKE THIS IN WASHINGTON. THESE STUDENTS COULD |

146

RETURN HOME OR LIVE IN FORSTER OR GROUP HOMES, IF THEIR PARENTS WON'T TAKE THEM.

THERE ARE PARENTS WHO REFUSE TO LET THEIR CHILDREN RETURN WHEN THEY HAVE BEEN TRAINED IN THE FEW PROGRAMS THE INSTITUTION OFFERS. AND MANY FAMILIES NEVER VISIT THEIR RELATIVES. SOME FAMILIES EVEN BECOME LOST BECAUSE OF A POOR RECORD SYSTEM.

ON THE OTHER HAND, A FEW PEOPLE PAY UP TO $17.50 A DAY TO KEEP A CHILD HERE.

IF THESE MORE COMPETENT RESIDENTS COULD FIND HOMES, IT WOULD FREE STAFF TO WORK WITH THE SEVERELY RETARDED, LIKE THE BOYS AT POPLAR COTTAGE.

**STAFF ASSISTANT:**
**(TEACHING BOYS**
**TO LACE SHOES)**

NO, THAT'S THE WRONG HOLE.

**CRAWFORD:**
**V/O SCENES OF BOYS**
**DOING PERSONAL**
**HYGIENE**

FORTY-SIX ARE IN A PROGRAM FINANCED BY THE FEDERAL GOVERNMENT. DESPITE THE USUAL FOREST HAVEN UNDERSTAF-FING AND OVERCROWDING, THE BOYS HAVE LEARNED FEEDING, TOILET, AND PERSONAL-CARE SKILLS. THE TEACHING METHOD IS CALLED CONDITIONING. EACH CORRECT ACTION IS REWARDED. IT WORKS. BUT MR. ATKINSON THINKS IT WOULD WORK BETTER WITH THE BOYS IF THERE WERE MORE STAFF. THOUGH HE'S BEEN ABLE TO RECRUIT A FEW PEOPLE SINCE HE TOOK OVER LAST FALL, THERE'S NOW NO HOPE OF GETTING ENOUGH STAFF TO RUN ANY KIND OF REAL PROGRAM FOR THE REST OF THE RESIDENTS.

HE COULD FREE PRESENT STAFF MEMBERS IF RESIDENTS WHO DON'T BELONG COULD FIND OTHER HOMES. BUT THERE'S ONLY ONE HALFWAY HOUSE AND NO GROUP HOMES AND NO WORKING FOSTER-PARENT PLACEMENT PROGRAM. SO THESE PEOPLE, WHO HAVE COMMITTED NO CRIMES, STAY IN AN INSTITUTION. AND, SADLY, SOME BECOME ADJUSTED TO THE LIMITED LIFE HERE.

SOME DO MAKE IT TO THE OUTSIDE WORLD. IT'S HARD TO GET OUT OF FOREST HAVEN BECAUSE UNTIL RECENTLY, THE ONLY WAY TO GET IN WAS BY COURT COMMITMENT. NOT LONG AGO MR. ATKINSON WAS ABLE TO GET A RESIDENT RELEASED FROM HIS COM-

MITMENT. THE RESIDENT HAD BEEN
WORKING FOR OVER A YEAR AS A CLERK
FOR THE GOVERNMENT.

**BOGGS:**
**STUDIO**

ON MONDAY, THE NEWS 4 PROBE TEAM WILL
INTERVIEW THE FOREST HAVEN
SUPERINTENDENT AND HIS BOSS, WHO DIF-
FER SERIOUSLY ON THE INSTITUTION'S
PROBLEMS. THE TEAM WILL ALSO DISCUSS
WHO IS RESPONSIBLE FOR CARING FOR
THESE PEOPLE WHO NEED SPECIAL HELP.

## EPISODE 6—MONDAY

**RINKER:**
**STUDIO**

TONIGHT CLARE CRAWFORD AND THE NEWS
4 PROBE TEAM CONTINUE THEIR REPORT
ON THE CARE AVAILABLE TO RETARDED
AND OTHER HANDICAPPED PEOPLE IN THE
DISTRICT OF COLUMBIA. THEY VISITED
WASHINGTON FAMILIES WITH RETARDED
CHILDREN, AND THE DISTRICT'S ONLY
INSTITUTION FOR THEM, FOREST HAVEN.
THEN THE PROBE TEAM FOUND OUT
WASHINGTON IS THE ONLY JURISDICTION IN
THE UNITED STATES WITH NO LAWS MEN-
TIONING SUCH PEOPLE.

**CRAWFORD:**
**CLOSEUP**

THIS MEANS RETARDED CHILDREN AND
PEOPLE WHO NEED SPECIAL HELP TO LIVE
WITH OTHER PEOPLE ARE IN A LEGAL
LIMBO. THEY ONLY GET HELP ON A CATCH-
AS-CATCH-CAN BASIS WITH NO REAL PLAN-
NING AHEAD. MOST PEOPLE DON'T GET ANY
HELP AT ALL.

**DISSOLVE TO**
**SHOTS OF GIRL**
**WATCHING TV**

FIRST THERE IS VIOLA. SHE'S 17 AND HAS
NEVER BEEN TO SCHOOL. THERE IS NO DAY-
CARE OR RECREATION PROGRAM FOR HER.
THERE IS NO COUNSELING FOR HER
MOTHER. VIOLA IS STRONGER THAN HER
MOTHER AND HER MOTHER DOESN'T KNOW
WHAT SHE CAN DO, OR WHAT'S GOING TO
HAPPEN TO VIOLA.

**SCENE OF IMMOBILE**
**CHILD**
**IN CRIB**

THERE IS DANIELLE. SHE'S 7 BUT STILL AT
INFANT LEVEL. HER LIFE EXPECTANCY IS
11, AND HER MOTHER HOPES SHE CAN TAKE
CARE OF HER UNTIL THEN. THERE IS NO
OTHER CARE FOR DANIELLE AND THERE IS
NO HELP FOR HER MOTHER.

**CRAWFORD:**
**INTERVIEW**
**SOUND ON FILM**

THIS IS DR. ESSEX NOEL. HE'S THE DIREC-
TOR OF THE DISTRICT MENTAL HEALTH
SERVICES WHICH TAKES CARE OF SOME
CHILDREN LIKE VIOLA AND DANIELLE. HE
THINKS THERE ARE PROBABLY ABOUT 24

| | |
|---|---|
| | THOUSAND RETARDED PEOPLE HERE. HE DOESN'T KNOW WHERE THEY ARE OR HOW THEY ARE GETTING ALONG. |
| DR. NOEL: | I AM SURE THAT THEY ARE NOT ALL BEING CARED FOR BY DISTRICT FACILITIES. MANY RETARDED PEOPLE ARE TAKEN CARE OF BY THEIR OWN FAMILIES. AND WE ENCOURAGE THIS. AS A MATTER OF FACT. WE THINK THIS IS THE IDEAL SITUATION. |
| CRAWFORD: | DR. NOEL. HOW DOES THE DISTRICT OF COLUMBIA RANK NATIONALLY IN ITS CARE OF THE RETARDED? |
| DR. NOEL: | WELL. THE DISTRICT OF COLUMBIA. I'M VERY HAPPY TO INFORM YOU. STANDS IN A VERY FAVORABLE POSITION IN THIS AREA. I CAN'T GIVE YOU THE EXACT FIGURES BUT WE DO HAVE ONE OF THE BETTER PROGRAMS IN THIS AREA. |
| CRAWFORD: INTERVIEW SOUND ON FILM TWO-SHOT | THIS IS RIMSKY ATKINSON. HE RUNS FOREST HAVEN AND IT'S THE DISTRICT'S ONLY REAL FACILITY FOR THE RETARDED. AND HE DOESN'T AGREE WITH HIS BOSS. DR. NOEL. THAT THINGS ARE GOOD IN THE DISTRICT FOR THE RETARDED. |
| ATKINSON: | I'M NOT SATISFIED. |
| CRAWFORD: | WHAT ARE SOME OF THE DEFICIENCIES THAT YOU HAVE DISCOVERED? |
| ATKINSON: | WELL. I DARESAY THE MOST GLARING DEFICIENCY THAT I NOTICE IS REALLY THE SHORTAGE OF STAFF HERE. WE HAVE AN ABYSMAL LACK OF STAFF. BUT ASIDE FROM MERELY THE ISSUES OF A LACK OF STAFF. ARE THE PROBLEMS OF A LACK OF PROGRAMS. FOR EXAMPLE. I SUPPOSE ONE OF THE THINGS THAT IMPRESSED ME WHEN I FIRST ARRIVED HERE WAS THE LARGE NUMBER OF PERSONS WHOM I SAW SITTING AND ROCKING. TO PUT IT BLUNTLY. |
| CRAWFORD: INTERVIEW SOUND ON FILM | THIS IS TERESA FELTON. SHE IS THE HEAD OF A CITIZEN'S TASK FORCE WHICH HAS BEEN TRYING TO IMPROVE THINGS AT FOREST HAVEN. HER DAUGHTER USED TO BE A RESIDENT THERE. |
| FELTON: | SHE'S PRESENTLY AT SAINT E'S. SHE'S UNDER RESTRAINT ORDERS RIGHT NOW. BUT THERE'S A POSSIBILITY OF HER BEING TRANSFERRED BACK TO FOREST HAVEN WITHOUT MY KNOWLEDGE. IF THE DOCTORS SEE FIT TO DO SO. |
| CRAWFORD: | DO YOU WANT TO GO BACK TO FOREST HAVEN? |

149

| | |
|---|---|
| **FELTON:** | DEFINITELY NOT. I HATE THAT PLACE AND THE WAYS THEY ABUSE MY CHILD. BY NO MEANS I DO NOT WANT HER THERE. I'D RATHER SEE HER DEAD THAN SEE HER AT FOREST HAVEN AS THE CONDITION EXISTS AT THE PRESENT TIME. |
| **CRAWFORD:** | WHAT IS THE FUTURE OF A RETARDED CHILD BORN TODAY IN THE DISTRICT OF COLUMBIA WHO WILL NEED A FULL-TIME PROGRAM TO BECOME A SELF-SUPPORTING MEMBER OF THE COMMUNITY? |
| **MAN:** | I WOULD SAY THAT THE CHANCES ARE MUCH BETTER NOW THAN THEY HAVE BEEN AT ANY TIME IN THE PAST. |
| **CRAWFORD:** | CONGRESS GIVES DR. NOEL THE MONEY TO RUN FOREST HAVEN. AND IT WOULD BE CONGRESS WHO WOULD HAVE TO VOTE MONEY FOR DAY-CARE CENTERS FOR THE RETARDED AND COUNSELING SERVICES FOR THEIR PARENTS. LAST SUMMER DR. NOEL TOLD CONGRESS HOW HE FELT THINGS WERE AT FOREST HAVEN. HE TOLD CONGRESS, "I AM HAPPY TO SAY WE ARE MOVING FORWARD VERY RAPIDLY TO MAKE THIS INTO A MUCH BETTER FACILITY AND ONE IN WHICH WE HOPE TO BE ABLE TO DEVELOP THE MAXIMUM POTENTIAL OF THE INDIVIDUALS IN THE DIRECTION OF REHABILITATION."

HE ALSO TOLD CONGRESS, WHICH GIVES HIM THE MONEY FOR SALARIES TO HIRE PEOPLE, "WE HAVE RECRUITED SO THAT OUR RATIO OF STAFF TO PATIENTS NOW IS MUCH MORE ATTRACTIVE AND IS AP-PROACHING THAT SUGGESTED BY THE AUTHORITIES."

BUT TODAY FOREST HAVEN IS STILL OVERCROWDED AND UNDERSTAFFED. AND THERE IS NO PROGRAM TO HELP MOST OF THE RESIDENTS GET BETTER. AND THERE ARE THOUSANDS OF RETARDED. NOT EVEN IN FOREST HAVEN. RECEIVING NO HELP—A CRUSHING BURDEN ON THEIR FAMILIES AND COMMUNITY.

CLARE CRAWFORD FOR NEWS 4 WASHINGTON. |
| **RINKER:**<br>**STUDIO** | TOMORROW NIGHT THE PROBE TEAM GOES TO A DISTRICT JUNIOR HIGH SCHOOL WITH A STUDENT WHO NEEDS SPECIAL EDUCATION. HE IS NOT GETTING IT. EVEN THOUGH THE BOY IS PHYSICALLY PRESENT IN THE CLASSROOM. HE IS MENTALLY ABSENT. |

# EPISODE 7—TUESDAY

**BOGGS:**
**STUDIO**
**V/O SHOT OF FILM CREW**

CLARE CRAWFORD AND THE NEWS 4 PROBE TEAM'S SCHEDULED REPORT IN THE SERIES ON THE MENTALLY RETARDED WILL NOT BE SHOWN TONIGHT. TODAY, AFTER SEEING THE SERIES, DISTRICT HUMAN RESOURCES DIRECTOR JOSEPH YELDELL ANNOUNCED THAT HE PLANS TO INVESTIGATE THE SITUATION. CLARE CRAWFORD HAS DETAILS.

**CRAWFORD:**
**INTERVIEW**
**SOUND ON FILM**

MR. YELDELL SAID THE INVESTIGATION WILL START A WEEK FROM THURSDAY AFTER HE GETS A REPORT ON HOW MUCH MONEY IS AVAILABLE TO CORRECT THE PROBLEMS BROUGHT OUT ON THE NEWS 4 SERIES. OVER THE PAST WEEK, I HAVE REPORTED THAT THERE IS NO HELP FOR PARENTS WITH RETARDED CHILDREN AND THAT THE DISTRICT'S ONLY INSTITUTION, FOREST HAVEN, IS UNDERSTAFFED AND OVERCROWDED AND HAS VIRTUALLY NO PROGRAM. YELDELL SAYS HE PLANS TO ATTACK EACH PROBLEM.

**YELDELL:**

I THINK THE SERIES HAS DONE A CREDITABLE JOB. AND WHAT WE'RE DOING SPECIFICALLY AS IT RELATES TO MENTAL HEALTH IS THAT, ONE, WE ARE MEETING WITH THE SCHOOL BOARD TO BETTER UNDERSTAND AND DEFINE THE WHOLE POPULATION OF PEOPLE IN THIS CITY WHO REQUIRE SPECIAL EDUCATION AND WHO HAVE NOT BEEN RECEIVING IT. TWO, WE HAVE EXEMPTED FOREST HAVEN FROM THE BUDGET CUT—PHASE 1. PHASE 2 BUDGET CUTS—SO THAT WE CAN STAFF THE PROGRAM UP THERE AND BEGIN TO GET ON AND DEFINE SOME BASIC KINDS OF PROGRAMS. THIRDLY, OF COURSE, WE HAVE MADE THE FOREST HAVEN SITUATION A TOP-PRIORITY ITEM, NOT JUST FOR MENTAL HEALTH BUT FOR THE DEPARTMENT OF HUMAN RESOURCES, WHICH MEANS THAT I WILL BE LOOKING ACROSS THE BOARD AT RESOURCES THAT CAN BE PUT INTO FOREST HAVEN TO BEGIN TO SOLVE THE PROBLEM THERE.

MY ATTENTION WAS DRAWN TO IT BY THE SUITS THAT HAVE BEEN FILED BY PARENTS OF CHILDREN WHO HAD BEEN BURNED AT FOREST HAVEN. IN WATCHING THE SERIES AND, OF COURSE, AFTER THE VISIT THAT I MADE OUT TO FOREST HAVEN WITH YOU, I BECAME ACUTELY AWARE THAT IT'S PART OF A LARGER PROBLEM AND THAT IS OF

|  | PROVIDING THE KIND OF CARE AND EDUCATION FOR THESE CHILDREN AND ADULTS. IN SOME CASES. THAT JUST HASN'T BEEN THE PATTERN IN THE DISTRICT OF COLUMBIA. |
| --- | --- |
| CRAWFORD: | YELDELL SAID HE ALSO PLANS TO LIFT THE JOB FREEZE AT FOREST HAVEN AND HE EXPECTS THE FULL COOPERATION OF EVERYONE IN HIS DEPARTMENT. INCLUDING MENTAL HEALTH DIRECTOR DOCTOR ESSEX NOEL. WHO LAST NIGHT ON NEWS 4 SAID HE FELT THE DISTRICT'S PROGRAM WAS ONE OF THE BEST IN THE AREA. |
| CLOSE | CLARE CRAWFORD FOR NEW 4 WASHINGTON. |

## EPISODE 8—WEDNESDAY

| CRAWFORD: V/O SHOTS OF CHILDREN IN A WOODWORKING SHOP, SEWING CLASS AND OTHER ACTIVITIES | THERE ARE AT LEAST 15 THOUSAND CHILDREN WHO ARE NOT GETTING HELP IN THE SCHOOL SYSTEM: CHILDREN WHOSE FUTURE IS NOT VEGETATING IN AN INSTITUTION FOR THE MENTALLY RETARDED BUT WHO FACE A FUTURE EVEN MORE BLEAK. THEY UNDERSTAND ENOUGH TO KNOW THEY DON'T UNDERSTAND. THEY GET BORED AND. IF THEY'RE ACTIVE. CAUSE TROUBLE. FIRST DISRUPTING THE SCHOOL AND LATER DISRUPTING THE COMMUNITY. IF THEY ARE QUIET THEY DON'T GET ATTENTION OR HELP AND THEY DON'T GET JOBS WHEN THEY LEAVE SCHOOL. |
| --- | --- |
| BOY WORKING ON WOOD PROJECT IN CLASS | THESE CHILDREN DON'T LOOK DIFFERENT. THIS YOUNG MAN IS 14. HE'S ON HIS WAY TO SCHOOL. AS HE'S DONE ALMOST EVERY DAY FOR 8 YEARS. BUT IT IS THE WRONG SCHOOL. HE SHOULD BE IN A PRIVATE SPECIAL SCHOOL. HE IS ONE OF 574 STUDENTS ON THE WAITING LIST FOR A TUITION GRANT TO A SPECIAL SCHOOL. AND THOUGH HE CAN BARELY READ. WRITE. OR COUNT. SCHOOL OFFICIALS DIDN'T TELL HIS MOTHER HE NEEDED SPECIAL HELP UNTIL LAST YEAR. |
| BOY THUMBING THROUGH BOOK | HE'S OFFICIALLY IN THE SEVENTH GRADE. HIS SHOP TEACHER SAID HE HASN'T MADE ANYTHING IN CLASS THIS YEAR. HE JUST SPENDS EVERY DAY THUMBING THROUGH BOOKS OR STANDING AROUND. |
| SCENES OF CHILDREN IN CLASSES | THE SCHOOL SYSTEM COUNTS ALMOST 5 THOUSAND STUDENTS AS ATTENDING SPECIAL CLASSES. BUT NOT EVEN HALF |

THAT NUMBER ARE IN A FULL-TIME PROGRAM. MOST ARE IN A CLASS. LIKE THIS STUDENT. WHICH GIVES HIM 1 HOUR A DAY IN A SMALL GROUP. HERE THE TEACHER TRIES TO HELP THE STUDENTS WITH EVERYDAY PROBLEMS LIKE COUNTING MONEY. BUT THIS IS ALMOST IMPOSSIBLE TO DO IN AN HOUR A DAY WITH A PUPIL WHO FUNCTIONS AT ABOUT A FIRST-GRADE LEVEL. I ASKED THIS YOUNGSTER'S MOTHER HOW WELL HE READS.

**MOTHER: INTERVIEW SOUND ON FILM**   HE'S VERY SLOW. VERY SLOW.

**CRAWFORD:**   WHAT CAN HE READ?

**MOTHER:**   NOTHING MUCH. HE CAN'T READ. BUT HE TRIES TO...I MEANS I TRY TO TEACH HIM DIFFERENT WORDS AND HE SEEMS TO GET CONFUSED OR SOMETHING.

**CRAWFORD:**   HOW IS HIS MATH?

**MOTHER:**   HE DOESN'T KNOW ANYTHING ABOUT ARITHMETIC.

**CRAWFORD:**   WHAT DO YOU THINK THE FUTURE FOR HIM IS?

**MOTHER:**   I REALLY DON'T KNOW.

**CRAWFORD:**   CAN YOU THINK OF ANY JOB HE MIGHT BE ABLE TO HOLD DOWN?

**MOTHER:**   TO TELL YOU THE TRUTH. I DON'T THINK HE'LL BE ABLE TO HOLD ANY.

**CRAWFORD:**   WHO IS GOING TO TAKE CARE OF HIM?

**MOTHER:**   THAT'S A PROBLEM. TOO. HIS FATHER WILL HAVE TO TAKE CARE OF HIM—UNTIL HE GETS TO A CERTAIN AGE. ANYWAY. BUT I THINK HE WILL HELP HIM AS MUCH AS HE CAN. AS LONG AS HE HAS TO. ANYWAY. I DON'T THINK HE WOULD JUST PUT HIM OUT. OR ANYTHING. YOU KNOW. HE WOULDN'T BE ABLE TO MAKE IT ON HIS OWN.

**CRAWFORD:**

**CLOSEUP**   IT'S NOT COMPLETELY CLEAR WHY THE DISTRICT'S SPECIAL EDUCATION SYSTEM IS SO INADEQUATE. A REPORT IN DECEMBER BY A SCHOOL SYSTEM TASK FORCE SAID THAT PARENTS HAVING TO CONTINUALLY COMPETE FOR TUITION AND HELP FOR THEIR CHILDREN WAS AN UNENDING OBSCENE NIGHTMARE.

**CLOSE**   CLARE CRAWFORD FOR NEWS 4 WASHINGTON.

# PERCEPTIVE PHOTOGRAPHY

Charles (Chuck) Fekete is a cameraman for WRC-TV who is making the crossover from film to videotape. He spent 9 years as a still and motion picture photographer for the United States Air Force. Then he served a 4-year apprenticeship as an assistant TV cameraman before coming to WRC-TV.

The basic difference between shooting news footage and a mini-documentary series, according to Fekete, is that for straight news the event determines what you're going to film, whereas for a mini-documentary, preplanning is involved. However, he points out, there is much more extensive planning for a full-length documentary. Also, mini-documentary episodes are comparatively brief, limiting creativity with your camera.

In the final chapter, devoted to a survey of television stations around the country, it is noted that many stations cover the same topics. Obviously, many communities face similar problems. And, if a titillating subject produces a higher rating for a TV station, a competing station will attempt to meet the competition with a similar treatment. Therefore, it is not unusual to find that each of the Washington, D.C. TV stations has presented mini-documentaries on prostitution.

Like the other photographers at competing stations, the WRC-TV cameraman has had to resort to undercover techniques for his mini-documentary series on prostitution. Fekete states that he would "shoot from inside a car. I would get in the back of the car and shoot through open windows. I would try to get the nighttime effect. I would try to get people silhouetted against store windows to give me an interesting type of exposure."

Fekete uses the CP-16, a single-system sound camera for both undercover and normal shooting of news events. At times, highly specialized equipment has to be employed. For example, in the mini-documentary series, *Uncle Sam is a Slumlord*, we have noted that in order to obtain shots of a rat coming out of a hole in one of the slum apartments, an image intensifier, similar to a nightscope on a rifle, was used. That produced a greenish film rather than true color, but it did afford an image.

For mini-documentaries, Fekete uses a double system and always has a sound technician with him. In this respect, he is in complete agreement with his colleagues at the other Washington stations, who believe that a good sound man frees the photographer to concentrate on the filming. "You have control over the sound and what it is you want but you don't *have* to use a sound man. It's a visual medium and it's the photographer who is conveying the visual impact and he has to be free to do that."

There is excellent rapport between cameraman and sound man, each intent on a highly satisfactory product and each searching for the best effect. In the mini-documentary series on the mentally retarded, it was the studio technician who came upon an inmate of the institution who made some strikingly dramatic remarks. The sound man immediately pointed out the potential scene and the photographer focused his camera on the youngster to obtain an image as effective as the audio. "You don't disregard the impact of the spoken word," Fekete says, "but if you don't have the picture, you have radio." The key word is relevancy: how relevant is the sound to the picture, and the picture to the sound?

Fekete also agrees that no photographer likes to shoot talking heads. Nevertheless, there are instances when a talking head may be essential. If a sequence in a mini-documentary series concerned unsanitary conditions in a restaurant, it might be necessary to film a closeup interview with the manager who had insisted that the complaints were unjustified. Cutaways can be employed but again they should be relevant to the subject the interviewee is discussing.

At WRC-TV, the cameraman, usually, is not present during the early planning sessions. He will go out on location with the reporter or the producer. By that time, the story line is all set. The next step is to decide what type of photography is required. There is seldom a cued script for shooting sequences for a mini-documentary series. There is a basic idea and a story outline, but once on location, ideas change—scenes do not line up the way they have been visualized originally.

Flexibility is a key element of the mini-documentary crew: the ability to adapt to rapidly changing situations and the capacity to integrate changing ideas into the structure of the mini-documentary series. As Fekete commented, "It's not a Hollywood production where you control everything. You may start out doing one thing and then end up doing something entirely different."

In exploring Fekete's concept of the role of the cameraman in relation to mini-documentaries, his reaction was that he had always thought of himself as a creative photographer, not as a journalist. But his practical experience has since changed his thinking. He has witnessed and photographed the riots and the demonstrations in the nation's capital. He discovered then that he was a photo-journalist. "It was more than the photographer being out on the street by himself, and it was his own judgment in getting the story."

The structure of the mini-documentary series, as we have reiterated, calls for each episode to be complete in itself. It can present a problem to the cameraman and the film editor. "The danger," Fekete points out, "is that sometimes you have a

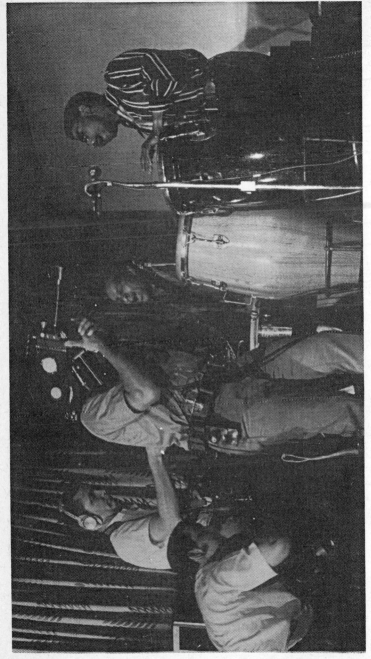

Cameraman Fekete and sound men "join the combo" for a closeup.

Contemporary videotape equipment is just now showing up at metropolitan TV news departments. (A) Most small videotape cameras require tripods. Three different size color cameras are shown.

tendency to concentrate on sensational scenes for the ending of each episode. You do that in order to heighten people's interest and have them tune in the following day. The danger in this is that you might defeat your purpose in what you're trying to say. You can oversensationalize.'' Ideally, the cameraman should film the mini-documentary series in the context of its overall theme rather than in terms of single episodes.

(B) Small portable color camera with shoulder brace. Cassette recorder and camera control unit are at cameraman's feet.

Fekete is working with both film and videotape. He sees very little difference between the two media as far as the end result is concerned. He admits, however, that videotape still has a long way to go. The current video equipment is much bulkier and heavier than present-day film equipment. "Film has reached a point where, literally, you can stand on your head and capture a scene." Video constricts the cameraman to limited angles. Tripods are necessary. The lightweight film camera definitely has its advantages.

Still, he does not agree with some of his colleagues that videotape is best utilized for the immediacy of news events and that film is more satisfactory for documentaries. He has used videotape for documentaries. He admits that editors claim they have more problems with videotape than film, but he believes these technical problems will be overcome. From a budgetary standpoint, videotape has a decided advantage on location. You can view your photography immediately and avoid expensive return trips to the scene of the action.

The basic advice Fekete has for students of cinematography is to know the photographic equipment so thoroughly that they need not be concerned about such technical requirements as, for example, exposure. Those technical essentials should become second nature to the photographer. He or she should be free to

(C) Helical VTR with color adaptor records and plays back on batteries.

concentrate on creativity. In filming mini-documentary series, all types of situations will arise. The photographer must not be intimidated by either situations or participants. "Once you get behind that camera, you have to completely block out any emotions you have and concentrate on the job you're doing. You must know your subject. Don't take a shot just because it's a pretty shot. You have to know it's relevant."

"Any creative artist," Fekete added, "has a responsibility toward the audience to whom he's going to present his material." There are times when the photographer can permit himself or herself to be experimental "but if you're trying to be creative and communicative, you should present your material in such a way that people can readily understand what it is you're trying to say."

## THE CREATIVE FILM EDITOR

John Long, chief film editor for WRC-TV, has been with the station and the NBC network for fifteen years. He has garnered a wealth of experience. He is an innovator and a creative editor. He has worked on documentaries with one of the most sensitive and inspired writers, Lou Hazam, and with one of the finest producers, Ted Yates (who, unfortunately, was killed during the Six-Day War in the Middle East).

If our readers will allow, we are going to invoke an ancient admonition: "Speak for yourself, John." From his absorbing discourse on film editing, particularly in relation to the mini-documentary, we have culled the essence of his commentary; some of his statements are paraphrased, much of what you will read in the following pages are his own words.

Sociologists and psychologists say you're a product of your environment. I believe it. I grew up in television, as it were, working closely with documentary writers and producers. I learned a great deal from them and I have come to think in documentary terms. When I joined the news department at WRC-TV, I felt the newscasts needed more production: more than just sound effects and voice-over narration. I introduced double-system editing; in which film and magnetic sound are taken simultaneously on camera and recorder. I used more actualities, more music. That's what the double system allowed me to do.

Reporting is always more effective when you can pick up right from the location where the event is occurring. People are more animated during the action than after the fact. I always consider I can, as a film editor, make the sequence more interesting to the viewer. With double-system editing, I can bring in all the background sound. I can use music to the fullest extent.

When the scene cannot be done live, I can put a reporter in a booth and project the film. If he is a true journalist, he will become animated by seeing the film.

Our *probe* unit was organized in 1969 for the production of mini-documentaries. It was an immediate success. It concerned itself with in-depth investigative reporting. For instance, when we presented a mini-documentary on evictions, we reported all sides: the evicted people, the landlord, the legal aspects. In the mini-documentary on food stamps, we also covered all angles: the men and women who receive food stamps, the supermarkets where they buy food, the farmers who raise the food, the welfare issue. Although food stamps are a topic of national interest, we focused on one local area: Washington County, Maryland.

John Long thinks of a mini-documentary as "dealing with a problem and then concluding with a sequence on what, if anything, is going to be done about that problem." Of course, there isn't always a solution, as John notes:

> Many times we are just posing the problem. Also, I would say that about 80% of the time we have returned to the subject to see what the situation is. There is always so much to say about these community problems.
>
> I know that not everybody watches every episode, so I always start each episode with a brief film sequence from the preceding episode. In that respect, each segment should have a beginning, a middle, and an end. However, the viewing audience is much more sophisticated today. You don't need to spend a great deal of time telling them what they saw.

Practically everyone at WRC-TV suggests ideas for mini-documentaries, Long says. The crew just recently began work on a mini-documentary that was suggested by a station electrician.

Not all good ideas can be followed up; some are simply too costly to develop. And sometimes there are other problems:

> We are planning to do a mini-documentary on the Eagle Squadron, an all-black unit that fought in World War II. Little or nothing is known about the unit. Very little footage exists. But we have interviewed some of the old squadron fighter pilots. They are very powerful interviews. I know they will carry the program, even without many visuals. It will be a mini-documentary that is not only entertaining but educational. That's what I believe a mini-documentary should be—*entertaining* and *educational*.

Long often goes out with film crews, does all his own editing. In his career, he's edited as may as 3000 mini-documentary episodes and gone through millions of feet of film.

> I try to bring all my creative instincts to bear on every program... Technique has become subconscious with me: my conscious is busy evaluating the content. I work as a team with the reporter, the producer, the cameraman, the sound man. We all try to get the best results we can, not the most sensational but the most effective. There is a creativity to sound, too. A good sound man can greatly enhance a mini-documentary.

Experimentation is something Long believes in. Some editors, he says, feel that they can gain a great deal by studying feature films. But Long says television editing is a great deal more difficult. There is no script telling what shots and what sound to use. It's a matter of "feeling" one's way from frame to frame.

The writer may come to me and say he's working on a script and needs some specific footage. I may not have the footage. I will say to the writer, here is what I can give you for the most impact. Then the writer faces a challenge to make the scene as effective as possible based on the footage available. On the other hand, the writer or writer reporter faces difficulties in having a wealth of material which must be compressed within a brief time. As a film editor, I face an analogous situation when I have some beautiful footage that I would love to use but can't when I know they would not enhance the editorial value of the story.

It is important that nothing in the visual distract the viewer from the content of the mini-documentary. A bad cut, raucous sound, poorly recorded narration—these are elements that will disturb the viewer. The editorial and the visual, Long feels, must mesh as smoothly as a $200,000 commercial.

I believe, as I have said, that a film editor should be knowledgeable about the subject matter. For example, if I were working on a film about sky-diving and decided on a wide shot which did not show the diver pulling his ripcord, I can assure you the station would get a hundred calls from sky-divers protesting that the man did not pull his ripcord. We'd be asked, don't you people know his parachute won't open otherwise?

There is not always the time do as much research for a mini-documentary as for a full-length documentary. Yet the impact, the honesty must be there. Long believes that a reporter has to be as honest with his audience as a doctor with his patients—especially when surveys show that more people watch television than read newspapers. They depend on television for news. And the qualities of integrity and truth are required of the film editor as much as they are of the reporter:

Let's go back to the riots of 1968. There were bloody confrontations—head bashings. Suppose we shot 2000 feet of film and we only have a minute-and-a-half on the air. If our cameras were at 5 locations and each one of those locations was the scene of a violent confrontation, then it would look like a blood bath to the audience. In order to keep myself aware of the entire situation, I read the wire copy, I listen to radio reports, I talk to the cameramen who shot the footage. In that way I can visualize how to put my film together without bias.

With regard to videotape versus film, John Long firmly believes that tape is not as flexible as film:

People in the industry will point out that film has to be processed, which generally takes about 40 minutes. The fact is, however, you can learn to look at film at a very high speed. You cannot look at tape at high speed. You cannot do double-system editing with tape. Also, let us suppose that station A uses a film camera and station B a tape camera. Station B may get its tape footage back to the studio in quicker time than the film. But I can assure you that when I, as a film editor, present my sequence on the air, I will be able to show 60 shots to the tape's 20. I will be able to bring to my viewers a mixed track animated with actualities.

In the future, Long says, tape may become more flexible and film ultimately will be eliminated. Management tends to look at

Moviola's new film editor is quite a contrast to the small squint boxes still in use at many stations.

Helical VTR with editing capability.

the situation from an economic view: no processing is necessary, so the number of editors can be decreased. Tape does unquestionably have a great potential for immediate feedback and for some types of location shots. And the fact is that more and more television stations are installing tape equipment. Perhaps, Long says. it will be the wave of the future.

# Chapter 6

# The Mini-Documentary Approach of CBS Affiliate WTOP- TV

WTOP-TV in Washington, D.C. is affiliated with the Columbia Broadcasting System and owned by the *Washington Post*. Its news department is very active in the production of mini-documentaries. To John Baker, executive producer, the mini-documentaries are as essential to a newscast as the traditional weather and sports, and he believes news programs would lose much of their flavor and authority without the mini-documentary.

Although full-length documentaries are critically well received, Baker states they do not reach as large an audience as the mini-documentaries. "You preempt a network program that has a 20 rating to put on a local documentary that gets a 5 rating. Any newscast would double or triple that rating." A more comprehensive public service is performed, therefore, by the mini-documentary precisely because it reaches a larger segment of the community. Another factor is that a local station, except in rare instances, cannot compete with a network in documentary production. As far as a mini-documentary series is concerned, the public is apt to judge it more by content than production values.

Like other television stations, WTOP-TV receives suggestions for mini-documentaries from many sources: staff reporters, the news director, the managing editor, the viewing audience. Sometimes a single-shot news feature might possess the elements for a series. WTOP-TV mini-documentaries are not an extension of the station's editorial policy. Often editorials stem from an investigative series.

The station has had excellent viewer response to its mini-documentaries. When a troublesome situation is explored, many calls come in from people who want to help. And the mini-documentaries have resulted in specific action; for example, the series on outdated drugs and baby foods prompted additional regulatory activities by the agencies concerned.

Have sponsors brought pressure to bear when their products are involved? No sponsor, Baker asserts, believes he could really influence a controversial mini-documentary. If the sponsor or its agency bring up the issue to a time salesman, his response would simply be that he could not interfere with the news department.

Although Baker is not arbitrary about the time length of mini-documentary episodes, he does feel that anything over 3 or 4 minutes, unless emotionally powerful, is too long. He believes that if you have to go into greater length, you might as well develop a half-hour documentary.

Some form of recapitulation is used to introduce each episode, but the episode must be able to stand by itself, possess its own beginning, middle, and end. The subject dictates the type of visuals. They should be exciting and dramatic, whenever possible, but Baker insists that substance must not be sacrificed for visual impact.

There is no restrictive deadline to hamper the production of the mini-documentary. It depends on the complexity of the subject and the expertise of the reporter. At times, a field producer accompanies the crew but often the reporter serves also as producer/director.

Like his colleagues, Baker points out the the mini-documentaries have been produced for many years. They were developed because station management urged that if a community problem was important enough, it ought to be presented at optimum viewing time. Or a newsman insisted that the subject could not be fully portrayed as a single-shot feature. After one or two mini-documentaries were produced and received widespread response, the tendency was to incorporate them as a continuing element of the newscast. It is the old adage that nothing succeeds like success. Actually, the presentation of television newscasts has changed dramatically in the past decade.

Baker is of the opinion that turning a 5- or 6-part series into a half-hour documentary does not work out too well. And neither would the reverse, that is, filming a half-hour or hour documentary and dividing it into segments. He asserts that production of mini-documentaries is becoming more sophisticated; eventually they will be much more impressive and have even greater impact.

But—and other news directors have made the same observation—when students who have majored in broadcasting apply for a position and are asked what they would most like to do, the response is invariably: "Produce award-winning documentaries." They are referring, of course, to the half-hour or hour documentary, the elite programing format of broadcasting. It is natural for young people to be idealistic and to want to become part of an endeavor that may be the means or a catalyst for changing existing conditions. The mini-documentary, particularly the investigative report, does afford such an opportunity.

## REPORTING

Jim Michie, as an outstanding reporter for WTOP-TV and producer of many first-rate, hard-hitting mini-documentaries, preferred to be his own producer. And most of the topics for his series were his own suggestions. Usually, he submitted 5 or 10 ideas and then did some preliminary research to determine the feasibility of the investigation. "You do not punch a time clock as a reporter," he says. "Many times your contacts are made at night or over weekends. You have to build up sources of information. After a while you find these sources call you about stories."

For his mini-documentary series on land investment, *Only One Hour from the Beltway*, Michie began his research at the Department of Housing and Urban Development (HUD). He went to the Office of Interstate Land Sales and searched through its files. There were numerous complaints and he learned that the office had too few personnel to handle adequately the volume of grievances. But the number of disgruntled and discouraged land buyers was enough to let Michie know he was onto a problem that needed airing.

Land sales for vacation sites is a nationwide industry and the subject is of national interest, but Michie concentrated on land buyers who resided in the Washington metropolitan area, which gave the series its local flavor. He was fortunate that he could team up with his wife and in this way carry on field research in the guise of a couple interested in a land purchase. They found that some salesmen were forthright but others were uninformed or given to exaggeration and half-truths in order to force a sale. To be absolutely certain they were not going to misquote anyone, Michie and his wife carried concealed tape recorders.

The reporter called several complainants and made arrangements to interview them. With his cameraman and sound technician, he accompanied one of the unhappy families to their site so he could examine the situation first-hand. When the camera was set up, a salesman attempted to prevent them from filming, at which point Michie recorded a statement to the effect that he was being harassed. The salesman hastily conferred with the project manager and Michie was permitted to continue his filming. He offered the manager an opportunity to rebut.

On other trips to land development areas, Michie took with him copies of the prospectus which was on file at HUD. He found that very often the prospectus differed widely from the promises the salesmen were making. This time his cameraman was taking stills which enabled Michie to determine the visuals he wanted. He was, perforce, encountering opposition to filming on site. He overcame that by renting an airplane and having his crew shoot aerial footage.

You can surmise from the above that the production of this mini-documentary series was costly. However, WTOP-TV is a firm believer in public service. Countless thousands of families are interested in vacation or home building sites and many of them invested their life's savings. *Only One Hour from the Beltway* was bound to evoke wide audience response and it did. The WTOP switchboard was flooded with calls. Michie mailed over a hundred transcripts. And it was not long after the series was broadcast that the HUD office stepped up its public information programs and increased the Land Sales Registration staff.

Any legal problems involved in the presentation of this mini-documentary series, particularly concerning statements by salesmen and land developers, were checked out with the station's attorneys. Since the series was broadcast as Michie had planned it, there were no legal stumbling blocks, and no repercussions.

From the production standpoint, each episode of this 5-part series ran about 4¼ minutes and the series was broadcast on a somewhat once-weekly basis rather than a daily schedule. We say somewhat because even the weekly schedule varied. The first two episodes were aired during the Monday evening newscasts—a week apart. Episodes 3 and 4 aired on Wednesday and Friday of the same week, and episode 5 on a Monday evening a week later.

Now, for study purposes, we are reproducing part 1 and part 4 of *Only One Hour from the Beltway*.

## PART 1

| INTRODUCTION ANCHORMAN: STUDIO | SPRING IS THE SEASON OF RENEWAL, WITH FLOWERS, TREES, AND ALL THAT. BUT IT ALSO MEANS THE RENEWAL OF SALES CAMPAIGNS BY LAND DEVELOPERS. |
|---|---|

| | |
|---|---|
| **MUSIC OVER SILENT FILM SCENES OF MOUNTAINS, FORESTS, OCEANSIDE** | FAMILIES IN THE WASHINGTON AREA AND ACROSS THE NATION ARE BEGINNING TO RECEIVE PHONE CALLS AND MAILINGS INVITING THEM TO "BUY A PIECE OF AMERICA." |
| | EYEWITNESS NEWS CORRESPONDENT JIM MICHIE BEGINS A SERIES OF REPORTS TONIGHT ON THE PITFALLS OF BUYING VACATION LAND. IT'S ENTITLED "ONLY ONE HOUR FROM THE BELTWAY." |
| **SEGMENT OF SALESMAN'S PITCH TO PROSPECTIVE LAND BUYERS: SHOT OF FAMILY ON CLIFFSIDE** | WHAT'S GOING TO HAPPEN DOWN IN HERE IS THIS IS DROPPING, AND AS IT DROPS, DROPS INTO YOUR SHUFFLE BOARD AREA, YOUR BARBECUE PIT, AND YOUR SNACK BAR, WHICH WILL BE RIGHT… |
| **MICHIE:** | IMAGINATION IS WHAT MOST LAND DEVELOPMENT SALESMEN REQUIRE OF THE BUYER. THE LAKE AND SANDY BEACH AREN'T THERE YET. NEITHER IS THE MARINA NOR THE UTILITY HOOKUPS. BUT DREAMS ARE BUILT ON IMAGINATION. THE CITY DWELLER WANTS TO GET AWAY FROM IT ALL. THE RETIREE WANTS A PLACE TO RELAX IN THE SUN. THE INVESTOR IS LOOKING FOR HIS CHANCE OF A LIFETIME. |
| **V/O MONTAGE OF FREE-GIFT ADS** | |
| | THE LAND SALES INDUSTRY IS A MULTIBILLION-DOLLAR BUSINESS AND STILL GROWING. THE INDUSTRY IS SO COMPETITIVE THAT MOST DEVELOPERS OFFER PROSPECTIVE LAND BUYERS SOMETHING FOR NOTHING—FREE GIFTS. ALL YOU HAVE TO DO IS LISTEN TO THE SALES PITCH. |
| | BUT IF THE DEVELOPER IS TO STAY IN BUSINESS, HE MUST SELL THE LAND. LOTS COME IN ALL SHAPES, SIZES, AND SOMETIMES, AS I DISCOVERED, ON STEEP HILLSIDES. AS IN EVERY OTHER BUSINESS, SOME DEVELOPERS ARE MORE HONEST THAN OTHERS. SOME DON'T OR CAN'T MAKE GOOD ON THEIR PROMISES OF LAKES, GOOD ROADS, AND GOLF COURSES. AND THERE IS LITTLE PROTECTION FOR THE BUYER. |
| | THE DEVELOPER MAY ADVERTISE LOW-PRICED LOTS AS SUITABLE FOR BUILDING A VACATION HOME. THAT WAS THE CASE WITH THIS LOT WHICH I INSPECTED AS A PROSPECTIVE BUYER. |
| **AUDIO SEGMENT OF SALESMAN'S PITCH:** | SEVERAL GOOD PIECES, I THINK, ARE FOR PEOPLE WHO WANT TO CAMP. YOU KNOW, |

| | |
|---|---|
| **SHOTS OF MICHIE CLIMBING CLIFFSIDE** | AGAIN BECAUSE I ASSUME YOU'RE A CAMPER. YOU'RE NOT ONE OF THESE GUYS THAT WANTS A POOL TABLE. YOU KNOW, THE PERFECTLY FLAT PIECE THAT YOU CAN GET RIGHT IN THE CENTER OF... |
| **MICHIE:** | NO. NO. |
| **LAND BUYER 1: SOUND ON FILM SHOTS OF BUYER LOOKING OVER LAND SITE** | IF I HAD KNOWN WHEN WE CAME DOWN HERE WHAT KIND OF A PLACE THIS WAS AND WAS GOING TO TAKE THAT LONG, WE WOULD HAVE WAITED AND THOUGHT ABOUT IT TWICE BEFORE WE SIGNED ON THE LINE. I'D DO JUST WHAT I SAID: I'D LIKE TO GET RID OF IT. |
| **LAND BUYER 2:** | THE ROADS ARE SO BAD HERE. |
| **MICHIE:** | THE ROADS? |
| **LAND BUYER 2: SHOTS OF ROADS** | THEY'RE JUST FULL OF HOLES. AND THE MAN WHEN WE BOUGHT THE LAND FROM HIM, HE PROMISED HE'D TAKE CARE OF IT WITH STONES AND FIX THE HOLES AND ALL, WHICH HE DIDN'T. |
| **LAND BUYER 3: FILM OF WOMAN ON HER LOT; SHOTS OF MOBILE HOME AND BEACH** | WE WERE ALSO TO GET A SANDY BEACH AND THEY CAME IN AND PUT DOWN A LITTLE SAND ON THE BANK OF THE LAKE AND THAT WAS CALLED A SANDY BEACH. THAT'S ALL THEY DID. AND IN A LITTLE WHILE THE GRASS HAD GROWN RIGHT UP THROUGH THE SAND. |
| **MICHIE: V/O EXTERIOR OF HUD BUILDING DISSOLVE TO INTERIOR SHOWING OFFICES WITH DESKS STACKED HIGH WITH PAPERS** | WHO IS RESPONSIBLE FOR GIVING SOME PROTECTION TO THE PROSPECTIVE LAND BUYER? IT'S THE OFFICE OF INTERSTATE LAND SALES REGISTRATION, AND THAT OFFICE HAS A STAFF OF ONLY 5 PEOPLE TO DEAL WITH THOUSANDS OF LAND DEVELOPERS AND STACKS OF COMPLAINTS. |
| | I ASKED REX GLASPEY, WHO HEADS THE ENFORCEMENT SECTION, WHETHER HE IS ABLE TO DO AN ADEQUATE JOB. |
| **REX GLASPEY: SOUND ON FILM** | ABSOLUTELY NOT. THERE IS TOO MUCH WORK COMING INTO THE OFFICE FOR US TO HANDLE. I HAVE ONE PERSON WORKING FOR ME. |
| **MICHIE:** | YOU SAY THERE ARE ONLY TWO PEOPLE— YOU AND ANOTHER PERSON—TO TAKE CARE OF THE ENTIRE NATION? |
| **GLASPEY:** | AND FOREIGN COUNTRIES. I'VE BEEN WORKING ON ONE RECENTLY IN ISRAEL. |
| **RAYMOND WALSH: (CHIEF OF COMPLAINTS SECTION)** | THE FILES ARE IN PRETTY BAD SHAPE. THERE ARE DOCUMENTS MISSING WE DON'T KNOW WHETHER WE HAD IN THE FIRST PLACE. I SUSPECT THAT WITH THE VOLUME |

|  |  |
|---|---|
| | OF FILES THAT WE HAVE. THAT THEY NEVER CAME IN. WE NEVER HAD THE DOCUMENT. |
| MICHIE: | AND SO WHAT'S GOING TO HAPPEN? |
| WALSH: | I DON'T THINK I'M THE ONE TO ANSWER THAT. I KNOW THAT MY DESK IS JUST PILED HIGH WITH LETTERS FROM PEOPLE WHO WRITE IN AND SAY WE HAVEN'T HEARD FROM YOU. WE NEVER GOT YOUR LETTER. WE WROTE YOU THREE TIMES AND WE STILL HAVEN'T HEARD ANYTHING. ETC. |
| SALESMAN'S PITCH: SLIDES OF LAND WITH MOVEMENT SIMULATION | YOU KNOW THIS TYPE OF PROPERTY. IF YOU'VE BEEN TO RECREATIONAL DEVELOPMENTS BEFORE. JIM. YOU'VE BEEN BEAT TO DEATH. AND IT'S—WELL. I WON'T EVEN SAY IT. THERE'S A LADY IN THE CAR. BUT I'LL TELL YOU WHAT THE LAND INDUSTRY IS KNOWN AS. |
| MICHIE: | WHAT'S THAT? |
| SALESMAN: | IT'S THE DIRTIEST INDUSTRY THAT YOU CAN FIND TODAY. BECAUSE SO MANY PEOPLE IN IT WOULD SIT HERE AND LIE TO YOU. TELL YOU THIS. THAT. AND THE OTHER. JUST TO SELL YOU A PIECE OF PROPERTY. |
| MICHIE: V/O SHOTS OF COUPLE AT DEVELOPMENT EXAMINING LOT | THIS COUPLE WOULD AGREE WITH THAT LAND SALESMAN'S COMMENT. IN FUTURE REPORTS. THEY'LL TELL OF THEIR DISSATISFACTION WITH A DEVELOPER AND WITH THE OFFICE OF INTERSTATE LAND SALES. WE'LL EXAMINE DEVELOPMENTS THAT HAVE HAD PROBLEMS IN DELIVERY ON PROMISES. THE LACK OF PROTECTION FOR THE LAND BUYER IN SPITE OF A 4-YEAR-OLD FEDERAL LAW. AND WE'LL MAKE SUGGESTIONS ON WHAT THE PROSPECTIVE LAND BUYER CAN DO TO PROTECT HIMSELF. |
| CLOSE: | THIS IS JIM MICHIE. EYEWITNESS NEWS. |

## PART 4

|  |  |
|---|---|
| INTRODUCTION ANCHORMAN: STUDIO | OVER THE PAST TWO WEEKS. EYEWITNESS NEWS HAS BEEN RUNNING A SERIES OF STORIES ENTITLED. "ONLY ONE HOUR FROM THE BELTWAY.'' TONIGHT. CORRESPONDENT JIM MICHIE HAS HIS FOURTH REPORT. IT'S ABOUT A FEDERAL AGENCY'S INABILITY TO ADEQUATELY POLICE THE MULTIBILLION-DOLLAR VACATION LAND INDUSTRY. AND IT'S ABOUT A VACATION LAND DEVELOPMENT THAT'S ACTUALLY 2 OR 3 HOURS FROM THE BELTWAY. |

| | |
|---|---|
| **SALESMAN:**<br>**AUDIO SEGMENT**<br>**AERIAL FOOTAGE OF**<br>**DEVELOPMENT** | EVERYBODY WANTS TO OWN A PIECE OF AMERICA. BUT YOU KNOW WHAT YOUR PRO RATA SHARE WOULD BE IF THEY TAKE AWAY THE GOVERNMENT LAND? IT WOULD BE ONLY ONE-FIFTH OF AN ACRE. WATERFRONT'LL GO UP NOW. I DON'T THINK YOU'LL BE ABLE TO TOUCH WATERFRONT PROPERTY HERE 10 YEARS FROM NOW FOR UNDER 80 THOUSAND. |
| **MICHIE:**<br>**V/O AERIAL FOOTAGE OF**<br>**DEVELOPMENT**<br>**SLIDES OF MICHIE AND**<br>**WIFE WITH SALESMAN** | PROMISES OF A HUGE INVESTMENT RETURN ARE OFTEN MADE. LAND IS BECOMING SCARCE. THESE ARE UNSUBSTANTIATED SALES PITCHES OFTEN USED AT VACATION LAND DEVELOPMENTS. SUCH WAS THE CASE ON APRIL THIRD WHEN MY WIFE AND I VISITED CAPTAIN'S COVE. A TWO-YEAR-OLD DEVELOPMENT ON THE VIRGINIA COAST. |
| | WE WERE GIVEN A PROPERTY REPORT AS SOON AS WE ARRIVED. THE REPORT. REQUIRED BY FEDERAL LAW. SHOULD BE AN OUTLINE OF THE DEVELOPER'S PLANS AND HIS ABILITY OR INABILITY TO GUARANTEE THEM. |
| **SLIDES OF**<br>**DEVELOPMENT**<br>**SIMULATED**<br>**MOVEMENT** | ONE OF THE BIGGEST SELLING POINTS IS A MARINA THAT DOES NOT AND MAY NEVER EXIST. LAST YEAR THE DEVELOPER PLEADED GUILTY TO HAVING ILLEGALLY DREDGED AND FILLED SOME OF THE LAND IN THE CONSTRUCTION OF THE MARINA AND CANALS. THE FEDERAL GOVERNMENT HAS NOT DECIDED WHETHER IT WILL ALLOW THE PROJECTS. ALL THIS IS IN THE PROPERTY REPORT. BUT THE SALESMAN IN-DICATED HE HAD SOME INSIDE IN-FORMATION. |
| **SALESMAN:**<br>**AUDIO SEGMENT**<br>**SLIDES OF**<br>**DEVELOPMENT**<br>**SIMULATED**<br>**MOVEMENT** | BUT WE'VE GOTTEN VERBAL APPROVAL FROM EVERYBODY. IN OTHER WORDS. INTERIOR DEPARTMENT HAS ALREADY AP-PROVED US. THE MARINE RESOURCES COM-MISSION HAS ALREADY APPROVED US. WE'VE HEARD. AND THIS IS OFF THE RECORD. THAT OUR PERMITS HAVE BEEN APPROVED BY THE LOCAL CORPS OF ENGINEERS FROM NORFOLK AND HAVE ALREADY BEEN SENT ON FOR REGIONAL APPROVAL IN WASHINGTON. AND WE SHOULD HAVE OUR PERMITS WITHIN THE NEXT 30 DAYS. MAXIMUM. |
| **MICHIE:**<br>**V/O AERIAL SHOTS OF**<br>**DEVELOPMENT** | THE U.S. ARMY CORPS OF ENGINEERS SAYS NO APPROVAL. VERBAL OR OTHERWISE. HAS BEEN GIVEN. AND THE INTERIOR DEPARTMENT HAS NOT APPROVED THE PROJECT. |

THE SALESMAN TRIED OUR CAPACITY FOR IMAGINATION BY ATTEMPTING TO SELL US A SWAMPY LOT FOR 65 HUNDRED DOLLARS.

| | |
|---|---|
| SALESMAN:<br>AUDIO SEGMENT<br>SLIDES OF<br>DEVELOPMENT | THIS IS A CHOICE PIECE OF PROPERTY, BUT YOU HAVE TO USE A LITTLE OF YOUR IMAGINATION WITH IT RIGHT NOW. A LOT OF PEOPLE DON'T HAVE ANY. YOU KNOW WHAT I'M TALKING ABOUT. IN OTHER WORDS, YOU HAVE TO LOOK AT IT LIKE IT'S FILLED IN. IN OTHER WORDS, THIS IS WHAT YOU CALL VIEW PROPERTY. IT'LL BE UNOBSTRUCTED ALL THE WAY. YOU KNOW, YOU CAN WALK OUT YOUR BACK DOOR AND YOU CAN WALK DOWN TO THE BEACH. IN OTHER WORDS, THESE BEACHES WILL BE MAN-MADE BEACHES. YOU KNOW, RIGHT ON YOUR WATERFRONT OUT THERE. |
| MRS. MICHIE: | THEY'RE NOT THERE YET? |
| SALESMAN: | NO, MA'M. |
| MICHIE:<br>V/O SLIDES OF<br>PROPERTY | BUT THE PROPERTY REPORT OUTLINING THE DEVELOPER'S PLANS SAYS NOTHING ABOUT BEACHES. THE SALESMAN DID NOT CHANCE DRIVING US ON THE STREET TO OUR LOT. |
| SALESMAN: AUDIO<br>SHOTS OF PEOPLE<br>WALKING<br>ALONG "ROAD" | BUT YOU CAN KINDA TELL THAT THE ROADS HAVE JUST BEEN PUT IN HERE. IN FACT, WE HADN'T EVEN GOT THEM ALL THE WAY IN YET. |
| MICHIE:<br>V/O SUPER OF<br>QUOTATION | HOWEVER, IN THE STATEMENT OF RECORD FILED WITH THE DEPARTMENT OF HOUSING AND URBAN DEVELOPMENT, THE DEVELOPER STATES, "ALL LOTS WILL BE ABLE TO BE REACHED BY CONVENTIONAL AUTOMOBILE BEFORE BEING OFFERED FOR PURCHASE TO BUYERS." |
| INTERIOR SALES<br>OFFICE | FINALLY, I ASKED THE SALESMAN FOR A COPY OF THE SALES CONTRACT TO TAKE TO A LAWYER. |
| SALESMAN: | CAN'T DO IT. |
| MICHIE: | WHY NOT? |
| SALESMAN: | THE ONLY WAY THAT WE ALLOW THEM TO GO OUT IS IF YOU BUY PROPERTY, JIM. |
| MICHIE: | WELL, I KNOW, BUT MAN, I'M NOT A LAWYER. I WANT TO GET THIS STUFF CHECKED OVER. |
| SALESMAN: | A TWO-YEAR-OLD CAN UNDERSTAND IT COMPLETELY. |
| MICHIE: | WELL, I BEG TO DIFFER WITH YOU. |

| | |
|---|---|
| SALESMAN: | IT'S DRAWN UP THAT SIMPLY. NO. THIS IS THE ONLY WAY WE CAN DO IT. AND ANOTHER THING I CAN ASSURE YOU. YOUR PROPERTY THAT YOU SAW WILL NOT BE AVAILABLE... |
| MICHIE: | YOU SAY I CAN'T TAKE THE CONTRACT? |
| SALESMAN: | NO. YOU CAN'T. THIS IS COMPANY POLICY. THEY DON'T EVEN ALLOW... |
| MICHIE: | EVEN IF YOU JUST MARKED VOID ON IT? |
| SALESMAN: | THEY DON'T ALLOW IT. |
| MICHIE: V/O EXTERIOR SCENES OF DEVELOPMENT | THE NEXT DAY A CAPTAIN'S COVE OFFICIAL SAID HE COULD NOT UNDERSTAND WHY THE SALESMAN REFUSED TO GIVE ME A COPY OF THE SALES CONTRACT. HE SAID: "I'VE NEVER HEARD OF SUCH A THING." |
| | RICHARD HEIDERMANN IS HEAD OF THE COMPLAINTS AND COMPLIANCE DIVISION IN THE H-U-D OFFICE OF INTERSTATE LAND SALES REGISTRATION. |
| HEIDERMANN: SOUND ON FILM | IF SOMEONE WOULD REFUSE TO LET ME TAKE THE SALES DOCUMENTS ALONG WITH ME TO THINK ABOUT IT ON A MULTITHOUSAND-DOLLAR PURCHASE. I WOULD JUST WALK AWAY FROM IT. |
| MICHIE: V/O FILM | THE OFFICE IS CHARGED WITH IMPLEMEN-TING THE FOUR-YEAR-OLD INTERSTATE LAND SALES ACT—A CONSUMER-PROTECTION LAW. |
| SHOTS OF OFFICES; RECORD FILES BULGING | THE H-U-D OFFICE CHECKS TO SEE THAT THE PROPERTY REPORT IS AN ACCURATE SUMMARY OF A LENGTHY STATEMENT OF RECORD FILED WITH THE OFFICE. BUT SOMETIMES GLARING INCONSISTENCIES ARE MISSED. FIRST CHARTER LAND SALES CORPORATION. THE DEVELOPER OF CAP- |
| SUPER STATEMENT OF PROPERTY REPORT | TAIN'S COVE. SAYS CORRECTLY IN ITS STATEMENT OF RECORD TO H-U-D THAT THE NEAREST GENERAL HOSPITAL IS 40 MILES FROM THE DEVELOPMENT. BUT IN THE PROPERTY REPORT THE DEVELOPER TELLS THE BUYER INCORRECTLY THAT HOSPITAL FACILITIES ARE AVAILABLE IN GREENBACKVILLE. VIRGINIA. FOUR MILES FROM THE SUBDIVISION. AND MORE EXTENSIVELY IN POCOMOKE CITY. MARYLAND. 15 MILES FROM THE SUB-DIVISION. |
| SHOTS OF EMPLOYEES WORKING | OFFICIALS AND WORKERS AT THE H-U-D OF-FICE SAY THIS TYPE MISTAKE GETS BY THEM ALL TOO OFTEN. THEY PLACE MOST OF THE BLAME ON A SEVERE LACK OF |

173

| | |
|---|---|
| **FILM OF INTERVIEW** | PERSONNEL. THERE ARE PROBABLY MORE THAN 10 THOUSAND LAND DEVELOPERS IN THE NATION. THE H-U-D OFFICE OF INTERSTATE LAND SALES REGISTRATION HAS BEEN HELD TO A STAFF OF 55 PEOPLE. GEORGE BERNSTEIN IS ADMINISTRATOR OF THE OFFICE. |
| **MICHIE:** | DO YOU THINK THAT 55 PEOPLE WERE ENOUGH FOR THIS PAST YEAR? |
| **BERNSTEIN:** | I DON'T WASTE MY TIME ARGUING HOW MANY FAIRIES CAN DANCE ON THE HEAD OF A PIN. MY JOB IS TO IMPLEMENT THIS LAW WITH WHAT I'VE GOT AND WHAT I CAN GET. AND I TRY TO GET AS MANY AS I CAN TO THE EXTENT THAT I THINK I NEED THEM. I DON'T GO AROUND COMPLAINING TO REPORTERS OR OTHER PEOPLE THAT I NEED MORE PEOPLE. THAT'S A WASTE OF TIME. |
| **MICHIE:** | DO YOU THINK THAT CEILING IS REALISTIC? |
| **BERNSTEIN:** | YES. |
| **HEIDERMANN: SOUND ON FILM** | WELL, ALL I KNOW IS THAT WE'VE GOT MORE WORK THAN WE CAN POSSIBLY COPE WITH NOW. THE NUMBERS OF COMPLAINTS CONSTANTLY INCREASE. |
| **MICHIE: SOUND ON FILM** | YOU THINK THEN THAT YOU'VE BEEN ABLE TO DO AN ADEQUATE JOB WITH 55 PEOPLE? |
| **BERNSTEIN:** | YES. I DO. |
| **HEIDERMANN: FILMED INTERVIEW** | THERE ARE MANY, MANY CASES THAT HAVE TO TAKE LOWER PRIORITY AND WE CONFINE, I'M AFRAID, OUR PROSECUTIVE EFFORTS TO WHAT I'D CONSIDER THE GREAT FRAUDS. |
| **MICHIE:** | DOES THIS MEAN THAT DEVELOPERS, IF THEY CHOOSE TO, CAN AFFORD TO BE CROOKED TO A CERTAIN EXTENT? |
| **HEIDERMANN:** | THEY CAN TAKE A CALCULATED RISK. IT'S LIKE NOT FILING YOUR INCOME TAX RETURNS... |
| **MICHIE:** | DO THEY? |
| **HEIDERMANN:** | ...OR... |
| **MICHIE:** | DO THEY? |
| **HEIDERMANN:** | I'M AFRAID THAT THEY DO. HUMAN NATURE BEING WHAT IT IS, I THINK THEY DO. |
| **MICHIE:** | DO YOU THINK SOME ARE TAKING ADVANTAGE OF YOUR SITUATION? |
| **HEIDERMANN:** | I'M SURE THEY ARE. |

| MICHIE:<br>V/O | THE H-U-D OFFICE OF INTERSTATE LAND SALES REGISTRATION WILL BE GIVEN AN ADDITIONAL 19 PEOPLE NEXT FISCAL YEAR. THAT'S A 40 PERCENT INCREASE. BUT PEOPLE IN THE OFFICE SAY THAT'S A DROP IN THE BUCKET COMPARED TO THEIR NEEDS. |
|---|---|
| INTERIOR SCENES OF OFFICES | BASED ON MY 4 WEEKS OF RESEARCH AT THE H-U-D OFFICE. IT'S APPARENT THAT THE LAND BUYER IS RELYING TOO MUCH ON OBTAINING HELP FROM THAT AGENCY. |
| CLOSE<br>EXTERIOR SHOT OF<br>LAND DEVELOPMENT | IN OUR NEXT REPORT. WE'LL EXAMINE SOME SUGGESTIONS ON HOW THE PROSPECTIVE LAND BUYER CAN PROTECT HIMSELF. THIS IS JIM MICHIE. EYEWITNESS NEWS. |

## UNDERCOVER TECHNIQUE

If you ask Jim Michie whether he considers himself an investigative reporter, he responds that the term is redundant. He believes the very definition of a reporter is one who seeks information and attempts to discover the whys and wherefores of an occurrence.

The mini-documentary series we have chosen for study, *Only One Hour from the Beltway* and *The Miracle Merchants*, required special techniques to produce. The participants, particularly in *The Miracle Merchants*, were hardly receptive to cameras and sound recorders delving into their inner sanctum.

In order to be sure of his facts, Michie used an "undercover" assistant to do on-the-scene research. She assumed the role of a distraught woman who was very much in need of help. With a hidden recorder, she was able to tape the conversations between herself and each "miracle merchant." After this evidence was studied, an appointment was made for one of the miracle merchants to visit an elderly woman who, presumably, was looking for help. Actually this was a sublet apartment and a hidden video mini-camera was installed to tape the meeting between the miracle merchant and her client.

The question arises: what considerations are involved in using hidden equipment? Here again, the legal aspects were checked out with the station's attorneys. The justification was that the miracle merchants were offering a service to the public. Many of them advertised on radio. If they could accomplish what they promised then they had nothing to hide. Otherwise, they were bilking poor, gullible people out of their generally pitiful savings. All the miracle merchants were given an opportunity to respond. They chose not to.

The use of hidden cameras is a technique employed by crusading reporters at other stations around the country. In the

*TV Guide* issue of September 21, 1974, Howard Whitman has written a forceful article on investigative reporting by personnel of three Miami, Florida television stations. "Newsmen," he relates, "have hovered about in disguised trucks, taken shots with a camera ingeniously concealed in an Ian Fleming type briefcase and have even shot with a mini-camera tucked into a cigarette pack." Another time, "one crew pulled up with a flatbed truck carrying a photographer hidden in a refrigerator packing case." The hidden cameras were essential in ferreting out illegal gambling activities. "Lawmen," Whitman states, "have worked closely with them (investigative reporters), often exchanging news tips and sometimes actually collaborating in stakeouts."

Obviously, when you are working with hidden equipment, your shots are very restricted. In some cases when no camera could be used, an artist, who could draw from memory, was hired as an undercover reporter. When the artwork was shown on screen, it was backed by audio: the conversation between the reporter and the miracle merchant. The standard technique of zooming and panning the stills was used to simulate movement and avoid utterly static visuals.

The length of time to produce mini-documentary series such as *Only One Hour from the Beltway* or *The Miracle Merchants* is considerable. From inception to airing required approximately 3 months. However, many half-hour or hour documentaries take longer to produce; so much depends on the simplicity or complexity of the subject matter. The more complex, the more research is required. Michie submitted a progress report once or twice a week. Sometimes plans have to change even in the midst of a series because a sequence does not work out as envisioned. Flexibility is necessary. The reporter/producer is always motivated by his twin goals of quality and accuracy.

An in-house producer gets into the picture when it comes to editing the footage. Like his reporter colleagues, Michie insists on having the last word concerning content. The in-house producer or the film editor may decide on the final visuals. Essentially, it becomes a team effort with the news director making the ultimate decision on the completed film.

The reporter and the producer usually come to a joint agreement on how many episodes the series will require. They attempt a balanced time for each episode, eliminating an episode running a minute-and-a-half and another taking 9 minutes. Each installment is self-contained, but as you will note from the episodes following, a recapitulation is used preceding each episode.

Jim Michie entered television directly from Louisiana State College, where he majored in journalism. He covered politics for a station in the Midwest and was a general assignment reporter. "I don't think you can jump into mini-documentaries cold," he says. "You have to learn about film, learn to edit, to put things together. You should do general assignments for several years." Mini-documentaries, he finds, are very rewarding.

Now here are transcripts of the mini-documentary series, *The Miracle Merchants*. We might note that there is nothing sacrosanct about having a series kick off at the beginning of the week. The first episode of *The Miracle Merchants* was presented on a Wednesday and ran through Friday. The next 5 episodes ran Monday through Friday.

## THE MIRACLE MERCHANTS: EPISODE 1—WEDNESDAY

| | |
|---|---|
| **INTRODUCTION ANCHORMAN: STUDIO** | VIRTUALLY EVERYTHING COSTS MONEY THESE DAYS. IN THIS AGE OF COMMERCIALISM, THERE IS EVEN A MARKET FOR MIRACLES OR PROMISED MIRACLES. AND AN EYEWITNESS NEWS INVESTIGATION SHOWS THAT A SUBSTANTIAL NUMBER OF PEOPLE IN THE D.C. AREA PAY THOUSANDS OF DOLLARS ANNUALLY TO MERCHANTS CLAIMING MIRACULOUS POWERS. |
| | CORRESPONDENT JIM MICHIE HAS THE FIRST IN A SERIES OF REPORTS ON "THE MIRACLE MERCHANTS." |
| **REV. WAYNE PARKS: ON FILMED SEGMENT OF REVIVAL MEETING (COURTESY WCCO-TV)** | I COMMAND YOU TO BE MADE WHOLE IN THE NAME OF JESUS... I SHALL BRING DELIVERANCE TO THEE AND I SHALL PROVE UNTO THEE THAT I AM A MIRACLE WORKER. SAYETH THE LORD THY GOD UNTO THEE. WOOOOO...I'M GOING TO STAY HERE ANOTHER WEEK. I'M GOING TO STAY THROUGH AUGUST THE 12TH...A WHOLE 'NOTHER WEEK OF HOLY GHOST, TONGUE-TALKING, HEALING, AND BLESSING...SAVING AND DELIVERING HOLY GHOST REVIVAL. PRAISE GOD...IF YOU'RE GLAD, PUT YOUR HANDS UP AND SAY, YEAA...GO AHEAD, MAMA...GO AHEAD...SHOUT YOUR SHOUT, HONEY...SHOUT YOUR SHOUT...DANCE YOUR DANCE...WOOOO..." |
| **MICHIE: V/O STREET SCENE, D.C.** | THE REVEREND WAYNE PARKS PRACTICES FAITH HEALING IN A KHAKI TENT ON THE OUTSKIRTS OF EVERY TOWN THAT WILL LET HIM IN. THE LAME, THE FRIGHTENED, THE BORED, AND THE BLIND COME IN DROVES, HOPING TO BE HEALED THROUGH PRAYER. |

| | |
|---|---|
| **SHOTS OF HOUSES,**<br>**STORE FRONTS** | IN THE DISTRICT OF COLUMBIA. THE MIRACLE MERCHANTS OPERATE IN MORE SUBSTANTIAL QUARTERS: AN OLD BROWNSTONE. A STORE-FRONT PARLOR. A SECOND-STORY WALKUP. BUT THE PRODUCT IS MUCH THE SAME. AND SO IS THE PITCH. |
| | THEY PROMISE HOPE. HEALTH. HAPPINESS. AND SUCCESS...FOR A PRICE. |
| | TWO-THOUSAND-SIX EYE STREET. NORTHWEST: THE PROPRIETOR: REVEREND MOTHER DAY. THE PRODUCT: MARITAL BLISS. |
| **CANDLE CITY**<br>**STORE;**<br>**LONG SHOT** | CANDLE CITY: ONE OF FOUR SUCH STORES WHERE PROPHET SAMUEL SELLS SUCH RELIGIOUS ARTICLES AS FREEDOM-FROM-EVIL BATH OIL. |
| **EXTERIOR OF**<br>**HOUSE** | REVEREND MARY CALLS HER LOCATION AT 4-SEVENTEEN-AND-A-HALF 11TH STREET. NORTHWEST. "THE MIRACLE PLACE." THE PRODUCT: WHATEVER YOU WISH. |
| **EXTERIOR OF**<br>**HOUSE** | FIFTY-ONE-NINETEEN GEORGIA AVENUE IS HEADQUARTERS FOR REVEREND SISTER KING. SHE PROMISES TO CURE OR FIX ANYTHING THE OTHER MERCHANTS CAN'T. |
| **SHOTS OF**<br>**MS. AMEEN**<br>**WALKING ALONG**<br>**CITY**<br>**STREETS** | DURING OUR TWO-MONTH INVESTIGATION. NYCEMAH AMEEN OF THE EYEWITNESS NEWS STAFF WAS OUR UNDERCOVER CONSUMER. SHE SHOPPED THE WARES OF THESE AND OTHER REVERENDS IN THE DISTRICT. SHE WAS TOLD THAT SHE WAS HEXED. THAT SHE WAS HEADED FOR A NERVOUS BREAKDOWN. THAT OLIVE OIL WOULD RID HER OF TUMORS AND THAT CANDLES LIT FOR A PRICE OF $200 WOULD REMOVE A CURSE AND BRING HER HUSBAND BACK. |
| **MICHIE:**<br>**AT REV. DAY'S**<br>**DOORSTEP**<br>**SOUND ON FILM** | HELLO. IS REVEREND DAY IN. PLEASE? I'M JIM MICHIE. I'M A REPORTER WITH W-T-O-P AND I'M DOING A SERIES OF STORIES ON SPIRITUALISTS. I WAS WONDERING IF I COULD COME IN AND HAVE AN INTERVIEW WITH YOU. |
| **REV. DAY:** | COME IN. |
| **MICHIE:** | ALL RIGHT. THANK YOU. |
| **MICHIE:**<br>**V/O INTERIOR**<br>**REV. DAY'S**<br>**HOME** | THE MINISTRY OF REVEREND MOTHER DAY IS THE SUBJECT OF OUR NEXT REPORT.<br><br>THIS IS JIM MICHIE. EYEWITNESS NEWS. |

# EPISODE 2—THURSDAY

| | |
|---|---|
| **INTRODUCTION ANCHORMAN: STUDIO** | EYEWITNESS NEWS CORRESPONDENT JIM MICHIE HAS SPENT THE PAST TWO MONTHS INVESTIGATING A UNIQUE GROUP OF MERCHANTS IN THE DISTRICT OF COLUMBIA. THEY SAY THEY ARE MINISTERS. HOLY MEN. AND HOLY WOMEN WHO HAVE THE GIFT OF PERFORMING MIRACLES. BUT THEIR PATRONS MUST PAY A PRICE. |
| | TONIGHT. CORRESPONDENT MICHIE BEGINS EXAMINING THE MINISTRY OF REVEREND MOTHER DAY. HERE IS HIS SECOND IN A SERIES OF REPORTS ON "THE MIRACLE MERCHANTS." |
| **MICHIE: V/O VIEW OF DOORWAY** | BEHIND THIS DOOR ON ELEVENTH STREET IS REVEREND MARY. SHE PROMISES TO SOLVE PROBLEMS IN LIFE. LOVE. MARRIAGE. BUSINESS. AND HEALTH FOR A PRICE. |
| **EXTERIOR OF STORE** | PROPHET SAMUEL HAS THREE OTHER STORES LIKE THIS ONE. HERE YOU CAN BUY A BOTTLE OF "RUN-RUN-DEVIL FLOOR WASH" FOR $5. |
| **CLOSE UP REV. DAY** | AND THIS IS REVEREND MOTHER DAY. SHE SELLS PRAYERS AND GOOD LUCK. |
| | OUR UNDERCOVER CONSUMER. NYCEMAH AMEEN OF THE EYEWITNESS NEWS STAFF. VISITED HER AS A CLIENT. |
| **REV. DAY: AUDIO SEGMENT**<br><br>**DRAWINGS OF MS. AMEEN AND REV. DAY** | I KNOW YOU NOT RICH. I KNOW YOU WORK HARD FOR MONEY. YOU UNDERSTAND? BUT IF I DIDN'T KNOW THIS WAS GOING TO HELP YOU. I WOULDN'T WANT YOU TO PUT UP YOUR OWN MONEY. BUT YOU GONNA SEE. ONCE I'M GONNA DO THE WORK. THAT EVERYTHING GONNA BE GOOD FOR YOU. YOU UNDERSTAND?...THAT YOU GONNA HAVE YOUR GOOD LUCK. YOU GONNA HAVE YOUR PEACE OF MIND. BECAUSE THAT'S WHY YOU DO WHAT I TELL YOU AND LET ME DO THE WORK FOR YOU. AND I KNOW YOU NOT GONNA REGRET IT. UNDERSTAND? BECAUSE I'M GONNA GUARANTEE EVERYTHING IS GONNA BE ALL RIGHT. |
| **MICHIE: V/O EXT. REV. DAY'S HOME** | THAT WAS THE SALES PITCH OF REVEREND DAY. SEVERAL WEEKS LATER. I CALLED ON HER AND TOLD HER I WAS DOING A STORY ON SPIRITUALISTS. SHE INVITED ME IN. |
| **MICHIE: SOUND ON FILM** | WHAT. JUST WHAT DO YOU DO FOR PEOPLE? |

179

| | |
|---|---|
| REV. DAY:<br>SOUND ON FILM<br>INTERIOR REV. DAY'S<br>HOME | IN WAYS. WELL. THEY GET A BETTER UNDERSTANDING OF THEMSELVES WHEN I FINISH READING FOR THEM. AND A LOT OF TIMES IT HELPS THEM IN SOME KIND OF WAYS ON ACCOUNT OF ME GIVING THEM ADVICE ON WHAT THEY SHOULD DO. I GET PEOPLE TO, YOU KNOW, TO COME BACK TO ME AFTER I'VE READ THEM AND THEY TELL THEIR FRIENDS ABOUT ME SO APPARENTLY I MUST DO SOMETHING TO GIVE THEM SOME KIND OF SATISFACTION. |
| MICHIE: | WELL. FOR INSTANCE. DO THEY COME TO YOU EVER WITH PROBLEMS HAVING TO DO WITH THEIR MARRIAGE OR LOVE LIFE OR ANYTHING LIKE THAT? |
| REV. DAY:<br>CLOSEUP | YEAH. WELL I TRY TO ADVISE THEM THE BEST I CAN ON THAT. BUT I TELL THEM. REALLY. IF YOU DON'T CARE FOR THAT PERSON. WHY STAY WITH THAT PERSON? IF THEY REALLY IN LOVE. THEY WILL HAVE TO CHANGE FOR THAT PERSON. TO OVERLOOK A LOT OF THINGS THAT THAT PERSON WILL DO TO THEM. |
| MICHIE: | NOW TELL ME SOMETHING. I GUESS IN SOME WAYS YOU'RE ACTING SOMEWHAT LIKE A PSYCHIATRIST OR A PSYCHOLOGIST. AREN'T YOU? |
| REV. DAY:<br>CLOSEUP | WELL. IN SOME WAYS. I GUESS. BUT LIKE I SAY I NEVER GO INTO REALLY DESTROYING THEIR LIFE OR ANYTHING. YOU KNOW. I USUALLY LET 'EM MAKE UP THEIR OWN MIND FOR WHAT THEY WANT IN LIFE. I FEEL. WHATEVER THEY FEEL MAKES THEM HAPPY. THEY SHOULD DO. AND USUALLY. LIKE I SAY. IT WINDS UP THAT THEY'RE MORE HAPPY IN THE THINGS THAT THEY DO. SOME OF THEM JUST COME IN MAYBE FOR CURIOSITY. SOME OF THEM JUST COME IN. YOU KNOW. JUST TO BE READ TO SEE WHAT YOU HAVE TO SAY TO THEM. LIKE THAT. YOU KNOW. SOME OF THEM DON'T TAKE IT TOO SERIOUS AT ALL. |
| MICHIE: | NOW. IS THERE A SPECIAL TALENT? DO YOU FEEL THERE'S A SPECIAL TALENT FOR THIS. AND IF SO. WHERE DID YOU GET THIS TALENT? |
| REV. DAY:<br>MEDIUM CLOSEUP | WELL. LIKE I TOLD YOU. THIS HAS BEEN SOMETHING THAT HAS JUST GONE ON FROM GENERATION TO GENERATION. |
| MICHIE: | IN YOUR FAMILY? |
| REV. DAY: | IN MY FAMILY. YOU PICK IT UP AS YOU GO ALONG WITH IT. SO THAT'S WHY. LIKE I SAY. |

|  | THAT'S THE WAY I GOT IT. IT'S NOTHING THAT YOU COULD LEARN OUT OF A BOOK. THAT'S THE WAY I FEEL ABOUT IT. IT'S GOTTA BE SOME KIND OF GIFT GOING INTO YOU FOR IT. |
|---|---|
| MICHIE: | NOW WHY DO YOU CALL YOURSELF REVEREND DAY? |
| REV. DAY: | I...THIS IS THE CHURCH. AND I DO HAVE MY PROFESSIONAL LICENSE THAT I AM A REVERENDESS. |
| MICHIE: | YOU ARE A MINISTER? |
| REV. DAY: | YES. |
| MICHIE: | OF WHAT CHURCH? |
| REV. DAY:<br>CLOSEUP | THE CALIFORNIA CHURCH IN CALIFORNIA. THAT'S WHERE I LEARNED A LOT OF MINISTRY. AND NOW I'M IN WASHINGTON. |
| MICHIE: | IS REVEREND DAY YOUR REAL NAME. OR IS THAT A NAME YOU USE IN YOUR PROFESSION? |
| REV. DAY: | NO. THAT'S MY NAME. |
| MICHIE: | THAT'S YOUR REAL NAME? |
| REV. DAY: | YEAH. |
| MICHIE: | NOW WHAT ABOUT IN THE AREA OF EVIL SPIRITS AND CURSES AND THINGS OF THAT SORT. DO YOU DEAL WITH ANYTHING LIKE THAT? |
| REV. DAY:<br>MEDIUM CLOSEUP | NO...NO. I DON'T. I JUST GIVE CARD READINGS. PALM READINGS AND ADVICE. AND ALL. BUT NOTHING THAT HAS TO DO WITH BLACK MAGIC OR ANYTHING LIKE THAT. |
| MICHIE: | NOW WHAT DO YOU CHARGE? |
| REV. DAY: | WELL. I HAVE A 3-DOLLAR READING AND A 5-DOLLAR READING THAT TELLS YOU MORE. |
| MICHIE: | DO YOU EVER CHARGE ANY MORE THAN THAT? |
| REV. DAY: | NO. |
| MICHIE: | FOR HELP? |
| REV. DAY: | WELL. LIKE I SAY. I DON'T GIVE ANYTHING THAT HAS TO DO WITH HELP. IT'S JUST READINGS THAT I DO... |
| MICHIE:<br>FULL SHOT | DAVE (LIGHTING TECHNICIAN). WOULD YOU GO AND. EXCUSE ME. WOULD YOU GO AND GET ME ANOTHER CASSETTE. PLEASE? |

| MICHIE:<br>V/O CLOSEUP OF REV.<br>DAY | THIS WAS THE CUE FOR NYCEMAH AMEEN. OUR UNDERCOVER CONSUMER WHO WAS WAITING OUTSIDE. TO WALK IN ON THE INTERVIEW. |
|---|---|
| MICHIE: | DO YOU REMEMBER THIS YOUNG LADY? |
| REV. DAY: | YES. I BELIEVE SO. |
| MICHIE: | AND HOW MUCH DID YOU CHARGE HER? |
| REV. DAY: | I DON'T REMEMBER. |
| MICHIE: | WHAT DID SHE CHARGE YOU THE FIRST...WHY DON'T WE STEP OVER HERE...WHAT DID SHE CHARGE YOU THE FIRST VISIT? |
| MS. AMEEN: | SHE CHARGED ME $4. |
| MICHIE: | AND THE SECOND VISIT? |
| MS. AMEEN | TWENTY DOLLARS. |
| MICHIE: | THIRD VISIT? |
| MS. AMEEN: | NOTHING. SHE TOLD ME THAT I SHOULD BRING $200 WHEN I CAME BACK. |
| MICHIE:<br>V/O—THREE SHOT:<br>MS. AMEEN; DAY.<br>MICHIE | IN OUR NEXT REPORT. WE CONTINUE WITH REVEREND MOTHER DAY—PAST THE PROMISES AND TO THE TRUTH.<br><br>THIS IS JIM MICHIE. EYEWITNESS NEWS. |
| MS. AMEEN:<br>SOUND ON FILM<br>TEASER | AND I GAVE REV. DAY $4 FOR A READING. AND SHE TOLD ME THAT I HAD VERY SEVERE MARITAL PROBLEMS .. |

## EPISODE 3—FRIDAY

| INTRODUCTION<br>ANCHORMAN<br>STUDIO | THIS WEEK AND NEXT WEEK. EYEWITNESS NEWS IS RUNNING A SERIES OF REPORTS ENTITLED. "THE MIRACLE MERCHANTS." IT'S THE PRODUCT OF A 2-MONTH INVESTIGATION BY EYEWITNESS NEWS CORRESPONDENT JIM MICHIE.<br><br>TONIGHT. MICHIE CONTINUES HIS EXAMINATION OF THE MINISTRY OF REVEREND MOTHER DAY. WHO SELLS HER CLIENTS PRAYERS AND GOOD LUCK. |
|---|---|
| MICHIE:<br>V/O PAN OF D.C.<br>STREETS;<br>MS. AMEEN ASCENDING<br>STAIRWAY | TWO MONTHS AGO. REVEREND MOTHER DAY. A LICENSED FORTUNE TELLER IN THE DISTRICT. WAS LOCATED AT 917 SIXTH STREET. NORTHWEST. NYCEMAH AMEEN OF THE EYEWITNESS NEWS STAFF VISITED HER THREE TIMES AS AN UNDERCOVER CONSUMER. REVEREND DAY TOLD NYCEMAH SHE HAD A SERIOUS PROBLEM IN HER MARRIAGE. |

| | |
|---|---|
| REV. DAY:<br>AUDIO SEGMENT<br>DRAWINGS OF REV.<br>DAY | I TOLD YOU THAT YOU'VE BEEN GIFTED FROM THE GOD. YOU KNOW. LIKE THE GOD GIVES SOMEBODY GIFT TO SING OR TO DANCE OR TO WORK IN THE CHURCH OR TO BE A GOOD DOCTOR. YOU KNOW. YOU NEED HELP. HONEY. I FEEL SORRY FOR YOU. |
| MICHIE:<br>V/O MICHIE ENTERING<br>DAY'S HOME<br><br><br><br><br><br>SHOT OF MS. AMEEN<br>ENTERING | UNAWARE THAT NYCEMAH AND I WERE WORKING TOGETHER. REVEREND DAY GRANTED ME AN INTERVIEW SEVERAL WEEKS LATER AT HER NEW ADDRESS ON EYE STREET. IN THE BEGINNING OF THAT INTERVIEW. REVEREND DAY TOLD ME SHE NEVER DEALS WITH CURSES OR EVIL SPIRITS. THAT HER REAL NAME IS REVEREND DAY, AND THAT SHE NEVER CHARGES HER CLIENTS MORE THAN $5 FOR A READING. ON A PREARRANGED CUE. NYCEMAH. WHO WAS WAITING OUTSIDE. WALKED IN ON THE INTERVIEW AND CON-FRONTED REVEREND DAY... |
| MICHIE:<br>FILMED INTERVIEW | DO YOU REMEMBER THIS YOUNG LADY? |
| REV. DAY: | YES. I BELIEVE SO. |
| MICHIE: | HOW MUCH DID YOU CHARGE HER? |
| REV. DAY | I DON'T REMEMBER. |
| MICHIE: | WHAT DID SHE CHARGE YOU THE FIRST...WHY DON'T WE STEP OVER HERE...WHAT DID SHE CHARGE YOU THE FIRST VISIT? |
| MS. AMEEN: | SHE CHARGED ME $4. |
| MICHIE: | AND THE SECOND VISIT? |
| MS. AMEEN: | TWENTY DOLLARS. |
| MICHIE: | THIRD VISIT? |
| MS AMEEN: | NOTHING. SHE TOLD ME I SHOULD BRING $200 BACK WHEN I CAME BACK. BUT I DIDN'T COME BACK. I VISITED HER THE FIRST TIME AROUND THE MIDDLE OF NOVEMBER. |
| REV. DAY: | WHERE DID YOU...WAS THAT HERE? |
| MS. AMEEN: | IT WAS AT 917 SIXTH STREET. I GAVE HER $4 FOR A READING. AND SHE TOLD ME THAT I HAD VERY SEVERE MARITAL PROBLEMS. THAT SHE HAD A SPECIAL GIFT FROM GOD. AND THAT SHE COULD TELL I HAD VERY SEVERE MARITAL PROBLEMS. |
| MICHIE: | ON THE THIRD VISIT DID SHE ASK YOU FOR $200? |
| MS. AMEEN: | YES. WHEN I CAME BACK THE THIRD TIME. |

| | |
|---|---|
| **MICHIE:** | NOW. REVEREND DAY. EARLIER IN THE INTERVIEW. YOU SAID YOU CHARGED 3 TO 5 DOLLARS. WHY WOULD YOU ASK THIS YOUNG LADY FOR $200? |
| **REV. DAY:** | WELL. BECAUSE I ASKED HER FOR THE CANDLES...IF SHE WANTED ME TO PRAY FOR HER WITH CANDLES. |
| **MICHIE:** | DIDN'T YOU. IN FACT. TELL HER THAT SHE HAD A CURSE ON HER THAT TWO WOMEN PUT A CURSE ON HER AND...SO HAD AN OLD WOMAN IN NORTH CAROLINA? |
| **REV. DAY:** | I DON'T REMEMBER THAT. |
| **MICHIE:** | YOU DON'T REMEMBER THAT. |
| **REV. DAY:** | I DON'T REMEMBER ANYTHING LIKE THAT. |
| **REV. DAY:** **AUDIO SEGMENT** | YOU SEE. FOR THE WORK THAT NEED TO BE DONE. BECAUSE I GOTTA PRAY FOR YOU FOR 9 WEEKS AND 9 MORE WEEKS IN ORDER FOR THAT... |
| **DRAWINGS OF REV. DAY AND MS. AMEEN** | |
| **MS. AMEEN:** | $200? |
| **REV. DAY:** **END OF AUDIO SEGMENT** | YES. HONEY. LOOK. THAT'S NOT BIG MONEY FOR YOUR LIFE AND HAPPINESS. YOU UNDERSTAND? |
| **MICHIE:** **FILMED INTERVIEW** | NOW. WHY DOES IT TAKE $200 REVEREND DAY? |
| **REV. DAY:** | WELL. WHY DOES EVERYTHING ELSE TAKE MONEY IN THE WORLD? YOU HAVE TO BE BORN IN LIFE. YOU HAVE TO PAY FOR SOMETHING. WHEN YOU'RE DEAD. YOU HAVE TO BE BURIED. YOU HAVE TO PAY FOR THAT LIKE EVERYTHING ELSE IN LIFE. |
| **MICHIE:** | I KNOW. THAT'S WHAT YOU TOLD MS. AMEEN. |
| **REV. DAY:** | RIGHT. YOU KNOW. WHEN YOU GO TO THE CHURCH. YOU HAVE TO PAY TO BE THERE AND TO BURN THE CANDLES. SAME WAY. IT'S GOTTA BE FOR HER. TOO. |
| **MICHIE:** | SO. IN OTHER WORDS. WHEN YOU TOLD ME YOU CHARGED ONLY 3 OR 5 DOLLARS AT THE MOST. THAT WASN'T ACCURATE. WAS IT? |

184

| | |
|---|---|
| REV. DAY: | WELL. THAT'S PRIVATE BUSINESS. THAT'S SOMETHING THAT ONLY ME AND THE PEOPLE THAT I WORK WITH...THAT'S LIKE GOING TO THE DOCTOR AND YOU TELLING HIM SOMETHING SPECIAL. NOBODY IS SUPPOSED TO KNOW ALL YOUR BUSINESS. |
| MICHIE: | IS YOUR NAME REVEREND DAY OR IS IT SALLY ZERO? |
| REV. DAY: | I DON'T THINK IT'S ANY OF YOUR BUSINESS. IF YOU REALLY WANT TO KNOW. SEE. YOU CAME IN TO TRICK ME ON THE QUESTIONS AND THINGS LIKE THAT. IS THAT WHAT IT WAS? |
| MICHIE: | NO. NO. I CAME IN... |
| REV. DAY: | SEE. WHAT YOU'RE DOING NOW IS COMPLETELY DIFFERENT FROM WHAT YOU TOLD ME. AND I'M NOT EVEN GOING TO LET YOU TAKE THIS TO THE TELEVISION BECAUSE I'LL CALL UP MY LAWYER AND TELL HIM ABOUT THIS. |
| MICHIE: | WELL. YOU HAVE A PERFECT RIGHT TO CALL YOUR LAWYER. REVEREND DAY. BUT I'M ASKING YOU. IS YOUR NAME SALLY ZERO OR IS IT REVEREND DAY? |
| REV. DAY: | IT'S SALLY ZERO. |
| MICHIE: | WELL. NOW. HOW MANY CANDLES...YOU ASKED HER FOR $200. HOW MANY CANDLES DOES IT TAKE...$200 WORTH OF CANDLES TO BURN IN ORDER TO REMOVE A CURSE? |
| REV. DAY: SHOWING MICHIE TO DOOR | WELL. I DON'T WANT TO ANSWER ANYTHING ANY MORE BECAUSE YOU PEOPLE DIDN'T DO RIGHT. SO YOU JUST LEAVE. |
| MICHIE: | ALL RIGHT. ALL RIGHT. REVEREND DAY. WE'LL LEAVE. |
| MR. ZERO: AT DOORWAY | SEE. MY WIFE IS A GODLY WOMAN. SHE IS WITH THE CHURCHES. |
| MICHIE: | YEAH. |
| MR. ZERO: | THIS WOMAN DID NOT ASK MY WIFE FOR ANY WORK THAT SHE DOES FOR HERSELF. THE $200 WERE FOR A CANDLE BURNING. YOU CAN CHECK WITH HER PAST RECORD. I |

|  |  |
|---|---|
|  | THINK SHE IS REGISTERED HERE IN TOWN WITH THE CITY OF WASHINGTON. D.C. |
| MICHIE: | AND ARE YOU ROBERT ZERO? |
| MR. ZERO: | YES. |
| MICHIE: | AND ARE YOU ALSO A MINISTER? |
| MR. ZERO: | YES. I AM. |
| MICHIE: | JUST HOW OFTEN DO YOU CHARGE PEOPLE THAT AMOUNT OF MONEY? |
| REV. DAY: | WELL. I TELL YOU. THAT'S MY BUSINESS. THAT'S MY PRIVATE BUSINESS. I CAN'T TELL YOU EVERYTHING ABOUT MY PRIVATE BUSINESS. |
| MICHIE: | IF YOU HAVE ANY QUESTIONS. PLEASE FEEL FREE TO CALL THE STATION. |
| MICHIE: V/O | REVEREND MOTHER DAY SELLS PRAYERS AND SAYS SHE BURNS CANDLES. |
| EXTERIOR OF CANDLE CITY STORE | THE DO-IT-YOURSELFER CAN ELIMINATE THIS MIDDLE MAN OR WOMAN BY GOING TO A PLACE CALLED CANDLE CITY—A CHAIN OF STORES IN THE DISTRICT THAT WILL SELL YOU THE CANDLES ALONG WITH HAIR-GROWING TONIC AND "FREEDOM-FROM-EVIL BATH OIL." PROPHET SAMUEL IS THE FOUNDER AND PROPRIETOR OF CANDLE CITY. |
| PROPHET SAMUEL: INTERIOR OF STORE SOUND ON FILM | ...TAUGHT PEOPLE AGAINST PROPHETS DOWN FOR 2 THOUSAND YEARS. LIKE JOAN OF ARC—THEY KILLED HER. LIKE JESUS CHRIST—THEY HUNG HIM. AND A LOT OF PEOPLE ARE AFRAID OF SPIRITUAL PEOPLE. THEY THINK WE TALK TO THE DEAD. AND THIS IS WHY THEY CALL YOU NAMES: FORTUNE TELLERS. WITCHCRAFT. VOODOO. HOODOO—ANYTHING THEY CAN THINK OF. YOU KNOW. BUT THERE'S NO VALUE TO IT. IT DOESN'T BOTHER ME. I WAS BORN A PROPHET. SO WHY SHOULD I FEAR? |
| MICHIE: V/O INT. OF STORE | I'LL TALK WITH PROPHET SAMUEL IN OUR NEXT REPORT. THIS IS JIM MICHIE. EYEWITNESS NEWS. |

## EPISODE 4—MONDAY

|  |  |
|---|---|
| INTRODUCTION ANCHORMAN: STUDIO | EVERY YEAR THOUSANDS OF DESPERATE. LONELY. AND SICK PEOPLE TRY TO BUY MIRACLES FOR HUNDREDS. SOMETIMES THOUSANDS OF DOLLARS FROM IN-DIVIDUALS WHO CLAIM TO HAVE SPECIAL POWERS. BUT IN WASHINGTON THERE IS A PLACE THAT CATERS TO THOSE WHO CAN'T |

186

AFFORD THE EXPENSIVE MIDDLEMAN. IT'S CALLED "CANDLE CITY." OWNED AND OPERATED BY PROPHET SAMUEL.

HERE IS EYEWITNESS NEWS COR-RESPONDENT JIM MICHIE WITH THE FOURTH IN A SERIES OF REPORTS ON "THE MIRACLE MERCHANTS."

**PROPHET SAMUEL:**
**INTERIOR OF STORE**
**SOUND ON FILM**

I DON'T READ CARDS. TEA LEAVES. CRYSTAL BALLS. OR PALMS. I READ THE PEOPLE. NOW YOU ASK ME HOW I DO IT: I COULDN'T TELL YOU. BUT FOR $7. I'LL GIVE YOU A READING.

**MICHIE:**
**V/O PAN OF STORE**
**SHOWING**
**PRODUCTS AND**
**CUSTOMERS**

MOST MIRACLE MERCHANTS SELL PRAYERS AND PROMISES. BUT SOME DEAL IN ACTUAL PRODUCTS. AND WHEN IT COMES TO BOT-TLES AND JARS. NOBODY HAS MORE TO OF-FER THAN PROPHET SAMUEL.

HE'S THE BISHOP OF THE LORD'S HOUSE OF PRAYER WHICH OWNS AND OPERATES A CHAIN OF FOUR STORES CALLED "CANDLE CITY." CUSTOMERS HAVE THEIR CHOICE OF PACKAGED MIRACLES. ALL FOR A PRICE: LOVER'S SPRAY. JINX-REMOVING BATH OIL. RUN-RUN-DEVIL FLOOR WASH. FINANCIAL BLESSING INCENSE. AND MANY MORE. CANDLE CITY HAS HOME DELIVERY AND ITS WARES ARE TOUTED DAILY ON PROPHET SAMUEL'S RADIO SHOW.

**PROPHET SAMUEL:**
**INTERIOR OF STORE**
**FILMED INTERVIEW**

WELL. THE FREEDOM-FROM-EVIL BATH OIL. THE JINX-REMOVING BATH SALTS ARE TO ENCOURAGE THE PEOPLE TO CONTINUE TO BATHE. FOR CLEANING ONESELF UP RELIEVES ONE OF THE EVIL FORCES. EVIL SPIRITS AND AN EVIL BODY GO TOGETHER.

**MICHIE:**

DO YOU BELIEVE THAT THESE PRODUCTS ACTUALLY REMOVE EVIL SPIRITS AND SO ON?

**PROPHET SAMUEL:**

WELL. THEY HELP ME. AND I DON'T SELL NOTHING I HAVEN'T TRIED.

**MICHIE:**

LET'S TAKE JINX-REMOVING BATH OIL. WHAT IS THIS MADE OF?

**PROPHET SAMUEL:**

I COULDN'T TELL YOU. THAT'S A PHARMACEUTICAL. IT'S A PHARMACY. WE JUST BLESS IT AT THE CHURCH. IT'S A REGULAR BATH OIL. BUT IT'S BLESSED AT THE CHURCH.

**MICHIE:**

ALL RIGHT. AND WHAT DOES THIS BLESSING DO?

**PROPHET SAMUEL:**

I HOPE IT HELPS PEOPLE TO GET WELL. IT REMOVES THE JINX.

| | |
|---|---|
| MICHIE: | DO YOU EVER PRESCRIBE ANYTHING OF ANY KIND TO BE TAKEN INTERNALLY? |
| PROPHET SAMUEL: | NO, THAT'S AGAINST THE LAW. WE DON'T DO THAT. THAT'S FOR A DOCTOR, NOT FOR ME. |
| MICHIE: | YOU DON'T EVER PRESCRIBE ANYTHING AT ALL FOR SOMEONE TO TAKE? |
| PROPHET SAMUEL: | NO. NO! NO MORE THAN THE PATENTED HERB TEAS THAT YOU SEE UP HERE. |
| MICHIE: | BUT NOTHING ELSE? |
| PROPHET SAMUEL: | THAT'S NOT PRESCRIBED. THEY COME IN AND ASK FOR WHAT THEY WANT. |
| MICHIE: V/O | FOR A $7 FEE, WHICH HE CALLS A DONATION, PROPHET SAMUEL GIVES PRIVATE READINGS TO HIS PATRONS. |
| MCU PROPHET SAMUEL | SEVERAL WEEKS PRIOR TO MY INTERVIEW WITH THE PROPHET, OUR UNDERCOVER CONSUMER, NYCEMAH AMEEN OF THE EYEWITNESS NEWS STAFF, HAD VISITED PROPHET SAMUEL AS A CLIENT. SHE TOLD HIM SHE WAS CONCERNED ABOUT TWO TUMORS A DOCTOR HAD DISCOVERED IN |
| MS. AMEEN ENTERING STORE | HER UTERUS. PARTWAY THROUGH MY INTERVIEW NYCEMAH WALKED IN AND CONFRONTED PROPHET SAMUEL WITH WHAT HE HAD TOLD HER. |
| MICHIE: FILMED INTERVIEW | A MOMENT AGO YOU SAID YOU DIDN'T PRESCRIBE THINGS FOR PEOPLE TO TAKE INTERNALLY. |
| PROPHET SAMUEL: | ONLY THE TEA...ONLY THE TEA... |
| MICHIE: | BECAUSE YOU'RE NOT A DOCTOR, RIGHT? |
| PROPHET SAMUEL: | RIGHT. |
| MICHIE: | NOW, DID HE PRESCRIBE ANYTHING FOR YOU? |
| MS. AMEEN: TO PROPHET SAMUEL | WELL, THE FIRST TIME I CAME IN I TOLD YOU I HAD TWO BENIGN TUMORS. |
| PROPHET SAMUEL: | TWO WHAT? |
| MS. AMEEN: | TWO BENIGN TUMORS THE DOCTOR TOLD ME I HAD. |
| PROPHET SAMUEL: | WHAT'S THAT? |
| MS. AMEEN: | TUMORS? THEY'RE GROWTHS. |
| PROPHET SAMUEL: | YEAH... |
| MS. AMEEN: | AND YOU PRESCRIBED OLIVE OIL AND HERBS THAT YOU HAD SPECIALLY BLESSED. |
| PROPHET SAMUEL: | WHAT KIND OF HERBS WERE THEY? |

188

| | |
|---|---|
| MS. AMEEN: | I HAVE NO IDEA. YOU SAID THEY WERE SPECIAL. |
| AUDIO SEGMENT MS. AMEEN: DRAWINGS OF MS. AMEEN AND SAMUEL | WELL. THE DOCTOR JUST TOLD ME THAT I HAVE TWO TUMORS ON MY UTERUS AND THAT THEY SHOULD BE REMOVED. AND I'M REALLY IN A TURMOIL AS TO WHETHER I SHOULD HAVE AN OPERATION OR NOT. |
| PROPHET SAMUEL: | I DON'T SEE YOU HAVING TO HAVE THIS OPERATION, GIRL. NOT IN THE NEAR FUTURE. I DON'T. OKAY, SWEETHEART. IS IT HURTING YOU NOW? |
| MS. AMEEN: | YES. |
| PROPHET SAMUEL: | IT IS HURTING YOU. DOES IT STING YOU LIKE PINS? |
| MS. AMEEN | NO. IT'S SORT OF A DULL HURT. |
| PROPHET SAMUEL | OKAY. YOUR OLIVE OIL WILL BE READY FOR YOU. IN FACT. I WILL GIVE YOU SOME OLIVE OIL THAT'S ALREADY BEEN BLESSED. THIS IS SOMEBODY'S OLIVE OIL. I WANT YOU TO TAKE A TEASPOON EVERY NIGHT BEFORE YOU GO TO...EVERY OTHER NIGHT. TAKE IT ONLY AT BEDTIME BECAUSE IT'S NAUSEATING IF YOU ARE NOT ACCUSTOMED TO IT. ONLY AT BEDTIME. |
| DRAWING OF OLIVE OIL BOTTLE | |
| END OF AUDIO SEGMENT | |
| MICHIE: FILMED INTERVIEW | PROPHET SAMUEL. WHY WOULD YOU PRESCRIBE THIS OLIVE OIL? |
| PROPHET SAMUEL: | OLIVE OIL IS ONE OF THE BEST THINGS IN THE WORLD FOR STOMACH CONDITIONS. YOU CAN GET IT IN ANY DRUG OR GROCERY STORE. |
| MICHIE: | OH. IN OTHER WORDS. THEN. YOU DO PRESCRIBE THINGS FOR PEOPLE TO TAKE INTERNALLY. |
| PROPHET SAMUEL: (END OF FILMED INTERVIEW) | NO! NO! NO!... OLIVE OIL... I TELL HER TO TAKE OLIVE OIL BECAUSE IT'S FOR HEALING. IT'S A HEALING OIL. IT'S NOT A MEDICINE. |
| MS. AMEEN: AUDIO SEGMENT DRAWINGS OF MS. AMEEN AND SAMUEL | YOU SAID DON'T EAT ANY PORK. BRING THE OIL BACK FOR YOU TO BLESS. AND THAT YOU WOULD GIVE ME...THAT I SHOULD BUY SOME SPECIAL HERBS. |
| PROPHET SAMUEL: | WELL. YOU CAN BUY THOSE TODAY. HOW MUCH DID I TELL YOU TO BRING? |
| MS. AMEEN: | WELL. I ONLY HAVE $10. |
| PROPHET SAMUEL: (END, AUDIO SEGMENT) | THEN GIVE IT TO ME. |

| PROPHET SAMUEL:<br>(FILMED SEGMENT) | AND YOU GOT THE HERBS? |
| --- | --- |
| MS. AMEEN: | I HAVE THE HERBS. |
| PROPHET SAMUEL: | NOT FROM HERE. YOU DIDN'T. |
| MS. AMEEN: | YES. I HAVE THE HERBS. |
| PROPHET SAMUEL | NO. I BEG TO DIFFER WITH YOU. (ASKS CLERK) YOU HAVE ANY 10-DOLLAR HERBS? NO. |
| MS. AMEEN | WELL. PROPHET SAMUEL. I... |
| PROPHET SAMUEL:<br>(END OF FILM SEGMENT) | SO IF YOU PUT THIS ON THE AIR. I BEG TO TELL HER SHE'S LYING. |
| MICHIE:<br>V/O<br>BAG OF HERBS BEING OPENED<br>AND DUMPED ON COUNTER | BOTANISTS AT THE SMITHSONIAN INSTITUTION SAY AS FAR AS THEY CAN DETERMINE. PROPHET SAMUEL'S 10-DOLLAR BAG OF HERBS CONTAINS GROUND UP TREE LEAVES AND A COMMON WEED THAT GROWS ALONG HIGHWAYS. |
| SHOT OF AMBULANCE ON WAY TO HOSPITAL | THE EASIEST SALE FOR THE MIRACLE MERCHANT IS TO THE SERIOUSLY ILL— PEOPLE WHO GRASP AT ANY HOPE. AN EXAMINATION OF THAT PROBLEM IN OUR NEXT REPORT. |
|  | THIS IS JIM MICHIE. EYEWITNESS NEWS. |

## EPISODE 5—TUESDAY

| INTRODUCTION ANCHORMAN:<br>STUDIO | FOR THE PAST WEEK EYEWITNESS NEWS CORRESPONDENT JIM MICHIE HAS BEEN DETAILING THE ACTIVITIES OF SO-CALLED MIRACLE MERCHANTS IN THIS AREA— PEOPLE WHO SAY THEY ARE MINISTERS AND PROMISE TO SOLVE ALL KINDS OF PROBLEMS...FOR A PRICE. |
| --- | --- |
|  | TONIGHT. MICHIE'S REPORT ON "THE MIRACLE MERCHANTS" DEALS WITH THOSE WHO ARE MORE LIKELY TO PAY FOR THESE PROMISES. AND HOW EASY IT IS TO BECOME A MINISTER IN THE DISTRICT OF COLUMBIA. |
| MICHIE:<br>V/O EXTERIOR OF HOSPITAL<br>PEOPLE STANDING AROUND | PEOPLE TURN TO MIRACLE MERCHANTS THROUGH SUPERSTITION. WORRY. LONELINESS. AND IGNORANCE. AND THE EASIEST MARK IS THE PERSON WHO IS SICK. THE FEAR OF ILLNESS AND DEATH MAKE THE HOSPITAL CLIENT THE MOST VULNERABLE OF ALL. CHAPLAINS AT D.C. GENERAL HOSPITAL SAY SOME MIRACLE MERCHANTS HAVE BEEN KNOWN TO PROWL THE HOSPITAL WARDS SELLING PROMISES TO AN EASY PREY. |

| | |
|---|---|
| **DR. BROWNE:**<br>**(CHAPLAIN)**<br>**SOUND ON FILM**<br>**STANDING OUTSIDE OF**<br>**HOSPITAL** | THERE WAS A LADY WHO WAS HEALING PATIENTS THAT APPARENTLY...WELL. ONE CASE. THE PERSON WAS DYING OF CANCER AND SHE HAD PROCEEDED TO GO FROM ONE ROOM TO ANOTHER. CHARGING $50 PER CURE. AND WHEN SHE WAS SENT DOWN TO MY OFFICE. SHE TOLD ME THAT GOD HAD SENT HER IN TO DO THIS TYPE OF HEALING. |
| **FATHER GRIFFIN:**<br>**(CHAPLAIN)**<br>**FILMED INTERVIEW**<br><br><br><br><br><br><br><br>**CLOSEUP PAMPHLET**<br>**GRIFFIN TURNING**<br>**PAGES** | WELL. WE HAVE A PROBLEM THROUGHOUT THE HOSPITAL THAT I SEE AS WELL-INTENTIONED. BUT MISGUIDED IN-DIVIDUALS COMING INTO A SITUATION WHERE PEOPLE ARE ALREADY FRIGHTENED AND FEEL SOMEHOW THREATENED. AND AS A CONSEQUENCE I FEEL THAT THEIR PRIVACY IS INVADED BY PERSONS COMING IN AND GIVING THEM LITERATURE THAT IS GOING TO FRIGHTEN THEM. AS A MATTER OF FACT. IT'S DESIGNED TO FRIGHTEN. FOR EXAMPLE. THIS TYPE OF THING HERE. AND MORE ESPECIALLY. WE HAVE A LITTLE PAMPHLET THAT HAS AS ITS PURPOSE REALLY TO SCARE THE LIVING DAYLIGHTS OUT OF AN INDIVIDUAL AND TO CAUSE THEM TO REPENT AND TO COME CLOSER TO GOD. |
| **MICHIE:** | SCARING THEM ABOUT THE FACT THAT THEY'RE IN THE HOSPITAL? |
| **FATHER GRIFFIN:**<br>**CLOSEUP** | WELL. YES. THAT AND SCARING THEM INTO THINKING THAT THEIR SITUATION IS GRAVE. THAT THEY'RE NOT GOING TO RECOVER. AND THAT AS A CONSEQUENCE THEY'RE ABOUT TO FACE THEIR MAKER IM-MEDIATELY. |
| **MICHIE:**<br>**CLOSEUP** | IS THERE ANY PRACTICAL WAY AT ALL TO STOP THIS PRACTICE IN THE HOSPITAL AND TO KEEP THESE PEOPLE OUT. I MEAN THESE SO-CALLED MINISTERS WHO ARE AC-TUALLY TRYING TO GOUGE PEOPLE? |
| **FATHER GRIFFIN:**<br><br><br><br><br><br>**END OF FILMED**<br>**INTERVIEW** | I REALLY DON'T THINK THAT THERE IS. IT'S EXTREMELY DIFFICULT TO POLICE THE EN-TIRE HOSPITAL. AND. FURTHERMORE. THOSE PERSONS WHO DO COME IN. IF THEY SEE SOMEONE LIKE ME, FOR EXAMPLE, THEY PUT THEIR LITERATURE AWAY AND TRY TO BLEND INTO THE WOODWORK. AS IT WERE. AND WAIT UNTIL I'VE GONE BY; AND THEN THEY START OVER AGAIN. |
| **MICHIE:**<br>**STANDING IN STREET** | WITH A LITTLE STYLE AND A LOT OF IMAGINATION. ANYONE CAN BE A MIRACLE MERCHANT. EVEN SOMEBODY LIKE ME. |

191

| | |
|---|---|
| SUPER CERTIFICATE | A SHORT LETTER. A 20-DOLLAR BILL AND 8 CENTS POSTAGE: THAT'S ALL I NEEDED TO BECOME A MINISTER—A MAIL-ORDER MINISTER. MY CERTIFICATE SAYS I WAS ORDAINED ON DECEMBER 3. 1973 IN THE UNIVERSAL LIFE CHURCH BASED IN MODESTO. CALIFORNIA. |
| | FUNNY AS IT MAY SEEM. THIS CERTIFICATE IS NOT A JOKE IN THE NATION'S CAPITAL. USING IT. SOME MIRACLE MERCHANTS HAVE EVEN OBTAINED OFFICIAL RECOGNITION AS MINISTERS FROM D.C. SUPERIOR COURT. THIS ALLOWING THEM TO APPLY FOR TAX EXEMPT STATUS AND TO PERFORM MARRIAGES. |
| | LAST DECEMBER 19TH. I FOUND OUT HOW SIMPLE IT IS... |
| MICHIE: V/O EXTERIOR SUPERIOR COURT | ALL IT TOOK WAS A BRIEF VISIT TO THE D.C. MARRIAGE BUREAU WITH MY SIGNED ENDORSEMENT FROM ANOTHER UNIVERSAL LIFE MINISTER AND PAYMENT OF A 1-DOLLAR FEE. FROM THERE TO SUPERIOR COURT WHERE MY APPLICATION WAS APPROVED. AND 15 MINUTES LATER. CHIEF DEPUTY CLERK ROBERT NASH PRESENTED ME WITH MY D.C. MINISTER'S CERTIFICATE. |
| MICHIE ASCENDING STEPS | |
| NASH: FILMED INTERVIEW | MR. MICHIE. YOUR PAPERS SEEM TO BE IN ORDER. THIS IS A LICENSE TO PERFORM MARRIAGES IN THE DISTRICT OF COLUMBIA. IT'S GOOD FOR A LIFETIME. |
| MICHIE: | THANK YOU. SIR. COULD YOU HAVE REFUSED TO GIVE ME THIS CERTIFICATE? |
| NASH: | NO. SIR. |
| MICHIE: | WHY NOT? |
| NASH: | BECAUSE YOU MET ALL THE REQUIREMENTS OF THE D.C. CODE. |
| MICHIE: | AND IT'S JUST THAT SIMPLE? SO IT DOESN'T MATTER THAT I SENT OFF $20 AND RECEIVED MY ORDINATION CERTIFICATE IN THE MAIL? |
| NASH: | I'M NOT INTERESTED IN THAT. ALL I'M INTERESTED IN IS THAT YOU SHOW ME THE RIGHT CREDENTIALS CERTIFYING THAT YOU ARE AN ORDAINED MINISTER. AND I CAN GIVE YOU A LICENSE TO MARRY PEOPLE IN THE DISTRICT. |
| MICHIE: | IS THERE SOME OTHER REASON? WHAT ABOUT IN THE TAX AREA? |
| NASH: | IT IS MY UNDERSTANDING THAT ONCE YOU...THAT IS. THE PREREQUISITE TO GET- |

| | |
|---|---|
| | TING D.C. TAX EXEMPTION IS THAT YOU HAVE TO HAVE A LICENSE TO MARRY PEOPLE IN THE DISTRICT. I GOT THIS ANSWER FROM... |
| MICHIE: | THE TAX OFFICE? |
| NASH: | THE TAX OFFICE IN THE D.C. TAX DEPARTMENT. |
| MICHIE: | DO YOU SUSPECT THEN THAT SOME OF THESE BOGUS MINISTERS ARE OBTAINING THESE CERTIFICATES JUST SO THEY CAN GET TAX EXEMPTION? |
| NASH: | YES. I DO. |
| MICHIE: | DO YOU THINK IT'S TOO SIMPLE? |
| NASH: | YES. I DO. I THINK WE SHOULD HAVE SOME RULES WHERE YOU SHOULD SHOW ME SOME CREDENTIALS OTHER THAN A PIECE OF PAPER SAYING THAT YOU'RE AN ORDAINED MINISTER. YOU SHOULD SHOW ME SOMETHING FROM SOME ACCREDITED COLLEGE OR SOME RELIGIOUS SOCIETY SHOWING THAT YOU HAVE MET THE |
| END OF FILMED INTERVIEW | REQUIREMENTS OF THAT SOCIETY—OTHER THAN A PIECE OF PAPER SAYING THAT YOU'RE AN ORDAINED MINISTER. |
| MIRACLE BUYER: CLOSEUP OF GNARLED HANDS | SO THAT'S HOW IT STARTED. THAT WAS THE FIRST VISIT. |
| MICHIE: V/O BACK OF HEAD OF ELDERLY WOMAN | IN OUR NEXT REPORT. THIS 73-YEAR-OLD WOMAN TELLS ABOUT HER VISIT TO A MIRACLE MERCHANT—A VISIT WHICH SHE SAYS COST HER $250. |
| CLOSE | THIS IS JIM MICHIE. EYEWITNESS NEWS. |

## EPISODE 6—WEDNESDAY

| | |
|---|---|
| INTRODUCTION ANCHORMAN: STUDIO | TONIGHT. ANOTHER REPORT ON WASHINGTON'S MIRACLE MERCHANTS— THOSE WHO PEDDLE SPIRITUAL PANACEAS FOR HUNDREDS OF DOLLARS IN THE D.C. AREA. DISAPPOINTED SHOPPERS FOR MIRACLES SELDOM COMPLAIN TO POLICE BECAUSE OF FEAR AND EMBARRASSMENT. |
| | TONIGHT. EYEWITNESS NEWS COR-RESPONDENT JIM MICHIE REPORTS ON ONE OF THE FEW CASES TO RESULT IN AN AR-REST. |
| MIRACLE BUYER: VIDEOTAPE INTERVIEW | ..CHARGED ME $10. |

| | |
|---|---|
| MICHIE: | THE FIRST VISIT? |
| MIRACLE BUYER: | THE FIRST VISIT SHE CHARGED ME $10 AND THEN SHE CHARGED ME 10 MORE. |
| MICHIE: V/O SHOT OF ELDERLY WOMAN BACK OF HEAD THEN CLOSEUP OF HANDS | THIS 73-YEAR-OLD WOMAN IS ONE OF THE FEW MIRACLE BUYERS WHO HAVE COMPLAINED TO THE POLICE. SHE DECLINED TO BE IDENTIFIED BECAUSE OF HER EMBARRASSMENT. BUT SHE TOLD HER STORY HOPING IT WOULD BE A LESSON TO OTHERS. |
| MICHIE: VIDEOTAPE INTERVIEW | SO THE FIRST VISIT SHE GOT $20 FROM YOU? |
| MIRACLE BUYER: | TWENTY DOLLARS. |
| MICHIE: | HOW DID SHE KNOW? DID SHE TELL YOU HOW SHE KNEW YOU HAD A LOT OF TROUBLES? |
| MIRACLE BUYER: | NO. SHE DIDN'T TELL ME HOW. BUT SHE SAID SHE KNEW THAT I WASN'T WELL. SHE SAYS IT'S ALL IN YOUR STOMACH. AND SHE SAYS YOU COME BACK TOMORROW OR THE NEXT DAY. I DON'T REMEMBER. AND SHE SAYS, CAN YOU BRING MORE MONEY? AND I TOLD HER NO. I DON'T SEE HOW I COULD BUT SHE TALKED ME IN TO COMING BACK AND BRINGING HER $500. AND I GAVE IT TO HER AND THEN SHE BURNED THIS PAPER AND THEN THIS SNAKE CAME OUT. AND I'VE SEEN THAT TRICK BEFORE AND I SHOULD HAVE KNOWN BETTER. BUT ANYWAY SHE TOLD ME THAT THAT HAD COME OUT OF MY BODY. |
| MICHIE: | THE SNAKE? |
| MIRACLE BUYER: CLOSEUP WOMAN RUB-BING HER HANDS PAN OF ROOM FULL SHOT OF MICHIE | THE SNAKE. THAT'S THE POISON IN THE SNAKE THAT'S COMING OUT OF YOUR BODY. SHE SAID. THEN SHE HAD THIS STRING AND I TIED KNOTS IN THE STRING. AND THEN SHE TOOK THE STRING FROM ME AND KEPT TALKING TO ME BUT SHE WAS RUBBING THIS STRING IN THE PALM OF HER HAND. YOU KNOW. AND THEN WHEN SHE HANDED IT TO ME SHE SAID. NOW SEE IF THERE'S ANY KNOTS IN THERE. WELL. THERE WEREN'T. BUT OF COURSE. THAT'S ANOTHER TRICK AND I SHOULD HAVE KNOWN BETTER THEN. BUT SHE HAD MY $500. SO I WAS WORRIED AND THEN SHE PROMISED TO GIVE THIS MONEY BACK TO ME. SHE SAYS YOU'RE GONNA GET IT ALL BACK. I'M GONNA GIVE IT ALL BACK TO YOU. AND THEN SHE WANTED MORE MONEY. SHE WANTED 2 THOUSAND. BUT THAT WAS OUT OF THE QUESTION. AND |

THEN SHE GOT IT DOWN TO 900. AND I KNEW I WASN'T GONNA GET 900 AND BRING IT THERE. SO I WAS WORRIED AND I MET MY FRIEND IN TOWN AND SHE SAID. "WELL. YOU BETTER TELL THE POLICE."

**MICHIE:**
**V/O FOOTAGE OF**
**LAURA MARKS**
**ESCORTED BY POLICE**
**OFFICER TO WAITING**
**PATROL CAR**

LAURA MARKS. WHO CALLS HERSELF REVEREND MARY. WAS ARRESTED ON NOVEMBER 27TH. THE CHARGE WAS STEALING BY TRICK FROM THE 73-YEAR-OLD WOMAN. WHOSE ONLY INCOME IS A SMALL PENSION. THE MONEY INVOLVED. $520. WAS A SUBSTANTIAL PART OF THE VICTIM'S LIFE'S SAVINGS. THE POLICE ALSO CONTEND THAT LAURA MARKS IS A FORTUNE TELLER. OPERATING WITH THE $250 LICENSE REQUIRED BY DISTRICT LAW.

**MIRACLE BUYER:**
**VIDEOTAPE**
**CLOSEUP HANDS**
**TWISTING**
**NERVOUSLY**

OH. SHE PROMISED ME GOOD HEALTH AND AT THE TIME I WAS VERY WORRIED ABOUT MY DAUGHTER BECAUSE SHE'D BEEN SICK SO LONG AND JUST COULDN'T SEEM TO GET WELL. AND SHE SAID THAT SHE WOULD BE OKAY. SHE WOULD MAKE HER WELL. AND SHE SAID. "EVERYBODY. I'LL TAKE CARE OF YOUR FAMILY FOR YOU. THEY'LL BE ALL RIGHT." AND SHE SAID "I'M GONNA GET YOU A HUSBAND. HE'S GONNA BE RICH AND HE'S GONNA TAKE YOU AROUND THE WORLD. HE'LL TAKE YOU. YOU KNOW. TOURING. AND YOU'LL HAVE FINE HAPPINESS AND A GOOD LIFE AND I'M GOING WITH YOU." SHE WAS VERY NICE TO ME AND THAT'S WHY I WAS SO GULLIBLE.

**MICHIE:**
**V/O EXTERIOR**
**OF HOUSE**

NINE DAYS AFTER LAURA MARKS' ARREST. OUR UNDERCOVER CONSUMER. NYCEMAH AMEEN OF THE EYEWITNESS NEWS STAFF FOUND THAT REVEREND MARY WAS BACK IN BUSINESS.

**REV. MARY:**
**AUDIO SEGMENT**
**DRAWINGS OF REV.**
**MARY**
**AND MS. AMEEN**
**SIMULATED**
**MOVEMENT**
**SHOWING EXCHANGE**
**OF MONEY**

THROUGH THE FIRST LINE. DEAR. I SEE THAT YOU GOT A LONG LIFE TO LIVE. YOU GOT GOOD LUCK FROM GOD. BUT YOU AIN'T GOT MUCH GOOD LUCK FROM CERTAIN PEOPLE. NOW. I WORK THROUGH THE GOOD LORD AND I ALSO WORK THROUGH CANDLES. DEAR. MY WORK BELONGS TO THE GOOD LORD. MONEY. LOVE. HEALTH. HAPPINESS IS COMING TO YOU. HOW MUCH ARE YOU WILLING TO PUT UP TOWARDS THIS CANDLE? LOTTA PEOPLE. LIKE I TOLD YOU. PUT 20—30—$40. $50. $60— BECAUSE MONEY IS NOT EVERYTHING. MONEY WASN'T CREATED BY THE GOOD LORD. BUT MONEY WAS CREATED BY THE DEVIL HIMSELF. I GOT TO BURN THESE CANDLES FOR YOU. DEAR. BECAUSE THAT'S THE WAY THESE

| | |
|---|---|
| | PEOPLE HAVE DONE TO YOU THIS BAD LUCK. THEY USED MONEY TO DESTROY YOUR LIFE. YOUR HEALTH. YOUR LOVE. AND YOUR HAPPINESS. AND WE ARE TO DO THE SAME THINGS. WHAT THESE PEOPLE HAVE DONE TO YOU. |
| **MICHIE:**<br>**V/O FOOTAGE**<br>**OF ARREST**<br>**SCENE** | ON JANUARY 17TH. A MONTH AND HALF AFTER HER ARREST. THE U.S. ATTORNEY'S OFFICE DROPPED THE LARCENY CHARGE AGAINST LAURA MARKS. I ASKED THE ASSISTANT U.S. ATTORNEY WARREN KING WHY. |
| **KING:**<br>**FILMED INTERVIEW** | WELL. THE CASE WAS UP FOR A PRELIMINARY HEARING AND AT THAT TIME WE WEREN'T PREPARED TO GO FORWARD WITH A PRELIMINARY HEARING. |
| **MICHIE:** | WHY NOT? |
| **KING:** | I DON'T KNOW THE ANSWER TO THAT. THE CASE IS NOW PENDING BEFORE A GRAND JURY AND THE GRAND JURY HAS IT UNDER CONSIDERATION. AN INVESTIGATION IS BEING CONDUCTED. THAT'S ALL I CAN SAY ABOUT THE CASE. |
| **MICHIE:**<br>**V/O TWO SHOT MICHIE**<br>**AND KING** | BUT AFTER A MONTH AND A HALF OF INVESTIGATING. THE ASSISTANT U.S. ATTORNEY HANDLING THE MARKS CASE WAS NOT EVEN AWARE THAT THE DISTRICT REQUIRES LICENSING OF FORTUNE TELLERS—UNTIL HE WAS INFORMED BY EYEWITNESS NEWS. ASKED WHAT WOULD BE DONE WITH THIS NEW PIECE OF INFORMATION. ASSISTANT U.S. ATTORNEY KING SAID. "WE'RE LOOKING INTO THAT NOW." |
| | IN MY NEXT REPORT. A LOOK AT THE ADVERTISING TECHNIQUES OF THE MIRACLE MERCHANTS. |
| **CLOSE** | THIS IS JIM MICHIE. EYEWITNESS NEWS. |

## EPISODE 7—THURSDAY

| | |
|---|---|
| **INTRODUCTION**<br>**ANCHORMAN:**<br>**STUDIO** | EYEWITNESS NEWS CORRESPONDENT JIM MICHIE HAS THE SEVENTH IN A SERIES OF REPORTS ON THE DISTRICT'S "MIRACLE MERCHANTS." |
| | TONIGHT. MICHIE TALKS WITH OUR UNDERCOVER MIRACLE SHOPPER AND EXAMINES AN ADVERTISING TECHNIQUE USED BY SOME OF THE PANACEA PEDDLERS. |

196

| | |
|---|---|
| **MICHIE:**<br>**V/O SHOTS OF**<br>**ADVERTISING**<br>**FLYERS** | ADVERTISING IS A MUST FOR MOST EN-TREPRENEURS. THE DISTRICT'S MIRACLE MERCHANTS INCLUDED. SOME ADVERTISE ON THE RADIO OR WITH STREET SIGNS. OTHERS HAND OUT FLYERS LIKE THIS ONE. ON IT ARE THREE TESTIMONIALS AND PIC-TURES OF PEOPLE TELLING HOW THEY WERE HELPED BY REVEREND SISTER KING. |
| **FLYER VISUAL** | "I'VE HAD HARD LUCK AND BEEN UNDER EVIL INFLUENCE FOR MANY YEARS..." |
| **FLYER VISUAL** | "I WAS FLAT ON MY BACK SUFFERING FROM AN INCURABLE DISEASE..." |
| **FLYER VISUAL** | "I WAS UNSUCCESSFUL IN MARRIAGE AND SEPARATED MANY YEARS..." |
| **MONTAGE OF**<br>**FLYERS** | BUT STRANGELY ENOUGH. THE IDENTICAL TESTIMONIALS APPEAR ON FLYERS FOR MOTHER ANDORA. REVEREND SISTER TERESA. SISTER GAYLORD. REVEREND MARGO. AND POCAHANTAS. EVEN THE SAME PICTURES WERE USED ON SEVERAL OF THE FLYERS. |
| **DRAWINGS OF MS.**<br>**AMEEN**<br>**VISITING REV. KING** | REVEREND KING'S FLYER SAYS THERE'S A $1 CHARGE TO SEE HER. BUT FOR OUR UNDERCOVER CONSUMER NYCEMAH AMEEN OF THE EYEWITNESS NEWS STAFF. THE FIRST VISIT COST $15: THE SECOND VISIT. $40. THE THIRD VISIT. REVEREND KING TOOK $300 MORE TO REMOVE A CURSE SHE SAID HAD CAUSED AN IMAGINARY MARITAL PROBLEM FOR NYCEMAH. |
| **REV. KING:**<br>**AUDIO SEGMENT**<br>**DRAWINGS OF REV.**<br>**KING**<br>**AND MS. AMEEN** | DIDN'T I TELL YOU? DON'T YOU WANT RESULTS IN WORK. HAPPINESS AND SUC-CESS? IS THAT RIGHT? IS THAT RIGHT? WHEN I DO THIS WORK. IT'S GOT TO WORK OUT FOR YOU. EVERYTHING IS GONNA WORK OUT THE RIGHT WAY. DO YOU HEAR ME? UNDERSTAND ME? EVERYTHING IS GONNA WORK OUT FOR YOU THE RIGHT WAY. I GUARANTEE I WILL SATISFY YOU. DON'T WORRY ABOUT IT. DON'T WORRY. |
| **MS. AMEEN:** | DOES IT HAVE TO BE AS MUCH AS $300? |
| **REV. KING:**<br><br><br><br>**END OF AUDIO**<br>**SEGMENT** | YES. IT'S GOT TO BE. DON'T CRY FOR THE 300. IF YOUR HOME IS BROKEN UP. YOU'RE DESTROYED. YOU CAN ALWAYS MAKE MONEY. THE KIND OF WORK YOU DO. MONEY WILL ALWAYS COME TO YOU. DO YOU KNOW THAT? |
| **MICHIE:**<br>**V/O** | I ATTEMPTED TO REACH REVEREND KING FOR AN INTERVIEW. BUT WAS TOLD SHE WAS NOT INTERESTED. |

| | |
|---|---|
| **MICHIE:**<br>**FILMED INTERVIEW**<br>**IN STUDIO** | NYCEMAH AMEEN. OUR UNDERCOVER CONSUMER. HAS TRAVELED ALL OVER THIS CITY IN SEARCH OF "THE MIRACLE MERCHANTS."<br><br>NOW WHAT ABOUT THIS TYPE OF BUSINESS. NYCEMAH. JUST HOW MUCH OF IT IS THERE IN THE DISTRICT? |
| **MS. AMEEN:** | WELL. IT'S MY IMPRESSION AFTER HAVING SHOPPED THESE PLACES FOR THE LAST TWO MONTHS THAT IT IS WIDESPREAD AND DEEPLY ENTRENCHED IN THE WASHINGTON AREA. IT'S IN THE HEART OF THE BUSINESS DISTRICT AS WELL AS IN POORER SECTIONS OF THE CITY IN NORTHWEST. SOUTHEAST. SOUTHWEST. AND NORTHEAST. |
| **MICHIE:** | WHAT ABOUT THE VOLUME OF BUSINESS? DO MANY PEOPLE GO IN AND SEEK THESE SERVICES? AND WHAT TYPE OF PEOPLE ARE THEY? |
| **MS. AMEEN:**<br>**CLOSEUP** | I GET THE IMPRESSION THAT SOME OF THESE MIRACLE WORKERS DO A BOOMING BUSINESS. ONE PLACE IN PARTICULAR: THE DAY I VISITED THERE WERE 30 OR 40 PEOPLE THERE FOR GROUP SESSIONS. AFTER THE SESSION I HAD TO WAIT AT LEAST 3 HOURS FOR A PRIVATE CONSULTATION BECAUSE THERE WERE SO MANY PEOPLE AHEAD OF ME. I THINK THE TYPE OF PEOPLE WHO FREQUENT THE PLACES ARE THOSE WHO ARE GULLIBLE. WHO HAVE LOST ALL HOPE. WHO ARE LOOKING FOR AN INSTANTANEOUS SOLUTION TO SOME OF THEIR PROBLEMS. |
| **MICHIE:**<br>**TWO SHOT**<br>**MICHIE AND**<br>**MS. AMEEN** | BASED ON YOUR OBSERVATIONS AS A CLIENT—HAVING VISITED A NUMBER OF THESE PEOPLE—WOULD YOU SAY THAT THERE'S A COMMON THREAD THAT RUNS THROUGH THESE TYPES OF OPERATIONS? |
| **MS. AMEEN:**<br>**CLOSEUP** | YES. DEFINITELY. SOME OF THEM LURE YOU IN WITH PROMISES OF INSTANT SOLUTIONS TO YOUR PROBLEM FOR A MINIMUM FEE—LIKE 5 OR 10 DOLLARS. THEN. DURING THE CONSULTATION. THEY ADD DRAMA AND MYSTERY TO THE SITUATION BY SAYING THAT YOUR PROBLEMS ARE SO COMPLEX. THEY ARE SO DARK AND DEVIOUS. THEY ARE OF SUCH MAGNITUDE THAT THEY DEFY IMMEDIATE SOLUTION. THEY MUST CONSULT THEIR SPIRITS AND BURN CANDLES AND. OF COURSE. THIS COSTS SUBSTANTIALLY MORE THAN THE ORIGINAL. SAY 5 DOLLAR FEE. THEY REQUESTED. IT MAY BE EVEN HUN- |

198

| | |
|---|---|
| | DREDS OF DOLLARS MORE. IN SOME INSTANCES WE KNOW OF. THEY'VE EVEN REQUESTED THOUSANDS OF DOLLARS. IT'S NOT A NICKEL-AND-DIME OPERATION. DEFINITELY. THEY'RE OUT TO GET AS MUCH MONEY AS THEY CAN. |
| TWO SHOT<br>MICHIE<br>AND MS. AMEEN | THEY ALSO TELL YOU WHAT YOU WANT TO HEAR: YOU'RE INTELLIGENT. YOU'RE BEAUTIFUL. KIND. YOU'RE NICER TO OTHER PEOPLE THAN THEY ARE TO YOU. AND SOMETHING VERY IMPORTANT: WHATEVER YOUR PARTICULAR PROBLEM IS. YOU ARE NOT RESPONSIBLE FOR IT. SOME FORCE OR PERSON OUTSIDE OF YOU IS RESPONSIBLE FOR YOUR PREDICAMENT. THEY'VE PLACED A CURSE ON YOU. AND ONLY THEY. THE "MINISTER." CAN REMOVE THIS CURSE. |
| MICHIE:<br>V/O SHOT OF SISTER<br>STEVENS AND CLIENT | IN OUR NEXT REPORT. SISTER STEVENS MAKES A HOUSE CALL AND REACTION FROM CHURCH AND COURT OFFICIALS TO OUR FINDINGS. |
| | THIS IS JIM MICHIE. EYEWITNESS NEWS. |

## EPISODE 8—FRIDAY

| | |
|---|---|
| INTRODUCTION<br>ACHORMAN:<br>STUDIO | FOR THE PAST WEEK-AND-A-HALF EYEWITNESS NEWS CORRESPONDENT JIM MICHIE HAS BEEN REPORTING ON THE PRACTICES OF THOSE WHO PROMISE MIRACLES FOR A PRICE IN THE DISTRICT OF COLUMBIA. "MIRACLE MERCHANTS." HE CALLS THEM. |
| | TONIGHT. MICHIE CONCLUDES HIS SERIES ON THE "MIRACLE MERCHANTS" WITH THIS REPORT. |
| MICHIE:<br>V/O DRAWINGS OF MS.<br>AMEEN<br>AND LAURA MARKS | OVER THE PAST WEEK-AND-A-HALF. WE'VE SHOWN THROUGH ARTWORK AND RECORDINGS HOW MIRACLE MERCHANTS CHARGE SPECIFIC PRICES FOR THEIR PROMISES—PROMISES TO FIX PROBLEMS WITH ILLNESS. MARRIAGE. MONEY. EVIL SPIRITS. AND CURSES. |
| SISTER STEVENS AND<br>CLIENT AT CLIENT'S<br>APARTMENT | THIS IS AN ACTUAL ENCOUNTER FILMED WITH A HIDDEN EYEWITNESS NEWS CAMERA. IT'S A HOUSE CALL BY SISTER STEVENS—A LICENSED FORTUNE TELLER IN THE DISTRICT. HER CLIENT WAS AWARE OF THE HIDDEN CAMERA. BUT NOT SISTER STEVENS. |
| SISTER STEVENS:<br>VIDEOTAPE | YOU UNDERSTAND? I WILL PRAY FOR YOU. YOU SAY. PRAY FOR ME. SISTER. SAY. PRAY FOR ME. SISTER.... |

199

| | |
|---|---|
| CLIENT: | PRAY FOR ME. SISTER. |
| SISTER STEVENS: | FOR THE GOOD LORD'S HELP. |
| CLIENT: | FOR THE GOOD LORD'S HELP. |
| SISTER STEVENS: | I WANT TO BE OFF THE BAD WISHES... |
| CLIENT: | I WANT TO BE OFF THE BAD WISHES... |
| SISTER STEVENS: | ALWAYS... |
| CLIENT: | ALWAYS... |
| SISTER STEVENS: | AND HAVE GOOD LUCK... |
| CLIENT: | AND HAVE GOOD LUCK... |
| SISTER STEVENS: | ALL THE TIME... |
| CLIENT: | ALL THE TIME... |
| SISTER STEVENS: | I'M NOT GOING TO CHARGE YOU NO MORE. |
| CLIENT: COUNTING OUT MONEY END VIDEOTAPE | THERE'S TWENTY. THIRTY. THIRTY-ONE. THIRTY-TWO. THREE. AND HERE'S THIRTY-FIVE. FORTY. FIFTY. THAT'S ALL THE MONEY I HAVE TO GET ALONG ON.... |
| MICHIE: V/O SHOT OF SISTER STEVENS TAKING MONEY | FIFTY DOLLARS PRESSED INTO SISTER STEVENS' BIBLE: THE PRICE FOR HER PROMISE OF PRAYER AND A SMALL WHITE CANDLE. |
| | LATER. I CALLED AND ASKED SISTER STEVENS FOR AN INTERVIEW. SHE DECLINED. |
| | WHAT DO ESTABLISHED CHURCHMEN THINK OF WASHINGTON'S MIRACLE TRADE? I PUT THAT QUESTION TO THE REVEREND CORTEZ TIPTON. EXECUTIVE DIRECTOR FOR THE COUNCIL OF CHURCHES OF GREATER WASHINGTON. |
| REV. TIPTON: VIDEOTAPE INTERVIEW | IT MIGHT BE INTERESTING FOR YOU TO KNOW THAT I WAS WALKING UP TO THE POST OFFICE UP 14TH STREET THE OTHER DAY AND THIS PERSON. WHO'D BEEN ON THE RADIO AND WHOSE NAME HAD BEEN IN THE PAPER. HANDED ME THIS LITTLE SLIP HERE. |
| MICHIE: | LET'S SEE THE FRONT OF IT...WHAT IS IT. A FLYER? |
| REV. TIPTON: | IT MIGHT BE CALLED A FLYER. AND IT PROMISED ME PIE IN THE SKY. IT HAS NO PRICE ATTACHED TO THE CONSULTATION. BUT SHE TRIED TO GET ME TO GO TO HER OFFICE IMMEDIATELY FOR A CONSULTATION. SHE GUARANTEED TO RESTORE MY LOST NATURE. SHE GUARANTEED TO HELP MY STOMACH |

| | |
|---|---|
| | WHERE EVIL EXISTED. SHE JUST ASSUMED THAT ALL OF THESE THINGS WERE WRONG WITH ME. MAYBE I'M UGLY ENOUGH. BUT I DIDN'T THINK ALL OF THOSE THINGS WERE WRONG WITH ME. AT ANY RATE, THESE ARE THE KINDS OF THINGS THAT PEOPLE WITH PERHAPS MORE PROBLEMS THAN I HAVE |
| CLOSEUP MICHIE | WOULD FALL FOR. AND I THINK WE CHURCH PEOPLE SHOULD BE PARTICULARLY CONCERNED ABOUT THIS KIND OF FALSE REPRESENTATION OF ANY KIND OF RELIGION, WHETHER IT BE THAT OF CHRIST OR WHATEVER THE RELIGION OF THE PERSON IS OR WHATEVER THE ORGANIZATION MIGHT BE. WE SHOULD HAVE MORE PRIDE IN IT THAN TO WANT SCORES AND SCORES AND HUNDREDS AND HUNDREDS OF PEOPLE IN OUR COMMUNITY TO BE GETTING AWAY WITH REPRESENTING THEMSELVES AS BEING A PART OF THE |
| CLOSEUP TIPTON | RELIGIOUS COMMUNITY. AND AT THE SAME TIME THEY ARE DUPING PEOPLE AND TAKING THEM IN AND INCONVENIENCING THEM CONSIDERABLY MORE THAN THEY WOULD HAVE BEEN INCONVENIENCED IF THEY HAD NOT MET THE PERSON. IT'S A TERRIBLE THING THAT'S HAPPENING IN |
| END OF VIDEOTAPE | OUR COMMUNITY. |
| MICHIE: V/O FOOTAGE OF POLICE ENTERING BUILDING | D.C. POLICE DETECTIVE ROBERT ELDRIDGE SAYS, "IT'S JUST ANOTHER VERSION OF THE OLD CONFIDENCE GAME: USING RELIGION TO GET MONEY OUT OF PEOPLE. AND IN LOTS OF WAYS IT'S MORE EFFECTIVE AND MUCH SAFER THAN USING A GUN." |
| EXTERIOR OF COURT HOUSE | THE DISTRICT DOES HAVE LAWS DESIGNED TO PROTECT PEOPLE FROM CON GAMES. BUT FEW CASES INVOLVING RELIGION HAVE EVER BEEN PROSECUTED BY THE U.S. AT-TORNEY'S OFFICE. |
| WARREN KING: FILMED INTERVIEW SEGMENT CLOSEUP OF KING | WELL, PRINCIPALLY, OF COURSE, IS THE FACT THAT RELIGION IS INVOLVED. AND THE DIFFICULTY IS IN SEPARATING OUT FROM THE RELIGIOUS ASPECT OF THE RELATIONSHIP BETWEEN THE PARTIES AND THE FRAUD ITSELF. SO THAT IS THE FIRST HURDLE WE MUST OVERCOME. ONCE WE HAVE OVERCOME THAT. AND IT'S A VERY DIFFICULT ONE TO OVERCOME. BUT ONCE WE'VE OVERCOME THAT, WE HAVE OFTEN PROBLEMS WITH FAILING MEMORIES OF THE VICTIMS—LACK OF ATTENTION TO DETAIL BY THE VICTIMS IN THAT SOME VERY IMPORTANT FACT IS SIMPLY NOT RELATED TO US. IT'S ESSENTIAL FOR PROSECUTION. BUT IT'S PERHAPS NOT IM- |

| | |
|---|---|
| **END OF FILMED SEGMENT** | PORTANT TO THAT PERSON. SO THE NATURE OF THE VICTIM AND THE RELIGIOUS ASPECT OF IT ARE THE KEY PROBLEMS. BUT YOU MUST UNDERSTAND THAT THE REALLY BIG HURDLE IS THE SEPARATION OF THE RELIGIOUS PORTION OF THE SWINDLE FROM THE ACTUAL FRAUDULENT PORTION OF THE SWINDLE. |
| **MICHIE: SUPER SCENE OF POLICE ARREST** | FEAR, SUPERSTITION. EMBARRASSMENT, POVERTY. THESE ARE THE REASONS FOR SO FEW COMPLAINTS FROM MIRACLE SEEKERS WHO FEEL THEY'VE BEEN CHEATED OR TRICKED OUT OF THEIR MONEY. |
| | BOTH THE POLICE AND THE U.S. ATTORNEY'S OFFICE SAY THEY CAN DO LITTLE TO SOLVE THAT PROBLEM. BUT IT'S APPARENT TO ME THAT THERE IS VIRTUALLY NO ENFORCEMENT OF THOSE FEW LAWS AND REGULATIONS APPLICABLE TO THE DISTRICT'S MIRACLE MERCHANTS. |
| **MICHIE WALKING ALONG STREET** | SOME OF THESE PANACEA PEDDLERS WHO ARE ACTUALLY MEDIUMS OR FORTUNE TELLERS CONTINUE TO OPERATE WITH THE 250-DOLLAR LICENSE REQUIRED BY DISTRICT LAW. OTHERS GET AWAY WITH IGNORING THE DISTRICT REQUIREMENT FOR AN OCCUPANCY PERMIT. |
| | OVER THE PAST WEEK AND A HALF. WE'VE SHOWN THAT THERE ARE PITFALLS IN HIRING A MIRACLE MERCHANT...THAT IF YOU'RE IN THE MARKET FOR A MIRACLE. YOU MAY BE IN FOR THE MOST EXPENSIVE DISAPPOINTMENT OF YOUR LIFE. |
| **MITCHIE: CLOSE** | THIS IS JIM MICHIE. EYEWITNESS NEWS. |

## COMMENTARY

Although *The Miracle Merchants* may not represent a theme paramount to the interests of a wide segment of the community, it is an offshoot of the ancient confidence game which has affected a great many people throughout the years. P.T. Barnum's perceptive dictum that there's a sucker born every minute attests to the gullibility of countless victims. And so, in that respect, the subject matter of *The Miracle Merchants* has a universality to it that is unfortunate.

By having before you the transcripts of the entire series, you can observe the comprehensive research that must have gone into the making of this mini-documentary. Reporter Jim Michie has tapped a wide array of sources. The very opening uses footage obtained from television station WCCO. It is a portion of a revival meeting which had been presented on the CBS network. Michie had seen the program and believed the footage would make a very effective opening for his series.

The first episode consists of a montage of the actual "miracle merchants" who are the subjects of the investigatory series. Each episode begins with an introduction by one of the anchormen to set the scene, and to serve as a brief recapitulation. In episode 3, we have a rather extensive summation of preceding events which provide catchup information to viewers who may have tuned in for the first time. Nevertheless, the various segments are planned to tell complete stories in themselves. Each episode employs a teaser at the conclusion, generally a very brief visual from the following episode.

The interview technique is an attempt to elicit the truth from the miracle merchants. When the subject equivocates, an audio segment of his or her actual statement is played. We explored the use of undercover methods in the beginning of this chapter. Some perils are involved: note the confrontation between the reporter and Reverend Day in which she threatens to call her lawyer to prevent the television interview from being shown. Obviously, the threat was never carried out.

In our chapter on the interview, we quoted the observation of one reporter: "You have to have the technique of a trial lawyer: the ability to elicit information from a hostile or uncooperative witness." This is particularly exemplified in episode 4, where the reporter is, in essence, cross-examining Prophet Samuel.

In another episode we learn that the reporter has gone to the extent of obtaining a certificate of ordination as a minister in his effort to prove the mockery of this type of certification which, because of ineffectual city ordinances, is acceptable in the District of Columbia.

The reporter had to deal with reluctant witnesses in both of the foregoing mini-documentary series. For the series, *One Hour from the Beltway*, Michie had to overcome the generally self-serving statements of the bureaucrats and win their confidence in order to obtain an honest appraisal of the on-going situation.

Visually, *The Miracle Merchants* used a simplistic approach. Emphasis was on content. Undercover techniques restricted camera movement and in many instances no camera could be used; artwork was substituted, transferred to 16 mm film and pans and zooms employed to simulate movements.

Many of the mini-documentaries, as we have noted, resulted in definitive action being taken by a community. But, as the Assistant U.S. Attorney pointed out in the case of the miracle

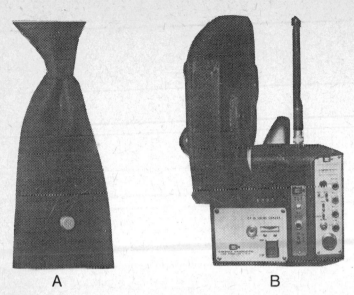

A                    B

Unobtrusive condenser mike can be covered by a tie or other clothing for undercover reporting. When mike is used with FM transmitter, built-in wireless receiver and camera unit shown in (B) make a convenient pair for getting the story.

merchants, often the solution is not simple. The mini-documentary did serve its purpose, however, in unearthing the problem and presenting it to a wide audience. If corrective action cannot be forthcoming at the moment, a mini-documentary can arouse a surge of sentiment in the community that will force proper steps to be taken.

## PHOTOGRAPHIC TECHNIQUE

Bob Boyer, cameraman and editor for WTOP-TV, majored in broadcasting at Southern Illinois University, with a minor in cinematography. His first job was that of a news film photographer for a television station in Baltimore, then the same sort of assignment in Philadelphia. After 4 years of news filming experience, he applied for his current assignment with WTOP-TV. where he has worked for more than 6 years in the news department and with the documentary film unit.

Boyer uses the CP-16 camera, which is light in weight and in which all of the elements of an effective camera are incorporated: the battery slides into the side of the camera; the magazines are simple to load and are made of lightweight material. An amplifier fastens directly onto the camera, eliminating any necessity for lugging cables and battery packs. The CP-16 is therefore highly maneuverable.

For specialized types of camera work, such as aerial shooting, Boyer uses the Bell and Howell 70DR, a silent hand-held camera: Boyer explains:

> It has been basic equipment for news photography for 20 years. It was a combat camera before that. It's simply a hand-held camera that's spring wound and has three lenses. When you're shooting from a helicopter, for instance, you set the speed for 48 frames per second as opposed to the normal 24 frames. That minimizes the amount of vibration. When you're filming from the airplane, you shoot at 32 frames per second. There is a substantial difference in the vibration of a helicopter as against an airplane. Light readings would be the same as they are on the ground. If there is haze, you use a haze filter or you just shoot through the haze. When you locate the area you want to film, you instruct the pilot regarding the flight pattern you want him to follow.

WTOP-TV employs a sound technician as part of the mini-documentary crew, which is advantageous to the cameraman. He can concentrate on the visual while the sound man handles the audio. "With two people, you can more readily accomplish a mission," Boyer says. But he is pessimistic about the future. Economy requirements and the advent of highly mobile single-system cameras may reduce crews to one man. He believes that situation would affect the creativity of the cameraman and, particularly, his attention to detail.

The technique of news filming, as he has experienced it, involves shooting interviews, talking heads, and then shooting

For aerial photography, cameraman Boyer switches to his silent hand-held Bell & Howell 70 DR.

film to support or illustrate the contentions of the interviewee. Or it may consist of simply shooting a spot news story with silent film.

There is quite a difference in filming a mini-documentary series. You may go out on location for periods varying from 1 to 5 days. You shoot a great many more details than you would for news film. You do include talking heads. Actually, most of the film is shot around the sound track. But you shoot much more illustrative material. "For instance," Boyer relates, "we did a mini-documentary series on house trailers. I spent one full day just shooting details of house trailers. For a news film, I would have concentrated on only one element of the story."

Boyer also feels that shooting mini-documentaries may require special camera equipment, particularly for good closeup, detail shots. Common to all creative endeavors, there never appears to be enough time. Spot news is generally shot as it is occurring; the requirement is *competence* rather than *creativity*.

206

Boyer's preference for undercover shooting is the Beaulieu 6P-48 with zoom lens.

When undercover shooting is necessary for a mini-documentary series, the cameraman can equip himself with a slender 16 mm camera that has a wide-angle lens and can be placed in an attache case which has an opening cut into it. The camera would have to be battery-operated. It may have to run for long periods of time. A fast lens is required with the aperture opening up more than "normal" to allow more light to reach the film. In undercover operations, you are generally working in low-light-level areas. On other occasions, it is possible to obtain coverage by stationing yourself a great distance away from the subject and filming with a zoom lens. The Beaulieu 16 mm single/double system sound camera with 12—120 mm zoom lens is often used by Boyer.

In his book, *The Five C's of Cinematography*, Mascelli states that "composition reflects personal taste. A cameraman with artistic background, inherently good taste; an inborn feeling for proper balance, form, rhythm, space, line, and tone; an appreciation of color values; a sense of the dramatic; may create good composition intuitively. Even a mechanically minded cameraman, with limited artistic inclination, can learn to apply the basic principles of good composition by developing a better understanding of visual and emotional elements involved in recording story telling images."

Boyer's concept of composition is certainly in agreement with Mascelli's:

A good photographer always picks the best background, whether it be for news or documentary. The visual has to blend with the aural. You don't want something that's going to detract from the subject. You want it to blend but you want it to be as perfect visually as you can get it. A good photographer should always be cognizant of that goal.

At WTOP-TV, the cameraman does not take part in the initial planning conferences for a mini-documentary series. He may be asked for his opinion on the technical feasibility of a proposed scene, and his advice may be sought on the question of the most economical way of getting the required shots. Economy is always a factor.

In the production of a mini-documentary series, the relationship between the reporter and the photographer is a sensitive one. There are bound to be differences of opinion. The optimum collaboration occurs when both members of the documentary unit have faith in each other's judgment. As Boyer expresses it:

> In my particular case, the reporter trusts the cameraman's ability. He will tell the cameraman what he needs and then let him alone to get the proper footage. When it comes to the amount of footage shot, it is usually the reporter's responsibility. If he rambles on and on during an interview with an overload of questions, the photographer can do nothing but let the camera run.

There is another equally important relationship: the film editor with the camera crew. The film editor is responsible for putting the footage together so that it is logical in presentation and communicates explicitly to the audience. The content of the mini-documentary series is the reporter's domain.

There are advantages to having a cameraman who is also an editor. An editor may not know how to shoot and a cameraman may not know how to edit. But a cameraman/editor, as Boyer notes, "thinks like an editor and shoots what the editor needs."

In Boyer's experience, there is a great deal more pressure placed on the camera crew in the production of a mini-documentary series than in the production of a full-length documentary. There have been instances when segments of a mini-documentary series went on the air the very day editing of those segments was completed. However, a film editor who can edit swiftly and still maintain creativity can turn out a high-quality product.

The mini-documentary series is designed to reach the news audience and hold it over a sustained period of time. Boyer thinks it does that effectively.

Like his colleagues at the other Washington stations, he points out that original film is used in editing mini-documentaries. In that respect, mini-documentaries follow the same editing procedure as newsfilm. For the full-length documentary, as we have noted, original footage is not cut.

Generally, there is a separate sound track, and A and B rolls are used for printing. "When newsfilm is put together," Boyer explains, "the A roll and the B roll are run in two separate projectors and the two are combined when the film is aired. You take your chance for error: human error or machine error."

He believes that eventually videotape will replace film. However, the current state of the art requires the use of both videotape and film. Some stations now have their cameramen and film editors working with both media, which provides for an efficient crossover. With the advent of mini-cameras, one-man operations may become more frequent. It would be advisable for both student and professional to be multifaceted: achieve a good background of experience in television production and film- and video-camera operation.

Boyer believes that students at colleges and universities which offer courses in cinematography should take full advantage of them. "Shoot films of college football games. Do studio work for your closed-circuit TV station. Get to know every aspect of TV studio operation." After that, a job as a cameraman for a TV station that has a small staff is an excellent learning experience. Such stations may not pay very well, but they will hire photographers with little experience. They expect these tyros to move up in the television world after perhaps two years of intensive news and documentary experience.

## FILM EDITING

Toby Weaver is executive film editor for WTOP-TV. He began his career in the Navy, where he was trained at its photo school in Pensacola. Afterwards, he worked in commercial film laboratories, then at WRC-TV and now at his present assignment for WTOP-TV.

There is definitely a difference in editing mini-documentaries as opposed to straight news film, Weaver says. The mini-documentary has a continuous story to tell. It is entertainment over and above its news value. Editing technique should be in keeping with modern concepts. Weaver sees as many feature films as he has time for, to study trends and techniques of master film editors. Then he attempts to adapt the new techniques to the mini-documentaries.

Weaver's opinion is that newscasts a decade ago, or even less, were very dry. Today's news program is much more interesting, more entertaining than its predecessor. Feature stories abound in current newscasts. The fact is the market is highly competitive. Viewers are more demanding, more sophisticated in their tastes. You cannot give them the product they accepted 10 years ago. News stories have to be more complete, more in-depth. The mini-documentary is one of the ways to meet the current demand.

He believes that the mini-documentary series has more impact than the local half-hour or hour documentary. The local documentary has to be very heavily promoted to buck network competition. On the other hand, the audience to local newscasts is substantial.

Since the mini-documentary compresses a great deal of editorial content into a comparatively brief time, it presents a distinct challenge to the film editor. He works very closely with the reporter but they do not always see eye to eye. Out of the counter suggestions, however, a better product results. "I can't remember any mini-documentary that wasn't changed in its final form from the way it was originally conceived," Weaver reveals.

On occasion, the film editor accompanies the production crew, but most often he does not have the time. Editing for the daily newscasts is an all-encompassing job. He does find time, nevertheless, to submit ideas. One of his suggestions has been developed as a mini-documentary on commentators: who they are, why they are so influential, what makes them acceptable as pundits.

The technique of Weaver's approach is to start with good sound—jarring sound that attracts an audience and holds attention. He works under the premise that if he "can keep them for the first 30 seconds, I've got them all the way." Then comes concentration on the pictorial matter to maintain steadfast interest. In the series on fire alarms, for example, the opening episode began with the scream of a fire siren and the sight of a burning house.

But it is not a simple task. One mini-documentary series the station presented was on the subject of rape. The visuals available were all talking heads. To eliminate completely static scenes, the camera crew was sent out on location to recreate a scene: the woman arriving at her apartment house. Viewers saw the back of the woman as she opened the door. After that, the camera took over and, figuratively, became the victim. The woman, herself, was no longer seen. There were shots of the ascending stairs, the door opening into the flat, the violent movements of the camera in the rooms, all backed by appropriate music. It turned out to be a very effective sequence.

Another series on child abuse also had a great many talking heads. And there were many shots of mutilated children. In contrast, a scene was inserted of a lovely looking child reciting his prayers before going to bed.

Weaver believes that every mini-documentary has some sound or picture content which, with skillful editing, can offer an ear-catching or eye-catching opening. It is basic with him. He also has to think in terms of developing each episode so that it is complete in itself and yet an integral part of a 5- or 10-part series. It is the challenge of bringing a beginning, a middle, and an end to each sequence and yet having it blend with the rest of the series. Usually, a teaser is used at the end of each episode to intrigue the viewer into watching the following night—a technique employed successfully, as we have observed, for *The Miracle Merchants*. That series posed a special problem because of the use of the hidden video mini-camera. It was necessary to incorporate film with the videotape. This restricted the flexibility in editing that one has in working solely with film.

Although experimentation and the use of imaginative techniques by the film editor are to be commended, *technique must not overwhelm content*. Otherwise the viewer may be so fascinated by the technique that he will lose sight of the content. Weaver believes in striking a balance, i.e., use as much technique

Small console film editor (Magnasync/Moviola).

as does not overwhelm content. There should be room in nearly every story for experimentation. Pacing is also very important because pacing can improve a poor segment of film.

Editing has reached a high level of sophistication. The first television newscasts are almost as far removed from today's productions as the modern screen epic from the ancient silents. The problem for the film editor is time. He works under tremendous pressure. He may be cutting a film while the newscast is in progress.

Weaver's advice to tyro film editors is that he or she learn basic techniques before attempting any experimentation. An analogy may be drawn here: A would-be artist may be intrigued by abstract, action, or nonobjective painting which appears formless and often deceptively simplistic. But the great artists first learned the basics of composition, form, line, and color. All of them could and often did paint realistic landscapes or pleasing portraits before they began to experiment and develop their own creative expression. Weaver's philosophy is that "if you discover a technique you like, you'll find a place to use it."

# Chapter 7
# The Mini-Documentary Approach of Independent WTTG

WTTG is part of the Metro-Media complex, but it is independent of the networks. It is rated as one of the top independent stations in the country. However, its budget for programing does not compare with the more affluent network affiliates. The station has been producing mini-documentaries for the part 6 or 7 years, both investigative and informational. News director Stan Berk believes mini-documentaries are the "greatest way to reach a large audience."

WTTG does not editorialize. Its highly rated news program is scheduled from 6 to 11 p.m. It does not have any early (6 p.m.) newscast to compete with the other Washington stations. The 10 o'clock newscast does give the station an edge over the competing 11 o'clock programs of the network affiliates, and both the Nielsen and Arbitron ratings showed WTTG ratings as high as—and, in some instances, higher than—the 6 p.m. newscasts of its competitors. However, when a competing network station programs a very popular movie or sporting event that runs from 9 to 11 p.m., it cuts the viewing audience of the 10 p.m. newscast drastically.

The news department is run informally and ideas for mini-documentaries come from all sources. WTTG has only 3 film crews. Therefore, the station works on a much tighter schedule than the network affiliates. Mini-documentaries must be completed in a comparatively brief time—perhaps a week or two—and the series may go on the air before all episodes are in the can. Also, a series seldom runs longer than a week.

The length of each segment does vary, depending on the interest value. But each episode must be able to stand by itself. WTTG, like the other stations, uses follow-ups. For example, the mini-documentary series on resort land included a total of 45 reports over a period of several months.

Film crews consist of a cameraman and sound technician. The reporter almost always acts as field producer. Sometimes if the idea for the mini-documentary is his, the film editor may accompany the crew.

Berk knows he has the backing of station management on mini-documentaries. A series on unscrupulous auto repair shops brought repercussions from automotive sponsors who actually withdrew their accounts. This was even after a spokesman for the auto repair industry was given time to state his case. The news director believed he was right in airing the series—a television station must have a sense of commitment. Some time later, the automotive companies renewed their sponsorship.

Where a participant's livelihood may be involved or the theme is highly controversial, the news director checks with the station's attorneys for a ruling.

Berk asserts that the mini-documentary evokes tremendous response, particularly when a series concerns the consumer's income. The series on resort land had its effect on the Department of Housing and Urban Development (HUD), which modified its regulations to more fully assist the land buyer. Transcripts of the series were sent to HUD and also were reprinted in the *Congressional Record*.

It should be noted that the topics of resort land sales and auto repair overcharges, as we have seen in foregoing chapters, were the themes of mini-documentaries produced by other Washington stations. Both subjects are of widespread interest. In a metropolitan area of 3 to 4 million people, each station can compete for its own large audience. Programs do have their loyal followers so that those who watch the 6 p.m. or 11 p.m. newscasts may not watch the 10 p.m. newscast, and vice versa. Also, television stations are not about to reveal their plans for mini-documentaries to other stations. It is altogether possible for 2 or even 3 stations in the same city to develop similar ideas, especially when the subject is one that is very much in the public eye.

An aid to WTTG has been the George Washington University Law School, whose students staff the station's consumer HELP center. With student research assistance, WTTG produced a series on career schools, the vocational establishments which promise their enrollees jobs after completing the course, and, more often then not, fail to make them good. Interviews were held with many students who paid, in some instances, $2000 for a computer course or other types of courses that were supposed to lead to jobs but the positions never materialized. Viewers were made to realize that they were indirect participants, since many of the career schools were government accredited and student loans were guaranteed—loan defaults that had to be paid came out of the taxpayers' money.

Advice was sought from the Federal Trade Commission's consumer protection bureau, which launched a campaign to warn prospective students about the pitfalls to be encountered at some of the career schools. The mini-documentary made excellent use of the professional broadcasters, the academic world, and government officials to bring a valuable service to the community.

## REPORTER/PRODUCER/WRITER

Meryl Comer considers herself a jack of all trades at WTTG. She is a newscaster, an anchorwoman, a reporter, a producer, a writer. Her background includes a law school education, but she never entered the legal field. She was attracted to broadcasting and her first job was as a radio announcer—which she admits she obtained because she was willing to arise at 4 a.m. to do a 6 a.m. program and accept very little pay. Later she worked with a film crew for Guggenheim Productions on many political documentaries—after that, a stint with the *Philadelphia Enquirer* writing women's features. WTTG gave her her first assignment several years ago and she has been with the station ever since.

As far as mini-documentaries are concerned, she believes she does best when she selects her own subjects. She chooses a theme because she feels very strongly about it. Sometimes the idea will come from personal experience. Her series on euthanasia was inspired by a visit to her grandmother, who was devastated by a terminal illness. She was concerned about her grandmother's emotions and about the reactions of the other elderly residents of the nursing home. It was heart-rending to watch a loved one die. But it was an experience she knew was undergone by many, and she felt that the entire subject of euthanasia—controversial as it was—should be publicly aired. As it happened, a competing station was presenting a series called *The Right to Die*.

Ms. Comer, although pressed for time and limited in budget, set out to do as thorough a job as she could, interviewing doctors, nurses, women who were dying of cancer, researching what had been written on the subject. She did have the assistance of a student intern but she had to do most of her research alone.

Meryl Comer, anchorwoman/reporter at WTTG.

When she tackles a controversial issue, she does some soul searching: "I have to sit back and ask myself, am I being fair? Am I being biased because I feel so strongly about the subject?"

Again, the question of objectivity is at issue. The honest reporter must never be accused of showing bias. It is not a simple issue. How can a reporter be truly objective when he or she feels so strongly about the subject? In Ms. Comer's case, her conscience, as the cliche goes, is her guide, but the subconscious feelings are there and she must tread carefully.

What finally emerges on the air is the result of a subjective decision. "You have to rethink and ask yourself: are you serving the public interest?" She is also of the opinion that a woman makes her subjective choices differently from a man. She tends more to choose medical topics, to be more sensitive to people's reactions.

After the series on terminal illness, *A Way to Say Goodbye*, was aired, many viewers commented that it was too depressing. But others, who were undergoing a similar experience—i.e., watching a loved one die—said they were encouraged by what they saw. Many of the terminal patients confessed they did not want to be isolated; they wanted to be part of living as long as there was a spark of life within them.

Meryl Comer's philosophy is one of commitment to the larger issues, the problems that affect a great many people. It was with some misgiving that she undertook to write and produce a mini-documentary series on transsexuals. It was not a topic of her choice. She felt it was too narrow in scope. Only a tiny minority was affected. Nevertheless, it did offer a challenge. She wanted to present the poignant, not the bizarre; these are humans who face a special problem. She was conscious of the fact that many of the participants might overreact and reveal unnecessary intimacies. But she feels herself very attuned to the people she interviews and she was able to present the series very sympathetically. She will delete statements that place participants in an embarrassing light as long as she can maintain the honesty of the film report. She believes in investigative reporting, but not in sensational exposes. The upshot was that the series was highly praised and won a local Emmy.

Another series she worked on was called *When ABC's Spell Trouble*. It dealt with special learning difficulties of children; how to spot potential problem areas; how to deal with children in the critical preschool period. The series was so well received by parents that it was rescheduled 6 months later.

Despite the impact of the mini-documentaries, Ms. Comer feels that the kind of investigative reporting she would like to do would fall more readily within the scope of a full-length documentary. The mini-documentary, to her, is too concentrated in time.

As a reporter/producer, she is in complete agreement with Reuven Frank's dictum: "The best interviews are of people reacting—not people expounding." She wants to show emotion. She wants reactions to come about naturally without directing people. But she knows that envisioned scenes have to be planned. She avoids extraneous background or establishing shots such as panning across a room. Her mini-documentaries are concerned with people and their inner feelings about problems of major interest. The drama is the actuality.

Her shooting schedule is limited by budgetary restrictions and her other duties so that she cannot spend more than 1 or 2 hours filming each day. She needs a full day in the studio to prepare for her anchorwoman chores. The mini-documentaries are devised so that they generally encompass a week's run, i.e., 5 episodes. Sometimes the series may consist of only 3 segments. Each episode is tailored to be complete in itself and she prefers not to have any recapitulation because it is time-consuming. Most of the segments average between 3 or 4 minutes. However, she will fight for additional time if she believes an episode warrants it.

Her technique in putting the finished production together is to identify the strong scenes. She types a draft of a scenario and makes notations as she screens the entire footage. She uses a counter to mark the footage she wants. Then she goes over the footage to again mark the sequences. This is a sort of double-check on herself, a confirmation of her original choice. She lists the various shots: Are they closeups? Are they clear? Are they poor? Can they be edited without getting a jump cut? She works closely with her film editor. "Sometimes you need someone else to be with you. You're so wrapped up in it, you no longer can tear it apart, but someone else can."

She knows she should be able to work far enough in advance so that "everything's in the can" before the series is aired. But with her tight schedule this is not always possible. Nevertheless, her experience and her workload are perhaps the best guide for students and aspirants. They may well find themselves at independent stations where they will be required to perform many functions rather than concentrating on one assignment as do the investigative reporters for many of the network affiliates.

As far as audience is concerned, Meryl Comer's observation is that "You're reaching people in a newscast who may not be primarily interested in the theme of the mini-documentary so you do reach a wider public that way. The full-length documentary will mainly appeal to people who are interested in the subject and take the trouble to check the time it is going to be shown."

## A WAY TO SAY GOODBYE

This mini-documentary series deals with a highly controversial subject: euthanasia. It required a very sensitive approach. Most of us avoid talking about death, although it is true that recently there have been university courses devoted to the subject. Jessica Mitford has written a devastating book on the commercialization of death. But the issue of whether a terminal patient should be maintained in a state of vegetation as long as he or she is breathing is one that arouses as much ire as a debate on abortion.

It is remarkable that Meryl Comer found terminal patients who were willing to speak of their plight frankly and unsentimentally. They were filmed with a great deal of awareness. There were no closeups. We see the patients only in profile or in silhouette.

The handling is different with the boy who has leukemia. We see him full face by himself and with his family. There are no signs of fear in his facial expressions. A precocious understanding comes through that not only awakens the sympathy of the viewer but, assuredly, evokes a reaction of *why can't we conquer this affliction*?

*A Way to Say Goodbye* was aired in 5 brief sequences that add up to a poignant presentation of a perplexing dilemma.

## EPISODE 1—MONDAY

COMER:
SUPER TITLE
STUDIO
CLOSEUP

"NEITHER THE SUN NOR DEATH CAN BE LOOKED AT STEADILY"—THE WORDS OF AN 18TH CENTURY POET. WITH ALL OUR MODERN SOPHISTICATION, WE STILL HAVE TROUBLE COPING WITH THE INEVITABLE STATE OF MAN. WE PERSIST IN MAKING DYING A LONELY PROCESS—SHUT IT OFF IN WAITING ROOMS. HOSPITAL WARDS. NURSING HOMES. AND INTENSIVE-CARE UNITS. WE DO MUCH BETTER AS A SOCIETY WITH VIOLENT AND ACCIDENTAL DEATH. WE ARE APPALLED AND THEN IT IS OVER. WHAT WE DON'T HANDLE WELL IS TERMINAL ILLNESS. IT FORCES US TO WATCH THE DYING PROCESS TOO CLOSELY. IT ASKS TOO MANY DECISIONS FROM DOCTORS AND FAMILIES AND THEN THE PATIENT. DECISIONS ABOUT ONE'S OWN LIFE ARE OFTEN ASSUMED BY OTHERS WHEN ONE IS DYING OR THE PROGNOSIS IS TERMINAL. OUR ADVANCED MEDICAL TECHNOLOGY—MAN-MADE MIRACLES—ARE NO LONGER OF COMFORT. THEY ENABLE US TO PLUG LIFE IN. NURSE WHAT'S LEFT. PROLONG THE INEVITABLE. THE QUESTION: IS IT LIVING? ARE WE CARING? HOW MUCH TIME ARE WE BARGAINING FOR AND AT WHAT PRICE? WHILE A HEALTHY SOCIETY ASKS FOR REDEFINITION. TIME TO RECONSIDER THE PATIENT'S RIGHTS. THERE ARE THOSE FOR WHOM MIRACLES AND CURES WON'T WAIT. THEIR TIME IS OF THE MOMENT. THEY ARE OUR CONCERN.

PATIENT:
HEARTBEAT IN
BACKGROUND

SUPER SHOT
OF INFANT
WIRED UP TO MEDICAL
INSTRUMENTATION

THE NATURE OF MY ILLNESS I KNEW ABOUT TWO YEARS AGO. TERMINAL. I THINK. JUST MEANS TO ME SOMETHING THAT WILL EVENTUALLY PROBABLY DEFEAT ME. I THINK THAT PATIENTS WHO HAVE TERMINAL DISEASES OR MAYBE ANY KIND OF DISEASE HAVE GREAT FEARS AS I DO. I THINK THAT THE PROFESSION DOES. TOO. AND THAT THE

CONFRONTATION OF TWO SCARED PEOPLE—
BOTH AFRAID MAYBE TO SAY THINGS—
CERTAINLY DOESN'T HELP THE PATIENT. I
DON'T KNOW WHAT IT DOES TO THE DOCTOR.

DR. ROSS:
V/O PAN OF WIRES
HOOKING
UP CHILD TO
INSTRUMENTS;
SHOT OF INTRAVENOUS
APPLICATION

DYING IS REALLY SOMETHING THAT THE
PATIENT IS GOING TO DO BY HIMSELF. BUT
HE WOULD LIKE THE SUPPORT OF THOSE HE
LOVES AND THOSE HE HAS GIVEN THE
RESPONSIBILITY OF TAKING CARE OF HIM.
WHEN PEOPLE AVOID THE TOPIC, WALK OUT
OF THE ROOM OR SAY EVERYTHING'S GOING
TO BE FINE WHEN HE KNOWS OTHERWISE.
IT JUST MAKES HIM GO INTO A SHELL.

YOU CANNOT LIE TO A DYING PATIENT OVER
A LONG PERIOD OF TIME. THEY KNOW IT.
THEY SENSE IT. THEY KNOW THAT YOU
CAN'T TALK ABOUT IT. THEY DON'T EVEN
TALK WITH YOU ABOUT IT. BUT IF YOU GO TO
THEIR ROOM, YOU SIT DOWN, AND LISTEN TO
THEM, THEY WILL TELL YOU.

DOCTOR:
V/O CLOSE SHOTS OF
HOSPITAL
TECHNOLOGY

ALL OF US HAVE HAD THE EXPERIENCE
WHERE WE'RE CONVINCED SOMEONE'S
GOING TO BE DEAD WITHIN A MATTER OF
DAYS. THEN, A FEW YEARS LATER THINGS
ARE STILL GOING ALONG AT A REASONABLE
LEVEL AND THE PATIENT IS ABLE TO
FUNCTION. I THINK IT'S NOT ONLY CRUEL
BUT UNREALISTIC TO TOTALLY WIPE OUT
ALL HOPE FROM A PATIENT. NO MATTER
HOW STRONGLY WE MAY SCIENTIFICALLY
FEEL THAT THE END IS AT HAND.

TERMINAL PATIENT:
V/O HOSPITAL SCENE

WE LEARN TO TAKE ANY RISK WITH THE
SIDE EFFECTS. ONLY BECAUSE WE'RE
BUYING TIME ANY WAY WE CAN.

TERMINAL PATIENT:
V/O MEDICAL CHARTS

NO, I WOULD NOT PREFER TO BE KEPT
ALIVE JUST TO BE BREATHING AT ALL. I'M
NOT IN FAVOR OF THAT WHEN YOU CAN DIE
WITHOUT HAVING YOUR FAMILY WATCH.
YOU SUFFER AND YOU'RE MISERABLE AND
PERHAPS JUST BE A VEGETABLE.

DOCTOR:
V/O PAN OF INFANT IN
HOSPITAL BED

I KNOW OF NO PHYSICIAN WHO IS WILLING
OR FEELS THAT HE SHOULD TAKE ANY
POSITIVE ACTION TO SHORTEN ANYONE'S
LIFE. AND I DON'T THINK THAT'S
SOMETHING WE HAVE A RIGHT TO TAMPER
WITH. BUT I DON'T THINK THAT WE ARE
OBLIGED TO GRIND UP A WHOLE BUNCH OF
TECHNOLOGY TO KEEP SOMEONE ALIVE
WHO MERELY WILL BE JUST THAT—ALIVE—
WITHOUT BEING ABLE TO COMMUNICATE OR
FUNCTION AS A HUMAN BEING.

| | |
|---|---|
| **DR. ROSS:**<br>**V/O INFANT MOVING**<br>**ABOUT IN**<br>**HOSPITAL CRIB,**<br>**RESTRICTED BY**<br>**MEDICAL**<br>**HOOKUPS** | MERCY KILLING HAS NOTHING TO DO WITH A GOOD DEATH. I'M VERY OPPOSED TO ANY FORM OF MERCY KILLING. I HAVE NO USE FOR IT. NOT ONLY FOR RELIGIOUS OR MORAL REASONS...BUT IF YOU REALLY TAKE CARE OF DYING PATIENTS. IF YOU GIVE SUFFICIENT PAIN RELIEVERS WITHOUT WAITING UNTIL PATIENTS CRY FOR RELIEF...WITH GOOD PHYSICAL, EMOTIONAL, AND SPIRITUAL HELP. THERE IS NO NEED FOR MERCY KILLING. |
| **COMER:**<br>**V/O CLOSEUP OF**<br>**INFANT** | HOW TO MAKE MORE MERCIFUL WHAT'S LEFT TO LIFE INVOLVES DECISIONS THAT MUST BE FACED BY DOCTORS, PATIENTS, AND FAMILIES. THESE ARE THE PEOPLE WHO CONCERNED US, WHOM WE TALKED TO, AND ALL HOPED THAT WHAT THEY SAID WOULD MAKE A DIFFERENCE FOR OTHERS SUFFERING NOW OR WHEN THE TIME COMES. |
| **COMER:**<br>**CLOSEUP** | TOMORROW. A TIME TO TELL WHEN THE END IS NEAR. |

## EPISODE 2—TUESDAY

| | |
|---|---|
| **COMER:**<br>**V/O PROFILE OF**<br>**PATIENT**<br>**SUPER TITLE** | WHOM ARE YOU PROTECTING BY NOT LETTING PEOPLE SEE A VERY ATTRACTIVE WOMAN? |
| **PATIENT:**<br>**IN PROFILE** | THAT'S A TOUGH QUESTION. I THINK MY FIRST THOUGHT WAS I DON'T WANT MY CHILDREN HEARING ME TALK ABOUT DEATH HEAD-ON. I DON'T EVEN KNOW IF THAT'S WHY. MAYBE I DON'T WANT SOME OF MY FRIENDS TO HEAR IT EITHER BECAUSE I THINK THEY WOULD BE DISCOMFITED BY IT. I'M TIRED OF GOING THROUGH THAT ROUTINE OF: "I DON'T WANT TO HEAR THOSE REMARKS" OR "OH, COME ON, WE ALL KNOW THAT REALLY ISN'T SO." BECAUSE I KNOW IT IS SO. |
| **DR. ROSS:**<br>**CLOSEUP** | I THINK THE MOST IMPORTANT THING TO REMEMBER IS THAT PATIENTS DO KNOW WHEN THEY'RE DYING. AND I'M NOT TALKING ABOUT CAR ACCIDENTS. YOU KNOW, WHEN THEY HAVE MAYBE HALF AN HOUR BETWEEN ACCIDENT AND DEATH. I'M TALKING ABOUT HOSPITALIZED PATIENTS WHO HAVE AT LEAST TWO WEEKS BETWEEN THE ONSET OF THE ILLNESS AND THEIR ACTUAL DEATH. THOSE PATIENTS KNOW WHEN THEY'RE CLOSE TO DYING. AND I THINK WHAT YOU HAVE TO DO IS TO SAY TO |

SOMEONE. "LISTEN TO THEM AND ASK IF THEY FEEL LIKE TALKING ABOUT IT." THEY'RE USUALLY VERY GRATEFUL BECAUSE THEY REALLY SUFFER FROM THIS ISOLATION. LONELINESS. AND CONSPIRACY OF SILENCE.

COMER:
V/O GROUP OF
PARENTS
IN LIVING ROOM

WHAT IS DIFFICULT FOR ADULTS IS MADE MORE SO WHEN THE PATIENT IS A YOUNG CHILD. FAMILY MEMBERS ARE FULLY AWARE OF THE TERMINAL IMPLICATIONS OF THE PROGNOSIS. THE CHILD UNDERSTANDS THE PAIN. IS SELF-CONSCIOUS THAT HE IS DIFFERENT. PARENTS ARE TORN BETWEEN TELLING THE TRUTH. AND THE PROTECTIVE INSTINCT TO LIVE A WELL-MEANT LIE. THOSE HERE ARE MEMBERS OF CANDLELIGHTERS. A GROUP THAT LOBBIES FOR CANCER RESEARCH FUNDS. THEIR CHILDREN ARE SUSTAINED BY HIGHLY TOXIC AND EXPERIMENTAL DRUGS. AWAITING A CURE OR A CONTROL. OR THOSE WHOSE CHILDREN HAVE DIED WAITING.

ON SCREEN

THEY HAVE ASKED NOT TO BE IDENTIFIED.

ADDRESSING GROUP

WHY DID YOU WAIT SO LONG?

MOTHER 1:

BECAUSE INITIALLY WHEN HE WAS DIAGNOSED AT CHILDREN'S HOSPITAL THEY SPENT A GOOD DEAL OF TIME TELLING US

PAN OF OTHER
PARENTS
LISTENING INTENTLY

NOT TO TELL HIM. THEY TOLD HIM THAT HE HAD ANEMIA. HE WAS SIX. GOING ON SEVEN AT THE TIME. AND THEY EMPHASIZED THAT WE SHOULD GO ALONG WITH THIS. THEY TOLD US NOT TO TELL OUR NEIGHBORS OR THE SCHOOL OFFICIALS OR MOST OF OUR FRIENDS. MAYBE JUST OUR CLOSEST RELATIVES. FOR EXAMPLE. HIS GRANDPARENTS. MAINLY BECAUSE HE DIDN'T KNOW AND THEY DIDN'T THINK HE SHOULD LEARN FROM OUTSIDE SOURCES. THEY SAID THAT SOMETIMES WHEN NEIGHBOR CHILDREN KNOW. THEY WON'T PLAY WITH THE CHILD. THE NEIGHBORING PARENTS WILL TELL THEIR CHILDREN NOT TO PLAY WITH THE CHILD WHO IS AF-FLICTED. SO HE BECOMES A SORT OF NEIGHBORHOOD ODDITY.

COMER:

BUT YOU MADE A DECISION AT A CERTAIN POINT TO LET YOUR SON KNOW WHAT HE HAD. IS IT HELPFUL TO YOU THAT HE KNOWS?

FATHER 1:

YES. IT IS HELPFUL TO US. WE DON'T FEEL AS THOUGH WE HAVE TO KEEP SECRETS FROM HIM. HIS ATTITUDE. HOWEVER.

|  | DOESN'T SEEM TO BE TOO DIFFERENT FOR SOME REASON. I GUESS HE PREFERS NOT TO THINK ABOUT IT. AND, IN A WAY, THAT'S THE WAY WE ARE ABLE TO COPE WITH THE SITUATION. |
|---|---|
| FATHER 2: | OF COURSE. THE DISEASE IS LESS DEBILITATING ON THE CHILD THAN THE DRUGS THAT THE CHILD RECEIVES. DRUGS MAKE THE CHILD SO SICK FOR DAYS AFTERWARDS THAT YOU WONDER. YOU REACH A POINT SOMETIMES. WELL, MAYBE IT'S BETTER JUST TO TAKE THE CHILD HOME, TAKE THE CHILD OUT OF THE STERILE AND TERRIFYING ENVIRONMENT AND LET HER COME TO THE COMFORTABLE SURROUNDINGS THAT SHE KNOWS SO FAMILIARLY WITH HER MOTHER AND HER FATHER RIGHT THERE WITH HER AND FRIENDS COMING IN. IF SHE'S GOING TO DIE, LET HER DIE RIGHT HERE WITH US. |
| MOTHER 2: | WALKING DOWN THE HALL JUST EVEN NOW HE SAID, "MOMMA, I'VE GOT LEUKEMIA." OH! YOU KNOW, I SAID, "SON, NO, NO, DON'T SAY THAT. LET'S WAIT AND LET THE DOCTORS TELL US. WHY DO YOU THINK THAT?" AND HE SAID, "BECAUSE I'VE READ IT IN MY SCIENCE BOOK. I KNOW WHAT IT IS." BUT FOR SIX MONTHS, HE WOULD NOT SAY THE WORD AGAIN. HIS OLDEST SISTER ONE DAY SAID ABOUT THREE MONTHS LATER, "MOMMA, EXACTLY WHAT IS IT THAT STEPHEN DOES HAVE? WHAT'S ITS NAME?" STEPHEN SAID, "IT DOESN'T HAVE A NAME." |
| COMER: | ARE YOU HAPPY THE WAY IT ENDED? IF THERE IS SUCH A HAPPINESS... |
| FATHER 2: | YES, WE FEEL BETTER ABOUT THE FACT THAT HE WAS ABLE TO GET HIS LAST WISH. HIS LAST DESIRE: TO SPEND SOME TIME AT HOME BEFORE HE DIED. AND ALTHOUGH HE SPENT THE WEEKEND IN BED, HE WAS THERE WITH HIS SISTERS, WITH US, AND WITH HIS DOG. AND WE FEEL LIKE THAT BEING THERE MEANT A LOT TO HIM. |
| COMER: V/O PANEL OF DOCTORS AT NIH | AT THE NATIONAL INSTITUTE OF HEALTH'S CANCER RESEARCH CENTER, THE DECISION OF A FAMILY TO TELL OR NOT TO TELL A LOVED ONE THAT HE OR SHE IS DYING IS REMOVED. THERE IS NO MASQUERADE. IT IS HOSPITAL POLICY THAT ALL PATIENTS, NO MATTER WHAT THEIR AGE, KNOW THEIR DIAGNOSIS. |
| PSYCHIATRIST: CLOSEUP | WELL, CHILDREN COPE, IN MY OPINION, EXTRAORDINARILY WELL WITH |

223

KNOWLEDGE THAT THEY ARE VERY SICK—
INDEED, WITH KNOWLEDGE OF WHAT THEY
HAVE. WITH KNOWLEDGE OF THE
NECESSARY TREATMENTS AND
PROCEDURES, DISCOMFORTS, CHANGES IN
THEIR LIFE THAT THEY HAVE TO BE
SUBJECTED TO. WHAT THEY DON'T COPE
WELL WITH IS PEOPLE NOT BEING
STRAIGHT WITH THEM. NOT SHARING IN-
FORMATION WITH THEM. GETTING INTO THE
COMPLEXITIES OF WELL-MEANT DECEP-
TIONS THAT ARE, UNFORTUNATELY, AGAIN
BY MY STANDARDS, FAIRLY COMMON.

**COMER:** DO YOU FIND THEM PREOCCUPIED WITH
THEIR ILLNESS AND THE POSSIBILITY OF
DEATH?

**NURSE:**
**CANCER WARD** NOW THIS IS ONE PREOCCUPATION THAT
THE PATIENTS NEVER SEEM TO HAVE. IN
FACT, I CAN REMEMBER ONE INSTANCE
WHEN OUR SOCIAL WORKER WAS GOING TO
TAKE THE CHILDREN OUT AND ONE LITTLE
BOY ABOUT 11 TOLD ANOTHER ONE ABOUT 7,
"I CAN'T GO OUT ON A TRIP TODAY, I'M
DYING." AND HIS ROOMMATE SAID, "WELL,
YOU'RE NOT DEAD YET. GET YOUR COAT
AND COME ON."

**COMER:**
**V/O LONG SHOT** LIVING GOES ON. FOR THE PATIENT IT
**HOSPITAL CORRIDOR** MEANS MAKING THE MOMENTS BETWEEN
**PAN TO EMPTY BED** THE PAIN AND OPPRESSION COUNT. THE
PATIENTS' LIFELINE INTRICATELY HOOKED
UP WITH DOCTORS, NURSES, AND THE
HOSPITAL.

**CLOSE** TOMORROW, THE BEDSIDE MANNER. THIS IS
MERYL COMER REPORTING.

## EPISODE 3—WEDNESDAY

**COMER: SUPER TITLE** THE LIFELINE FOR THE TERMINAL PATIENT
**V/O SHOTS OF NURSES** IS THE HOOKUP TO DOCTORS AND
**MOVING PATIENT IN** RESEARCHERS EQUIPPED WITH THE
**HOSPITAL BED** MEDICAL TECHNOLOGY CAPABLE OF PUM-
PING HUMAN FUNCTIONS THROUGH A
LIFELESS FORM. A MAN-MADE CAPACITY WE
HAVE THAT MORE AND MORE CONTEND
ONLY PROLONGS THE DYING PROCESS; IT
DOES NOT REALLY EXTEND LIFE.
COMPLICATIONS SET IN. DRUGS THAT ARE
TOO TOXIC, SIDE EFFECTS MORE
FOREBODING THAN EVEN THE FEAR OF
DEATH. PAIN. DEPRESSION, THE OFTEN
ASKED, "HOW MUCH TIME DO I HAVE LEFT?"
THE PATIENT—DOCTOR—HOSPITAL LINK
STRAINS WHERE IT SHOULD COMFORT.

| | |
|---|---|
| **PATIENT:**<br>**SEATED IN CHAIR**<br>**PROFILE VIEW** | I THINK THAT ONE MUST BE IN A POSITION OF DYING TO UNDERSTAND FULLY WHAT IT MEANS. AND I HAVE HAD THE EXPERIENCE IN A DOCTOR'S OFFICE SITTING NAKED AND WAITING WHILE HE DISCUSSES WITH HIS WIFE SOME INANE PROBLEM LIKE CHECK BOUNCING OR MINOR PETTY PROBLEMS THAT HE'S CAUSED. AND I SAY. "AREN'T YOU ASHAMED? I AM DYING AND YOU ARE TALKING ABOUT A HUNDRED DOLLARS. DO YOU KNOW WHAT I WOULD GIVE YOU IF YOU COULD FIND A CURE FOR ME TODAY?" |
| **TERMINAL PATIENT:**<br>**SILHOUETTE** | PATIENTS ARE PEOPLE. I WAS ONCE TOLD THAT FOR AN OUT-PATIENT WAITING FOR AN X-RAY SETUP, I HAD TO STAY IN A BOOTH AND WAIT FOR MY NAME TO BE CALLED. THAT I COULDN'T COME OUT AND USE THE WAITING ROOM BECAUSE THEY COULDN'T HAVE ALL THOSE BODIES AROUND THERE. WELL. I MAY BE A BODY, BUT I AM A PERSON. PARTICULARLY WITH PEOPLE WHO HAVE TERMINAL ILLNESSES. THERE'S A FANTASTIC NEED TO FEEL THAT YOU EXIST WHILE YOU STILL HAVE THE TIME. |
| **NURSE:**<br>**CLOSEUP** | THE FIRST STAGE THAT A PATIENT GOES THROUGH. AS WELL AS THE FAMILY. IS DENIAL—I KNOW THIS CAN'T BE HAPPENING TO ME. OH, NOT ME. THERE MAY BE A TIME WHEN THE PATIENT WILL REFUSE TREATMENT. THEY WON'T STAY IN BED. AND IN TERMS OF THE FAMILY. THEY WILL BE TOLD THE PATIENT IS DYING AND THEY WON'T BELIEVE THE DOCTOR. THEY'LL LOOK AROUND FOR ANOTHER DOCTOR WHO CAN TELL THEM SOMETHING DIFFERENT. |
| **DOCTOR:**<br>**CLOSEUP** | IF I TELL THEM SOMETHING UNTRUTHFUL TODAY I DON'T REMEMBER TOMORROW WHAT I TOLD THEM YESTERDAY. SO. IF WE START OUT ON A TRUTHFUL BASIS—TRUTH WITH HOPE—THEN BOTH THE PATIENT AND THE PHYSICIAN CAN WORK TOGETHER TOWARDS TRYING TO BENEFIT THE PATIENT. AND I THINK ONCE THEY REMOVE THE UNKNOWN AND TELL THEM WHAT'S GOING ON. THEY COME TO GRIPS WITH IT. I MEAN, THEY CAN HANDLE IT. BY AND LARGE. |
| **COMER:**<br>**OFF SCREEN** | IF THEY CAN HANDLE IT. CAN THEIR FAMILY USUALLY HANDLE IT? |
| **DOCTOR:**<br>**CLOSEUP** | NOT NECESSARILY. THIS IS WHERE PART OF THE PROBLEM IS. IF THE PATIENT HAS THE INFORMATION AND THE FAMILY HAS IT TOO. THIS CREATES A POTENTIAL CHANNEL OF |

COMMUNICATION WHICH MAY BE VERY PAINFUL FOR THE FAMILY BECAUSE THEY MAY THEN HAVE TO TALK TO THE PATIENT ABOUT THE POSSIBILITY OR THE EVENTUALITY OF DEATH. THIS IS A DIFFICULT THING FOR FAMILIES IN OUR LIFE CULTURE TO HANDLE. I THINK THIS IS ONE OF THE REASONS THAT MANY FAMILIES INSIST THAT THE PATIENT NOT BE TOLD. BECAUSE AS LONG AS THEY'RE NOT TOLD THEN THEY CAN LIVE THIS GAME OF "WELL, EVERYTHING IS EVENTUALLY GOING TO BE OKAY."

**COMER:**
**OFF SCREEN**

IN WHAT INSTANCES DO YOU FEEL THAT A PASSIVE EUTHANASIA IS APPROPRIATE? IN WHAT CASES?

**ANESTHETIST:**
**CLOSEUP**

I THINK IN THOSE CASES WHERE IT IS IM POSSIBLE TO RESUSCITATE A FUNCTIONAL BEING. WHERE ALL THAT YOU HAD LEFT WOULD BE A BIOLOGICAL PREPARATION.

**COMER:**
**OFF SCREEN**

THE ISSUE IS NOT WHEN TO PULL THE PLUG?

**PSYCHIATRIST:**
**CLOSEUP**

NO. THE ISSUE IS WHEN NOT TO HOOK PATIENTS UP ON MORE AND MORE EQUIPMENT AND MACHINES. THIS IS SOMETHING THAT YOU HAVE TO TEACH IN MEDICAL SCHOOL EARLY. WE TEACH THE SCIENCE OF MEDICINE TO OUR MEDICAL STUDENTS. WE TEACH THEM TO CURE. TO TREAT. THE ONLY INSTRUCTION THEY GET THAT HAS TO DO WITH DEATH AND DYING IS HOW TO ASK FOR AN AUTOPSY. HOW IN THE WORLD ARE THOSE PEOPLE SUPPOSED TO COMFORT PEOPLE WHO ARE DYING?

**DOCTOR:**
**CLOSEUP**

MANY PATIENTS HAVE SAID TO ME. "AS LONG AS I'M FUNCTIONING. AS LONG AS I AM ABLE TO BE ABOUT. AND BE WITH MY FAMILY. FINE. I WANT THINGS TO CONTINUE WITH TREATMENT AND SO FORTH. BUT AT THE TIME THAT I HAVE TO BE MAINTAINED BY HOSPITALIZATION. BY INTRAVENOUS FLUIDS. AND BY TUBES IN MY NOSE. THEN I DON'T WANT TO LIVE THAT WAY. AND I WANT YOU TO PROMISE ME THAT WHEN THAT HAS TO HAPPEN. THAT YOU WILL KEEP ME COMFORTABLE AND DON'T DO ANYTHING TO PROLONG MY AGONY."

**COMER:**
**OFF SCREEN**

BECAUSE OF THE TREATMENT YOU'VE SPOKEN OF IN THE HOSPITAL. HAVE YOU EVER THOUGHT THAT WHEN THE END WAS NEAR WHERE YOU'D LIKE TO BE? WOULD YOU RATHER BE HOME OR IN A HOSPITAL?

| | |
|---|---|
| PATIENT:<br>SILHOUETTE | OH. I'D RATHER BE HOME. I THINK HOSPITALS ARE DREADFUL. I'D LIKE TO BE HOME. I DON'T KNOW IF THAT'S POSSIBLE BUT THERE'S NO QUESTION IN MY MIND. YOU CAN SAY, DO ANYTHING, KEEP ME ALIVE ONE MORE DAY. I THINK THIS IS WHAT I'M LIKE. I DON'T KNOW ABOUT TOMORROW. BUT WHEN THERE ARE OTHER PEOPLE WHO SAY, "I CAN ONLY STAY ALIVE UNDER CERTAIN CONDITIONS AND THEN I'D LIKE TO GO OUT AND SAY GOODBYE, FOLKS, BUT WITH MY DIGNITY." |
| COMER:<br>V/O FOOTAGE OF BOY<br>IN HOSPITAL BED | A 9-AND-A-HALF-YEAR-OLD BOY. A VICTIM OF LEUKEMIA SINCE 4...5 YEARS OF PAIN-FUL TREATMENT. RELAPSES. PARENT AND CHILD REFUSING TO GIVE UP. BUYING TIME TO A CONTROL. HAVING TO GIVE UP HOPE FOR A CURE. TOMORROW HIS STORY. |
| CLOSE | THIS IS MERYL COMER REPORTING. |

# EPISODE 4—THURSDAY

| | |
|---|---|
| COMER: SUPER TITLE<br>V/O SHOTS OF JEFF<br>GETTING OFF SCHOOL<br>BUS | WHEN JEFF POPPER, AGE 9-AND-A-HALF, GROWS UP, HE WANTS TO BE A DOCTOR. A DOCTOR LIKE THE ONE THEY HAVE AT N-I-H...AND HE'S EVEN PICKED OUT A SPECIALTY. ONE HE'S PERSONALLY WELL ACQUAINTED WITH. IT'S CALLED LEUKEMIA. SCHOOL FRIENDS. NEIGHBORS. TEACHERS. KNOW OF HIS TERMINAL ILLNESS. HE'S SICK. BUT HE GETS TO HIS SCHOOL. EVERYONE TRIES TO KEEP THINGS AS NORMAL AS POSSIBLE. |
| MOTHER:<br>V/O SCENES OF<br>CHILDREN<br>WALKING TO SCHOOL | WE WERE TOLD TO TELL HIM AS SOON AS WE COULD. EVEN AS YOUNG AS HE WAS. HE KNEW FROM THE VERY BEGINNING THAT HE HAD BAD CELLS IN HIS BLOOD. WHAT THAT MEANT TO HIM, I'M REALLY NOT SURE. BUT HE HAS COME THROUGH THE PHASES VERY EASILY. HE ADAPTED VERY WELL TO THE POINT WHERE NOW HE USES THE WORD LEUKEMIA FREELY AND IT'S NOT A FEAR FOR HIM. |
| COMER: OFF SCREEN | IS DEATH A FEARFUL THING FOR HIM? |
| MOTHER:<br>V/O CHILDREN GOING<br>TO SCHOOL | NO. THERE ARE LOTS OF TIMES HE TALKS LIKE HE'D WELCOME DEATH. HE'S NOT AFRAID OF IT. WHICH REALLY HELPS US. HE FEELS IT WILL BE THE END TO HIS PROBLEMS. THE END TO NEEDLES. THE END OF ILLNESS. THE END OF CLINIC VISITS. HE SEES OTHER CHILDREN SUFFERING. HE SHARES VERY DEEPLY THE LOSS OF HIS FRIENDS. |

227

| | |
|---|---|
| JEFF:<br>V/O FOOTAGE OF BOY IN<br>HOSPITAL BED;<br>INTRAVENOUS EQUIPMENT | WELL, JUST A COUPLE OF DAYS AGO, I LEARNED IT WAS PART OF CANCER. I DIDN'T THINK IT WAS A PART OF CANCER. I THOUGHT IT WAS A WHOLE AREA BY ITSELF—LEUKEMIA—BUT I KNOW IF I DON'T GET THE MEDICINES, I WILL JUST WITHER DOWN TO NOTHING. I KNOW THAT LEUKEMIA CAN BE VERY PAINFUL IN SOME WAYS. |
| SHOTS OF HOSPITAL CORRIDOR; BOY AND MOTHER WALKING | I DON'T REALLY MIND AFTER THEY PUT THE NEEDLE IN OR STUFF LIKE THAT. IT'S JUST THAT WHILE THEY'RE DOING IT THAT HURTS ME THE MOST. |
| COMER:<br>OFF SCREEN | DO YOU EVER GET TIRED OF GOING THERE AND WISH IT WOULD ALL STOP? |
| JEFF:<br>OFF SCREEN | YEAH. |
| MOTHER:<br>V/O FULL SHOT<br>PLAYROOM<br>AT HOME | SOME OF THE DRUGS MAKE YOU VERY STIFF. THEY ALSO EAT YOUR DIGESTIVE TRACT. THE THINGS THAT BOTHER A CHILD MOST IS THE FACT THAT THEY ARE DIFFERENT FROM THE OTHERS. |
| COMER:<br>OFF SCREEN | DO THE KIDS BOTHER YOU AND GIVE YOU A HARD TIME? |
| JEFF:<br>IN PLAYROOM | IN FIRST GRADE THEY DID. I'D WALK UP THE HALL AND THEY'D RUN BY ME AND SAY, "HEY, BALDY." |
| COMER: | AND HOW DID YOU HANDLE THAT? |
| JEFF: | I'D JUST WALK ON. I DIDN'T LIKE IT. |
| COMER: | AND NOW THEY DON'T BOTHER YOU? |
| JEFF: | NOW THEY DON'T BOTHER ME. |
| COMER: | DO YOU THINK THERE'S A CURE FOR WHAT YOU HAVE? |
| JEFF: | I DON'T THINK SO YET. BUT I THINK THEY'LL FIND ONE. |
| COMER: | WHAT MAKES YOU THINK THEY'RE GOING TO FIND ONE? |
| JEFF: | I JUST GOT FAITH IN THE DOCTORS. |
| COMER: | ARE THEY GOOD TO YOU? |
| JEFF: | YES. I THINK THEY KNOW WHAT THEY'RE DOING. |
| MOTHER:<br>IN KITCHEN<br>CHILDREN SEATED<br>AT TABLE | I FEEL THAT THEY'RE A RESEARCH INSTITUTION AND WE KNEW THAT WHEN WE WENT THERE AND PART OF RESEARCH IS TRYING NEW TECHNIQUES AND NEW DRUGS. THE THING THAT ALWAYS SUSTAINED US IS THE FACT THAT IF THEY DO COME UP WITH SOMETHING, JEFF WILL GET IT FIRST. AND HE WILL HAVE THAT MUCH MORE OF A |

| | CHANCE. I DON'T THINK THAT THERE'S ANYTHING I'LL OPPOSE IF IT'S IN HIS BEST INTEREST. |
|---|---|
| COMER:<br>OFF SCREEN | HOW DO YOU MAKE EACH DAY COUNT AS A FAMILY? WHAT DO YOU DO? |
| FATHER:<br>IN LIVING ROOM | WE TRY TO MAKE THE BEST OF THE GOOD TIMES. WE'VE TAKEN UP SAILING. WE TRAVEL WHENEVER WE CAN—TRY TO LEAD AS NORMAL A LIFE AS POSSIBLE. |
| COMER:<br>OFF SCREEN | DO YOU UNDERSTAND HOW IMPORTANT THE DRUGS AND THE TREATMENT ARE TO YOUR HEALTH? |
| JEFF:<br>CLOSEUP | YES. I DO. BECAUSE IF I DIDN'T HAVE THEM. I MIGHT ALL OF A SUDDEN GO DOWN TO A LITTLE NOTHING. |
| COMER:<br>OFF SCREEN | WHAT HAPPENS WHEN SOME OF YOUR FRIENDS AT THE CENTER DIE? HOW DO YOU FEEL? |
| JEFF:<br>CLOSEUP | I FEEL MORE THAN SAD. I FEEL SORT OF ALONE 'CAUSE MOST OF THE FRIENDS THERE ARE MY BEST FRIENDS. I WOULDN'T MIND IT IF SOMEONE I DIDN'T KNOW DIED. IT ALWAYS USUALLY IS MY FRIENDS THAT DIE. |
| COMER:<br>V/O SHOTS OF FAMILY IN LIVING ROOM | THE POPPERS CONSENTED TO THIS INTERVIEW TO GIVE OTHER FAMILIES IN SIMILAR SITUATIONS STRENGTH. IT'S BEEN 5 YEARS NOW SINCE JEFF HAS BEEN DIAGNOSED—5 YEARS MORE OF LIVING THAN THEY EVER THOUGHT THEY HAD. JEFF'S PARENTS KNOW A CURE IS OUT OF THE QUESTION. ALL THEY'RE PRAYING FOR NOW IS TIME AND A CONTROL. EVEN IF IT MEANS A REGIME OF DRUGS AND TREATMENT FOR THE REST OF JEFF'S LIFE. JUST SO HE LIVES. THAT'S ALL THEY WANT. |
| CLOSE | THIS IS MERYL COMER REPORTING. |

## EPISODE 5—FRIDAY

| COMER:<br>SUPER TITLE<br>V/O SHOT OF HOSPITAL PATIENT IN BED | WHY IS IT NECESSARY TO TALK ABOUT DYING? ASK SOME OF OUR LISTENERS. DEATH IS DEPRESSING. WE WILL ALL FACE IT EACH IN OUR OWN WAY WHEN THE TIME COMES. BUT THOSE WHO ARE FACING THE PROSPECT OF TERMINAL PATIENTS TELL US IT SHOULD ALL BE TALKED ABOUT NOW. SO WE'RE BETTER PREPARED. SO WE CAN. WITH THE PRESENCE OF MIND. ASK BEFORE IT'S TOO LATE. FOR SOME DIGNITY FROM |

OUR MEDICAL TECHNOLOGY. WE GO TO ANY LENGTHS TO AVOID IT OURSELVES OR POSTPONE IT INDEFINITELY IN OTHERS.

**REVEREND:**
**CLOSEUP**

I THINK WHEN PEOPLE COME TO A HOSPITAL THEY BRING THEIR RELIGION WITH THEM. IF IT'S SOMETHING MEANINGFUL. IT WILL BE MEANINGFUL HERE. IF IT'S SOMETHING THAT'S BEEN PUT IN A SPARE CLOSET PERHAPS IT'S NOT AS HELPFUL. FOR SOME. RELIGION CAN BE MAGIC. AND MAGIC DOESN'T WORK IN A HOSPITAL. FOR OTHERS IT CAN HAVE A SENSE OF DEPTH AND MEANING AND SYMBOLIZATION FOR THEM THAT CARRIES THEM THROUGH.

**PSYCHIATRIST:**
**CLOSEUP**
**THEN DISSOLVE TO**
**SCENES IN HOSPITAL,**
**NURSE TREATING**
**PATIENT**

ONE OF THE PROBLEMS WE HAVE AS A RESEARCH INSTITUTE IS MORE ACTIVELY DEALING AND BEING CONFRONTED MORE WITH THE PROBLEM. WHEN DO YOU STOP TREATMENT? WHEN IS ENOUGH. ENOUGH? WHEN ARE YOU INTERFERING WITH THE QUALITY OF WHAT LIFE REMAINS? AND NOT ONLY IS IT A PROBLEM FOR US AS THE TREATING MEDICAL TEAMS. IT IS A PROBLEM FOR THE FAMILIES BECAUSE OF THE MAGIC OF THIS PLACE. MAYBE WE SHOULD TRY THIS NEW DRUG. MAYBE WE SHOULD TRY THIS NEW PROCEDURE A LITTLE BIT FURTHER. MAYBE SOMETHING SUDDENLY WILL HAPPEN. EVEN THOUGH ALL THE INFORMATION PRESENTS A COMPLETELY DIFFERENT PICTURE AND SOMETIMES WE GET CAUGHT UP IN ALMOST A REINFORCING CYCLE WHERE EVERYBODY IS HELPING EVERYBODY ELSE TO BE UNREALISTIC. OFTEN TO THE DETRIMENT OF THE PATIENT. AND SOMETIMES THERE HAVE BEEN PATIENTS WHO HAVE BEEN WISER THAN US. LIKE ONE PERSON YOU REMEMBER RECENTLY WHO JUST SAID. "ENOUGH. ENOUGH."

**COMER:**
**OFF SCREEN**

HOW DO YOU COPE WITH THE KNOWLEDGE THAT THERE IS NO CURE AT THE MOMENT FOR THEIR ILLNESS BUT IF YOU COULD ONLY HANG IN THERE LONG ENOUGH MAYBE THERE WILL BE.

**PATIENT:**
**SILHOUETTE**

OFTEN I COPE WITH IT VERY BADLY. I'M QUITE ANGRY ABOUT THE WHOLE THING. OTHER TIMES I HAVE A SORT OF PHILOSOPHICAL—AT LEAST I'M WORKING TOWARD ONE—ACCEPTANCE WHICH LETS ME THINK IN TERMS OF WHAT MY LIFE HAS BEEN. TO HOPE THAT I COULD LEAVE A LITTLE SOMETHING. I HAVE A SENSE OF A

PRESS OF TIME. TO DO A LOT OF THINGS THAT I HAVEN'T DONE YET.

COMER:
OFF SCREEN

WHAT ABOUT YOUR FAMILY? FOR A WHILE YOU DIDN'T INCLUDE THEM IN THE KNOWLEDGE.

PATIENT:
MEDIUM CLOSEUP
SILHOUETTE

I'VE NEVER NOT INCLUDED THEM. EVERYONE KNEW I HAD A MALIGNANCY. WHAT I HAVE DONE—AND THIS HAS BEEN SINCE THE SEMINAR WITH DR. ROSS—IS TO MY KIDS. I HAVE A 21-YEAR-OLD AND A 17-YEAR-OLD. I DO NOT IN ANY WAY PERPETUATE THE IDEA THAT I HAD SOMETHING AND I BEAT IT. AND HIP-HIP-HOORAY. AND THAT'S THE END OF IT. I SPOKE TO THEM VERY RECENTLY AND I SAID, ARE YOU AWARE THAT I MAY NOT HAVE THIS AT ALL. AND THAT IF I DO DIE I WOULD LIKE THEM TO FEEL THAT IF THERE WAS SOMETHING THEY DID WANT TO DO, HAVE WANTED TO DO, THEY SHOULD SAY OR DO IT. THEY SHOULD NOT HAVE TO HAVE THAT TERRIBLE FEELING: IF I HAD ONLY KNOWN. I WOULD HAVE LIKED TO HAVE SAID THIS TO MOM AND DONE THIS WITH MOM. I MEAN HERE WE ARE NOW. LET'S DO IT. WHAT I WOULD LIKE IS FOR PEOPLE JUST TO SAY SHE REALLY GAVE IT A GO WHILE SHE WAS HERE AND BE HAPPY FOR THAT. I STILL HAVE HOPE. I THINK ONE LIKES TO HAVE HOPE UNTIL THE VERY END. I HOPE THAT PERHAPS SOMETHING WILL HAPPEN IN A MONTH THAT WILL CURE AND MAYBE IT WILL. I'M NOT READY TO GIVE UP.

COMER:
OFF SCREEN

UNDER ANY CIRCUMSTANCE?

PATIENT:

YES. WELL. NO. I WILL NOT BE KEPT ALIVE BY MACHINES OR JUST BE A BURDEN TO EVERYONE. THAT I WOULD NOT WANT TO HAVE HAPPEN.

COMER:
FACING PATIENT

WOULD YOU WANT TO TALK ABOUT DEATH OR WOULD YOU RATHER TALK ABOUT LIFE?

PATIENT:

TO MY CHILDREN?

COMER:

YES.

PATIENT:
SILHOUETTE
THEN SHOTS OF
COMER CLOSEUP AT-
TENTIVE

OH...MUCH MORE ABOUT LIFE. BUT I THINK THEY MUST HEAR ABOUT DEATH. AND THEY MUST KNOW THAT I ACCEPTED IT AND WAS NOT FRIGHTENED, SO THEY CAN LIVE THEIR LIVES AND NOT BE FRIGHTENED THEMSELVES. THEY SHOULD NOT FEEL THAT THEIR MOTHER DIED FRIGHT-ENED.

| COMER: | YOU TELL ME THAT YOU'RE NOT AFRAID. |
|---|---|
| PATIENT:<br>SILHOUETTE | I'M NOT AFRAID OF DYING. I'M TERRIBLY SORRY THAT I WON'T SEE THE CHANGE OF SEASONS AND MY GRANDCHILDREN AND MY HUSBAND AND MY CHILDREN. ONE OF THE THINGS I NEVER THOUGHT IS WHY DID THIS |
| CLOSEUP COMER | HAPPEN TO ME. IT'S NOT FAIR. WHY ISN'T IT SOMEONE ELSE? AND AS THE ILLNESS GETS WORSE AND AS MY TIME GETS LIMITED, I BEGIN TO QUESTION, NOT WHY DID IT HAP-PEN TO ME, BUT DOES IT HAVE TO HAPPEN TO ANYONE? WHY CAN'T WE JUST EITHER BE DEAD OF A NATURAL LIFE OR BE RUN OVER BY A TRUCK? WHY DO WE HAVE TO GO THROUGH THIS TORMENT OF KNOWING. AND THE TREATMENT AND THE TYPE OF THING WE GET FROM FRIENDS. SOME THINGS FUNNY. SOME THINGS NOT SO FUNNY? I THINK THERE ARE PROBABLY BETTER WAYS TO DIE. |
| COMER:<br>V/O SHOT OF PATIENT<br>IN HOSPITAL BED<br>SURROUNDED BY<br>MACHINES | TERMINAL PATIENTS RESIGNED TO THEIR FATE...BUT IT IS UNBEARABLE TO WATCH A LOVED ONE DIE. WHAT WE WANT TO REMEMBER IS THAT VITAL HUMAN BEING WHO SHARED OUR LIVES, NOT WATCH WHAT'S LEFT LINGER ON. SUSTAINED INDEFINITELY BY MACHINES BECAUSE WE CAN'T BEAR THE PARTING. THERE MUST BE SOME DIGNITY TO DEATH—A BETTER WAY THAN THIS TO SAY GOODBYE. |

## THE PRESSURED PHOTOGRAPHER

Kenneth Resnick has been a cameraman for WTTG for more than 3 years. He was a photographer for the Maryland Center for Public Broadcasting, the National Broadcasting Company, and the United States Information Agency. Before that he worked for a documentary and industrial-film production company where he gained a great deal of experience in both cinematography and editing. Several of the documentary films he has been associated with have won awards in film festivals.

Obviously, film budgets play a large role in a cameraman's assignments, and Resnick is aware that he is more limited in working for an independent station than a network affiliate, particularly since he prefers shooting a large quantity of film to give him more leeway in his choice of shots. For example, he observes, you get your best pictures of an interviewee when he or she is relaxed and it does take time for a nonperformer to loosen up. "You can get some people on just one roll. Others may take 3 rolls before they really get into the meat of the documentary. Therefore, if you have an interviewee who proves difficult or is very uneasy, you do shoot a great deal of film." Where time and budget are too restrictive, a situation may arise when the reporter finds it necessary to prompt the interviewee in order to conserve time and film. In the long run, however, it is only the end product that is important.

There is a good deal more pressure on the cameraman at an independent station than at the network affiliates because the independent's staff is smaller and consequently the work load is greater. Also, a network, because of its more extensive resources, could cover, for example, an entire news conference and thus have a wider choice of excerpts. The independent's photographer does not have such largesse and sometimes it becomes a matter of instinct in shooting the precise highlights.

At WTTG, the cameraman is not brought in at the early planning stages of a mini-documentary series. At times, when an idea for a mini-documentary series is proposed by a film editor, he will discuss the proposal with the cameraman. The fact is that at an independent station, where the staff doubles up in its workload, there is not much time for any lengthy planning sessions. Neither is there the staff for research which is available at network affiliates. WTTG, however, does avail itself of interns, whenever it can do so, to assist in research. Usually, the mini-documentary reporter at WTTG, as we have seen, has to plan the series in addition to her duties as an anchorperson. The reporter also acts as the producer for the series. As far as the cameraman is concerned, generally, he is not informed of the requirements for the series until the day of the shooting.

Since WTTG is completely unionized, there are no crossovers. A sound man and an electrician always accompany the cameraman, and the latter does not do any of his own editing. Resnick is of the opinion that it would be very helpful to a newcomer to learn all the elements of filmmaking. He points out that when he was employed by a small film-producing company, he was engaged in all facets of the operation, including a great deal of film editing. The editing experience has been particularly helpful to him as a photographer. He is more aware of the editor's problems and the editor's importance in obtaining a quality product.

His basic equipment is the CP-16 camera. In the few instances where undercover work is essential, he will use a zoom lens, keeping himself at a discreet distance from the subject. The question of invasion of privacy can arise. In photographing sequences for a mini-documentary series on mistreatment of household pets, it was necessary to obtain shots in private residences of people accused of such mistreatment. In one instance, it entailed shooting through the window of a residence,

Cameraman Resnick shooting silent B roll footage for on-air mixing.

which certainly could have resulted in a lawsuit. Therefore, such requirements must be thoroughly checked for lawful procedure.

With only 2 editors and a very busy schedule, it is incumbent on the cameraman to confine himself to explicit filming. An overabundance of footage places a heavy burden on the film editor, since he is always facing a tight deadline. He may be forced to make a decision in favor of expediency rather than quality. The cameraman, particularly at the independent station, must be aware of these circumstances and confine his photography accordingly. In other words, he must not be an indifferent photographer who shoots at random with the expectation that the film editor will come up with a creative cutting job. The photographer must also think in terms of creativity.

Talking heads are a constant source of concern to every photographer. On the other hand, the journalistic imperative may call for a talking head because the "head" may be that of a prominent official who has some earth-shaking statement to make; therefore, *what he is saying* is of a great deal more importance than the visual. Nevertheless, Resnick tries to develop interest value by catching changes of expression, nuances of emotion:

If we're doing a mini-documentary series on the aged, then I will try to be subjective about my shooting, get myself completely involved in the subject. Of course, you have to realize that what you're doing is ephemeral. You capture a face, an emotion; it is only a few seconds in the mini-documentary...and then it's gone. But there is a great satisfaction in knowing that even if it's momentary, you have been able to get an extraordinary picture.

Rarely does the cameraman work from a script for the mini-documentary series. He must be keenly aware, listen closely to what is being said by the subject, ready to zoom in for a closeup when an important statement is being made. Without this awareness on the part of the photographer, there will be false shots and static pictures.

It is important, Resnick acknowledges, to know what your contemporaries are doing in the documentary field. But he thinks there may be a danger of becoming imitative:

That is, you may be viewing other films, other mini-documentaries or documentaries that are extremely well done; and perhaps consciously or subsconsciously you may find yourself copying those techniques. I believe you should develop your own technique. I want to bring to my films something that's particularly me, *innovative*—not *imitative*.

He employs what he terms a teaching approach in filming mini-documentaries. He does not take the audience's knowledge for granted. He attempts to make his visuals explicit, to communicate clearly, to teach the viewer. By using this method, he feels there is no problem in shaping each episode of the mini-documentary series to stand alone because in each episode the viewer is taught some aspect of the theme.

Resnick does not believe videotape will eliminate film. They will each have their uses. Film editors, as we have reiterated, find it more difficult to edit tape than film. And Resnick is of the opinion that even with the upsurge in the use of videotape, initial camera work may be accomplished with video equipment and then transferred to 16 mm film.

His advice to students is to obtain a well rounded background in television production. Knowing how to edit is of particular value to a photographer. It helps him in choosing his shots:

This does not mean that a cameramen also has to be a good editor. He may be an excellent cameraman but a poor editor. But he should have an awareness of the various other crafts that go to make up a quality production.

In filming a mini-documentary series, the cameraman must understand the journalistic needs of the story, but he also must be aware of the visual potentials. There are times when excellent visuals can make a dull story into a highly interesting one.

# Chapter 8

# Mini-Documentary Survey

To add to the scope of our findings on the mini-documentary, we have conducted a survey which was sent to 115 television stations in the United States. We have received an approximately 40% return. This may or may not be eminently satisfactory. We have our own reservations about projections based on percentage of returns. The rating systems by which television programs rise or fall utilize a tiny fraction of the population for their estimations. The fact that most television fare is mediocre or below must have one assume that the 12-year-old yardstick still prevails. There was a cartoon by Brickman in a daily newspaper recently which showed a man seated in an easy chair watching television and commenting, "I sure wish they'd stop giving the public what it wants."

Be that as it may, the following figures should give us some sort of insight, such as it is, into the proliferation of mini-documentaries.

Of the 40 stations responding, only a half-dozen stated they were not now producing mini-documentaries. Two of those holdouts did say they were hopeful of producing mini-documentaries in the future.

Who decides on the subject matter? To this question, the following responses were submitted:

| | |
|---|---|
| News director: | 16 |
| News director plus assignment editor: | 2 |
| News director plus reporter: | 2 |
| News director plus producer: | 1 |
| Editorial staff: | 15 |

*Are your mini-documentaries mostly informative or investigative in nature?*

| | |
|---|---|
| **Both types:** | **26** |
| **Mostly informative:** | **10** |

*What problems, if any, have you encountered in producing your mini-documentaries?*

| | |
|---|---|
| **Legal:** | **5** |
| **Limited staff:** | **13** |
| **Cost:** | **3** |
| **No problems:** | **15** |

For subject matter of mini-documentaries, each station listed 3 or 4 titles, some with brief explanatory remarks. The numerals beside some of the titles indicate the number of stations which produced mini-documentaries on the same theme.

| | |
|---|---|
| **Housing** | **5** |
| **Welfare** | **2** |
| | |
| **Constitutional amendment** | |
| **Mental health** | **2** |
| | |
| **Emergency ambulance service** | |
| **State and city budgets** | **2** |
| | |
| **Antifreeze shortage** | |
| **Energy crisis** | **3** |
| | |
| **Jesus freaks** | |
| **Euthanasia** | **2** |
| | |
| **Seabird sanctuary** | |
| **Illegal aliens** | **2** |
| | |
| **Cancer** | **2** |
| | |
| | |
| **Self-defense for women** | |
| **Fire regulation violations** | |
| **Police training** | **2** |
| **Food prices** | **3** |
| **Rape** | **5** |
| **Alcoholism** | **2** |
| **Traffic** | **5** |
| **Child abuse** | **2** |

Playground safety
Fraudulent promoters                 2

Animal birth control
Death row                            2

Divine light mission
Crime                                6


Runaways
Hitchhiking
Conflict in Northern Ireland
Employment agencies
Law and justice
Image makers
Heart disease                        3
Prostitution                         2
Solar energy
Resort lands
Gun control
Gasoline shortage
Amtrak
Problems of the aged
Foster homes
Fireworks
Postal system
Unique neighborhood
Nuclear energy
Prison for women
Medical center:
School bussing
Dam location
Deep water port
Massage parlors
The autistic child
Vasectomy
Meaning of machismo


Stations were also asked whether there were any instances where a mini-documentary influenced the community; perhaps an ordinance was passed or a fault rectified. The response was 27 stations in the affirmative; 9 could not point to any specific example.

News directors were asked: *On a local station basis, would you say you prefer the mini-documentary series to the full-length, half-hour, or hour documentary?* News directors from 32 stations replied that they preferred the mini-documentary to the locally produced full-length documentary. Three did not. One was not sure.

Do *you expect to continue producing mini-documentaries into the foreseeable future?* The response was unanimously positive.

## SUMMATION

The survey form we mailed to the various television stations was concise; we were aware that the news department is generally the busiest branch of a local TV station, and news directors would not or could not take the time to answer a very lengthy questionnaire. Nevertheless, we believe that the results of the survey, coupled with the in-depth study of the Washington, D.C. television stations, amply illustrate that the mini-documentary has become a way of life for newscasts.

WALB-TV, Albany, Georgia, states that the mini-documentary "gives you a flexible vehicle. You can start with a mini-documentary, then expand to a half-hour, if justified. Also, it is the best use of a very limited film budget."

WLTV-TV, Sarasota, Florida, has found through many years of documentary work that, too often, there "are interesting and worthwhile subjects which are too long for regular newscast presentation and too short in sustainable interest for a complete half-hour. The mini-documentaries, collectively, within our *On Assignment* time slots permit us to cover many more subjects in an interesting and fairly complete manner."

WNAC-TV, in Boston, prefers mini-documentaries "for wider exposure in our newscasts."

KIRO-TV, Seattle, Washington, asserts that "mini-documentaries are an important element of our news."

KJEO, Fresno, California, believes that full-length documentaries and mini-documentaries "are both very important to our format. Each one gives credit and believability to the other."

Al Schottelkotte, director of news and special events for WCPO-TV in Cincinnati, tells us that he has been presenting his *Spotlight Report* on the 11 p.m. newscast nightly for the past 15 years, "long before the term mini-documentary came into use... It gets into investigative subjects, political matters, but it is never politically partisan...it is even a humor piece on a topical matter."

In regard to the subject matter of the mini-documentaries, an examination of the topics listed in the foregoing pages gives some idea of the variety and scope of the themes investigated via mini-documentaries. There is hardly a subject of community or national interest, whether rape, vasectomy, housing, or heart disease, that has not found its way into a perceptive delineation by the mini-documentary. Its impact on the community is tremendous: 75% of the stations responding to the survey stated that the mini-documentaries they produced had a salutary effect.

KIRO-TV, Seattle, Washington, asserts that its "series on conditions in state veterans' homes resulted in corrective action by the legislature and the governor."

KENS-TV, San Antonio, Texas: "Our program on nursing homes initiated investigation by the state welfare department."

WALA-TV, Mobile, Alabama: "We had an old hotel closed because of fire violations and the fire code was updated."

WNAC-TV, Boston, Massachusetts: "A city council resolution followed up an investigation of playground safety."

KGO-TV, San Francisco, California: "Our series on handicapped persons produced [corrective] city legislation."

WBBM, Chicago, Illinois: "Our series on unscrupulous employment agencies resulted in a number of agency censures and legal action by the state."

KPRC-TV, Houston, Texas: "We believe we influenced the city's decision to establish first-class public emergency ambulance service...also, a county decision to establish an office to work on consumer frauds."

WWJ, Detroit, Michigan: "We influenced an investigation by HUD officials into false advertising claims of real-estate firms."

KHQ, Spokane, Washington: "Within 6 weeks after our mini-documentary series on unguarded railroad crossings, 3 new signals were installed at the worst crossings."

WWBT, Richmond, Virginia: "We were instrumental in achieving greater attention to the problems of the alcoholic in Richmond with a 7-part series called *Alcoholism: The Only Way Up Is Down*."

WTOL-TV, Toledo, Ohio: "We believe our series on rape influenced changes in police procedure."

KDFW-TV, Dallas, Texas: "Our series on dangerous intersections resulted in improvements being made."

WJW, Cleveland, Ohio: "We influenced legislation in the area of certain nonprescription drug sales."

From the above selected comments, it is reasonable to assume that the mini-documentary is a potent force in community relations. It is an image builder, if you will, for the television station. In its actuality drama, it induces empathy from the viewers and lets them know that the station is acting in the public interest. As a corollary, the investigative reporter becomes a public hero.

A mini-documentary can be news in its broadcast aspect; not merely a recording of an event but a depiction of the men and women involved and their emotional reactions. In that sense, the mini-documentary enlarges the scope of every newscast and acts as a catalyst for community participation.

Although investigative reporting has its hazards, as we have noted, no reporter we know of has been daunted, nor have news departments bowed to the will of a sponsor. Less than 10% of the television stations responding to our survey encountered legal problems in producing their mini-documentaries—and of these, none reported that legal obstacles prevented them from scheduling a mini-documentary.

The vast majority of television stations appear to prefer the mini-documentary to the full-length documentary. Bear in mind, however, that they are speaking on a local level. Obviously, a local station does not have the funds nor the talent that a network can bring to its production of documentaries. Assuredly, the local news director believes that the network documentary, informational or investigative, is an essential of good network programing. They believe, and rightly enough, that except in rare instances, the local full-length documentary cannot compete with the network production. Therefore, the mini-documentary becomes an extremely potent programing structure for the local TV station. The unanimous positive response of news directors to the question of continuing to produce mini-documentaries into the foreseeable future speaks for itself.

# Bibliography

Barnouw, Erik, *The Image Empire, Vol. 3*, Oxford University Press, 1970.

Bluem, A. William, *Documentary in American Television*, Hastings House, 1965.

Bluem, A. William & Manvell, Roger, *Television, The Creative Experience*, Hastings House, 1967.

Carlson, Verne and Sylvia, *Professional 16/35 mm Cameraman's Handbook*, American Photographer Book Publishing Co., 1970.

Dary, David, *Television News Handbook*, TAB Books, 1971.

Efrein, J. L., *Video Tape Production and Communication Techniques*, TAB Books, 1972.

Field, Stanley, *Professional Broadcast Writer's Handbook*, TAB Books, 1974.

Friendly, Fred W., *Due to Circumstances Beyond Our Control*, Random House, 1967.

Griffith, Richard, *The World of Robert Flaherty*, Duell, Sloan & Pearce, 1953.

Hardy, Forsyth, *Grierson on Documentary*, Praeger Publishers, 1971.

Hazard, Patric D., *TV as Art*, National Council of Teachers of English, 1966.

Levitan, Eli L., *An Alphabetical Guide to Motion Picture, Television and Videotape Production*, McGraw-Hill, 1970.

Madsen, Roy Paul, *The Impact of Film*, Macmillan, 1973.

Mascelli, Joseph V., *The Five C's of Cinematography*,

Cine/Grafic Publications, 1965.

Mickelson, Sig, *The Electric Mirror*, Dodd, Mead, 1972.

Reisz, Karel and Millar, Gavin, *The Technique of Film Editing*, Hastings House, 1968.

Reynertson, A.J., *The Work of the Film Director*, Hastings House, 1970.

Sherwood, Hugh C., *The Journalistic Interview*, Harper & Row, 1969.

Siller, Robert C., *Guide to Professional Radio & TV Newscasting*, TAB Books, 1971.

Small, William, *To Kill a Messenger*, Hastings House, 1970.

Souto, H. Mario Raimondo, *The Technique of the Motion Picture Camera*, Hastings House, 1967.

Steiner, Gary A., *The People Look at Television*, Alfred A. Knopf, 1963.

Stone, Vernon A., *Careers in Broadcast News*, Radio Television News Directors Association, 1972.

*Television News, Anatomy and Process*, Wadsworth Publishing, 1961.

*The Eighth Art*, Holt, Rinehart and Winston, 1962.

*Writing News for Broadcast*, Columbia University Press, 1971.

Young, Freddie & Petzold, Paul, *The Work of the Motion Picture Cameraman*, Hastings House, 1972.

# Index

# Index